"The history of Christianity in China will be a growing area of study in the coming years, when we will see China emerge as the largest Christian nation in the world. An important chapter of that history is the story of Christian monks in China, a chapter that until recently has not received sufficient treatment. Thanks to Matteo Nicolini-Zani, a monk of the Community of Bose who has published a number of studies of Chinese Christianity, we now have a sound study of that history. Distinguished scholars Sophia Senyk of the Pontifical Oriental Institute and William Skudlarek of Saint John's Abbey have rendered Nicolini-Zani's original Italian text very readable, giving English readers access to a fascinating story of Christian mission and intercultural dialogue. I recommend *Christian Monks on Chinese Soil* to students of Chinese history, Christian missions, and monasticism, as well as to anyone interested in intercultural dialogue."

—Timothy P. Muldoon, PhD
Boston College

D1599219

Christian Monks on Chinese Soil

A History of Monastic Missions to China

Matteo Nicolini-Zani

Translated by
Sophia Senyk
and
William Skudlarek, OSB

LITURGICAL PRESS
Collegeville, Minnesota

www.litpress.org

Cover design by Monica Bokinskie.

This book was originally published in Italian as *Monaci cristiani in terra cinese: Storia della missione monastica in Cina* by Edizioni Qiqajon s.r.l., Frazione Bose 6, I-13887 Magnano (BI), Italy, and is published in this edition by license of Edizioni Qiqajon s.r.l. All rights reserved.

1   2   3   4   5   6   7   8   9

Library of Congress Cataloging-in-Publication Data

Names: Nicolini-Zani, Matteo, 1975– author.
Title: Christian monks on Chinese soil : a history of monastic missions to China / Matteo Nicolini-Zani ; translated by Sophia Senyk and William Skudlarek, OSB.
Other titles: Monaci cristiani in terra cinese. English
Description: Collegeville, Minnesota : Liturgical Press, 2016. | Includes bibliographical references and index.
Identifiers: LCCN 2016010743 (print) | LCCN 2016034862 (ebook) | ISBN 9780814646991 | ISBN 9780814646007 (ebook)
Subjects: LCSH: Monasticism and religious orders—China—History. | Missions—China—History. | China—Church history.
Classification: LCC BX2723 .N5313 2016 (print) | LCC BX2723 (ebook) | DDC 266.00951—dc23
LC record available at https://lccn.loc.gov/2016010743

Contents

Abbreviations

AGOCD	Archivio Generale OCD (General Archive of the Order of Discalced Carmelites), Rome
AGOCSO	Archivio Generale OCSO (General Archive of the Order of Cistercians of the Strict Observance), Rome
ASA	Archive of the Benedictine Abbey of Sint-Andries (Saint-André), Bruges
BAV	Biblioteca Apostolica Vaticana, Vatican City
BCP	*Bulletin Catholique de Pékin*
BCUP	*Bulletin of the Catholic University of Peking*
BM	*Bulletin des Missions*
BO	*Benedictine Orient*
CA	*Contemplation et Apostolat*, supplement to the *Bulletin des Missions*
COCR	*Collectanea Ordinis Cisterciensium Reformatorum*
CSA	*Les Cahiers de Saint-André*
CSCO	*Corpus Scriptorum Christianorum Orientalium*. Louvain: Sécretariat du CorpusSCO, 1903ff.
MC	*Les Missions Catholiques*
MCJ	Jean-Marie Planchet, *Les missions de Chine et du Japon*. Peking: Imprimerie des Lazaristes, 1916–1933.
PL	*Patrologiae Cursus Completus. Series Latina*. Edited by Jacques-Paul Migne. Paris / Turnhout, 1844–1864.
RB	*Rule of Saint Benedict 1980*. Edited by Timothy Fry. Collegeville, MN: Liturgical Press, 1981.

RLB   *Rule of the Little Brothers of John the Baptist*

RPF   *Recueil des archives Vincent Lebbe*. [Vol. 4]: *La Règle des Petits frères de Saint-Jean-Baptiste*. Edited by Claude Soetens. Louvain-la-Neuve: Faculté de théologie, 1986.

SB   *Shengxin bao* 聖心報

SZ   *Shengjiao zazhi* 聖教雜志

YZ   *Yishi zhoukan* 益世周刊

YZB   *Yishi zhuri bao* 益世主日報

Preface

The origins of this work go back to 2002, the year I first learned about Christian monasticism in China. I was a novice at the time, and I made a visit to the Benedictine Abbey of La Pierre-qui-Vire in France together with some brothers from Bose. One of the monks learned of my research on the history of Christianity in China and showed me a book from the monastery library, *Une trappe en Chine*, written by the Lazarist Fr. Alphonse Hubrecht and published in 1933 in Peking (Beijing).[1] On our return to Bose, I discovered in our library a copy of another precious book, *Monaci nella tormenta*, edited by the Trappist Fr. Paolino Beltrame Quattrocchi and published in 1991. It is a richly documented account of the history of the Abbey of Our Lady of Consolation in Yangjiaping, in the mountains to the northwest of Peking, with the story of the martyrdom of thirty-three of its monks.[2]

I then spent ten years collecting, first somewhat haphazardly, later systematically, material about the various monastic foundations in China, with the intention of compiling an "outline history" of Christian monasticism in China. I followed the methodological rigor proper to historical research, including research in the area of the church's missionary activity, whose essential principle is absolute respect for history. As the historian of the church's missionary activity, Giovanni Battista Tragella, put it, "History is not a treatise

---

[1] Cf. Alphonse Hubrecht, *Une trappe en Chine* (Peking: Imprimerie des Lazaristes, 1933). Peking is the name in English by which the city currently called Beijing, meaning "northern capital," was known until the late twentieth century. By contrast, from 1928 to 1949, the city was known as Beiping or Peiping, meaning "northern peace." For consistency throughout this book, however, I will refer to the city as Peking.

[2] Cf. Paolino Beltrame Quattrocchi, ed., *Monaci nella tormenta. La "passio" dei monaci trappisti di Yan-Kia-Ping e di Liesse, testimoni della fede nella Cina di Mao-Tze-Tung* (Cîteaux: n.p., 1991).

on asceticism; it is what it is, and the first duty of the scholar is to *respect* it, rather than to alter it in order to make it more edifying."[3]

Originally, the purpose of my project was to summarize the events narrated in the numerous documents that were scattered widely and therefore difficult to access. In this endeavor I have benefited from the contributions of scholars who have already conducted research in this field or who are able to visit the different libraries and archives, and are thus in a better position to have access to existing materials. Many preserved documents still await careful study.

Many people have offered indispensable assistance to me as I sought to consult these materials, and here I wish to remember them and express to them my heartfelt thanks: the archivist at the Generalate of the Order of the Discalced Carmelites in Rome, Fr. Óscar Ignacio Aparicio Ahedo, who not only welcomed me to the archives but made it possible for me to scan many of the documents concerning the Carmelite foundations in China preserved in the Generalate; the archivist at the Generalate of the Order of Cistercians of the Strict Observance in Rome, Fr. Santiago Fidel Fernández Ordóñez, and the postulator general of the order, Sr. Augusta Tescari, who made available to me the materials collected over the years with great skill and patience by Fr. Paolino Beltrame Quattrocchi and now conserved in the archives at the Trappist Generalate; Frs. Victor Broekaert, librarian and subarchivist, and Olivier Raquez (d. 2012), of the Flemish Benedictine Abbey of Sint-Andries in Bruges, Belgium; Sr. Renee A. Rau and Mr. John Parker of the archives of St. Benedict's Monastery in St. Joseph, Minnesota, United States; Sr. Paula of the Trinity, prioress of the Carmelite monastery of Shen Keng, Taiwan; Sr. Marie-Bernard of the Carmelite monastery of Lisieux, France; Sr. Helen Wang of the Carmelite monastery of Oldenburg, Indiana, United States; the Little Brothers of John the Baptist in Taizhong, Taiwan; Fr. Fabrizio Tosolini, who made available to me the Chinese materials kept at the library of the theology faculty at Fu Jen Catholic University, Taipei, Taiwan; Dr. Claude Soetens, researcher at the Vincent Lebbe Archives in Louvain-la-Neuve, Belgium;

---

[3] Giovanni Battista Tragella, *Le Missioni estere di Milano nel quadro degli avvenimenti contemporanei*, vol. 1 (Milan: PIME, 1950), xii.

Dr. Adrian Dudink, researcher at the Department of Sinology at the Katholieke Universiteit of Leuven, Belgium; Fr. Roman Malek and Mr. Alek Stypa, librarian, at the Monumenta Serica Institute of Sankt Augustin, Germany; and Dr. Ng Ka Chai, researcher at the Chinese University of Hong Kong, China.

I wrote several articles based on the materials that I gradually collected on specific aspects of Christian monasticism in China. These I have now reworked, expanded, and integrated into the present work, which has been inspired by the spirit that Alphonse Hubrecht described as "a restless concern for truth, a great sympathy for this [monastic] undertaking [in China], and [attention to] the extremely interesting documentation."[4] The book is intended for two particular audiences. I offer it to that small but dynamic group of scholars whose field of research is the history of Christianity in China, in the hope that this "monastic piece" may contribute to the reconstruction of the various stages of the Gospel's entry into China. I also offer it to the ecclesiastical and, more specifically, the monastic world in the equally sincere hope that one day, God willing it be soon, monastic communities will again bloom from the seed still hidden beneath the earth of China. In the meantime we will do well to follow the counsel given by an expert on the contemporary ecclesial situation in China: "Some contemplative communities had existed in China, such as the Carmelites and the Trappists, but they were destroyed and dispersed, quite often dramatically and brutally, at the end of the 1940s, when Mao Zedong's troops conquered China. Today if one wants to approach realistically the restoration of contemplative communities in China, it is necessary to keep well in mind the recent tragic history."[5]

With this work I make my own the fervent wish already expressed more than seventy years ago: "May waves of fervent monks one day . . . spread the cool waters of prayer and love on the whole of China,

---

[4] Hubrecht, *Une trappe en Chine*, 9.

[5] Jeroom Heyndrickx, "Les communautés religieuses contemplatives revivent-elles en Chine? Signes d'espérance sur un long chemin," *Vies consacrées* 81, no. 1 (2009): 9–10.

where many souls thirst for God."[6] When the springs of monastic life once again gush forth in China, in peace and complete freedom, may those who draw water not forget the past, but rather cherish and learn from it. As the Chinese proverb puts it, "When you drink, do not forget those who drew the water from the well."

Bose, 12 July 2013

Memorial of the thirty-three Trappist monks of Our Lady of Consolation in Yangjiaping (China), martyrs.

---

[6] Albert Valensin, "Monastère Cistercien en Chine du Nord. Trappe de N.-D. de la Consolation, à Yang-kia-ping," MC 70 (1938): 117.

Introduction

It is precisely because we want to found a monastery
that is fully *Catholic* that we wish it to be *Chinese*.[1]

—Jehan Joliet

Monastic Life and Mission among the Nations

When Jean Leclercq (1911–1993), a Benedictine monk and one
of the greatest scholars of Western monastic history, was asked to
write about the relationship between Christian monasticism and
mission, he began by recognizing the "delicate and precise nature of
the question," as well as its complexity. "During the great missionary
period of the church since the sixteenth century Christian monastic
life has known a certain expansion; what relation has this had and
still have today to the church's missionary activity? . . . It is not
enough to affirm the presence of monasticism in various parts of the
world, but it is necessary to describe it, to discern its characteristics,
so as to show its place within all of what the church does for the
evangelization of peoples."[2]

In taking up the challenge of compiling a history of Christian monasticism in China, a brief introduction seems necessary to see why
the relationship of monasticism to mission has been the subject of so
much reflection and discussion within the church and the monastic
world. Such an introduction will also help to clarify the theoretical
background and the ecclesial and monastic context that led to the
extraordinary missionary dynamism in the history of Christianity,

---

[1] Cited in Henri-Philippe Delcourt, *Dom Jehan Joliet (1870–1937). Un projet de monachisme bénédictin chinois* (Paris: Cerf, 1988), 209 (emphasis added).

[2] Jean Leclercq, "Monachisme chrétien et missions," *Studia Missionalia* 28 (1979): 133.

1

which was accompanied by an exceptional flowering of monastic foundations "among the nations" (*ad gentes*), "in mission lands." Among these monastic foundations those in China were relatively recent. It is to them that this work is specifically dedicated.

In the history of the church and in the history of monasticism, the contribution of monks to the evangelization of lands not yet reached by the preaching of the Gospel has certainly been remarkable. The influence of monasticism on society, culture, and the life of the church has been crucial in both East and West. This was especially so during the first millennium and the beginning of the second:[3] "For upward of seven hundred years, from the fifth century to the twelfth, the monastery was not only the center of culture and civilization, but also of mission."[4]

The specific witness that the monastic community gives is of a radical Christian life naturally radiating outward, and thus it is implicitly missionary. On this basis, then, some monks have been explicit protagonists of the "missionary enterprise." "Although the monastic communities were not *intentionally* missionary (in other words, created for the purpose of mission), they were permeated by a missionary *dimension*. Even without knowing it and without intending it, their conduct was missionary through and through. Small wonder then that, increasingly, their implicitly missionary dimension began to spill over into explicit missionary efforts."[5]

Monk missionaries appear early in the history of Christianity both in the West and in the East: individuals such as Patrick (d. 460) in Ireland, Columbanus (520–597) in France and Italy, Boniface (ca. 675–754) in Germany, Ansgar (d. 865) in the north of Europe, Cyril and Methodius (ninth century) among the Slavic peoples, Bruno of Querfurt (974–1009) among the Prussians, and Anselm (1033–1109)

---

[3] See the summaries given in Stephen B. Bevans and Roger P. Schroeder, "Mission and the Monastic Movement (313–907): From Constantine to the Decline of the T'ang Dynasty," in *Constants in Context: Theology of Mission for Today* (Maryknoll, NY: Orbis Books, 2004), 99–136; David J. Bosch, "The Mission of Monasticism," in *Transforming Mission: Paradigm Shifts in Theology of Mission* (Maryknoll, NY: Orbis Books, 1991), 230–36.

[4] Bosch, "The Mission of Monasticism," 230.

[5] Ibid., 233.

in England.[6] Missionary monks also played an important role in the
extraordinary expansion of the Church of the East in much of Asia,
including China, beginning from the fifth century, as has been written of them: "The ascetic communities became the major dynamic
for missions in Asia."[7] One of the reasons for this was that in ancient
Asia the monastery was "the primary agent for mission."[8]

Nonetheless, what emerges from a reading of history, as Jean
Leclercq observes, is different. "There have been monk-apostles
. . . but monasticism, as an institution, was not apostolic. The
monk-apostles, once they became bishops, founded abbeys that were
by no means monasteries engaged in apostolic activity, but houses
of prayer and asceticism, of spiritual dissemination and, in addition,
of cultural influence on all levels, from the improvement of the land
to art and literature. . . . History, hence, confirms that the role of
monasticism is to be sought elsewhere, and not among missionary
institutions."[9]

Theological reflection—a kind of "monastic missiology"—has
attempted to determine whether or not the fundamental nature
of monastic life is compatible with a missionary perspective, but
a systematic approach to the question is quite recent. Among the
innumerable theological definitions of monastic life that could be
drawn on, I have chosen one that seems particularly apropos.

> The point of departure for monasticism is the desire to adhere
> totally to what Christ was, a conscious, considered, and exclusive
> desire concerning what originated at creation and was brought
> to its culmination in the incarnation. This ecstatic love is the
> foundation of every monastic vocation. This road leads to toil
> and to struggle. . . . To do this the monk knows that he must

[6] Cf. Edward Farrugia and Innocenzo Gargano, eds., *Monaci e missione* (Verucchio: Pazzini, 1999).

[7] Samuel Hugh Moffett, *A History of Christianity in Asia*, vol. 1: *Beginnings to
1500* (San Francisco, CA: Harper, 1992), 100. In addition to the treatment of this
topic, *infra*, pp. 47–57, and the works cited here, see two specific articles: Olaf Hendriks, "L'activité apostolique des premiers moines syriens," *Proche-Orient Chrétien*
8 (1958): 3–25; Olaf Hendriks, "L'activité apostolique du monachisme monophysite
et nestorien," *Proche-Orient Chrétien* 10 (1960): 97–113.

[8] Bevans and Schroeder, "Mission and the Monastic Movement (313–907)," 102.

[9] Leclercq, "Monachisme chrétien et missions," 135–36, 140.

make use of the means indicated by the tradition of those who preceded him on this road: the purification of the eyes, humility, continence, obedience to the Father in the Spirit, tears, the struggle against evil. It must also be remembered that every pastoral, charitable, or social aim is not the sense of the monastic life, but a consequence of union with Christ.[10]

Complementing this definition is an observation of the former archbishop of Canterbury, Rowan D. Williams. As he reflected on the experience of the early monastic mission of Augustine of Canterbury (d. 605) in England, he recalled its fundamental nature and therefore its one, true way of going about its mission.

What makes a [monastic] community effective in terms of mission and witness is [its] apostolic life. . . . The history of Benedictine mission in England is a history—at best—of how the apostolic life . . . , a life of simplicity, mutual dependence and service and committed worship conducted with thoughtfulness and imagination, has served to focus the evangelizing work of the church. [The monastic life] does so by presenting a new model of humanity, a model at odds with functionalist, anxious, impatient, would-be autonomous paradigms, offering a vision of the kind of humanity that finds its fulfilment in reciprocal service and shared joy. The monastic life represents in an intense way the Christological focus of the new humanity, holding together dependence and liberty, labour and contemplation. . . . The mission witness of the dedicated worshipping community exists because people fall in love with God, not because they are told that it is part of a strategy for evangelization. In all that we say about monasticism and mission, we have to keep first in mind the root of the monastic life in the plain sense of a calling into intimacy with God through life lived with brothers and sisters, nothing more, nothing less. There could have been no Gregorian mission to England had not Augustine and his brothers first sought the Lord for his own sake.[11]

Any talk of monastic mission, hence, must begin by seeing it as the natural and implicit radiation of Christian life when it is radically

[10] Claudio Gugerotti, "La comprensione teologica dell'identità della vocazione monastica," in *Riflessi d'Oriente* (Magnano: Qiqajon, 2012), 125–26.

[11] Rowan Williams, "Monks and Mission: A Perspective from England," http://www.archbishopofcanterbury.org/articles.php/2391/monks-and-mission-a-perspective-from-england, accessed 21 August 2013.

lived in a monastic way. The "missionary activity" of monks "was and is fundamentally spiritual. . . . Their apostolate is mainly one of radiation."[12] In other words, "the monastery itself is the 'word' of evangelization . . . , the monastic style of evangelization."[13]

The inseparability of monastic life and the mission of the church has been reiterated and developed in the years following Vatican II, with emphasis on community as the specific form of monastic witness.[14]

> Contemplation and mission are inseparable. . . . In this perspective, monasteries are both places of contemplation and places of activity and of mission, not in the sense that they allow themselves to become involved in the pastoral strategies of the church, . . . but in the sense that they are places in which prayer can extend as much as it needs, in which silence and listening offer a pedagogy to those who seek regeneration or who want to explore their own interior world. This is the mission entrusted to the monks in *Perfectae Caritatis* (1965): "Monasteries are like nurseries of edification for the Christian people." Through the liturgy and hospitality . . . contemplation becomes activity and mission.[15]

Monasticism, insofar as it is an ecclesial entity, partakes of the church's intrinsically missionary nature. To put it another way, monasticism participates in the life of the church, which is in itself mission.[16] On this basis, it will slowly but steadily become clear that

---

[12] José Cristo Rey García Paredes, "Missione," in *Dizionario teologico della vita consacrata*, ed. Angel Aparicio Rodríguez and Joan María Canal Casas (Milan: Àncora, 1994), 1047.

[13] Jeremy Driscoll, "Mission and Monasticism: Theological Reflections," in *Mission and Monasticism: Acts of the International Symposium at the Pontifical Athenaeum S. Anselmo, Rome, May 7–9, 2009*, ed. Conrad Leyser and Hannah Williams (Rome: Pontificio Ateneo Sant'Anselmo / Sankt Ottilien: EOS, 2013), 12.

[14] Cf. García Paredes, "Missione," 1049. Cf. also the summary of the theology of the contemplative/monastic life given in Leclercq, "Monachisme chrétien et missions," 142–47.

[15] Jean-Claude Lavigne, *Perché abbiano la vita in abbondanza. La vita religiosa* (Magnano: Qiqajon, 2011), 166–67. The quote is from Vatican Council II, *Perfectae Caritatis* 9; also found in John Paul II, *Vita Consecrata* 8.

[16] Cf. Sandra Mazzolini, "Missione e monachesimo. Una prospettiva missiologica," in Leyser and Williams, *Mission and Monasticism*, 197–210 (in particular 203–4).

a monastic foundation in a mission land is to become a place where those whom God has called to the monastic way of life can experience and live out the monastic life in their own country according to the cultural forms that are most congenial to them.

That the monastic life participates in the missionary nature of the church is verifiable in history, both in the East, where to this day most of the missionaries have been Orthodox monks,[17] and in the West, up to the Council of Trent.[18] However, the rise of large orders (primarily the Jesuits) and missionary societies (primarily the Paris Foreign Missions Society) in the sixteenth and especially in the nineteenth centuries, changed the picture. Missionary activity appeared more and more as an activity proper to some organizations specifically dedicated to this evangelization *ad gentes* by assignment by the Roman Apostolic See, which not by chance in 1622 instituted the Sacred Congregation of Propaganda Fide to organize and coordinate the church's specifically missionary activity, which in turn entrusted such activity to the missionary institutes that were being founded.[19]

Reflection on the monastic contribution to the mission of the church among the nations began to occur against this background and in partial reaction to it. Persons both inside and outside the monastic world engaged in such reflection, which was explicitly directed toward new monastic foundations in mission lands. The genesis

---

[17] Cf., e.g., Hlib Dynya, "Annunciare il vangelo nella vita monastica," in *Le missioni della chiesa ortodossa russa. Atti del XIV Convegno ecumenico internazionale di spiritualità ortodossa, sezione russa. Bose, 18–20 settembre 2006*, ed. Adalberto Mainardi (Magnano: Qiqajon, 2007), 295–322.

[18] For a summary of the relationship of monasticism to mission from an ecumenical perspective, see Ion Bria, "Monachisme et mission," in *Dictionnaire œcuménique de missiologie. Cent mots pour la mission*, ed. Ion Bria, Philippe Chanson, Jacques Gadille, and Marc Spindler (Paris: Cerf / Geneva: Labor et Fides / Yaoundé: CLE, 2001), 230–33.

[19] An Orthodox author makes an interesting observation in this regard: "For the West the traditional response to the question of how to implement the spread of the church is something like this: by means of some missionary organization, such as a religious order of the Roman Catholic Church, a missionary society or a board of the Protestant Churches. The Orthodox Church has never known such missionary organizations" because "the church itself is mission." Vsevolod Spiller, "Missionary Aims and the Russian Orthodox Church," *International Review of Mission* 52 (1963): 273.

and evolution of this rather recent reflection is directly connected with the presence of Christian monastic foundations in China.

In one part of the European monastic world signs of interest and action, both spiritual and material, of an explicitly missionary nature first appeared in the nineteenth century. These signs coincided with the great missionary thrust that made the nineteenth century "the great missionary century."[20] During this time the activity of the Holy See was characterized by the revitalization of missionary structures and religious orders, in particular the College of Propaganda Fide in Rome and the Society of Jesus; the institution of new works and missionary initiatives, such as the Society for the Propagation of the Faith and the Association of the Holy Childhood; and the setting up in mission countries of regions and of an ecclesiastical hierarchy, along with a movement to stimulate the formation of native clergy.[21] This activity, it might be noted, was also a response to the cultural, social, and political context of the time.

Despite an ever more determined effort on the part of the Holy See to detach missions from the French protectorate, France remained a major player on the nineteenth-century missionary scene. In France there was a particular ecclesiastical sensitivity to the missions that also began to "infect" the monastic world. It is significant that already in the preparatory phase of the First Vatican Council (1869–1870) a group of eleven French bishops presented a text concerning the missions, in which, among other proposals, they called for the establishment of monasteries in mission lands.[22] It is equally significant that already in the second half of the nineteenth century some French bishops who were vicars apostolic in mission areas visited their homeland to seek the presence of monastic communities in the ecclesiastical territories where they had jurisdiction. What was written about the Far East can be applied to the rest of the world as well. "Confidence in the prayer of the cloister is so widespread among

---

[20] Cf. Cyrill Schäfer, "Missionarietà delle congregazioni monastiche nei secoli XIX–XX," in Leyser and Williams, *Mission and Monasticism*, 99–123.

[21] Cf. Charles Molette, "Mission et missions. De la Révolution française à Vatican II," in *Dictionnaire de spiritualité, ascétique et mystique, doctrine et histoire*, vol. 10 (Paris: Beauchesne, 1980), 1390–404.

[22] Cf. ibid., 1395.

the superiors of the missions in the Far East that it leads them to seek not only the monks' intercession, but also the foundation of monasteries within the confines of their vicariates."[23]

Against this context, French Carmelite nuns established a monastery in Saigon in 1861. It was the first Carmel in a mission land. Eight years later, in 1869, the arrival of the first Catholic nuns on Chinese soil would mark the beginning of a story that would last for several decades (see chap. 2).

Around the same time, French Trappist monks also took the courageous step of founding a Trappist monastery outside Europe in response to the specific request of missionary bishops. Therefore the monks have not always allowed themselves to be used as tools of French colonial expansion under France's protectorate of the missions, as has been alleged.[24] The Trappists came to China in 1883, a few years after the Carmelites (see chap. 3).

Among the French Benedictines, both those inspired by the reform of Solesmes and others, "the will to make a foundation in mission countries was rarely manifested" at this time. "Almost all the French foundations of the nineteenth and the first part of the twentieth centuries consisted in 'retaking' ancient monasteries. . . . We see again a Benedictine expansion oriented more toward missionary activity than toward planting centers of prayer similar to those that existed in their homeland."[25]

This type of "Benedictine expansion oriented toward missionary activity," here understood as assuming responsibility for the evangelization and pastoral care of the new territories, also includes the foundations linked to German settlements in the United States of America in the mid-nineteenth century made by the pioneer Bavarian Benedictine Boniface Wimmer (1809–1887) and his missionary

---

[23] Alphonse Hubrecht, *Une trappe en Chine* (Peking: Imprimerie des Lazaristes, 1933), 44.

[24] I cannot agree with what in my view is an exaggerated conclusion of Jean Leclercq: "In France the Trappists accepted being used as instruments of expansion by the governments that succeeded each other, regardless of whether these governments were religious or antireligious." Jean Leclercq, "Le renouveau solesmien et le renouveau religieux du XIXe siècle," *Studia Monastica* 18, no. 1 (1976): 191.

[25] Ibid., 190–91. See also Leclercq, "Monachisme chrétien et missions," 136–40.

monks,[26] the Sylvestrine Benedictine mission in Ceylon that began in the same period,[27] the restoration of Brazilian monasteries by the Belgian Benedictine Gérard Van Caloen in the late nineteenth century,[28] and, in the early twentieth century, the birth and subsequent development of the German Benedictine congregations of Sankt Ottilien[29] and of Tutzing,[30] which were specifically intended for the foreign missions.

The *Pium Opus Messarum et Precum*

The Trappist Order of monks, especially in France, was thus the first to show some interest in the foreign missions. This interest initially took the form of a spiritual movement aimed to stimulate, support, and organize prayer and intercession for the conversion of peoples who were not yet Christian, especially the peoples of the Far East. As a member of the order put it, this was a movement that was "specifically Cistercian." It constituted the spiritual dimension of "Cistercian missiology" that had been taking shape for some time. "This work is specifically Cistercian, above all on account of its origins (our Trappist monastery in China), its means (prayer and

---

[26] Cf. Basilius Doppelfeld, *Mönchtum und kirchlicher Heilsdienst. Entstehung und Entwicklung des nordamerikanischen Benedektinertums im 19. Jahrhundert* (Münsterschwarzach: Vier-Türme-Verlag, 1974); Jerome Oetgen, *An American Abbot: Boniface Wimmer O.S.B., 1809–1887*, 2nd ed. (Washington, DC: The Catholic University of America Press, 1997).

[27] Cf. Andrea Pantaloni, "The Sylvestrine-Benedictine Congregation: A Monastic Pioneer in Modern Benedictine Mission," in Leyser and Williams, *Mission and Monasticism*, 133–42.

[28] Cf. Christian Papeians de Morchoven, *L'abbaye de Saint-André Zevenkerken*, vol. 1: *Un projet audacieux de dom Gérard Van Caloen (1853–1912)* (Tielt: Lannoo, 1998).

[29] On the history of the Benedictine congregation of Sankt Ottilien, see Godfrey Sieber, *The Benedictine Congregation of St. Ottilien* (St. Ottilien: EOS, 1992). On its founder, the Benedictine Andreas Amrhein, see his collected writings in Cyrill Schäfer, ed., *Der Gründer. Schriften von P. Andreas Amrhein OSB (1844–1927)* (St. Ottilien: EOS, 2006); Matilda Handl and Cyrill Schäfer, eds., *Der Gründer. Briefe von P. Andreas Amrhein OSB (1844–1927)*, 2 vols. (St. Ottilien: EOS, 2010).

[30] Cf. Bernita Walter, *Sustained by God's Faithfulness: The Missionary Benedictine Sisters of Tutzing*, vol. 1: *Founding and Early Development of the Congregation* (St. Ottilien: EOS, 1987).

sacrifice, especially the holy sacrifice of the Mass and Communion), its principal center (the Cîteaux Archabbey) and its secondary centers (all the abbeys of the strict observance of Cîteaux), and finally because from 1921 on it has been the object of encouragement continually renewed and ever more urged on the part of our general chapters."[31]

This movement "aroused a great deal of interest and prayer, not only with regard to the evangelization of the peoples of the East, but with regard to the contemplative life as such, which can be thought of as a carrier of the missionary presence of the church."[32] It was in the Far East, specifically in China, that this particular spiritual program originated. Its official name was *Pium opus messarum et precum*, but it was better known by its French name, approved by Pope Pius XI on 3 February 1925: *L'Extrême-Orient au Sacré-Cœur. Œuvre de messes et croisade de prières, en l'honneur de l'immaculée Vierge Marie, pour la conversion de la Chine, du Japon et des pays adjacents.*[33]

The concept and initial implementation of this "purely spiritual and missionary work, which soon took on global dimensions within the church,"[34] was the work of Fr. Maur Veychard, second abbot of Our Lady of Consolation in Yangjiaping. He explained his project in a newsletter dated 25 March 1914, which was sent to the bishops of China in response to requests they had previously made to the Trappist monastery of China.

> Many of you have honored us by writing, whether to ask for a foundation in your vicariate or at least to recommend your missions to the community's prayers. Not having been able, at least

---

[31] "Notre apostolat missionnaire monastique. Sa légitimité," COCR 6 (1939): 55.

[32] Paolino Beltrame Quattrocchi, ed., *Monaci nella tormenta. La "passio" dei monaci trappisti di Yan-Kia-Ping e di Liesse, testimoni della fede nella Cina di Mao-Tze-Tung* (Cîteaux: n.p., 1991), 50.

[33] On this movement, in addition to the published documents that are cited below, there is archival material that has not yet been published, contained in two dossiers to be found in Rome at AGOCSO, fondo postulazione generale [archive of the general postulation]. One of the dossiers contains letters, the other holds many issues of the *Bulletin du Pium opus*, which began publication in 1929, and annual reports of the same. This material was not part of the documentation given in the volume prepared by Fr. Paolino Beltrame Quattrocchi in 1991 (cf. Beltrame Quattrocchi, *Monaci nella tormenta*, 49–67) because it was discovered only after the volume had been published.

[34] Ibid., 49.

for the moment, to respond to the first part of your desires, we wish, as much as is possible, to satisfy fully the second, which consists in praying for the success of your works and the conversion of the poor pagans. This is what we have already sought to do from the moment of our establishment in China, because it is for this purpose that we have come, but we would like to do it in a more perfect manner now that our monastery . . . appears to be well established and our community sufficiently structured according to the rule and numerous. We have thought of a work consisting of Masses and prayers.[35]

The proposals included the construction within the Trappist monastery of Yangjiaping of a chapel destined for this pious work. Here, a Mass "for the missions and the conversion of the pagans" would be celebrated every day by a priest of the community in the presence of three other monks or lay brothers. Every visit to the Blessed Sacrament, prayer, or act of devotion freely made in this chapel by the members of the monastic community would be for the same intentions.[36]

On 1 January 1915, after the majority of the bishops of China had "fully endorsed and encouraged this project," the work proposed by Abbot Maur began to be carried out in the Trappist monastery in China.[37] The beginnings were modest, in part because of the war. After a few years, the project was altered and reproposed by the third abbot of Yangjiaping, Fr. Louis Brun. "Dom Brun undertook to reignite the wick, which was still smoldering, but, more audacious than his predecessor, he turned his gaze on the entire Christian world, which he wanted to win for the cause of the Chinese missions. . . . The *Pium opus*, timidly launched some years before, became a general mobilization, a large-scale campaign."[38]

[35] Letter of M. Veychard to the bishops of China, 25 March 1914, in AGOCSO, fondo postulazione generale, dossier "Pium opus messarum et precum," 1. Cited in Hubrecht, *Une trappe en Chine*, 45.

[36] Hubrecht, *Une trappe en Chine*, 45–46.

[37] Letter of M. Veychard, 8 December 1914, in AGOCSO, fondo postulazione generale, dossier "Pium opus messarum et precum," 2. E.g., Msgr. J.-B. de Guébriant, vicar apostolic of Canton, wrote, "The pious society you have recommended to me appears to be divinely inspired and responds to one of the most urgent needs of the church in China." Cited in Hubrecht, *Une trappe en Chine*, 46.

[38] Hubrecht, *Une trappe en Chine*, 56–57.

The day after his abbatial election in 1921, Fr. Louis solicited the interest of the general chapter of the Trappist Order, which, that year for the first time, spoke about it in glowing terms and encouraged the dissemination of the *Pium opus* to all Trappist monasteries. "The special characteristics of the *Pium opus of Masses and prayers for the conversion of China*, based in the Abbey of Our Lady of Consolation, are worthy of the full attention of the general chapter. Our monasteries are invited to collaborate effectively with this work, from which all the bishops in China expect prolific results."[39]

Abbot Brun's travels throughout Europe in late 1922 and the early months of 1923 provided him with a signal opportunity to promote vigorously the *Pium opus* throughout the Trappist Order, the Congregation of Propaganda Fide, and the Vatican.

On 5 April 1923 Fr. Louis was able to present the work directly to Pope Pius XI in a private audience. Since the pope too wanted to promote the conversion of the peoples of the Far East, he judged the enterprise to be most opportune. In fact, he gave it a special sign of his personal approval by becoming the first person to commit himself, in writing, to celebrate Mass on the fifteenth day of each month for the intentions of the *Pium opus*.[40] A few months later, on 26 June 1923, a papal rescript gave the work canonical recognition and, at the request of Abbot Brun, transferred the administrative center of this work from Yangjiaping to Cîteaux, placing it under the direction of the abbot general, who in turn delegated the vicar general of the order as its director. In the following year the same pope, in a letter from Cardinal Pietro Gasparri to the abbot general of the Trappists dated 20 August 1924, again approved the work, "*vehementer*," as he wrote in his letter.

Expressions of official approval from other circles came in the following months. In the same year the synod of bishops of China, which met for the first time in Shanghai, enthusiastically recommended "to all missionaries and all Christians the remarkable work organized by the Order of Reformed Cistercians" and strongly urged

---

[39] Cited in "Notre apostolat missionnaire monastique," 130.
[40] Cf. Hubrecht, *Une trappe en Chine*, 56.

"all the faithful to join this very beneficial association."[41] On 20 April 1925 the cardinal prefect of Propaganda Fide informed the abbot general of the Trappists that the congregation over which he presided wished "wholeheartedly to accept under its special protection" the *Pium opus*.[42] The general chapters of the Trappist Order held in 1923, 1924, 1925, 1926, and 1927 constantly commended the work to all the houses of the order, asking them to support it in every way.[43] Finally, in addition to the strong support given by the first apostolic delegate in China, Archbishop Celso Costantini (1922–1933), his successor, Archbishop Mario Zanin (1934–1946), also gave his support and called the work "not only good, but necessary."[44]

In the meantime, a work called *Croisade de prières pour la Chine*, founded by the Jesuit Fr. Alphonse Gasperment (1871–1951), a missionary in China, which was similar to the *Pium opus*, merged with the Trappist work that had recently received official approval.[45]

The *Pium opus*, now fully recognized and encouraged by ecclesiastical and monastic authorities, was a well-organized operation with its main center in Cîteaux and secondary centers in all the other monasteries of the order throughout the world, whose abbots, priors, or chaplains became its promoters. There were two conditions for membership of the *Pium opus*: having one's name entered in the register of the *Pium opus* at one of the centers and celebrating Mass or having a Mass celebrated every year, or, in place of a Mass, receiving Communion twelve times a year. Members were granted plenary or partial indulgences under specific conditions.[46] A Cistercian author, summarizing the characteristics of the work, said that it was first

[41] "Notre apostolat missionnaire monastique," 129. Cf. also Hubrecht, *Une trappe en Chine*, 59.

[42] "Notre apostolat missionnaire monastique," 128.

[43] Cf. the documents cited in "Notre apostolat missionnaire monastique," 130, 226.

[44] Ibid., 129.

[45] Cf. Un religieux cistercien, "L'Extrême-Orient au Sacré-Cœur. Œuvre de Messes et Croisade de Prières pour la conversion de la Chine, du Japon et des pays adjacents," in *Action missionnaire d'arrière-garde. Conférences* (Godewaersvelde: Abbaye Sainte-Marie-du-Mont, 1930), 53. See also the related documents in AGOCSO, fondo postulazione generale, dossier "Pium opus messarum et precum."

[46] Cf. Un religieux cistercien, "L'Extrême-Orient au Sacré-Cœur," 57–59.

and foremost an *apostolic* work ("Its purpose is the conversion of the East. . . . It is, therefore, a missionary work"); it was a *eucharistic* work ("It is above all through Masses and Communions that it intends to achieve its end"); it was a *Marian* work in that it drew its spiritual strength from the intercession of the Mother of the Lord; finally, it was a *sacrificial* work, because it was nourished by personal sacrifice, added to that of the Mass and of spiritual practices that were proposed for more fervent souls.[47]

The comprehensive structure of *Pium opus* helped it to spread rapidly throughout the world. According to statistics, the number of those enrolled in the work in 1925 was 354,466;[48] in 1929 that number had already more than doubled, to a total of 832,846;[49] and the following year it reached one million.[50] According to some documents, however, already in 1931 there were requests to transfer the responsibility for the work to another religious order. These requests continued until the 1950s, when the work came to an end.[51] Being part of *Pium opus* was one of the main reasons for the persecution unleashed against the Trappist monks in the forties. "In 1947 the prayers of the *Pium opus* became the material . . . for a presumptuous pretext for unleashing a persecution against the community of Yang-Kia-Ping [Yangjiaping], when, artificially distorted as activity against Communism, they were adopted in the formal charge against

---

[47] Cf. ibid., 55–56.

[48] Cf. Letter of Fr. Bernard, secretary of the abbot of Timadeuc, Dominique Nogues, delegated director of the *Pium opus*, 15 December 1925, in AGOCSO, fondo postulazione generale, dossier "Pium opus messarum et precum," 47.

[49] Of these, 14 were cardinals, 291 bishops, 8,562 secular priests, 171,336 men and women religious, 652,643 laypeople. Cf. *L'Extrême-Orient au Sacré-Cœur. Œuvre de Messes et Croisade de Prières. Compte-rendu pour l'année 1929* (n.p.: n.p., [1930]), 2.

[50] Cf. Beltrame Quattrocchi, *Monaci nella tormenta*, 50. In a letter from L. Brun to H.-J. Smets, 20 July 1931 (in AGOCSO, fondo postulazione generale, dossier "Pium opus messarum et precum," 58), we find the following enthusiastic statement: "Taking all things into consideration, under our direction, the *Pium opus* has been a success, a huge success. More than a million members in eight years. Who could have imagined something like this?"

[51] Cf. the documents in AGOCSO, fondo postulazione generale, dossier "Pium opus messarum et precum," 59–61, 64–75.

the monks and their abbot, thus making clear the evident anti-religious root of the entire procedure."[52]

The Encyclical *Rerum Ecclesiae*, the Work *Contemplation et Apostolat*, and the Journal *Bulletin des Missions*

Although the first seeds of monastic missionary vitality, particularly as regards spiritual commitment, were already present in the late nineteenth and early twentieth centuries, in general, "at the time of the great missionary thrust of the nineteenth century, monastic orders were not greatly interested in expanding outside of Europe," and a turning point occurred only after 1926.[53]

The person who decisively encouraged this change was Pope Pius XI. During his pontificate (1922–1939) he translated into action the urgent missionary concerns that his predecessor Benedict XV (1914–1922) in his encyclical *Maximum Illud* (30 November 1919) had already voiced concerning the missions and the creation of a native episcopate.

Among various initiatives in the mission field, first and foremost being the ordination of the first native bishops in some Asian countries[54] and a redrawing of ecclesiastical boundaries, some "showed more clearly the link between the contemplative life and missionary activity."[55] Besides fervent support for the creation and spread of *Pium opus* in 1923, as mentioned above, and the proclamation in 1927 of Therese of the Child Jesus co-patron, with Francis Xavier, of the missions, Pius XI sent his "missionary appeal" to the monastic world in two magisterial documents.[56] The first was the constitution *Umbratilem*, addressed to the Carthusian Order on 8 July 1924, in which the pope emphasized the crucial importance of the monks' prayer for the effectiveness of direct missionary action. His words

---

[52] Beltrame Quattrocchi, *Monaci nella tormenta*, 50.

[53] Leclercq, "Monachisme chrétien et missions," 141.

[54] In 1923 Pope Pius XI ordained the first Indian bishop, in 1926 the first six Chinese bishops, in 1927 the first Japanese bishop, and in 1933 the first Annamite bishop.

[55] Molette, "Mission et missions," 1399.

[56] Cf. "Sa sainteté Pie XI," COCR 6 (1939): 1–5.

were a further incentive to nurture the spiritual dimension of the monastic missionary apostolate. The second document, much more universal in scope, was the short but significant encyclical *Rerum Ecclesiae*, promulgated on 28 February 1926, which was directed to the "promotion of the missions" (*de missionibus provehendis*), addressed to bishops around the world.

> There still remains for us in this context to commend to your zeal a plan which, if it should be put into operation, we believe would greatly help in the wider diffusion of the faith. In what high esteem we hold the contemplative life is made abundantly clear in the apostolic constitution [*Umbratilem*] of two years ago, whereby we most gladly confirmed by our apostolic authority the rule of the Carthusians which had been revised to conform with the new Code of Canon Law. . . . Now, as we exhort from our heart the major superiors of similar contemplative orders, so you too in like manner give them repeated evidences of the fact that they, by *founding* such houses in the mission field, can *spread and promote the more austere types of contemplative life*. These contemplatives, too, will obtain from heaven for you and for the work to which you are devoted an abundance of graces. Nor is there any danger that such monks will not find *conditions for their mode of life satisfactory*. The inhabitants, particularly in certain places, although pagan in large majority have *a natural inclination towards solitude, prayer, and contemplation*. In this special connection may we call to your notice that great monastery which the Reformed Cistercians of La Trappe founded in the Vicariate Apostolic of Peking. In this monastery there are nearly one hundred monks, *the major portion of whom are Chinese*. As they, by the exercise of the most perfect virtue, by constant prayer, by the austerity of their lives, by manual labor placate the Divine Majesty and bring down the mercies of God both upon themselves and their pagan neighbors, so also *by the force of their example* they win these very pagans to Jesus Christ. It is, therefore, not to be questioned that these hermits, while they *guard intact the spirit of their holy Founder* and therefore *do not engage in an active life*, nevertheless they prove themselves of *great assistance in the successful work of the missions*. If, perchance, the superiors of any of these orders should heed your requests and establish houses for their subjects in places judged best by common agreement between you, they shall do something which will be, in the first place, very beneficial to the

great multitudes of pagans and which will be, secondly, more pleasing to us personally than any words can express.[57]

This text presented a summary of all the issues involved in the relationship between monasticism and mission that had been raised and discussed within the contemplative orders in those years. It strongly urged those same orders to continue theoretical reflection on missiology and, above all, to consider what concrete missionary practices could be undertaken by monastic foundations in mission lands. The encyclical presented three arguments to show why there was such an urgent need for monastic foundations.

The first and most "traditional" argument is that the presence of monks brings the *promise of spiritual intercession* to "obtain from heaven an abundance of graces" on pastors and the churches entrusted to them. As we have seen, the missionary dynamism that emerged from the monastic world in the previous decades had emphasized this spiritual role of the missionary monastery.

The second is that the monastic life, with the prayer, work, and asceticism that is proper to it, is an *effective example* in itself and does not need to "distort" itself by engaging in an active apostolate. By giving witness to a complete and radical Christian life, the form of Christian life that is proper to monasticism is of "great use for the success of the missions." Theological and, more specifically, missiological reflection over the decades leading up to Vatican II will emphasize the "magnificent witness" that monasticism can give. This same understanding of the missionary dimension of the monastic life is developed in a passage of the council's Decree on the Missionary Activity of the Church, *Ad Gentes* (7 December 1965).

> Institutes of the contemplative life, by their prayers, sufferings, and works of penance [*tribulationes*] have a very great importance in the conversion of souls, because it is God who sends workers into His harvest when He is asked to do so (cf. Matt 9:38), God who opens the minds of non-Christians to hear the Gospel (cf. Acts 16:4), and God who fructifies the word of

---

[57] Pius XI, *Rerum Ecclesiae* 28 (translation from the Vatican website; emphasis added). The Latin text of the encyclical was originally published in *Acta Apostolicae Sedis* 18, no. 3 (1926): 77–83.

salvation in their hearts (cf. 1 Cor 3:7). In fact, these institutes
are asked to found houses in mission areas, as not a few of them
have already done, so that there, living out their lives in a way
accommodated to the truly religious traditions of the people,
they can bear excellent witness among non-Christians to the
majesty and love of God, as well as to our union in Christ.[58]

The third argument is more properly monastic and regards a monastic foundation as an essential means of spreading the monastic way
of life. In fact, monasteries are urged to "spread the more austere forms
of contemplative life," knowing that among many peoples in mission
lands there is already a fertile ground prepared by the natural inclination
of many persons toward a way of life that values "solitude," "prayer,"
and "contemplation." Of the three arguments, this is undoubtedly the
one that will take decades to be fully realized. Indeed, it was only in
response to the issuing of another papal document, the encyclical *Fidei
Donum* (21 April 1957), in which Pius XII summoned all Catholics to
deploy their resources for the spread of the faith throughout the world,
that Benedictines and Cistercians began to think seriously about the
missionary thrust of monastic foundations. In 1961 the jointly created
secretariat for missions called "Aide à l'implantation monastique"
(AIM) was established for the purpose of supporting new monastic
foundations and fostering the human, cultural, and spiritual development of monasteries throughout the world.[59]

As Jean Leclercq put it so well, it finally became possible to conceive of a "non-missionary [monastic] presence in the missions."[60]
There was a clearer understanding that "the role of monasticism is
to bring monastic life to the missions, with all that it entails for the

[58] Vatican Council II, *Ad Gentes* 40 (translation from the Vatican website).

[59] This secretariat, which in 1976 changed its name to "Aide inter-monastères" and
in 1997 was reorganized, taking the name "Alliance inter-monastères," has its center
in Vanves (France) at the priory of Sainte-Bathilde. It publishes a biannual bulletin
(*Bulletin de l'AIM*) and has an internet site (http://www.aimintl.org). For a history of
the secretariat, see Jean Leclercq, *Nouvelle page d'histoire monastique. Histoire de
l'AIM. 1960–1985* ([Vanves]: AIM, 1986); Irene Debalus, "AIM: Fifty Years and More
of Sustaining the Momentum of Monastic Life in Asia," *AIM Bulletin* 102 (2012):
30–42; *So Far yet So Near: Monasticism for a New World; Alliance for International
Monasticism* (Sankt Ottilien: EOS, 2013).

[60] Leclercq, "Monachisme chrétien et missions," 151.

life of a church, and not to do something else there."[61] As this point became even clearer, attention was also given to the question of the inculturation of monasticism in other cultural and spiritual settings, but this reflection was still in an embryonic stage.

The encyclical *Rerum Ecclesiae* became a point of reference for those in the monastic world who were willing to further the development of one or both dimensions, the theoretical and the practical, of monastic mission. The main organ of this missionary dynamism in the monastic world was the organization *Contemplation et Apostolat*, and its prime means of communication was the journal *Bulletin des Missions*. The organization and the journal were located at the Belgian Abbey of Saint-André in Bruges, and their two leading figures were Théodore Nève, abbot of Saint-André, and Édouard Neut, a monk of the same abbey.

During his long tenure as abbot (1912–1958), Théodore Nève typified the missionary ideal of the "monk-apostle" that he had inherited from his predecessor, the founder of Saint-André, Gérard Van Caloen. In 1916 Abbot Nève made an impassioned entry in his diary. "God is asking great things of us. Saint-André must be a nursery of *monk-apostles*, who will not only carry the light of the Gospel everywhere that the church will send them, but will cause the virtues of our predecessors to flourish in new solitudes."[62]

This monastic and missionary ideal was judged, at least in principle, to be at the center of what was an essential element of the monastic life. There is no monastic life without genuine fraternal life and communal liturgical prayer. As the abbot of Saint-André said in 1928, when he conferred the mission cross on two brothers who were being sent to the monastery in Xishan, "The monk exercises his ministry not in his name but in the name of the monastery; it is the monastery that evangelizes."[63] On this same occasion he also declared: "May the recitation and singing of the Divine Office be regulated before every other occupation. May delicate fraternal

---

[61] Ibid., 146.

[62] Cited in Christian Papeians de Morchoven, *L'abbaye de Saint-André Zevenkerken*, vol. 2: *Un défi relevé par dom Théodore Nève* (Tielt: Lannoo, 2002), 56 (emphasis added).

[63] Édouard Neut, "Le Moine Apôtre," BM 6 (1920–1923): 123.

charity rule all your relations, may observance rule all your activity, both within and outside the monastery."[64]

Abbot Nève stressed the central position of common prayer as an important condition for the fecundity of the monastic mission a few years later when he reflected on the experience of making a foundation in China.

> To show the Chinese religious life as it is practiced in the Catholic Church, to introduce and develop it in China, to combat with its help the fascinating influence of pagan superstitions—this is and this remains the primary goal of our Benedictine foundation. Moreover, the principal work of monks finds its highest expression in psalmody and the chanting of the Divine Office. The *"nihil operi divino praeponatur"* of Saint Benedict is carried out daily in Si-Shan [Xishan]. Seven times during the day and once during the night the triple gong before the oratory is struck and its echoes resound in the valley. The monks go to the choir. By their solemn liturgical prayer they desire to draw abundant blessings on China, on its church, on its prelates, its priests, and its missionaries and thus they hope to give their share to the immense apostolic work spread over the Chinese Empire in order to win it totally to Christ.[65]

The abbot of Saint-André opened another way for the monastic community to be apostolic when he said, "Si-Shan ought to engage in apostolic action in its locality."[66] "But while the Benedictine monk has lent his voice to the church to chant the divine praises, he can also ask to participate directly in such fruitful labors of preparing souls: his task remains in harmony with his obligations of the monastic life and is only more orderly and more productive. After the tribute of divine praises, Si-Shan offers to its monks the attractive work of education and instruction."[67]

The real challenge for the "missionary monastery," as we will see from detailed study of the monastic mission in China, will be maintaining a balanced implementation of these two dimensions.

---

[64] Cited in Papeians de Morchoven, *L'abbaye de Saint-André Zevenkerken*, 2:57.

[65] Théodore Nève, "Le monastère des SS. Pierre et André de Si-Shan," BM 15 (1936), supp. no. 1: *Le Courrier de l'Apostolat Monastique*, 9*.

[66] Ibid.

[67] Ibid., 9*–10*.

Endowed with a talent for writing, Édouard Neut publicized the
ideas of Saint-André and its abbot passionately and tirelessly. When
he took over the editorial direction of the *Bulletin des Missions* in
the 1920s—it had begun publication in 1905—he made the ideals of
the "monk-apostle" and the "apostolate of the monks" its dominant
themes. More generally, Fr. Édouard's missionary zeal was directed to
making known the missionary teachings of Popes Benedict XV and
Pius XI, in which they espoused a new way of engaging in mission,
which was clearly oriented in the direction of what is now called "inculturation" and whose main exponent was Fr. Vincent Lebbe. Neut
regarded Lebbe with "profound and overwhelming admiration."[68]
Beginning in the early 1920s, China, with all its problems, was the
region covered the most by the magazine, and Édouard Neut did all
he could to give voice and support to the new directions for mission
that were at their height in the ecclesiastical and monastic world.
He wrote at the beginning of 1923: "In widening the scope of our
journal beyond the immediate activity of the abbey and of the Order
of Saint Benedict, we want to acquaint our readers with the great
problems confronting the evangelization of the world."[69]

This goal was pursued steadfastly—notwithstanding the objections
of many readers that the *Bulletin* had become the organ of a new
missionary movement, controversially referred to as the "Belgian
missionary movement"—because it was propagating the prophetic
intuitions of Lebbe and the ideas contained in the papal documents
inspired by him.[70]

Interestingly, the *Bulletin des Missions* was the main publication
paying attention to the specific contribution of the monastic world to
reflection regarding monasticism and mission. It did so, first of all,
by accepting responsibility for the movement called *Contemplation
et Apostolat*. This movement was created by a priest of the Society
of African Missions, but it was similar to a project that was dear to
Abbot Nève and that had received the spiritual support of the Carmel
of Lisieux already in 1925. This movement was originally conceived

[68] Papeians de Morchoven, *L'abbaye de Saint-André Zevenkerken*, 2:162.
[69] BM 6 (1920–1923): 389.
[70] Cf. Papeians de Morchoven, *L'abbaye de Saint-André Zevenkerken*, 2:162–82.

of as the "spiritual adoption" of a mission territory on the part of a contemplative monastery that would, in turn, ensure constant prayer for the growth of the Christian community in that area of the world. The movement, thus, was a way of "putting the spiritual forces of contemplative houses directly at the service of evangelization."[71] The main characteristics of the work were well described in the *Bulletin des Missions*.

> We are trying to arouse in all contemplative monasteries a real love of Christ the Apostle. We are trying to arouse in missionary milieus a real love of Christ Praying. We are asking missionary bishops if they would not like us to find for them a contemplative monastery that would agree to adopting their mission and their seminary spiritually. Such adoption would not mean any special exercise; it would demand an effective intention and an active interest. Relations by letters would be established between missionaries and contemplatives. These relations would render charity alive.[72]

Enthusiastic support for the work came from monasteries and also from vicars apostolic and prefects. One of them, for example, commended it in these terms: "The work of *Contemplation et Apostolat*, through the mighty means of prayer, is destined to give growth to and to crown every apostolate by ensuring God's blessing on our poor endeavors."[73]

The movement, which had the *Bulletin des Missions* as its "humble instrument for establishing ties" and which was also supported by the Benedictine sisters of Bethany (Lophem, Bruges), was officially established in 1926 at the Abbey of Saint-André. It began functioning shortly thereafter, establishing dozens of "spiritual twins."[74] From the very beginning, however, in addition to seeking prayerful support for

---

[71] Un religieux cistercien, "Une œuvre d'adoption spirituelle des missions par des communautés de contemplatifs," in *Action missionnaire d'arrière-garde*, 65.

[72] Édouard Neut, "Le Christ apôtre cherche des contemplatifs," BM 9 (1928–1929): 300.

[73] Letter from A. Vignato, apostolic prefect of the Equatorial Nile (1923–1934), to the administration of *Contemplation et Apostolat*, cited in *Contemplation et Apostolat* (Lophem-lez-Bruges: Abbaye de Saint-André, 1927), 9.

[74] Cf. *Contemplation et Apostolat*, 5–8.

their work, ordinaries and heads of missions requested that monasteries be founded in the territories entrusted to their pastoral care.[75] One example of such a request was that made by Msgr. Jean-Baptiste de Guébriant, superior of the Paris Foreign Missions Society.

> If in a mission that I love and for which I am more or less responsible, in China, in Tibet, in Japan, in Annam, in the Indies, I would be given the choice between two forms of good news: either that 10,000 new Christians have been baptized this year or that a monastery was opened by the Cistercians, the Carthusians, or the Benedictines—I would choose the second alternative. This would give me more joy, because it would open for me vaster prospects. What I say today, I would already have said forty years ago, but with how much more conviction today, after the appeal of the pope to the superiors general of contemplative orders to introduce and extend ever more this form of more austere life in mission countries by founding monasteries there.[76]

Contemplation et Apostolat proposed "creating a movement of public opinion" as well as "serving as an intermediary for missionaries and communities that so wish, providing them with all the means that are proper to it."[77] In a letter approving the movement, Cardinal Willem Van Rossum, prefect of Propaganda Fide, stated: "If tangible results, and above all, results that we await with impatience, are to be obtained, mission countries themselves must have monasteries of contemplatives who day and night intercede before the Divine Majesty to obtain the graces that we have spoken about. These monasteries will be an integral part of the church founded in these countries."[78]

Through the magazine that bore the same name as the movement, *Contemplation et Apostolat*, which was first published at Saint-André as an extract of the *Bulletin des Missions* and then, after 1933, as

[75] Cf. Neut, "Le Christ apôtre cherche des contemplatifs," 304–7.

[76] J.-B. de Guébriant, "Le monachisme en pays de mission," *Annales des Missions Étrangères de Paris* (1929): 243.

[77] "L'œuvre 'Contemplation et Apostolat' sous le Pontificat de SS. Pie XI," CA 11 (1939): 18*.

[78] Letter from W. Van Rossum to the administration of *Contemplation et Apostolat*, 31 December 1928, given in Neut, "Le Christ apôtre cherche des contemplatifs," 308.

a supplement of the same journal, we can follow the projects and accomplishments of the movement. On 9 February 1932 the movement received the blessing of Pope Pius XI in a private audience. Then, over the years, the movement inspired an increasing number of spiritual adoptions[79] and supported monastic foundations in mission countries, which multiplied at an accelerated pace following the promulgation of the encyclical *Rerum Ecclesiae*. In the fourteen years between 1926 and 1939 eighty new foundations were made, of which twenty-three were Carmelite,[80] nine Benedictine (six of men and three of women), one Olivetan Benedictine, seven Cistercian, and three Trappist (two of men, one of women).[81] During this period the movement, unstintingly supported and promoted by the *Bulletin des Missions*, called on the monastic world to heed the need of mission among the nations by making monastic foundations, as the journal of the movement noted in 1939.

> In most of the [mission countries] aspirations to the contemplative life still wait to be satisfied. Contemplative life, however, is not an accessory of Christian life; it is rather an integral part of the church's physiognomy, so much so that if it is not established in mission countries, the church itself will appear without all its wealth and its vitality. It is the duty of those who follow this life and have received it from the Catholic Church to communicate it to these new lands. Charity demands that what one has received oneself, one must be ready to transmit to others, because ancient Catholic lands should not have a monopoly on anything in the church. Christ's words are addressed equally to contemplative convents: "Go and teach all nations" (Matt 28:19). It is up to them to teach new peoples the life of prayer and sacrifice in order to vivify the works of the active apostolate.[82]

The contribution of the *Bulletin des Missions* went beyond coordinating the activities of *Contemplation et Apostolat*. Its pages

---

[79] In 1929 the number of spiritual adoptions was 462, in 1933 there were 569, and in 1939, 783; also in 1939, some 256 seminaries were adopted; cf. "L'œuvre 'Contemplation et Apostolat,'" 9*.

[80] Cf. "La Carmélite Missionnaire," *Messager Thérésien* 21, no. 7 (1940): 159–60.

[81] Cf. "L'œuvre 'Contemplation et Apostolat,'" 12*–17*.

[82] Ibid., 19*.

included the contributions of those from the monastic world who were then reflecting on the various dimensions of "monastic missiology," namely, the reasons, methods, and problems related to the founding of monasteries in mission territories. In the issues of the *Bulletin des Missions* and its supplement *Contemplation et Apostolat* from the 1920s to the 1950s, articles of the abbot of Saint-André predominate. In 1926, during the fourth Missiology Week at Louvain, which brought together a number of influential scholars, the abbot gave a talk entitled "Regarding the Establishment of Monasteries in Mission Lands."[83] In it he systematically addressed the question of adaptation. In subsequent years he frequently returned to this topic in the pages of the *Bulletin des Missions.*

In this talk Abbot Nève set out to elucidate a seeming contradiction: "Contemplative life in mission—is it possible? It would seem that these two things are mutually exclusive."[84] He began by reviewing the contents of the recent papal document *Rerum Ecclesiae*, emphasizing one aspect in particular, namely, that monastic life can only be missionary if it radically lives out the *forma vitae* that is proper to cenobites.

> Monks form a *coenobium*, that is, a family-like grouping. It is in the *coenobium* that they pray, it is in the *coenobium* that they live, it is in the *coenobium* that they evangelize, and there resides the particular strength of their action. If they abandon this strength they lose the best thing they have. Certain transient circumstances may lead temporarily to a different apostolate, but the monks who definitively renounce giving their apostolate a cenobitic form lose their original character and stop acting like monks. . . . This monastic life must be proffered to all the peoples to whom the pioneers of the Gospel are today announcing salvation.[85]

Starting out from this fundamental conviction, Abbot Nève outlines the elements that a monastery in mission must ensure so

---

[83] Cf. Théodore Nève, "De la fondation de monastères en terre de mission," in *Autour du problème de l'adaptation. Compte rendu de la quatrième semaine de missiologie de Louvain (1926)* (Louvain: Éditions du Museum Lessianum, 1926), 36–46.

[84] Ibid., 36.

[85] Ibid., 37–38.

that "it can be planted and sprout," that is, become autonomous. Such autonomy is, in fact, the ultimate goal, for it is the sign that a community has roots and will develop. "What, then is the role of monasticism in mission lands today? First of all, it must be planted and sprout. The apostolic movement that urges a monastery to found others does not have for its object the establishment of branches of the motherhouse, but rather the establishment of new families, which, in the measure that they have *their own* recruitment, become autonomous."[86]

The life of an "apostolic monastery," as the author calls it, is based on two pillars: the Divine Office, by which a monastery carries out its apostolic activity as a school of prayer; and work, which in the case of monasteries that combine external activity with contemplation, "while remaining coenobitic, should be clearly apostolic, especially if the monastery is founded in a mission land, and should be ordered and regulated according to the circumstances of place, time, and people. . . . An apostolic monastery is a monastery that irradiates: it diffuses supernatural life by the carrying out of its liturgical life and, at the same time, it gains souls by divine words and by teaching. The monks . . . must establish around them a variety of works that penetrate the entire territory that is to be evangelized."[87]

Among the "works" that Nève finds especially appropriate for a mission monastery are education, which also includes the kind of intellectual work by which monks "devote themselves to the study of the language, history, customs, and philosophy and religion of the countries they evangelize,"[88] and hospitality, which also involves assistance to the poor and the sick through the establishment of hospitals, dispensaries, and orphanages.

Among later reflections that came from the Benedictine milieu and appeared in the periodical *Contemplation et Apostolat*, those of Jean Delacroix, the prior of the same Abbey of Saint-André, that appeared in 1947 deserve mention. They are the outcome of a trip to India and China that he made specifically for the purpose of de-

---

[86] Ibid., 40.
[87] Ibid., 41.
[88] Ibid.

termining "the possibility of monastic life in those countries as well as the best conditions for its development" and appear as the first tentative results of his study, still in its initial stages, of the inculturation of Christian monasticism in the spiritual context of Asia.[89] He distinguishes three settings that are more or less receptive to the establishment of a monastic life that is capable of "attracting" and incorporating a number of native elements.

The first setting is one where people have recently been drawn to the message of the Gospel—which was still the case, for example, in many regions of China. Such people "would have little attraction for the monastic life and little understanding of it." In such a setting, the author sees only one way that monastic life can be effective. "In these regions monasticism will be able to penetrate and to develop only by giving an example of some useful activity that will grant it admission and even appreciation. This benefit, which is secondary for the monks, will doubtlessly be the first thing examined by the people among whom they come to live. Obviously, the apostolic activity is to be chosen and apportioned in such a manner that it will not in any way contradict the monastic and contemplative ideal of the religious institute."[90]

As examples of activities that are compatible with the monastic life, he mentions schools of agriculture and the crafts and works of the "intellectual apostolate," such as teaching and publication. In such a setting the author thinks that the presence of foreign monks will be necessary for a relatively long time and "adaptation will not be realized immediately."

The second setting is one in which Christianity has already penetrated deeply, as had been the case in some northern and coastal regions of China or in various parts of India. In these christianized regions "monasticism is implanted very easily," for it answers a felt spiritual need. "In these regions the European element should not be very prominent, but from the beginning monastics should have a perfect knowledge of the language, customs, and spiritual needs

[89] Cf. Jean Delacroix, "Possibilités monastiques aux Indes et en Extrême-Orient," CA 12 (1947): 7–13.
[90] Ibid., 8.

of the Christian population of the region. Very soon the milieu itself will furnish the vocations necessary for the development of the
monastery. Adaptation, thus, must be as total as possible, from the
very beginning."[91]

The third setting, finally, is defined by the author as naturally
open, prepared for the contemplative and monastic life thanks to a
religious, spiritual, and mystical dimension of its own. Here he is
thinking especially of certain parts of India, where "monasticism
should be integrally presented for what it is, without resorting to this
or that particular way of penetration." It should present itself simply
as the true school for seeking God and take care to "take into account
the ascetical and mystical need that lies hidden in those souls."[92]

The pages of the *Bulletin des Missions* and its supplement *Contemplation et Apostolat* contain various reflections from Trappists, who,
together with Carmelites, were the leading players on the monastic
missionary scene. As one Trappist wrote at the end of the 1930s:
"With our six monasteries in the Far East we [Trappists] are clearly
at the head of the contemplatives who are heading to the missions."[93]

In the 1920s and 1930s the periodical of Saint-André along with
the *Collectanea Ordinis Cisterciensium Reformatorum* of the Trappist Order, which contained a special section on "Cistercian missiology," not only devoted pages to the sources, nature, and fruitfulness of
the missionary apostolate in general[94] but also published reflections
on the particular missionary vocation of a monastic order such as

---

[91] Ibid., 9.

[92] Ibid., 10.

[93] Jean-Marie Struyven, "Œuvre de messes et croisade de prières. À propos d'un
jubilé (1914–1939)," COCR 6 (1939): 259. It was not by chance that Pius XI addressed the Trappists again in 1930, encouraging them to proceed further with the
decision for "missionary action" they had taken in previous decades. "You who bear
the name of Cistercians of the Strict Observance have dedicated yourselves ever more
wholeheartedly to spread the Kingdom of Jesus Christ in China and Japan through
your *missionary action*." Apostolic letter sent by Pope Pius XI to the two abbots
general of the Cistercian Order on 20 July 1930, the centenary of the elevation of St.
Bernard of Clairvaux to the rank of Doctor of the Church, cited in "Notre apostolat
missionnaire monastique," 57 (emphasis added).

[94] Cf. "Le devoir de l'apostolat missionnaire," COCR 3 (1936): 36–37, 98–99,
168–69; 4 (1937): 31–33; "Les sources de l'apostolat missionnaire," COCR 4 (1937):
127–30, 210–13.

the Trappists. These reflections constantly emphasize the essential *modality* of a monastic missionary foundation, characterizing it as a presence that, by living out the vocation that is proper to it, radiates *by this very fact* the light of the Gospel to all in its vicinity.

> [The Cistercian monastery], beyond its apostolate through prayer and penance, . . . has preached the Gospel by the efficaciousness of its examples or, in a wider sense, by the *irradiation of its presence*. Charged with giving to souls "that seek God" a refuge where they can imitate and love Christ, with stimulating the faithful by the display of authentically Christian life, with showing pagans the true face of Catholicism, monasticism must be extended as far as Christianity itself. . . . The monastery also preaches fervor to the Christians who approach it. An existence in which prayer, work, mortification are marvelously balanced cannot but impress the faithful, show them the Gospel as lived, hence *evangelize* them.[95]

As already noted, many Trappist writers express the profound conviction that "the only motivation for a Trappist foundation in China is to give life to a new type of missiology: a life of prayer in the mission field."[96]

There were three prominent voices in those years. The first was that of Jean-Baptiste Chautard, abbot of Sept-Fons and father immediate of the Trappist monastery in Yangjiaping (1899–1935). In his exhortations to the monks to embrace the monastic apostolate of prayer and of penance he remained firm in his view that "the Trappists in China, as in any other place, should refrain from any apostolate outside the monastery." He believed that Trappists, by "remaining faithful to their vocation as contemplatives, will be most useful to the church by not engaging in activities to which they are not called by God."[97] The second voice was that of Louis Brun, abbot of the

---

[95] Frère M. Albert, "Notre vocation missionnaire," COCR 6 (1939): 131, 137.

[96] Paolino Beltrame Quattrocchi, "The Trappist Monks in China," in *Historiography of the Chinese Catholic Church: Nineteenth and Twentieth Centuries*, ed. Jeroom Heyndrickx (Leuven: Ferdinand Verbiest Foundation, K. U. Leuven, 1994), 315.

[97] Jean-Baptiste Auniord, "Dom Chautard, abbé de Sept-Fons. Vie intérieure et apostolat—Les trappistes en pays de mission," CA 6 (1935): 225. Here too Abbot Chautard "preferred prudence to boldness in making foundations." Ibid., 224.

Trappist monastery of Chinese Yangjiaping. He warned his monks: "All ministries are to be absolutely avoided. The monks come not *for a mission*, but *to a mission land*, and they come not to carry out an apostolic ministry, but to be perfect monks and to form disciples."[98]

The third voice was that of Gérard Haverbèque, abbot visitor of the Trappist monasteries in the East, who described the precise nature of the "silent preaching of monastic communities."

> Monastic life is essentially a life dedicated entirely to God's praise, love, and service. . . . Monastic communities have their clear place in mission lands, as much and even more than elsewhere, because they do all this *outstandingly*, they form persons for this *outstandingly*. . . . This essential role of the monastic life is closely tied to its apostolic efficacy. The latter depends on the former. Monks are so useful for the church and for the world because they love and serve God with all their heart, with all their soul, with their whole strength, because they fully carry out their acts of charity. . . . Contemplative communities contribute to the salvation of souls in the measure that they are *more faithful, more attached, more devoted* to the Father in heaven and to his Son Jesus.[99]

In his analysis, Abbot Haverbèque summarizes the three reasons already stated by Pius XI in *Rerum Ecclesiae* that indicate why monasteries appear "necessary, urgently necessary, in mission countries." The first reason is that they offer a place that can accommodate those who in a local church manifest "an attraction to and a capability for the contemplative life." The second reason is that they ensure that "a local church, even in mission countries, is equipped with all the ministries and structures necessary or useful for the full development of the supernatural life," including prayer and the asceticism proper to the monastic life. The third is that they ensure the presence among the nations of monastic communities that are a "living sermon, a particularly striking witness" to the Christian faith.[100]

[98] Louis Brun, "La vie contemplative en Chine," in Hubrecht, *Une trappe en Chine*, 101 (emphasis added).

[99] Gérard Haverbèque, "Pourquoi des monastères en Extrême-Orient," CA 6 (1935): 233–34 (emphasis added).

[100] Cf. ibid., 230–33.

Finally, we take note of an author who was not a Cistercian but who set out to evaluate the presence of Reformed Cistercians in East Asia. Writing in 1926, he presents a synthesis of the thinking of the Trappist founders in the Far East, showing that their thinking evolved between the time of the first foundations in the second half of the nineteenth century and those that had been made more recently.

> According to what the founders of the first Trappist monasteries in the Far East had in mind, the apostolic goal takes precedence over thought about personal sanctification. The monastery is conceived first of all as a work meant to support by prayer and example the missionaries in the conversion of pagans. . . . What takes precedence is the idea of apostolate among pagans: the monastery is first of all at the service of the missionary and of the pagan population. In recent foundations, however, this conception recedes. Here the monastery is considered as an institute of sanctification offered to the already Christian part of the mission and one that will allow the natives solicited by divine grace to tend toward evangelical perfection more easily and more surely.[101]

One last quote can serve as a bridge between a theoretical consideration of monasticism and mission and a discussion of monastic mission in China. The ideas expressed and the language used show that the foundation of monasteries in China was based on and directed by previous theoretical considerations. The words are those of Aurelius Stehle, abbot of the Benedictine Abbey of St. Vincent in the United States, in a speech to the monks of the American Cassinese Congregation in 1924, when monks from that congregation arrived in China. "The Benedictine is no mere preacher. He brings with him, in his monasticism, a complete miniature of the ideal Christian society. This is what makes him an apostle par excellence. . . . The religious is a soldier; the monk is a colonist, and herein lies the secret of the latter's apostolic efficacy. China has had many religious missionaries, but it is especially by the monastic missionary that its ultimate conversion will be achieved."[102]

---

[101] [Père] Peffer, "Les Cisterciens réformés dans l'Asie Orientale," in *Autour du problème de l'adaptation*, 49–50.

[102] "Archabbot Aurelius Stehle to the Monks of the American Cassinese Congregation on the Founding of the Catholic University of Peking. October 5, 1924,"

Toward a Chinese Christian Monasticism

With this missiological and monastic *reflection* in the background, we can better understand the courageous *establishment* of several communities and monastic orders on Chinese soil, the topic that constitutes the chapters of this book on the history of Christian monasticism in China. This history regards Christian *monastic foundations* in China in a period between roughly 1869, the year of the founding of the first Carmel on Chinese soil,[103] and 1955, the year when the last foreign nuns were forced to leave China.[104] Chapter 1 will present the "pioneers" of the Christian monastic presence in China: the monks of the Church of the East and their missionary adventure in China during the period between the seventh and thirteenth centuries. Brief and necessarily cautious references to monastic matters following the forced expulsion of foreign monks and nuns in the early 1950s will finally be given.

The common thread running through this historical research, as well as my principal intention, beyond the reconstruction of the main events relating to the monastic foundations in China, is to highlight the willingness of foreign monks to encounter the cultural

---

in Jerome Oetgen, *Mission to America: A History of Saint Vincent Archabbey, the First Benedictine Monastery in the United States* (Washington, DC: The Catholic University of America Press, 2000), 534–35.

[103] In fact, the Poor Clares of Manila had already founded a convent in Macau in 1633. The monastery of St. Clare continued in existence for two centuries, until 1835, when the law of suppression of women's religious orders promulgated by the Portuguese government the previous year was also applied in the Chinese colony. Cf. Manuel Teixeira, "Os Franciscanos em Macau," *Archivo Ibero-Americano* 38 (1978): 347–49. The Poor Clares are known in Chinese as *Sheng Jialan yinxiuhui* 聖佳蘭隱修會 (the contemplative order of St. Clare).

[104] Although it will not be discussed in detail, the presence in China of a monastery of the Sister-Servants of the Holy Spirit of Perpetual Adoration (SSpSAP) should be mentioned. This congregation, whose first group of novices was formed in 1896 in Steyl at the initiative of Arnold Janssen (1837–1909), founder of the Missionary Society of the Divine Word (SVD), became an independent congregation in 1917 with the aim of assisting the dissemination of the faith through the apostolate of prayer. The nuns' vocation involves a strictly contemplative cloistered life dedicated to prayer for the missions. In 1932 a group of seven nuns founded a monastery in China in Qingdao (Tsingtao) in the Shandong region. Cf. Karl Müller, *Kontemplation und Mission. Steyler Anbetungsschwestern 1896–1996* (Rome: apud Collegium Verbi Divini, 1996).

and spiritual realities of China and the degree of acceptance by the Chinese of the form of monastic life that was presented to them by the missionaries.

At this point I would like to summarize the reflections of some of the persons who were directly or indirectly involved in helping to initiate and then to continue the relations between Christian monastic life and Chinese culture. This was the first time in the history of Catholic missiology that consideration was given to the prospect of *Chinese Christian monasticism*,[105] and the reflection of these individuals focused mainly on the compatibility of Christian monasticism with the spirituality of China and the possibility of Christian monastic life taking root in Chinese soil.

It seems to me that what provoked this reflection was the unexpected yet clear awareness on the part of all involved in the Chinese monastic mission that the Chinese and, more generally, the peoples of the Far East could be called to the Christian monastic way of life. They have all that is needed to become good monks and, even more, they are naturally predisposed for such a form of life. Such was the initial and fundamental awareness of the *possibility* and *necessity* of an *indigenous monasticism* in China.

"Is the Far East suitable for monasticism?" asked Msgr. de Guébriant in 1929. His answer was: "It always has been, and today more than ever."[106] Among the many voices that echoed and developed this point of view, I cite only a few, mainly from the Trappist monastic world or related to it. It was said of the Trappist Abbot Jean-Baptiste Chautard that "he was able to see that the Chinese character is perfectly capable of adapting to the Cistercian life and of admiring the simple and strong virtues of some Chinese lay brothers."[107] Others, expressing themselves in the language of the time, said that "a person from the Far East may, in all respects, be as good a monk as someone from Europe."[108] "The Chinese are greatly attracted by the cenobitic life and the community exercises. They appear as perfect Christians

[105] "For a Chinese [Christian] Monasticism" was the title of an editorial in the *Bulletin des Missions* of 1927 ("Pour un monachisme chinois," BM 8 [1926–1927]: 257).

[106] Guébriant, "Le monachisme en pays de mission," 245.

[107] Auniord, "Dom Chautard, abbé de Sept-Fons," 223.

[108] Emmanuel de Meester, "Trappistes et Missions," CA 2 (1933): 74.

in the religious life. They generally understand very well the high supernatural force of renunciation and of sacrifice."[109]

> We have the experience of more than fifty years to show that our brothers of the yellow race have sufficient aptitude to become sons of St. Bernard. Both in the ancient Celestial Empire [i.e., China] and in that of the Rising Sun [i.e., Japan] monks and nuns are being formed today in Cistercian spirituality and know the benefits of the contemplative life. . . . The Trappists are the contemplative religious whose way of life best answers the aspirations and the temperament of the young people of the yellow race. . . . Could it not be affirmed that the Asian soul is naturally monastic? For more than two millennia the influence of the religions of Brahma, of Buddha, of Confucius have permeated the souls with prayer, asceticism, and a certain purity. Would not this be a propitious "climate" for the flowering of contemplative and penitential vocations in the light of Christ?[110]

A visitor of Our Lady of Consolation reported: "From the moment of my arrival in the Trappe of Our Lady of Consolation I had the impression that nowhere so much as in this out-of-the-way corner of China monastic life answered to this ideal [of the primacy of the spirit] and to this providential mission [of proclaiming this ideal]. . . . [The monks'] piety has peopled the monastery. The one hundred religious, who share the daily works and whose regular observance edifies me, prove the power of attraction of a fervent abbey."[111]

---

[109] M.-B. Delauze, abbot of Aiguebelle (1923–1946) and visitator of the Trappist monastery in Yangjiaping, cited in Peffer, "Les Cisterciens réformés dans l'Asie Orientale," 52.

[110] Frère M. Albert, "Notre vocation missionnaire," 135, 137. There were some Trappists who believed that the role of Christian monasticism was to counter Buddhist monastic life. "What do we have that is opposed to the Buddhist monastic life, which, in the eyes of half of southern and eastern Asia, incarnates the ideal lived by Buddha? It cannot only be an 'activism' that is incomprehensible to souls who reach out, more than we do, to the liberation of the whole being through the extinction of the passions and the practices of nirvana. . . . Christian monasticism could teach Asia that this release is not only the result of the negative practice of stripping away, but rather being granted access to the greater enrichment of all, as is the case of the disciple of the God-love who became man not to preach nirvana to us, but to give us life." François Vandenbroucke, "Monachisme missionnaire," CA 14 (1950): 15–16.

[111] Albert Valensin, "Une visite à Notre Dame de la Consolation, Yangkiap'ing. Chine," COCR 4 (1937): 259–60.

Who but Louis Brun, the third abbot of the Chinese Trappist monastery of Our Lady of Consolation, could better describe, on the basis of his experience of accepting dozens of young Chinese into the monastic life, the compatibility of Christian monasticism and Chinese life? In pages specifically dedicated to "the Chinese and the contemplative life" the abbot of Yangjiaping asks, "Are the Chinese capable of contemplation? Are they mature enough for contemplation?"[112] His response is that the Chinese, like men and women of all ethnic groups and all cultures, are certainly capable of contemplation and that God calls to this life, even in China, young people from different origins, social backgrounds, and levels of education. He admits that young Chinese have the same difficulties following the monastic way that is common to all the "sons of Adam," but he goes beyond this:

> It has been said that the Chinese would have a certain aptitude for contemplation and would be more disposed than other peoples for the contemplative life, and to support this are cited their sobriety, their hard life, the existence of many Buddhist or Taoist monasteries, the meditative character of the people, less given to action than Europeans. . . . We might also say what will seem a paradox to many, that the Rule of St. Benedict seems to have been composed for the Chinese. We mean that the Chinese Christian is at ease under the rule of the holy patriarch and quickly habituates himself to it. . . . Would we not be justified to say that our Chinese Christians find in the life of the Benedictine cloister, together with many points in common with their own mentality, all the means for developing and intensifying the good sides of their culture?[113]

Finally, we should take note of the acute observation of Vincent Lebbe. In 1932, a few years after the founding of the monastery of the Little Brothers of John the Baptist, he wrote that the "temperament common to many Chinese [shows] a natural disposition to the monastic life."

---

[112] Cf. Louis Brun, "Le chinois et la vie contemplative," in Hubrecht, *Une trappe en Chine*, 83–89.

[113] Ibid., 84, 87–89.

The great mass of the Chinese people is used to a frugal life. Even the pagans are familiar with the idea of submitting themselves to a *strict monastic discipline* and of bearing privations in order to obtain a spiritual benefit. It seems that a considerable number of peasants, of functionaries, and of the erudite, of Chinese of all conditions are naturally disposed for the monastic life. Consider: there are tens of thousands of Buddhist monks who lead an austere life in monasteries throughout the country. Doubtless, some are known to be dissolute, but the majority of them observe their vows of poverty, chastity, and obedience amidst a multitude of austerities, such as meditations at night, vigils, complete abstention from meat, eggs, tobacco, alcoholic drinks, and the like, with a scrupulous exactness that is not surpassed even by the most rigorous Catholic cloistered communities. Similarly, among the lay disciples of Buddhism many persons of our acquaintance observe a rule of life that strongly resembles that of the strictest bonzes. It is certainly in the interest of the Catholic Church to become aware of this temperament common to many Chinese and to benefit from it for its own situation. In Europe the work of evangelization that was able to traverse the centuries was founded on an indigenous monasticism. It was the monks who built and sustained the church of God in Europe. There is no good reason why the same thing cannot happen in China.[114]

The conviction of Fr. Lebbe leads to a second stage in the evolution of monastic reflection on the possibilities and conditions for the future of monastic life in China. At this stage, reflection will focus on the birth and development of an indigenous monasticism. For this to happen, it was necessary above all that the monks be and remain Chinese. The statement may seem obvious, but in fact for many years in mission countries candidates for the monastic life, and for religious life in general, were expected to separate themselves from their cultural roots and assume, if possible, those forms of religious life that had been developed in the West and were transplanted without change to mission lands.

The history of missions, even monastic missions, in the East had been mostly marked by this "colonialist" mind-set, sharply de-

[114] Cited in Clifford King, "Les Petits Frères de St Jean-Baptiste et les Petites Sœurs de Ste Thérèse," *Jeunesse chinoise. Bulletin de la Jeunesse catholique chinoise* 93–94 (1932): 514–15 (emphasis added).

nounced by Thomas Merton. Monasteries built in the late nineteenth century, he said, "became missionary branch offices of the big motherhouses in Europe," and the native monks who entered were forced to become "pseudo-Europeans."[115] Unfortunately, the history of the missions in China also presented many examples of this missionary approach. Vincent Lebbe was among those who strenuously opposed this practice, as recounted by one of "his" monks. "Fr. Lebbe found it natural that we Chinese should remain Chinese. . . . He taught us to love what made China great, its civilization, its literature, its art. . . . Our chapel was in Chinese style, our beautiful red and gold altar was admired by visitors. A little brother painted on the walls of the choir the blessed Chinese martyrs, whose feast we celebrate on 24 November with all the pomp possible. *There was nothing foreign to alter the Chinese aspect of the monastery and of our life.*"[116]

The ultimate goal of this process of "indigenization" was that over time the entire monastic community, including the superior, should be Chinese. "It is more natural and more in keeping with the Catholic spirit that a monastery be governed by a superior from that country," wrote the Trappist abbot Louis Brun, "and this is what we must strive for."[117] The question that, for the most part, remained in the background was: "*In what way* should the encounter between Western monastic life and the local cultural context take place?" In other words, just how should one go about the process of "adaptation," or "inculturation," as it was later called? "It is no longer possible to install in any place whatsoever a 'prefabricated' monastery because the contemplative life, more than any other, discovers that it is dependent on the 'human' conditions of life in a country, on its culture, its history, its customs, its religious tradition."[118]

Although it was certainly necessary to start from the Christian monastic tradition that had been developed up to that point west of

[115] Thomas Merton, "The Inner Experience: Prospects and Conclusions," *Cistercian Studies* 19 (1984): 339.

[116] Frère Alexandre, "Petits Frères de Saint Jean-Baptiste," *Perspectives de catholicité* 15, no. 3 (1956): 78 (emphasis added).

[117] Brun, "La vie contemplative en Chine," 95.

[118] "Conferenza di frère Christian," in *Frère Christian de Chergé e gli altri monaci di Tibhirine, Più forti dell'odio* (Magnano: Qiqajon, 2006), 120.

China, this tradition, stripped down to essential elements, in other words, stripped as much as possible of specifically Western cultural elements, was now carried over, transported, and delivered to the Chinese context, because that would allow it to be reborn in a *new form*. This process gradually became an imperative for all monasticism, not only in China. "Monasticism needs to demonstrate its capacity [in countries where Christianity has recently arrived] to assume forms different from those of ancient Christianity," a process that would be confirmed in the conciliar pronouncements of Vatican II.[119] "In fact, these institutes are asked to found houses in mission areas, as not a few of them have already done, so that there, living out their lives in *a way accommodated [modo accomodato]* to the *truly religious traditions of the people*, they can bear excellent witness among non-Christians to the majesty and love of God, as well as to our union in Christ."[120] "Retaining, therefore, the characteristics of the way of life proper to them, they should revive their ancient traditions of service and so *adapt* them to the needs of today that monasteries will become institutions dedicated to the edification of the Christian people."[121]

In the 1920s and 1930s this requirement became clear to the founders and leaders of the monastic communities who were already present in China. Among the Trappists, for example, this readiness to adapt was particularly evident at the time of the first monastic foundations in the Far East.

> What modifications occur in the rules, the usages, and the customs, in the very spirit of the Cistercian Order due to contact with local civilizations and mentalities? Or is it not rather the local mentality that should adapt itself to the customs and the spirit of the order?
> 1. Until recent times, due to the uniformity that necessarily reigns in an order as centralized as the Cistercian, not surprisingly, it was the second hypothesis that was carried out. In very

[119] Leclercq, "Monachisme chrétien et missions," 146–47.

[120] Vatican Council II, *Ad Gentes* 40 (translation from the Vatican website; emphasis added).

[121] Vatican Council II, *Perfectae Caritatis* 9 (translation from the Vatican website; emphasis added).

minor points certain details of the habit, of food, of the daily schedule, of that which jars the Chinese or Japanese temperament the most, have been modified. . . .

2. The Rule of Cîteaux, modified but lightly, to accord with the local mentality, has been taken in general as the norm for community life. This approach has been tried in Indochina, . . . in the Trappe of Our Lady of Annam. . . . The community, thus, adapts the way of life of the local inhabitants; is this now one of the reasons for its rapid expansion? In fact, after only seven years of existence it numbered already fifty members, while the Trappe of Peking after forty years has only ninety-six members. Is not this something to be considered? And does not this extraordinary growth suggest the thought that a community, the more it approaches in its organization and customs the mode of life and of thinking of the milieu where it exists, so much the more does it stand a chance of prospering?[122]

The history of the first foundations in the Far East gradually taught the Trappists to confront the necessity of adaptation and to understand what the abbot of Yangjiaping, Louis Brun, wrote in the 1930s. "Although the monastery depends on an order and is bound through its motherhouse with the Abbey of Cîteaux, . . . [it] is, nevertheless, a local and autonomous institution, which, transplanted from another place, must put out its roots in and be nourished by elements of the place where it finds itself and thus become a natural product of it. . . . The adaptation of Catholic monasticism to China, so that it becomes a natural product, cannot be the work of one day."[123]

A few years later, Abbot Marie Gabriel Sortais of Cîteaux, who was also the abbot general of the Trappists, would come to the following conclusion in an article specifically about the function of contemplative orders in mission countries:

It might happen that in order to be truly planted in a country, contemplative life will have to assume a *new form*. Particular circumstances of a place, of characters, above all of civilization might give rise to the birth of a religious family quite different from those that already exist in the church. Without in any way hastening to abandon a rule that has proved itself elsewhere,

[122] Peffer, "Les Cisterciens réformés dans l'Asie Orientale," 54–56.
[123] Brun, "La vie contemplative en Chine," 95–96, 103.

superiors must not refuse *a priori* to examine such a possibility and their first preoccupation should not be to extend their institute, but to serve the church by bringing the principles of the contemplative life where it does not yet exist. The whole difficulty will consist in resolving this problem: to preserve the authenticity of the contemplative life while making it at the same time *indigenous*.[124]

In the Benedictine world, however, Édouard Neut and Abbot Théodore Nève were still the main voices in this debate. In the late 1920s Neut wrote: "When cloistered life is established in new countries it must be impregnated with discretion and an evangelical attitude that is capable of *adapting its observances* without diminishing anything of what distinguishes it, its austerity, and its value; in fact, at times it may even emphasize them a little. Religious charity must continue in the mode of thinking, of speaking, and of loving proper to the native inhabitants."[125]

At around the same time Abbot Nève stated that what guarantees that a foundation will be able to "adapt" to the context in which it is located is its degree of autonomy and that the visible manifestation of this "adaptation" is "constructing a monastery in the style of the country in which it is built" and, above all, that the novitiate is "open and adapted to indigenous vocations."

> A monastery, in order to be a monastery, must plunge its roots into the deep strata of the soil on which it builds. As long as a monastery in a mission country lives only thanks to the continual addition of European blood, its life is precarious. Sooner or later our monasteries must *become indigenous*. . . . Thanks to this the monks and the abbot will quickly become natives and then they will be able to fine-tune regional adaptations of observance, to which the general lines of the monastic rule leave enough space so that it can really be a garb made to measure.[126]

The most prophetic Benedictine voice to speak in favor of the adaptation of Christian monasticism in China was undoubtedly that of

---

[124] Marie Gabriel Sortais, "Fonction des ordres contemplatifs en pays de missions," CA 22 (1954): 14 (emphasis added).
[125] Neut, "Le Christ apôtre cherche des contemplatifs," 309.
[126] Nève, "De la fondation de monastères en terre de mission," 43–44.

Jehan Joliet, whose project for a monastery that would be genuinely Chinese (cf. the texts of Joliet in app. 2) showed that he did not want "to import from the West a monasticism that was 'already complete' and apply it to China; rather, China, on its own, should restart the Christian monastic experience, and itself draw on the essential principles of the Rule of St. Benedict to produce a monasticism that is authentically Chinese."[127] Joliet was well aware of the daring nature of the task, as he confessed in a letter of 1928. "It is not to be thought that a real adaptation in practice, not one in letters and speeches, will be easy or agreeable. It is an effort continually renewed; it demands renunciation in many ways harder and more complete than that of religious vows because it is exercised in a field to which one has not vowed oneself explicitly and against which may arise the opposition of a holy and necessary sentiment of attachment to the customs of one's original community."[128]

This task was all the more difficult to realize because, as Jehan Joliet recognized when he wrote to Abbot Nève two years later, it called on the Western monastic, and particularly Benedictine, tradition to do away with the "Latin habit" that had been worn for centuries and to put on a "Chinese habit." "I know the present discipline of the Benedictine Order, but I believed that we were in China in order to adapt ourselves. . . . Gradually, more and more you want to have us copy what is done in Europe, in order to bring to [the Chinese] an up-to-date version, a ready habit, a modern ensemble of Western monasticism of the twentieth century, while the points of contact and of suture between China and monasticism lie much more in antiquity."[129]

The desire to resolve this basic tension seemed to motivate all Joliet's labors in China. As he bitterly noted, and as the events narrated in the following pages will show,[130] the degree of freedom and autonomy that he felt was needed in order to implement his proposal

[127] Delcourt, *Dom Jehan Joliet*, 197.
[128] Letter of J. Joliet to É. Neut, 2 October 1928, in Delcourt, *Dom Jehan Joliet*, 161–62.
[129] Letter of J. Joliet to T. Nève, 27 November 1930, in Delcourt, *Dom Jehan Joliet*, 202–3.
[130] Cf. *infra*, pp. 190–223.

for a Chinese form of monasticism was not always understood, and consequently not always granted, by superiors. He believed that if monasticism was to remain faithful to its own vocation it had to be "without works." A monastic presence in China, therefore, ought to remain without a direct mission, and monastic identity in China was not to be overshadowed by a missionary identity. An anonymous article in memory of Joliet that appeared in 1938 notes that this "monastic formula" of Joliet was one that many began to share, at least in theory.

> There was nothing in it that resembled a mission. The Benedictines who would be charged with establishing the first Chinese monastery would not be missionaries. They would not preach the Gospel, they would not teach catechism, they would not multiply courses right and left. They would be exclusively religious, attached to their convent and to their rule. They would chant the Office, they would have a library furnished equally with European and with Chinese works, so that the Europeans might learn to know and to appreciate Chinese civilization and the Chinese might come into contact with authentic Christian tradition. They would welcome the guests who might visit them, in conformity with the Rule of St. Benedict, and they would hope that among these guests God might inspire imitators of their life of prayer and study.[131]

Jehan Joliet believed that only in this way could the monastery fulfill its true function in China: "To be, through its capacity for intellectual and spiritual stimulation, a place of encounter and osmosis between Chinese culture and the Gospel."[132] Among the many problems surrounding this concept and the practice of adaptation that the different monastic families soon had to face was the question of how to admit young Chinese to the monastic structures that were born in the West but now had to be adapted to the social and cultural realities of China if they were to be effective. "It must be admitted: recruitment in the monastic orders in China is not without difficulty. The candidates who have the necessary qualities to be admitted to the canonical novitiate are rare; they, so to say, can be found only

---

[131] "Le R. P. Dom Jehan Joliet (1870–1937)," *La Vie diocésaine*, 2 April 1938.
[132] Delcourt, *Dom Jehan Joliet*, 306.

among seminary students or priests. Who would think of populating monasteries with fugitives from the clerical life?"[133]

The only community, as Abbot Nève admits, to successfully resolve this issue was that of the Little Brothers of John the Baptist—not surprisingly one that from the beginning was made up entirely of Chinese.

> Fr. Lebbe dreamed of a broader and easier recruitment. Like the founder of monasticism in the West, he did not try to collect intellectuals in his cloister but instead candidates of high moral virtue. Once the obstacle of Latin culture was removed, it was only a case of adapting the material life of the monks to the usages and customs of the land. This was not too complicated, because the conditions of the people's life in northern China are very simple. The monastery doors, hence, opened to all men of good will: rich and poor, masters and servants, traders and peasants came to join the ranks of the new monastic militia. As in the times of St. Benedict, they wanted to fight under a rule and under an abbot. The Little Brothers of St. John the Baptist, as the new monks were called, do not dedicate themselves to the study of Latin or of philosophy or of theology. They live their monastic life, to which is joined some small external ministry of catechesis.[134]

This freedom from Western structural forms, therefore, appears to be the main difference between the Western monastic foundations made in China by Carmelite, Trappist, and Benedictine monasteries, and the monastic foundation that Fr. Lebbe made in China, whose monks and nuns were all Chinese from the beginning and which for several years had an institutional structure that was very flexible (cf. chap. 5). The *Rule of the Little Brothers of John the Baptist* of the Monastery of the Beatitudes, which was amended several times over the years, is a unique example of how the spirit of the Rule of St. Benedict was adapted by the Trappist monastic tradition and transmitted to the cultural, social, and spiritual context of China (cf. app. 3). In this sense, the Monastery of the Beatitudes established by Vincent Lebbe in 1928 was undoubtedly exemplary.

---

[133] Théodore Nève, "L'œuvre monastique du Père Lebbe," CA 9 (1937): 1.
[134] Ibid., 2.

The "apostolic" dimension of the life of the Little Brothers, moreover, realized the ideal of the "apostle-monk" as propagated by Abbot Nève. While trying to live the monastic rule as faithfully and austerely as possible, the Little Brothers made themselves available to the local bishop to help in parishes. By directly contributing to the local community and to evangelization, they soon became known and respected. Future studies will be needed to assess, on the basis of the subsequent history of the congregation, whether and to what extent this "mixed" formula of monastic and apostolic life would have been able to maintain, over the long term, the quality of monastic life.

Because of external conditions, there were only twenty years in which to translate into projects, choices, and concrete achievements the awareness of the necessity for immediate adaptation and inculturation. Even the most successful undertakings remained, at best, in the experimental stage. There was no time for them to become institutionalized. The exodus from China imposed on foreign monks in the late 1940s and early 1950s and the inability of Chinese monks and nuns to live a monastic life in the subsequent years were thus the main obstacle to the development of a Chinese monasticism. However, it does seem that the monastic world itself, which over the centuries had been shaped by the Western tradition, was, at least in part, unprepared to accept, administer, and prudently accompany the first attempts to make Christian monasticism in China a Chinese Christian monasticism.

The case of the Benedictine monastic undertaking at Xishan is the most obvious example of this (cf. chap. 4). If there soon arose a lack of openness to dialogue between the "center" and the "periphery," between the impulse for innovation and the brakes of institutionalization, it cannot but be acknowledged that something was already lacking during the preliminary phase of the project. Even though it had been prepared over a long period of time by someone as insightful and committed as Jehan Joliet, his China project was unsuccessful because preparation for it was the work of a lone man who failed to engage his superiors and his community in an honest and open dialogue on its main components. As noted by one who was most familiar with the "Joliet project," "while Dom Joliet was personally prepared to face difficulties, what was lacking was communal reflection and preparation, a gathering that would have brought together superiors and members of a planning committee to discuss and come to a joint decision about a work that could only be successful if it was communally planned and implemented."[135]

The story told in the following pages basically shows that the process of inculturation of Christian monasticism in China required a bold spiritual attitude of openness to the future and a willingness to accept the transformation of monastic forms that had been received. These requirements, if heeded today, offer challenging questions for the whole of monasticism. "What will become of the seeds of the Trappe in countries recently opened to monasticism? . . . What resonance will their voice find in the heart of the local population? . . . What influence will the milieu exercise on newcomers who are plunged into it body and soul, and what transformations will ancient rules and the spirit of the order know from this contact with a civilization, a mysterious product made up of innumerable elements, of which only a few are barely known?"[136]

---

[135] Delcourt, *Dom Jehan Joliet*, 272.
[136] A. Limagne, *Les Trappistes en Chine* (Paris: J. de Gigord, 1911), 7.

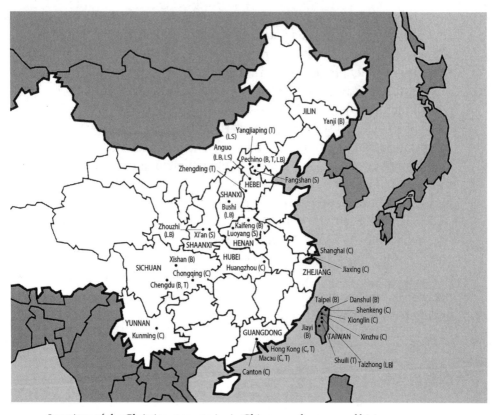

Locations of the Christian monasteries in China over the course of history.

(B)   Benedictine monastery

(C)   Carmelite monastery

(LB) monastery of the Little Brothers of John the Baptist

(LS) monastery of the Little Sisters of Therese of the Child Jesus

(S)   Syro-Oriental monastery

(T)   Trappist monastery

Chapter 1

||||||||||||||||||||||||||||||||||||||||||||||||

The Luminous Monks

Syro-Oriental Monasticism during the Tang Dynasty

When the first Trappist monks arrived in China in 1883 and settled at Yangjiaping, west of Peking, they were unaware that they were not the first Christian monks to live in the region around Peking.[1]

Historical and literary studies have shown that Christianity was first introduced into China already during the Tang dynasty (618–907) by the Church of the East. This church, which is known also as Syro-Oriental, Persian, or Assyrian, and polemically as the Nestorian Church,[2] had its headquarters in Seleucia Ctesiphon, near today's Baghdad. Even though today this is a small church existing mainly

---

[1] This first section is an abridged version of Matteo Nicolini-Zani, "Eastern Outreach: The Monastic Mission to China in the Seventh to the Ninth Centuries," in *Mission and Monasticism: Acts of the International Symposium at the Pontifical Athenaeum S. Anselmo, Rome, May 7–9, 2009*, ed. Conrad Leyser and Hannah Williams (Rome: Pontificio Ateneo Sant'Anselmo / Sankt Ottilien: EOS, 2013), 63–70. For a more detailed study, see Matteo Nicolini-Zani, *La via radiosa per l'oriente. I testi e la storia del primo incontro del cristianesimo con il mondo culturale e religioso cinese (secoli VII–IX)* (Magnano: Qiqajon, 2006).

[2] From Nestorius, patriarch of Constantinople (fifth century), the reference figure for the theology of this church. For an outline introduction to the history and theology of the Church of the East, see Eugène Tisserant, "Nestorienne (l'Église)," in *Dictionnaire de Théologie Catholique*, vol. 11/1 (Paris: Letouzey et Ané, 1931), 157–323; Raymond Le Coz, *Histoire de l'église d'Orient* (Paris: Cerf, 1995); Wilhelm Baum and Dietmar W. Winkler, *The Church of the East: A Concise History* (London: Routledge Curzon, 2003); Herman Teule, *Les Assyro-Chaldéens* (Turnhout: Brepols, 2008). For the misnomer given to this church, see Sebastian Brock, "The 'Nestorian' Church: A Lamentable Misnomer," *Bulletin of the John Rylands University Library of Manchester* 78, no. 3 (1996): 23–35.

in the diaspora, in the sixth century it was spread over the whole territory of the Persian Empire, and from the seventh century it experienced an extraordinary diffusion, from Persia southward into the Arabian peninsula and eastward through Central Asia and into India, Tibet, and China.[3]

According to various sources, China represented the easternmost outreach of the mission of the Assyrian Church. Since the Church of the East was threatened by Byzantine persecution and later by the advance of Islam, it spread out of Persia toward the east, following the Silk Road. Places such as Herat, Balkh, Merv, Bukhara, and Samarkand early on became centers for further missionary activities. This Central Asian space was therefore an important step of the journey of Christian missionaries to the East: it was here that an extraordinary encounter between cultural and religious traditions occurred. Christians, Manicheans, Zoroastrians, and Buddhists met each other and lived side by side with one another, being mutually confronted and transformed. In this pluralistic milieu Christianity was willing to enter into a dialogue with cultural and religious traditions very different from the ones in which it was born, namely, the Semitic and Greek-Hellenistic cultures.[4]

Christian missions from Persia and Central Asia were monastic missions, and the first Christian communities in China were structured around monasteries. Christian monasteries in Tang China were called "Persian monasteries" (*Bosi si* 波斯寺), then "Da Qin monasteries" (*Da Qin si* 大秦寺) or "Brilliant monasteries" (*Jingsi* 景寺), since Chinese Christianity in this period was called *Da Qin jingjiao* 大秦景教, "the Luminous Religion from Da Qin" (that is,

[3] Cf. François Nau, "L'expansion nestorienne en Asie," *Annales du Musée Guimet* 40 (1914): 193–383.

[4] Cf. Wolfgang Hage, *Syriac Christianity in the East* (Kottayam: St. Ephrem Ecumenical Research Institute, 1988; repr. 1996); Hans-Joachim Klimkeit, *Die Begegnung von Christentum, Gnosis und Buddhismus an der Seidenstraße* (Opladen: Westdeutscher Verlag, 1986); Ian Gillman and Hans-Joachim Klimkeit, *Christians in Asia before 1500* (Richmond: Curzon, 1999). About the dialogic attitude of the Church of the East toward other religions in Central Asia, see Wolfgang Hage, "Religiöse Toleranz in der nestorianischen Asienmission," in *Glaube und Toleranz. Das theologische Erbe der Aufklärung*, ed. Trutz Rendtorff (Gütersloh: G. Mohn, 1982), 99–112.

Syria).[5] On the basis of the text of the well-known Xi'an stele, dated 781, there were in China one or two monasteries in the western capital Chang'an (today's Xi'an), probably one also in the eastern capital Luoyang, a few monasteries in the region of Ningxia and other western regions of the Chinese Empire, and several other monastic communities in various unknown places of the empire.

According to the eulogistic text of the Xi'an stele, "the great emperor Gaozong (650–683) . . . ordered the building of brilliant monasteries [*Jingsi*] in every prefecture," hence "monasteries stood in one hundred towns."[6] The nature of this text, however, is apologetic and propagandist. In Chinese historical sources only one clear reference to the erection of a Christian monastery in the capital Chang'an can be found. An imperial edict, dated 638, ordered the building of a monastery in the western capital and the ordination of twenty-one people as monks for that community.[7]

I quote here an outline description of this first Christian monastic presence in China.

> The ecclesiastical organization of these Nestorians of the Far East was comparable to that of Irish monks in the West in the same period: *the monastery was the place of reference where*

---

[5] "Da Qin" is the generic term used by the Chinese for the eastern regions of the Roman Empire. This expression was coined by the Central Asian populations, who were in contact with both the Chinese Empire and the Roman Empire. For them, China was the Qin Empire, named after the dynasty that was the first to unify it (221–206 BCE). The Roman Empire, which in their eyes must have appeared larger and more powerful, was the empire of Da Qin, that is, the empire of the "Great China." The term "Da Qin" in the Chinese Christian texts perhaps refers specifically to Syria, the birthplace of the Syro-Oriental Church, rather than to Persia, the land of origin of the monks of that church, since Persia was already known as "Bosi."

[6] Cf. the text of the Xi'an stele, lines 15–16. The best study of the Xi'an stele remains Paul Pelliot, *L'inscription nestorienne de Si-ngan-fou*, ed. Antonino Forte (Kyoto: Scuola di Studi sull'Asia Orientale / Paris: Collège de France, Institut des Hautes Études Chinoises, 1996).

[7] Cf. Antonino Forte, "The Edict of 638 Allowing the Diffusion of Christianity in China," in Pelliot, *L'inscription nestorienne*, 349–73. The same edict is contained in the text of the Xi'an stele. It is not clear, however, why the number of the monks to be ordained was twenty-one, but it seems most probable that a rule for other religious communities, namely, Buddhist and Taoist communities, was simply applied also to Christians.

a bishop-monk resided; evangelization and the Christian life were organized around monasteries. The Nestorians presented the elements of the Christian faith in Chinese with great care to adapt them to the Chinese mentality, as the [Xi'an] stele witnesses. Thus, to speak of the liturgy and of the hierarchy expressions are borrowed from Buddhism, abstract notions are expressed in Taoist terms, while Confucian vocabulary is used for what concerns morality.[8]

The same Xi'an stele of the "Luminous Religion" describes the ideal Christian community as a community of monks/priests, called "eminent religious elevated above the matters of this world" and "luminous ministers dressed in white." According to this text, such a community is characterized by traditional monastic elements: the monks let their beards grow as a symbol of poverty and renunciation; ascetical practices, such as fasting, reclusion, meditation, *népsis* (vigilance), *hesychía* (quietness of body and mind), and *apátheia* (absence of passions), are fostered; liturgical services gather the community seven times a day for chanting the common monastic offices.

> Striking the wood,[9] [the Christian monks] diffuse a sound that incites goodness and benevolence. In their ceremonies they turn toward the east and they advance rapidly on the way of life and of glory. They let their beards grow as a sign of their public ministry and they shave the top of their heads to signify that they do not have interior passions.[10] They keep neither men nor women servants and hold in equal esteem people in high positions and people of humble origin. They do not accumulate wealth or riches, but give an example of radical renunciation. In addition to fasting, they cultivate solitude and meditation; they reinforce their discipline by quietness and vigilance.[11] Seven times a day they chant liturgical praises, in a great intercession for the living

[8] Henri-Philippe Delcourt, *Dom Jehan Joliet (1870–1937). Un projet de monachisme bénédictin chinois* (Paris: Cerf, 1988), 45 (emphasis added).

[9] In place of bells, the Eastern churches often use a hanging wooden board (called *nāqošā* in Syriac), which is struck to call monks to prayer.

[10] Tonsure, which was introduced after the monastic reform of Abraham of Kaškar (d. 586), was an element of monasticism in the Church of the East.

[11] The Chinese original text contains here several Buddhist and Taoist expressions to define the ascetical practices of Christian monks.

and the dead. Once every seven days they celebrate their cult, purifying their hearts and thus restoring to them their purity.[12]

The monastic essence of the first Christian presence in China is not surprising if we remember that in the church to which these first missionaries to China belonged monasticism always occupied a central position.[13] The missionaries sent by this church to China via Central Asia were monks, and the metropolitan bishops appointed as heads of the Far Eastern "external provinces" were in most cases monks trained in the monasteries of Mesopotamia and Persia. It was during the patriarchate of Timothy I (780–823) that the missionary impulse gained particular strength and the ecclesiastical organization of the missionary territories was established.[14] Patriarch Timothy generally chose the metropolitan bishops assigned to the "external provinces" from among the monks of the Monastery of Bet 'Abe, in the region of Marga, northeast of Mosul (today's northern Iraq). It seems that proven ascetics were chosen for distant lands because of the difficult nature of the task assigned to them. It was also important to have clerics well trained in the Scriptures and in theological matters, as were the monks of Bet 'Abe, because they would inevitably be involved in discussions with the leaders of other religions in the mission lands to which they were being sent. Usually it was the metropolitan himself who chose and ordained his bishops, again among the Mesopotamian or Persian missionary monks. What emerges from this picture, therefore, is a centralized ecclesiastical organization, even if the distances made the ties

---

[12] Cf. the text of the Xi'an stele, lines 8–10.

[13] Cf. Arthur Vööbus, *History of Asceticism in the Syrian Orient: A Contribution to the History of Culture in the Near East*, 3 vols., CSCO 184, 197, 500 (Louvain: Sécrétariat du CorpusSCO, 1958–1988); Sabino Chialà, *Abramo di Kashkar e la sua comunità. La rinascita del monachesimo siro-orientale* (Magnano: Qiqajon, 2005); Florence Jullien, *Le monachisme en Perse. La réforme d'Abraham le Grand, père des moines de l'Orient*, CSCO 622 (Louvain: Peeters, 2008); Florence Jullien, ed., *Le monachisme syriaque* (Paris: Geuthner, 2010).

[14] Cf. Vittorio Berti, "Cristiani sulle vie dell'Asia tra VIII e IX secolo. Ideologia e politica missionaria di Timoteo I, patriarca siro-orientale (780-823)," *Quaderni di storia religiosa* 13 (2006): 117–56; Jean Dauvillier, "Les Provinces Chaldéennes 'de l'extérieur' au Moyen Âge," in *Mélanges offerts au R. P. Ferdinand Cavallera* (Toulouse: Bibliothèque de l'Institut Catholique, 1948), 261–316.

between these peripheral territories and the Mesopotamian center very weak. Actually, this tie was reduced to a few reports sent every six years by the metropolitan to the patriarch, because the great distances of their sees from the center prevented the missionary bishops from participating in the synods of their church, which were held every four years in Seleucia Ctesiphon.

Looking closer at the China mission in this period, we find this ecclesiastical policy applied to the Chinese situation. Patriarch Timothy I in one of his letters says that "many monks cross the seas in the direction of India and China, bearing with them only a stick and a saddle bag."[15] Bishop Thomas of Marga reports in his *Monastic History* (ca. 850) that, among the bishops ordained in the Monastery of Bet 'Abe around 787, there was a certain Dawid (David, d. 810), metropolitan of Bet Ṣinaye (that is, the country of the Chinese).[16] The text of the Xi'an stele confirms this practice of appointing bishops from among the missionary clergy coming from Persia and Central Asia.[17]

Briefly put, the original core of the Christian communities in Tang China was represented by foreigners who had come to China for commercial or political reasons and who in a few cases settled in colonies inside Chinese towns, as in the capitals Chang'an and Luoyang.[18] To

[15] Timothy I, *Letters* 13, in *Timothei patriarchae I epistolae*, ed. Oscar Braun (Louvain: Sécretariat du CorpusSCO, 1953), vol. 1, p. 107 (text) and vol. 2, p. 70 (translation).

[16] Cf. Thomas of Marga, *Monastic History* IV, 20, in *The Book of Governors: The Historia Monastica of Thomas, Bishop of Margâ*, ed. E. A. Wallis Budge (London: Kegan Paul / Trench / Trübner, 1893), p. 238 (text) and p. 448 (translation). Thomas claims to derive this information from the letters of Timothy, but there is no mention of David in them. Perhaps he is referring to one of the lost letters of the patriarch. However, at the end of letter 13, where there appear to be some *lacunae* in the manuscript, there is a statement that may be related to this David of Bet 'Abe: "The Metropolitan of the Chinese has returned to the Lord. If there is [someone suitable] in the new convent [send him to us?]; In fact, I have heard that there is an outstanding monk there." Timothy I, *Letters* 13; Italian translation in Berti, "Cristiani sulle vie dell'Asia," p. 152, n. 14.

[17] For a detailed analysis of this aspect, see Nicolini-Zani, *La via radiosa per l'oriente*, 98–112.

[18] Confirmation of the spread of Christianity among the families of Sogdian origin who took on Chinese customs and resided in Luoyang comes from a funerary pillar with Chinese inscriptions, which was recently discovered. It is dated to the

provide what was necessary for the liturgical and spiritual life of the members of these colonies, groups of monks and individual clerics were sent at different times from Persia and Central Asia to China. As long as these communities, which were structured around the monasteries, were growing, they also welcomed a certain number of Chinese Christians.

These typically monastic communities were particularly meaningful in the religious context of that place and time. After the arrival of Buddhism the monastic community became the religious institution most visible and most powerful in China. The Christian monks, then, took from Buddhism most of the terms they used to define their institutions. Christian monasteries in this period were called *si* 寺 (pagodas), and the Buddhist term *seng* 僧 was borrowed by Christians to translate both the Syriac terms *iḥidāyā* for "monk" and *qašišā* for "priest," as the 781 inscription testifies. From the Buddhist vocabulary Christians borrowed also their Chinese ecclesiastical titles, such as "Great Virtue" (*dade* 大德) for a bishop, "Lord of the Doctrine" (*fazhu* 法主) most probably for a metropolitan bishop, and the common Chinese terms that Buddhists used for the prior of a monastery, *sizhu* 寺主 (Chinese translation of the Sanskrit word *vihārasvāmin*), and the abbot, *laosu* 老宿 (literally, "elder," a synonym of *shangzuo* 上座, translation of the Sanskrit word *sthavira*).

Finally, it is interesting to note that most of the names of the religious mentioned in the text of the Xi'an stele and in other contemporary epigraphic documents were chosen according to the Buddhist custom: two Chinese characters belonging to semantic fields such as light, knowledge, virtue, and peace. These terms were preferred by Buddhists and chosen by them as names for their monks. The character *jing* 景, "light," seems to have been particularly beloved by Christians, in evident relation to the Chinese denomination for Christianity as the "Religion of the Light," or "Brilliant Teaching" (*Jingjiao* 景教).

---

year 815 and was erected by a Christian family that originally came from the area of Bukhara. Cf. Matteo Nicolini-Zani, "The Tang Christian Pillar from Luoyang and Its 'Jingjiao' Inscription: A Preliminary Study," *Monumenta Serica* 57 (2009): 99–140.

After the Tang Dynasty until the Yuan

Between 843 and 845 a xenophobic reaction orchestrated by Taoists resulted in an edict issued by the emperor Wuzong outlawing all foreign religions present in China and ordering the closure of their monasteries. The Buddhists were the first to be affected by these measures, but Manicheans and Christians also fell under the ban.[19] The persecution of foreign religions was so severe that when the patriarch 'Abdišo' I sent a delegation of six monks to the Far East in 980 to make contact with communities that might have survived, one of the monks came back from the East to report that "for various reasons, the Christians in China have disappeared and perished; not a single one is left in the entire country."[20]

That report was not accurate. Christianity did not, in fact, disappear from China. The Syro-Oriental Church continued to exist there even after the fall of the Tang dynasty. At the end of the eleventh century Christians who may have been merchants from Persia could still be found in Canton, while in the north of the country new communities began to spring up, thanks to the Kitan, Turkish-Mongolian tribes that formed the kingdoms of Liao and Jin in the tenth, eleventh, and twelfth centuries. However, it was only with the invasion of the Mongols of Genghis Khan, when many nobles, kings, princes, and princesses became Christian, that the Syro-Oriental Church was revived in China. Among the converts was the first Mongol ruler Hülegü (1256–1265) and his wife Dokuz Khatun. With the Mongol conquest of China, Christianity thus strengthened its presence by being the religion of several members of the new ruling class. Evidence of the status of Christianity at this time can be found in the letters and historical descriptions of diplomats and Franciscan missionaries, such as Willem Van Rubroek, author of *Journey in the Kingdom of the Mongolians*, and Giovanni da Montecorvino, who was appointed archbishop of Khanbalik (present-day Peking) in 1307,

---

[19] This second section is an abridged version of Matteo Nicolini-Zani, "La via monastica al cristianesimo cinese," *Ad Gentes* 15, no. 1 (2011): 9–22, esp. 14–17.

[20] This information is given by the Arab historian Abū Zayd, who wrote in 987–988; cited in Pier Giorgio Borbone, *Storia di Mar Yahballaha e di Rabban Sauma. Un orientale in Occidente ai tempi di Marco Polo* (Turin: Zamorani, 2000), 45.

and in the fascinating tales of travelers and Western merchants such as Marco Polo, whose *Il Milione* contains references to Nestorian Christian communities in several areas of north-central China.

There are some indications that Christianity in China in those centuries was still characterized by the monastic way of life. On the whole, however, the church in the Mongol period seemingly was no longer as closely structured along monastic lines as it had been in the Tang period. Nevertheless, monasteries continued to be centers supporting the religious and intellectual life of Christians in the Yuan period.[21]

Archaeological evidence indicates that in the period between the eleventh and fourteenth centuries in the village of Fangshan, about forty kilometers southwest of Peking, some Christian monks lived in the "Monastery of the Cross" (*Shizi si* 十字寺). Some blocks of stone carved with crosses and bearing inscriptions in Syriac witness to a Christian presence at this site, which was later converted into a Buddhist monastery.[22]

Various sources show that other "monasteries of the Cross" existed in imperial territory. The main Chinese source, *Zhenjiang Zhishun zhi* 至順鎮江誌 (*Chronicle of Zhenjiang during the Zhishun period*, 1329–1332), describes the Christian monasteries in the region of Zhenjiang, south of the river Yangzi (Yangtze). In particular, a document that refers to Christianity and to Mar Sargis (Sergius), a native of Samarkand and a person "always intent on the propagation of the faith," says that he built seven Christian monasteries in that region around the year 1281.

> One night, in a dream, seven gates opened in the sky and two divine beings appeared who told him: "You must build seven monasteries." . . . When he awoke he felt inspired and later retired from his official position [in the court] and devoted himself

[21] Cf. Ian Gillman and Hans-Joachim Klimkeit, "Christian Monks and Hermits in Yuan China," in *Christians in Asia before 1500*, 295–98.

[22] Cf. Marco Guglielminotti Trivel, "Tempio della Croce—Fangshan—Pechino. Documentazione preliminare delle fonti epigrafiche 'in situ,'" *Orientalia Christiana Periodica* 71, no. 2 (2005): 431–60; Pier Giorgio Borbone, "I blocchi con croci e iscrizione siriaca da Fangshan," *Orientalia Christiana Periodica* 72, no. 1 (2006): 167–87.

to the construction of monasteries. . . . These seven monasteries were really the result of the good heart of his excellency.
He was loyal to the king and devoted to the empire, not trying
to call attention to himself, but to his monasteries. . . . Those
who made vows were all Christians (*yelikewen* 也里可溫).[23]

Interestingly, in the Chinese text the seven monasteries, in addition to Chinese names, also have Syrian-Turkish names and are
therefore called *humula* 忽木剌 (the phonetic transcription of the
Syriac *umrā*, which means "monastery"). They are also called *si*,
which is, as has already been noted, the term borrowed from Buddhism that had already been used in the period of the Tang dynasty.[24]

A Syrian source adds that the Öngüt monk Marqaws (Mark) also
came from the region around Peking. In 1280 he was elected metropolitan bishop of Cathay (North China) and of Ong (the country
of the Öngüt). In 1281 he was even chosen to be the catholicos
(patriarch) of the Syro-Oriental Church and given the name Mar
Yahballaha III (1281–1317).

The fascinating history of the pilgrimage of Mar Yahballaha III
and Rabban Sauma to Jerusalem, in the course of which they met
the pope and various European monarchs, is preceded by the story of
their life in China as solitary monks. Rabban Sauma, a priest in the
church of Khanbalik, early on felt the desire to withdraw from the
world. Like Antony in the Egyptian desert some centuries earlier, he
sold all his possessions and distributed them to the poor. He received
the monastic tonsure from the metropolitan of Khanbalik, Mar Gi-
wargis (George), and remained in his cell for seven years. Since he
was being disturbed by frequent visitors, he decided to seek solitude
in the quiet of a cave in the mountains of the region surrounding
the city. Even there, however, he was soon besieged by people who

[23] Cited in Arthur Christopher Moule, *Christians in China before the Year 1550*
(London / New York / Toronto: SPCK, 1930), 149–50. See also Yin Xiaoping, "On
the Christians in Jiangnan during the Yuan Dynasty according to 'The Gazetteer of
Zhenjiang of the Zhishun Period,'" in *Hidden Treasures and Intercultural Encoun-
ters: Studies on East Syriac Christianity in China and Central Asia*, ed. Dietmar W.
Winkler and Li Tang (Münster: LIT, 2009), 305–19.

[24] Cf. Louis Ligeti, "Les sept monastères nestoriens de mar Sargis," *Acta Orientalia
Hungarica* 26, nos. 2–3 (1972): 169–78.

sought his counsel. Among them was the young Mark, son of the archdeacon of Kawšang (Koshang or Olon Süme, in the region of Ordos), who wanted to be a monk and live as a hermit. After trying to discourage him by telling him about the rigors of the eremitical life, Rabban Sauma finally allowed him to be his disciple and join him in leading the ascetic life. After three years of apprenticeship, Mark received the monastic tonsure from the metropolitan of Khanbalik Mar Nestoris (Nestorius) and returned to live with the elder.[25]

The story of Rabban Sauma and Mark thus throws a small ray of light on the life of a hermit among the Syrian Christians in eastern China during the Yuan period. The ascetic discipline they practiced in solitude, but without isolating themselves from the church to which they belonged or breaking communion with their pastors, included fasting and other observances. The meaning of this ascetic life is well expressed in an account of their life, which says that both of them "practiced asceticism on the mountain, at the service of purity and holiness, and drew comfort from God, to whom they had made their vows."[26]

Unfortunately, we know nothing more precise about the organization of monastic life in those centuries, or about monastic attempts at inculturation and evangelization in those times.

[25] Cf. Borbone, *Storia di Mar Yahballaha e di Rabban Sauma*, 55–59.
[26] Ibid., 59.

Chapter 2

||||||||||||||||||||||||||||||||||||||||||||||

The Carmelites

In the mid-1900s a Carmelite priest had this to say about the contribution of his order to the missionary movement.

> The life [of the women's branch of the Carmelites] is purely contemplative. But their great apostolate consists precisely in this. There is no missionary who is not convinced of the usefulness and even of the necessity of contemplative orders. They always expect to receive the sap necessary for the growth of their plantings from sacrifice and prayer. For this reason numerous bishops have called on Theresian Carmelites, whose Carmels are for the missions centers of ardent charity. This spiritual treasure has produced much fruit: by the example of the contemplative life, souls have been called to a more intense Christianity and even to a total gift of oneself and of heroic virtue. . . . Without any exception, all [missionaries] have applauded the idea of reserving a place in each mission for the foundation of Carmels of men or of women, which by their own life and by the apostolate will be a real blessing for the new Christian communities. . . . The older [monastic] orders are not dispensed from furnishing their collaboration to the missionary life so characteristic of church life in the nineteenth and twentieth centuries. Some have done this spontaneously; they have broadened their cadre and have at their disposition a certain number of their members, without altering in any way the spirit of their founder. The Theresian Carmel is one of these. It has done this cautiously, watching so as not to impoverish their own spiritual life.[1]

---

[1] Avertanus, "Le Carmel thérésien aux missions," CA 13 (1949): 30–31. This chapter is based on an earlier study of the presence of the Carmelites in China: Matteo Nicolini-Zani, "'L'umile piccola falange sbarcò a Shanghai'. La storia del carmelo in Cina," *Teresianum* 61 (2010): 131–64.

Carmelite nuns were the first to respond to the missionary call for a monastic presence in China. These monastic communities were to be the nucleus of prayerful support for the missionary endeavors that were rapidly developing in the second half of the nineteenth century. The foundation of the first Carmel on Chinese soil was made in 1869 in the cosmopolitan city of Shanghai by a small group of French nuns.

Given the great missionary fervor in France in the nineteenth century, it is not surprising that the first monastic foundation to be made in China came from France. Prior to 1869, two important missionary organizations had been created in that country: the Society for the Propagation of the Faith, founded in Lyons in 1822, and the Pontifical Association of the Holy Childhood, founded in Paris in 1843. In 1860 France was made the "protector" of the Catholic missions in China.

It was mainly French nuns who made the Carmelite foundations in China—most of them from Normandy, the part of France from which many of the foundations in the Far East were made.[2] For example, Bishop Pierre-Lambert de la Motte, co-founder of the Paris Foreign Missions Society (MEP) and first vicar apostolic of Cochin-China, was born in Lisieux in 1624; and the first missionary foundation of the Carmel of Lisieux was made in Saigon, the capital of Cochin-China, a French colony located in the southernmost part of Indochina. The foundation was made in 1861 at the proposal of a vicar apostolic who was also a native of Normandy.[3] At the time, indications of this close relationship between Lisieux and the East was the personal bond of St. Therese of the Child Jesus (1873–1897) with Fr. Théophane Vénard, a young priest who in 1861 was martyred in Tonkin, the northernmost French protectorate of Indochina, and her correspondence with and prayers for her spiritual brother, Fr. Adolphe Roulland, a native of Normandy and missionary of the Paris Foreign Missions Society in Chongqing, China.[4]

[2] Cf. Pierre-André Picard, "Le climat missionnaire du diocèse de Lisieux au temps de Thérèse," *Vie Thérésienne* 187 (2007): 227–45.

[3] Cf. Gérard Moussay, "Mons. Lefebvre (1810–1865) et les Carmélites en Cochinchine," *Thérèse de Lisieux* 876 (2007): 2–3; Guy Gaucher, "La fondation des Carmels de Saïgon et d'Hanoï par le Carmel de Lisieux," *Vie Thérésienne* 39 (1999): 7–21.

[4] The link between Therese and the mission in Sichuan is also shown by the fact that she painted a picture for Fr. Roulland. The picture represents the Sacred Heart

In line with the spirit of St. Teresa of Avila, the reformer of Carmel, and the subsequent tradition of the Carmelite Order, Therese of the Child Jesus wrote about the specific link between the Carmelite vocation and the missionary apostolate: "A Carmelite who is not an apostle would abandon the essence of her vocation and would cease to be a daughter of the seraphic Saint Teresa."[5] She herself volunteered for the Carmel of Hanoi, the capital of Tonkin, which was founded by the Carmel of Saigon in 1895. Because of the progression of her illness, however, she was not able to realize this dream. On 14 December 1927, Therese of the Child Jesus, who had been canonized just two years earlier, was proclaimed principal patroness of the missions.

Finally, we should not forget that when *Contemplation et Apostolat*, a movement of prayer for the missions, was founded in September 1925, the Carmel of Lisieux immediately became a sponsor of the project.[6] The movement's newsletter regularly reported on its activity between the years 1926 and 1939; it also wrote about the extraordinary contribution of the Carmelite Order to the establishment of monastic foundations in mission territories. "One order stands out among the rest for its especially numerous foundations: this is the Carmelite Order, which has given to the church the patron saint of missions and which firmly desires to be the first to carry out her ideal. In fact, we count to the credit of the Carmelite sisters . . . a total of twenty-three foundations in fourteen years. This number added to the twenty-one Carmels that existed already before 1926

---

of Jesus, from which a drop of blood falls on the mission of Chongqing. Underneath is written a prayer composed by the saint: "O divine blood, water our mission that the elect may sprout forth." Cf. Mère Élisabeth, *Partir. Vers la Chine, en Chine, à Dieu la Chine* (Saint-Rémy: Monastère Saint-Élie, 1998), 57.

[5] Letter 198, to M. Bellière, 21 October 1896, in Thérèse de Lisieux, *Lettres à mes frères prêtres* (Paris: Cerf, 1997), 29. On the life of St. Therese of the Child Jesus as a model of the apostolic contemplative life, see Un religieux cistercien, "Un modèle de vie cloîtrée apostolique: sainte Thérèse de l'Enfant-Jésus," in *Action missionnaire d'arrière-garde. Conférences* (Godewaersvelde: Abbaye Sainte-Marie-du-Mont, 1930), 5–46.

[6] Cf. "L'œuvre 'Contemplation et Apostolat' sous le Pontificat de SS. Pie XI," CA 11 (1939): 3*.

brings to forty-four the total of Carmelite convents established in mission lands."[7]

A Garden of Tiny Flowers in Chinese Soil

A comprehensive and well-documented history of the Carmelite communities of women in China, where it was called the "monastic order of the holy habit" (*Shengyi yinxiuhui* 聖衣隱修會), has not yet been written. One reason for this is that their archives were dispersed or destroyed during the years when foreign nuns had to leave the country (1950–1955).[8] All that can be provided here, therefore, is some basic information regarding the various foundations; hopefully, future research will uncover more details about the history of each of the Carmelite communities in China.[9]

From the available sources it can be deduced that the Carmelite monasteries in China had close ties with one another. Evidence for this is the fact that when need arose, nuns were sent from one monastery to another. Carmelites also had close ties, spiritually and

[7] Ibid., 17*. See also "La Carmélite Missionnaire," *Messager Thérésien* 21, no. 7 (1940): 158–61.

[8] One of the few archives still preserved, though presumably only in part, is that of the Carmel of Shanghai, which in the mid-1950s was moved to Lucena in the Philippines. It includes the register of professions, letters, notebooks (including the one compiled by Mother Liesse containing a detailed account of the life of the Carmel of Shanghai), and the list of Chinese sisters present in the Carmel of Shanghai in 1955. Cf. Helen Wang, "An Account of My Journey on the China Mainland in Search of Our Carmelite Sisters" (unpublished typewritten manuscript, Indianapolis Carmel, 1996), 57–63. I was not able to consult this archive, but I did have access to the material conserved in the General Archive of the Order of Discalced Carmelites in Rome. For a description of the material of the nineteenth century, see Antonio Fortes, *Las Misiones del Carmelo Teresiano, 1800–1899. Documentos del Archivo General de Roma* (Rome: Teresianum, 2008), 192.

[9] The only detailed research, likewise an unpublished typewritten manuscript, is that of the Carmel in Shanghai. However, it only goes up to 1938. Cf. Edmond Molnar, "Recherches sur l'origine du carmel de T'ou-se-we" (unpublished typewritten manuscript, Zi-ka-wei, Chang-hai, 1938). A brief account of the Carmelite community in China may be found in Carmel de Cherbourg, *Généalogie des couvents de Carmélites de la Réforme de sainte Thérèse, 1562–1962* (n.p.: n.p., 1962), 39 (an English translation of this page appears in Wang, "An Account of My Journey," 65–66). Occasional references appear in *Contemplation et Apostolat* and in *Les Missions Catholiques*, the publication of the Society for the Propagation of the Faith.

materially, with the few other monastic communities in China. For example, every year the Carmel of Chongqing in southwest China received a gift of cheese produced by the Trappist monks of Yang-jiaping, located in northern China, thousands of kilometers away. "Once a year the Trappists of Our Lady of Consolation, in the North, want to give witness of their prayerful union with us by sending us their cheese . . . which we have to eat quickly."[10]

In general, the documents that are available to us show that the way of life of the Carmelite communities in China was minutely regulated by the constitutions and the liturgical usages of Europe, with very few attempts to adapt to the Chinese cultural context. The very few requests that the Carmelites in China made to Carmelite superiors in Europe or to the competent Vatican congregations had to do with such marginal concerns as setting the times for communal prayer, solemnizing some liturgical commemorations to make them correspond to the liturgical calendar used in France, or modifying their diet and vesture so they would be more suited to the climate of southern China.[11] One of the sources presents a succinct but informative picture of the practices followed in the largest and oldest Carmel in China, that of Shanghai.

> I will gladly tell you what our life is like in our humble Carmel in China. Our holy observances can be kept there integrally, without any mitigation. Rising and retiring are at the customary hours. It was necessary to make a modification in the morning schedule, since the reverend fathers of the Society of Jesus that are in charge of our mission could not assure us of a Mass at

[10] Mère Élisabeth, *Partir*, 46.

[11] See, e.g., letter of the undersecretary of the Congregation of Propaganda Fide to the superior general of the Discalced Carmelites, 6 May 1890 (AGOCD, sez. D, 184: "Monastero di Tou San Wei [Shang-hai]"); letter of Mother Isabelle de Jésus to the superior general of the Discalced Carmelites, 16 August 1936 (AGOCD, sez. D, 58: "Chung King"); letter of Mother Agnès du Bon Pasteur to the superior general of the Discalced Carmelites, 6 July 1936 (AGOCD, sez. D, 111: "Kun-Ming"); note of Sr. Marie-Cécile to the superior general of the Discalced Carmelites, no date (around the middle of the 1930s) about the Carmelite monastery that was transferred from Canton to Hong Kong (AGOCD, sez. D, 100: "Hong-Kong"); letter of the Carmelites of Hong Kong to the superior general of the Discalced Carmelites, 18 December 1951 (AGOCD, sez. D, 100).

such a late hour as our constitutions prescribe. Every exercise, however, is carried out fully. As for the habit, it is exactly the same as in our monasteries in France. During the great heat from July to September, however, a habit made of coarse brown cloth would be unbearable. During this summer period, hence, we wear lighter under and outer clothing. In all the seasons we keep woolen tunics and veils. We likewise in all seasons wear stockings and espadrilles. As concerns food, it is half Chinese, half French. That is, the same things are served the entire community (except for the necessary exceptions for the sick), but care is taken that everyone can be satisfied with the menu. At dinner there is always soup, a first course (French or Chinese), a second course (French or Chinese). We do not have the *frustulum* or refreshment at three o'clock. Only during the period of great heat it is permitted, to those that need it, to go during the day and before and after Matins to the refectory to take some water or cold tea. The exceedingly great heat causes abundant perspiration. This makes ablutions necessary after Matins, which reduces somewhat the time for rest. We have the hour of siesta according to custom. All our native sisters speak French. The Europeans, nevertheless, are learning Chinese. Reading in the refectory in the evening is exclusively in French, while in the morning it is half in Chinese, half in French. We have exhortations and retreat sermons in both languages.[12]

The only really significant request concerned the admission of Chinese applicants. In the early 1940s the Carmel of Kunming requested the apostolic delegate in China, Archbishop Mario Zanin, to grant permission to require an aspirancy of one or two years prior to the postulancy and novitiate of Chinese candidates to allow sufficient time to discern the genuineness of their vocations. This practice appears to have been common in several Chinese Carmelite communities.[13]

The Carmel of Shanghai

As has already been noted, the first Carmelite foundation in China was made in Shanghai at the request of Bishop Adrien-Hippolyte

---

[12] Letter of Sr. Marie-Cécile de Jésus, no date, pp. 1–3 (AGOCD, sez. D, 184).

[13] Cf. the notes in a letter of Mother Agnès du Bon Pasteur to the superior general of the Discalced Carmelites, 6 October 1944 (AGOCD, sez. D, 111).

Languillat, vicar apostolic of Jiangnan (Kiangnan, 1864–1878), the ecclesiastical territory that included Nanjing and Shanghai. During a visit to France in 1867, Bishop Languillat looked into the possibility of having a Carmelite community make a foundation in China. He first contacted two Carmelite monasteries in Paris, then Notre-Dame du Mont-Carmel in Laval. This last community, founded only a few years earlier, in 1856, and already flourishing, accepted the invitation of the Jesuit bishop without reservations and, with the consent of the local ordinary, appointed five nuns for the mission.[14]

These sisters embarked from Marseille on 19 December 1868, with the aim, in the language of religious life of those times, "of obtaining the salvation of China through their prayers, their penance, and their humble and hidden life."[15] Arriving in Shanghai on 3 February 1869, the sisters were housed for a few days at the convent of the Society of the Helpers of the Holy Souls.[16] They were then offered modest temporary accommodation in the suburb of Wang-katang (Wangjiatang), in quarters that the sisters of the Society of the Helpers of the Holy Souls had abandoned when they moved into their new convent. "This temporary lodging, a little Chinese house hardly suitable to serve as a monastery, was put in order, and the enclosure was solemnly inaugurated on 24 February."[17] During their stay at this convent the prioress of the Carmelites wrote to Bishop Languillat, "All of us are very happy and grateful for belonging to the mission in China and to be in the hands of your paternity. May the Lord grant us to fulfill the object for which you have called us. We can only rely on God's mercy and goodness, who, having called us, will continue, we believe, to help and to sustain us in our feeble efforts."[18]

---

[14] The French Carmelites, unlike those of some other geographical regions, were directly subject to the ordinary of the place, in accordance with legislation made after the French Revolution.

[15] Necrology of Sr. Catherine de Saint Louis de Gonzague, p. 2 (AGOCD, sez. D, 184).

[16] The Sisters of the Society of the Helpers of the Holy Souls in Purgatory (in Chinese *Zhengwanghui* 拯望會) arrived in Shanghai in 1867.

[17] Necrology of Mother Marie de Jésus, p. 6 (AGOCD, sez. D, 184).

[18] Letter of Mother Marie de Jésus to A. Languillat, no date (probably 1869), cited in Molnar, "Recherches," 30–31.

The nuns were warmly welcomed by the vicar apostolic and also by the superior of the mission of Jiangnan, who wrote in a letter that he was "happy to see the holy daughters of St. Teresa in the Far East to establish a Carmelite monastery for young Chinese women."[19] This small group of nuns lived in great poverty and for the first three years they had Mass only three times a week, but they prayed the Divine Office daily, singing it on Sundays and holy days.[20] The first Chinese novice was admitted in 1870, and at the end of 1871 two other nuns arrived from Laval to support the new foundation.[21] As some sources point out, the nuns were soon affected by diseases due to the unhealthy climate. "The climate and the illnesses that have visited us almost continually ever since we came to China make it much more difficult for us here than in France to carry out the austerity of the rule and even make it impossible for us to observe it fully."[22]

> Almost all the foundresses have paid their dues to the climate and have fallen ill. On some days the aspirants had to have their lesson at the bedside of their sick mistresses. Once or twice it was necessary to suspend the recitation of the Office, since only one religious remained well. . . . A new doubt arose: it could be questioned whether the life of Carmel was compatible for European women with the climate of China. No one of the foundresses thought of returning to France. Gradually [the European sisters] became acclimated, and the longevity of the Carmelites who came from Laval had all the signs of being providential.[23]

The temporary residence in Wangjiatang was surrounded by numerous canals and soon proved to be too humid and unhealthy to become the permanent residence of the Carmelites. Moreover, its isolation made it difficult for the Jesuits to come for the daily

---

[19] Letter of A. Della Corte to Mother Marie de Jésus, 5 February 1869, cited in Molnar, "Recherches," 32.

[20] Cf. Molnar, "Recherches," 34–37.

[21] They were Sr. Marie de Saint Louis de Gonzague (d. 1891), who lived in China for twenty years, and Sr. Marie de Saint Paul (d. 1920), who lived in China for forty-nine years.

[22] Letter of Mother Marie de Jésus to A. Languillat (1869), cited in Molnar, "Recherches," 40.

[23] Cited in Molnar, "Recherches," 40.

celebration of Mass and for spiritual direction. The location also "prevented us from attaining the goal we had proposed: that this Carmelite monastery become a center of the ascetical and mystical life, to which young Chinese Christian women, attracted by a high ideal of perfection, would have easy access."[24]

Construction work on a new Carmelite monastery lasted just over a year, from October 1873 to December 1874.[25] The new chapel and monastery of the Carmel of Saint Joseph, built on the property of the Jesuits in the most central suburb of Shanghai, Tushanwan (T'ousèwè), district of Xujiahui (Zikawei), were blessed on 8 December 1874.[26] From archival documents we know that the chapel, built in neo-Gothic style, had a raised altar surmounted by paintings, a Way of the Cross carved in wood, and numerous reliquaries.[27]

A total of sixteen nuns entered the new monastery, seven French and nine Chinese. Of the latter, seven were postulants to be choir nuns, and two were novices "in white veil."[28] The first prioress was Mother Marie de Jésus (1835–1908), who lived in China for forty years. The last of the founding nuns, Mother Saint Dominique du Mont-Carmel, after having served for several years as subprioress and treasurer, died in 1914 at age seventy-six, forty-five years of which she had spent in China.[29]

---

[24] Ibid., 48.

[25] Cf. August M. Colombel, *Histoire de la mission du Kiang-nan [1840–1899]*, vol. 3/2: *L'épiscopat de mgr Languillat, 1865–1878* ([T'ou-sè-wè]: n.p., 1900), 214.

[26] A description of the transfer of the community to T'ousèwè, the blessing of the monastery, and the inclaustration of the nuns can be found in Colombel, *Histoire de la mission du Kiang-nan [1840–1899]*, 3/2:252–55.

[27] Cf. the letter of Sr. Thérèse de Jésus (of the Carmel of Clamart), 5 September 1888 (AGOCD, sez. D, 184).

[28] The nuns in white veil were lay sisters, assigned to manual labor and service, primarily in the kitchen.

[29] Two documents, one handwritten, the other typed, from the General Archive of the Discalced Carmelites in Rome (AGOCD, sez. D, 184), give the names of the five founding sisters: Marie de Jésus (Marie Mousseron de la Chaussée), Clémence Éléonore des Martyrs (Clémence Chapdelaine), (Mother) Saint Dominique du Mont-Carmel (Cécile Victorine Marçais), Anne de Jésus (Joséphine Guillot), Louise Angéla de Saint Raphaël (Louise Caroline Duchène). Their necrologies can be found in the same archives.

In a document written in 1898 a nun from the monastery in Shanghai describes the events leading to the founding of this community and its beginnings.

> The Laval Carmel at that time counted a large number of young subjects who felt the need to devote themselves for the love of Him who had called them to the honor of His divine alliance. Our mothers, in seeing all these young people crowd around them, wondered what were God's designs. From the depths of many souls aspirations arose toward distant missions. The recent foundation of the Saigon Carmel had made a profound impression. . . . Nevertheless, God's moment had not yet come. Only some years later, in 1867, when Bishop Languillat came to the Laval Carmel asking for persons for his mission of Kiangnan [Jiangnan], our mothers saw in this unexpected request the answer to many secret prayers and aspirations and after mature reflection turned to Bishop Wicart,[30] who, himself moved by the divine will, immediately gave his full and complete assent. When this consent became known in our community, many hearts beat more quickly . . . and there were many requests [to leave for China]. . . . The departure took place on 19 December 1868, and the small and humble phalanx arrived in Shanghai on 3 February 1869. . . . Upon arrival the good Sisters Helpers of the Holy Souls showed us a most fraternal hospitality, and from that time we were bound to them with ties of faithful charity. . . . Three weeks later we were cloistered in a temporary house, sufficient for the beginning. . . . After six months of our stay in China we received a postulant for the white veil.[31]

The Jesuit historian of the mission in Jiangnan, the ecclesiastical territory entrusted to the Society of Jesus, where Shanghai is located, notes how ardently Bishop Languillat desired to have Carmelites in his vicariate: "In public [Bishop Languillat] used to give this reason: the mission had such need of prayers that he wanted to have a

---

[30] Casimir-Alexis Wicart, first bishop of the Diocese of Laval. A document in the archives adds that "Bishop Wicart of Laval designated Sr. Marie de Jésus as prioress and chose four of her companions to aid her in establishing a reformed Carmelite monastery in China." Necrology of Mother Marie de Jésus, p. 5 (AGOCD, sez. D, 184).

[31] Necrology of Sr. Louise Angéla de Saint Raphaël (d. 1898), one of the five founding nuns of the Carmelite monastery in Shanghai, p. 3 (AGOCD, sez. D, 184).

Carmel, which has always been a burning center from which this incense rose to heaven. Among intimate friends he said that St. Teresa was asking this of him in his deepest heart with such insistence that he could not resist."[32]

Mother Sophie de Saint Louis de Gonzague,[33] elected in 1878 as the second prioress, briefly described the first two decades of the first Carmel of China in a letter of 1888 to the superior general of the Discalced Carmelites.

> Since your paternity has regarded with benevolence this humble Carmel in China, it will perhaps be of some interest to you to know how it was founded. It was Bishop Languillat of blessed memory who called us here so that a perpetual prayer might cause grace to descend on a terrain that was responding only imperfectly to the labors of those cultivating it with so much zeal and devotion. Now it is already nineteen years since our foundation was born. We are now seven French and ten Chinese professed nuns. Our Carmel is loved, and devotion to our holy Mother [St. Teresa] is becoming popular. . . .[34] Thanks to the charity of the missionaries of the Society of Jesus we receive much spiritual assistance. The choir and the formation of native subjects is the object of all our cares. This formation demands not a little time and not a little labor. May the Lord grant that all those who have made and who will make profession in this humble Carmel to be true daughters of our holy Mother Teresa, animated by her spirit of prayer and of mortification and filled with her zeal for the glory of God and the salvation of souls![35]

[32] Colombel, *Histoire de la mission du Kiang-nan [1840–1899]*, 3/2:134.

[33] Cf. her necrology (AGOCD, sez. D, 184).

[34] An indication of the magnanimous reception the nuns received from various families is also given by Molnar, "Recherches," 41, and by J. de la Servière: "From the earliest days, the Christians of Chang-hai [Shanghai] and the surrounding area understood the blessings that the recently established center of prayer and sacrifice had brought to Kiang-nan [Jiangnan]. The best families were generous in giving alms and soon acquired the habit of asking the Carmelites to pray for them every time a serious situation arose, thereby assuring Bishop Languillat that the purpose for which the nuns had been asked to come had been fully achieved." Joseph de la Servière, *Histoire de la mission du Kiang-nan [1840–1899]*, vol. 2: *Mgr Borgniet (1856–1862), Mgr Languillat (1864–1878)* (Zi-ka-wei: Imprimerie de l'orphelinat, [1914]), 159.

[35] Letter of Sr. Sophie de Saint Louis de Gonzague to the superior general of the Discalced Carmelites, 2 April 1888 (AGOCD, sez. D, 184).

Meanwhile, the novitiate was canonically erected in January 1875, and on 8 December of the same year the first Chinese Carmelite, Sister Marthe (d. 1899), made her profession as a lay sister.[36] Over the course of thirty years, the number of nuns in the community grew slowly, thanks mainly to local vocations, mostly from fervent Shanghai families who had been Christian for several generations. The interest of young Chinese women in the Carmelite life was described in 1882.

> Soon they acquired the sympathy of the Christians, and the Holy Spirit made his voice heard in docile hearts, which responded to his call. Some young Chinese women showed eagerness to set out on the rough path of Carmel . . . . Gradually they became capable of being nourished by Teresa's celestial doctrine, and God, who loves to reveal himself to little ones, made them savor and understand it. China too has already given to the great Reformer of the sixteenth century daughters whom she appears to cover with particular tenderness, as the favorites of her family. Perhaps this is the place to say: this penitential, solitary, and contemplative life of Carmel is in perfect harmony with the customs and the spirit of China. It is understood, it is esteemed, it is loved. The Chinese respects only what is serious and austere. He admires everything that rises above that toward which his nature pulls him. Carmel, thus, for him is the ideal of Christian and religious perfection.[37]

However, the formation of these postulants and novices presented not a few difficulties, of which the prioress, Mother Marie de Jésus and Fr. August M. Colombel, the historian of the Jiangnan mission, give witness.

> Many [of the postulants] belonged to the best Christian families. They did not lack generosity, but for many of Chinese constitution the life of Carmel was too hard, and the majority of the first postulants had to give it up and return to their families or embrace a less rigorous religious observance. An anxious doubt plagued us in spite of ourselves. Would the Chinese ever have enough strength to practice the austerity of the Carmelite rule?

[36] Cf. her necrology (AGOCD, sez. D, 184).
[37] Cited in Molnar, "Recherches," 58.

This doubt seemed all the more well-founded, since it would have been necessary for the Chinese to add to the already rigorous trials of the postulancy three years of study, during which they would learn to speak French and at least to read Latin; their novitiate began only after it was shown that they could follow all the customary exercises of French monasteries.[38]

It was necessary to teach them to read and to follow the Office in Latin, and it was greatly desirable that they should know enough French to receive from the older religious the traditions of St. Teresa, to read books of spirituality that are not found in Chinese. To overcome this difficulty the Carmelites had to have the young girls who came to them undergo a long postulancy. The long period of trial tested the vocations, and after several years the chosen of God took the veil. In this way, in 1900 in the Carmel of Tou-sè-wei there were sixteen Chinese religious, twelve choir sisters and four of the white veil.[39]

Another, though lesser reason for the growth of the community was that nuns were sent to it from several French Carmelite monasteries (Tours, Angoulême, Orléans, Laval, Agen, Clamart) and from the Canadian Carmelite monastery in Montreal.[40] Among these monasteries, Tours was certainly the one most aware of the situation of the Carmelite monastery in Shanghai. The reason for this was that two prioresses of Tours were sisters of two Jesuit missionaries in Shanghai.[41]

In the early decades of the twentieth century the numbers of the sisters gradually began to decline. Between the years 1875 and 1900, there was a final monastic profession almost every two years.[42] In 1900 the community numbered twenty-five nuns (nine foreign and sixteen Chinese), in 1932 they were nineteen (six European and

---

[38] Letter of Mother Marie de Jésus to A. Languillat, 14 May 1871, cited in Molnar, "Recherches," 53.

[39] August M. Colombel, *Histoire de la mission du Kiang-nan [1840–1899]*, vol. 3/3: *L'épiscopat de mgr Garnier, 1879–1898; mgr Simon, 1899* ([T'ou-sè-wè]: n.p., 1900), 490.

[40] In the General Archive of the Order of Discalced Carmelites in Rome there is a letter with the list of the eight nuns from the Carmelite monastery in Tours who left for Shanghai between the years 1900 and 1946 (AGOCD, sez. D, 184).

[41] Cf. Colombel, *Histoire de la mission du Kiang-nan [1840–1899]*, 3/3:489.

[42] Cf. Molnar, "Recherches," 54.

thirteen Chinese),[43] in 1941 eighteen (seven European and eleven Chinese),[44] and in 1950 they were down to fourteen (six European and eight Chinese).[45] One of the reasons the number of the community decreased in the 1920s was that two new foundations were made in that decade, one in Chongqing and the other in Jiaxing.

In 1927 Shanghai was besieged by revolutionary Communist troops. The sisters were forced to leave the monastery; they took refuge for a few weeks in the main convent of the Sisters of Charity of St. Vincent de Paul, located in the protected territory of the foreign concession.[46]

As is noted in a 1927 circular letter, French continued to be the language that was spoken in the house and in which the young aspirants were taught. "French is the language we use when talking among ourselves; all our Chinese sisters, including those with the white veil, speak it and can also write it intelligibly."[47] The efforts made by the first nuns in Shanghai to try to learn Chinese, at least enough to make themselves understood, are to be commended. The obituary of Mother Marie de Jésus (d. 1908) states that "since her arrival in China, the study of Chinese took precedence over any other duty."[48] Three months after the arrival in China of Mother Sophie de Saint Louis de Gonzague (d. 1891) it is said that she "knew enough Chinese to make herself understood."[49] Sister Louise Angéla de Saint Raphaël (d. 1898) was praised for having "learned Chinese so quickly."[50]

Like other religious communities in China, the Carmelite community in Shanghai, headed by Sr. Marie-Cécile de Jésus, faced great

[43] Cf. *MCJ. Dixième année [1931–1932]*, 266.

[44] Cf. Lazaristes du Pétang, *Les missions de Chine. Seizième année (1940–1941)* (Shanghai: Procure des Lazaristes, 1942), 220.

[45] Cf. Zhou Xiufen, ed., *Lishi shang de Xujiahui (Zikawei in History)* (Shanghai: Shanghai wenhua chubanshe, 2005), 174–81.

[46] See the account of these events in the necrology of Sr. Marie-Louise de Jésus, pp. 4–6 (AGOCD, sez. D, 184).

[47] Ibid., p. 2.

[48] Necrology of Mother Marie de Jésus, p. 7 (AGOCD, sez. D, 184).

[49] Necrology of Mother Sophie de Saint Louis de Gonzague, p. 3 (AGOCD, sez. D, 184).

[50] Necrology of Sr. Louise Angéla de Saint Raphaël, p. 3 (AGOCD, sez. D, 184).

trials after 1949, yet it was the one that survived the longest. Documentary evidence that has been preserved clearly shows that the nuns were unanimous in their will to remain in China until the end, the only condition being that the essentials of regular monastic and community life be preserved. This led to the firm decision made by the nuns already in 1951 and confirmed by the superiors of the mission and the father general of the order.

> *We will remain here, all together as much as it is possible for us to have a normal religious life.* When it will no longer be possible, or *when we are no longer wanted here*, we will take refuge in Manila (at least the five foreigners), and our Chinese sisters will return *for the moment* to their families. I am worried about those who no longer have family and I am looking, together with our superiors, for means for them to find a refuge. Our sisters are truly courageous and full of confidence in the good God, our Father. In spite of the great suffering they feel for finding themselves in such extremity, they do not complain, but leave themselves [in God's hands]. . . . What has decided us to take refuge in Manila is its proximity to China and the really generous charity of our dear mothers there.[51]

All the sources agree that monastic life continued unabated until the beginning of September 1955.

> In spite of the persecution, at times veiled, at times violent, by the Communists, our life in Carmel after 1949 was calm, regular, happy. The exterior festivities, *very solemn*, attracted, gathered, comforted the Christians. The visits to the house by the Communists, rare at the beginning, became more frequent, longer, but respected our holy rule, the schedule set by our constitutions, our customs. . . . Since the material restrictions came gradually, we supported them gladly. Nothing caused us to foresee the "outstanding raid" that was to destroy our security, all our immediate and certain counsels.[52]

---

[51] Letter of Sr. Marie-Cécile de Jésus, 19 September 1951 (AGOCD, sez. D, 184). The emphasis occurs in the original as underlined text.

[52] "Le carmel de Tou-se-wei (Shanghai) du 8 septembre au 26 décembre 1955," typewritten by a French Carmelite of the monastery in Shanghai who had taken refuge in the Philippines, 16 July 1956, p. 1 (AGOCD, sez. D, 184). Emphasis in the original.

The precarious situation of the community did not allow it to accept new candidates for the monastic life, though they continued to seek admission. Mother prioress sadly noted this state of affairs in a letter written in 1952. One of the last European nuns at the Carmelite monastery in Shanghai also spoke of this situation in a letter she wrote in 1954.

> On account of the uncertain future I have been strongly urged, by those who have the right, to send our postulants to their families, as a measure of prudence. I cannot but follow this advice given with great supernatural wisdom, but it is a great suffering for me, because this is really to stop the growth of our community. These youngsters, by the way, have given us complete satisfaction, and we would have admitted them to the veil with joy. This is truly the hour of great sacrifices![53]

Another sister added: "Postulants present themselves, but we cannot have them enter. One of the three that we have had return to their families appeared to us to be quite seriously attached to her vocation. . . . If we no longer accept young candidates, we are destined for extinction!"[54]

The idea of sending some postulants to France for their formation, as expressed in a few letters from the early 1950s, could never be realized. The situation of insecurity and uncertainty, which the nuns faced bravely, entrusting themselves to the will of God as they looked for the best way to maintain their community life, came to an end on the night of 8 September 1955, when Communist soldiers burst into the monastery and occupied it, as was reported by the chronicler of *Contemplation et Apostolat*.

---

[53] Letter of Sr. Marie-Cécile de Jésus, 16 June 1952 (AGOCD, sez. D, 184). See also the letter of the same sister, 16 May 1952 (AGOCD, sez. D, 184).

[54] Letter of Sr. Marie-Liesse de l'Annunciation, 17 July 1954 (AGOCD, sez. D, 184). Some months later the mother superior of the Carmelite monastery in Shanghai planned to reopen the novitiate, but she was counseled not to do so by her superiors: cf. letter of Sr. Marie-Cécile de Jésus, 1 September 1954 (AGOCD, sez. D, 184). In this last letter she speaks of the possibility of permitting some postulants to participate in the life of the monastery during the day and then to return to their families at night. In this way their presence would not be as noticeable and they could avoid the law against changing one's legal residence.

> The Carmel of Zikawei, the last that still existed in Communist
> China, has not escaped the persecution that has raged in the last
> few months against Christianity and its holy bishop Ignatius
> Kiong [Gong Pinmei], in Shanghai. In the night between 8 and
> 9 November [September] 1955 groups of armed police with the
> aid of ladders scaled the high walls of the monastery of St. Joseph
> of T'ou-sè-wè and broke into the convent through the windows.
> The sisters were given the order to gather in a large room while
> all the cells and common rooms were thoroughly searched. The
> police took all papers, including the personal notes of the nuns.[55]

The nuns were forced to endure intense and prolonged sessions
of political indoctrination for the purpose, so it was claimed by the
Communists, of converting the monastery into a "patriotic Carmel."
"The Communists wanted to frighten, but they wanted to preserve
Carmel, *a patriotic Carmel.* 'The Christians love you,' they said,
'your disappearance would cause them pain. . . . We do not want
to send you away, you are an order that we esteem. You are not like
the others, your customs please us. Send away the foreigners who
remain, we will bring to you good young girls, we know some who
want to *be associated* with you.'"[56]

A detailed account of the tragic events that took place in the monastery between 8 September and 26 December 1955, the day the
last foreign nuns departed from China, was drawn up by one of the
nuns just a few months later. It provides a record of many occasions
when the whole community gave testimony of their loyalty and heroic steadfastness. One example is given under 11 September: "Sr.
Bernadette rose then and *cried out* loudly: 'We do not want to listen,
we will be faithful until death to our bishop, to our priests, to our
superiors.' At this all the sisters rose and gave their approval to this
declaration: 'Yes, yes, yes! Prison or death rather than abandoning
our beliefs and our spiritual superiors.' It was a fine show of courage,
of generous enthusiasm. All the Chinese sisters grouped themselves
by the door, and the non-Chinese followed them, saying, 'We will go
with our sisters wherever they are conducted.'"[57]

---

[55] CA 24 (1956): 11.

[56] "Le carmel de Tou-se-wei (Shanghai) du 8 septembre au 26 décembre 1955,"
10. Emphasis in the original.

[57] Ibid., 2.

Soon, however, the prioress, following the counsel of her superiors, even if reluctantly and hesitatingly, had to ask the superior general of the Carmelite Order to present the Holy See with the reasons that made it necessary to suppress the Carmelite monastery in Shanghai. The superior general, in a letter to Pope Pius XII dated 14 December 1955, listed those reasons as follows: "Inability to live the Carmelite life; being subject to the will of the Communists; pressure from the Communists to make them shift their allegiance to the national church . . . the vicar apostolic of Shanghai, under whose jurisdiction the monastery lies, is in prison."[58]

On 19 December 1955, seventy years after having been founded as the first Carmelite community in China, the Carmel of Shanghai was the last to be legally suppressed. The European Carmelite nuns were the last women religious from Shanghai to leave China. They were encouraged to do so by the Chinese sisters, who feared that under interrogation they might say something that would be detrimental to the European sisters.

> You cannot be of any help to us. Even the affection that you have for us no longer sustains us, but rather breaks our hearts. You are regarded as burdensome and despicable *objects*; you are treated like parasites. We are pressured to accuse you, we are forbidden to speak to you. Mother, ask for your exit visa. If you remain, you will be forced to declare that you have revealed the country's secrets, that you terrorize us, that you remain in order to prevent us from carrying out our civil duties, and so on. Mother, if you remain, you add to our anxieties, you increase the chances of our going to prison. . . . Leave! . . . After you cross the border you will be able to speak to our superiors, and . . . their advice will reach us through you. Your departure will bring us greater aid than your presence. . . . Leave, leave![59]

Having come together with the whole community in the chapel the night before to renew their vows, the last foreign nuns left for Hong Kong on 26 December and sailed to the Philippines where, in 1957,

[58] Letter of the superior general of the Discalced Carmelites to Pope Pius XII, 14 December 1955 (AGOCD, sez. D, 184).

[59] "Le carmel de Tou-se-wei (Shanghai) du 8 septembre au 26 décembre 1955," 13–14.

they refounded the St. Joseph Carmel in Lucena, "ready to return to China as soon as circumstances allow," as an archival document puts it with a hint of nostalgia.[60]

The Chinese sisters, eighteen in all, remained in China. Eight of them were solemnly professed, two simply professed, one a novice, four postulants, and three externs.[61] On 1 January 1956, they sent a poignant letter to the pope, asking him to enlighten them on the choices they should make. Since they, like many of the clergy, were torn between pressure to join the independence movement and loyalty to the universal church, they begged him to send them an authoritative word on what to do.[62] On 16 February 1956 the pope sent his response via the Secretariat of State to the superior general of the Discalced Carmelites. In his letter he expressed his participation in the suffering of the Carmelites of Shanghai, "who are now in the front ranks of the good fight," offering them words of appreciation for "their steadfastness, piety, and readiness to sacrifice," and encouraging them to remain members of the "holy militia of the Theresian Carmel of Shanghai": "The Lord, who . . . until now has given his spouses the grace not to stray off the right path of duty in perfect adherence to Jesus Christ and to his church, will not cease to assist and comfort them so that their witness to the Christian vocation may be perfect and glorious."[63]

The Chinese sisters would continue to live together until 1958, albeit with major restrictions, including the obligation to participate in political indoctrination sessions and the periodic arrests of some of them.

[60] Typewritten letter of Sr. Thérèse de Jésus to the superior general of the Carmelites, 4 July 1988 (AGOCD, sez. D, 184). Since the Carmelite monastery of Shanghai was formally suppressed, the canonical erection of the Carmelite monastery of Lucena was the responsibility of the Carmelite monastery of Quezon City. Five sisters from Shanghai made up the community at Lucena.

[61] Cf. letter of Sr. Thérèse de Jésus to the superior general of the Carmelites, 5 September 1988 (AGOCD, sez. D, 184).

[62] Cf. the original undated letter in Chinese, which is kept in the General Archive of the Order of Discalced Carmelites in Rome, along with a translation into Italian (AGOCD, sez. D, 184).

[63] Letter of A. Dell'Acqua, substitute of His Holiness, to the superior general of the Carmelites, 16 February 1956 (AGOCD, sez. D, 184).

As was the case for much church property, the old monastery complex was expropriated and became the property of the government, which assigned it to Shanghai Film Studios. Unlike other properties that were returned to the church in the 1980s, in 2001 this complex was bought by the Shanghai Film Group, of which Shanghai Film Studios was a part. In 2009 the Shanghai Film Group demolished the existing buildings and rebuilt the entire complex. The dormitory of the old Carmelite convent, which until then had miraculously escaped destruction and had been remodeled to house a museum of the film center then under construction, was inexplicably demolished, presumably at the end of 2009 or the beginning of 2010, only to be rebuilt, but twenty percent smaller than the original building.[64]

Excerpts from two official Chinese historical sources will serve to close this account of the history of the Carmelite monastery in Shanghai, the *Chronicles of the Suburb of Xuhui* and the *Chronicles of the Fahua District*.

In the eighth year of the Tongzhi era of the Qing [1869] the first group of French Carmelite sisters arrived in Shanghai and settled first with the sisters [of the Society of the] Helpers [of the Holy Souls]. In the thirteenth year of the Tongzhi era [1874] they moved to a large monastery of four floors, which today stands at number 595, Caoxibei Street. Carmel is based on mortification (*keji* 克己), spiritual perfection (*xiushen* 修身), and prayer. At its foundation Carmel remains open for three days, offering faithful women the possibility to visit it; once enclosure is established, those who have entered Carmel begin to live a monastic life separated from the world. Besides practicing religious activities such as attending Mass and receiving Communion, [the nuns] recite the Divine Office daily. On Sundays and feasts they sing the offices of Vespers and of the night. Another important practice is "flagellation" (*da kubian* 打苦鞭), carried out three evenings a week, which consists of flagellating the body in reparation for

[64] Cf. the information given by Adam Minter on his website *Shanghai Scrap*, where one can also find pictures of the Carmelite monastery: http://shanghaiscrap .com/2009/01/preservation-shanghai-style-pt-2; http://shanghaiscrap.com/2009/01 /event-better-than-the-real-thing-a-shanghai-scrap-correction; http://shanghaiscrap .com/2010/11/build-demolish-rinse-repeat-a-shanghai-scrap-carmelite-update, all accessed 21 August 2013.

others' sins. In the thirteenth year of the Tongzhi era [1874] the nuns of Carmel numbered seventeen, in the thirty-seventh year of the Republic [1948] they numbered eighteen.[65]

The Carmelite monastery, like the seminary, stands east of the Ciyun Bridge in Tushanwan. It was built at the beginning of the Tongzhi era as a place where virgins could practice self-betterment and seclusion throughout their life. It accepts both Chinese and Westerners. The aim of this order has for its basis spiritual perfection through mortification and the overcoming of self through prayer, which places it in the highest ranks of Catholic religious orders. Their rule is extremely severe; although they can meet parents, they may not converse long with them, they never go out of the monastery, and they do not eat meat. They observe severe fasts and lead a life of austerity from 15 September until the Resurrection of Jesus the next year. They pray day and night, imploring the Lord that he may make the country and the church prosper day after day.[66]

At about the same time that the first Carmelite monastery was established in China, the vicar apostolic in Peking, Bishop Louis-Gabriel Delaplace, did his best to bring Carmelites to his vicariate. Having received a sizeable donation from Count Caius de Stolberg, father of a young nun, for the foundation of a Carmelite monastery in the Vicariate of Peking, Bishop Delaplace approached several Carmelite communities in France between 1875 and 1878 in search of future missionary nuns. Even though the response of these communities was not positive, he did not delay implementing his proposal. In fact, he even began constructing quarters for a future Carmelite monastery in Tianjin (Tientsin). It was only after he had knocked on the doors of almost all the Carmelite monasteries in France that the community in Bayonne in southern France agreed to send three nuns to Tianjin. Unfortunately, just as they were about to embark for China, the project had to be abandoned because one of the nuns fell

[65] *Xuhui qu zhi* [Chronicles of the suburb of Xuhui] (Shanghai: Shanghai shehui kexueyuan chubanshe, 1997), 661.

[66] *Fahua xiang zhi* 法华乡志 [Chronicles of the Fahua district], in Zhang Xianqing and Zhao Ruijuan, eds., *Zhongguo difangzhi jidujiao shiliao jiyao* [References to Christianity contained in local Chinese chronicles] (Shanghai: Dongfang chuban zhongxin, 2010), 24.

ill. Seeing his many efforts come to naught, Bishop Delaplace concluded that this project was not the will of God. He suspended work
on the construction of a monastery in Tianjin and began looking
for other ways to use the funds he had received a few years earlier.[67]

The Carmel of Chongqing

In 1920, at the invitation of Bishop Célestin Chouvellon, a member of the Paris Foreign Missions Society and vicar apostolic of Eastern Sichuan, "who had long urged the Carmel of Shanghai to make
a foundation in his vicariate,"[68] the Carmel of the Sacred Heart of
Jesus was founded in the district of Chongqing (Chungking). It was
also known as the Carmel of Zengjiayan (Tsengkiagai), after the area
of the city where it was located. Popularly it was referred to as the
"Rock Carmel," since it was placed against a rock cliff. Thanks to the
memoirs of one of the nuns, Mother Marie-Élisabeth de la Trinité
(Marie Roussel, 1903–1996), who lived in this Carmel from 1933
to 1951, it is possible to give an "insider's" account of some of the
major events that marked the life of this community.[69]

The small group of founders who came from Shanghai to Chongqing in 1920 was made up of seven sisters. "In May 1920 . . . the
seven courageous missionaries arrived in Chung-King [Chongqing]:
four Europeans, one of whom could not bear the climate of Setchouan
[Sichuan] and shortly returned to Shanghai, while another, still quite
young, died, laid low by a terrible illness; three Chinese, of whom

[67] Cf. A. Thomas, "Projet de fondation d'un Carmel," in *Histoire de la mission
de Pékin*, vol. 2: *Depuis l'arrivée des Lazaristes jusqu'à la révolte des Boxeurs* (Paris:
Vald. Rasmussen, 1933), 564–65. As will be seen below, his search was then directed
with happy results to the founding of a Trappist monastery (cf. *infra*, pp. 115–19).

[68] Necrology of Mother Marie-Anne de Saint Paul (d. 1934), p. 4 (AGOCD, sez.
D, 58).

[69] Cf. Mère Élisabeth, *Partir*. After her expulsion from China and a short period in
Singapore, Mother Élisabeth returned to Nancy, where she became prioress. When
she finished her term as prioress in 1973, she and three other sisters of Nancy joined
the Carmel of Nogent-sur-Marne. They had already spent two years living together
in view of founding a Byzantine rite Carmel consecrated to prayer for Christian
unity. The foundation was made at Saint-Rémy in Burgundy, where, in 1981, the
monastery of Saint-Élie was recognized for five years *ad experimentum* and then
canonically established in 1986.

two were professed choir sisters with temporary vows and one sister very caring and devoted to Carmel as portress."[70]

The three French founders of the Carmelite monastery of Chongqing were Mother Marie-Anne de Saint Paul (Jeanne Hossart), a nun of the Carmel of Tours who had been in China since 1895 and was prioress of the Carmel of Chongqing from its foundation in May 1922 until 1929; Sr. Marguerite-Marie de l'Immaculée Conception (Lemoine), a nun of the Carmel of Enghien in Belgium, who had been in China since 1912; and Sr. Marie-Angèle de Jésus, a nun of the Carmel of Shanghai, who died in 1922, just two years after her arrival in Chongqing. In 1922, Sr. Blanche du Cœur de Marie, a nun of the Carmel of Lons-le-Saunier, along with two white-veiled nuns (lay sisters), were added to the group of founders. Sr. Blanche du Cœur de Marie was soon appointed subprior but died in 1927 at the age of thirty-three.[71]

The nuns resided in a temporary dwelling made available to them by a Catholic family until early 1925, when they could move into their new monastery, designed and built with the help of the Paris Foreign Missions Society. During the first decade of the community almost a dozen young Chinese women entered and became nuns. In 1927, at the request of Bishop Louis-Gabriel-Xavier Jantzen, vicar apostolic of Chongqing, a small group of the founders along with the Chinese nuns took refuge in Shanghai to flee the violence they might have been subjected to following a bloody uprising of xenophobic students. As one of the sisters reported, "It was so difficult to leave the mission, to abandon a work begun just when it seemed to be developing: two postulants had been admitted to clothing."[72]

The nuns of the Shanghai Carmel joyfully welcomed back the sisters who had departed seven years earlier.

> It was seven years since our dear mothers and sisters had left us
> for their beloved foundation of Tchong-king [Chongqing]. . . .

[70] Necrology of Mother Marie-Anne de Saint Paul, p. 5. Cf. also the following accounts of the foundation of the Carmel of Chongqing: "Xujiahui shengyiyuan xiunü fu Chongqing" [Nuns of the Xujiahui Carmel go to Chongqing], SZ 5 (1920): 234; "Shengyiyuan xiunü di Chuan" [Carmelite nuns arrive in Sichuan], SZ 8 (1920): 370–71.

[71] Cf. their necrologies (AGOCD, sez. D, 58).

[72] Necrology of Sr. Blanche du Cœur de Marie, p. 7 (AGOCD, sez. D, 58).

Since 27 April they have been here among us, forming truly one heart and one soul with those who are so happy to have them, and no shadow has yet come to trouble this beautiful harmony of union in charity. Our dear mothers and sisters will remain in T'ou-sè-wè until order is restored. . . . Until that time both of our groups live our life of missionary Carmelites, in silence and prayer, fully abandoned [to God's will], seeking our strength and our consolation in our dear holy observances, without troubling ourselves by noises from outside, "throwing all our cares into the bosom of our Father who is in heaven."[73]

In the absence of the nuns the monastery of Chongqing was managed by two externs and a Chinese postulant from the region and it did not suffer any damage.[74] The exile lasted only eighteen months, and the nuns were able to return to their monastery as early as 1929. In the same year Sr. Isabelle de Jésus (Poncelet, 1885–1967),[75] sub-prioress of the Carmel of Tournai in Belgium, and Sr. Marie-Thérèse de l'Enfant-Jésus, a young nun of the Carmel of Tourcoing in France, left Europe for Chongqing. Marie-Thérèse died prematurely that same year, while Isabelle was appointed prioress in 1930 and elected in 1933. In 1930 another nun of Tourcoing, Sr. Marie de Saint Joseph, went to Chongqing to replace the deceased Sr. Marie-Thérèse, but she also died a few months after her arrival in China.[76]

In October 1933 four newly professed Carmelite nuns left for the Carmel of Chongqing: two were from the Carmel of Nancy (Sr. Marie-Élisabeth de la Trinité, thirty years old, and Sr. Cécile) and two from the Carmel of Niort (Sr. Anne-Marie de Jésus, thirty-six years old, and Sr. Marie-Madeleine de Jésus, thirty-three years old). These four nuns were received by ten sisters—two of them European and eight Chinese, from different parts of China.[77] In 1936, they petitioned

---

[73] Necrology of Sr. Marie Louise de Jésus, p. 6 (AGOCD, sez. D, 184).

[74] The "externs" were sisters who, more often than not, did not take vows. They lived out of the cloister and performed services outside the community for the "intern" sisters, who were not allowed to leave the cloister.

[75] Cf. her necrology (AGOCD, sez. D, 58).

[76] Cf. the common necrology of Sr. Marie-Thérèse de l'Enfant-Jésus and Sr. Marie de Saint Joseph (AGOCD, sez. D, 58).

[77] Four of the Chinese sisters came from the Carmel of Shanghai. One of them, Sr. Saint Michel, was the widow of a Catholic mandarin from Shanghai. Her daughter,

Rome for an indult to allow them to leave their original Carmelite monasteries and become members of the Chongqing Carmel, thereby making explicit their determination to remain in China.[78]

In 1937, when Mother Isabelle was reconfirmed as prioress, a new French Carmelite, Mother Élisabeth de la Trinité, a professed nun of the Carmel of Reims, joined the Carmel of Chongqing after the closing of the Carmel of Jiaxing, where she had been prioress. In 1939 bombing began in Chongqing, causing severe damage to church buildings.[79] Concerned for their safety, Bishop Jantzen invited the nuns in the following year to move to the diocesan seminary outside Chongqing, but the community chose to remain where they were. In 1940, Mother Élisabeth de la Trinité was elected the new prioress.

Mother Isabelle was elected prioress once again in 1943, and she remained the superior of the community until 1948, when she resigned because of serious health problems. The chapter then elected Mother Marie-Élisabeth (from Nancy) as the new prioress. In 1944, Sr. Juliana du Sacré-Cœur (Wan Xizhen), the first Sichuan Carmelite, became the first Chinese nun to be appointed to the office of subprioress. At the end of 1946 four new European nuns arrived: two were French (Sr. Jeanne de Jésus-Maria, a nun of the Carmel of Boussu-les-Mons, but coming from the Carmel of Saint-Quentin,[80] and Marie du Sacré-Cœur, a nun of the Carmel of Aire-sur-la-Lys); the other two were Belgian (one from the Carmel of Liège-Cornillon and the other from the Carmel of Mehagne). One of the reasons these new members arrived was the proposed establishment of a Carmelite monastery in Chengdu, also in Sichuan province, but the war prevented the realization of this plan.

In 1949, at the time of the proclamation of the Republic, there were seven European nuns and a dozen Chinese sisters in the Carmel of Chongqing. After the bombing that led to the "liberation" of Chongqing on 29 November 1949, and that also damaged the

---

Anne, also became a nun of the Shanghai Carmel. She would be involved in the founding of the Kunming Carmel.

[78] Cf. the related documentation from the AGOCD, sez. D, 58.

[79] In 1938 Chongqing had become the seat of the central government, which had fled from Nanjing, and then became the new capital of the Republic of China.

[80] Sr. Jeanne de Jésus-Maria recounts her experience of a little more than four years in China in a long letter dated 12 February 1989 (AGOCD, sez. D, 58).

monastery, the effects of the Communist takeover were soon felt. Searches and interrogations began in 1950, and starting in 1951, political indoctrination sessions were also held in the monastery.

> Relations between the red police and Carmel were always correct, even during their several visits to the monastery. The European Carmelites were summoned four times, two of them secret, to the police for interrogation. They liked our great poverty at that time, and due to the absence of external works we were declared without "sin." Nevertheless, those responsible (prioress and subprioress) had to listen in the parlor to a more vehement talk, which denied the existence of God and of the soul and declared our beliefs and our hopes vain. It was a good occasion to confess our faith, which we did with all our heart, with profound emotion, interrupting the orators. This did not prevent them from inviting us to join them, happy to submit to women, often more capable than men to lead an army: here you command twenty persons, with us . . . you will command 2,000, 20,000. . . . The matter did not stop there, because after having tried in vain to obtain the presence of a delegate of Carmel at their meetings or marches (a novice, however, was obliged to be present at a labor feast), they imposed attendance at a Marxist studies circle on the Chinese sisters. The first meeting took place inside the enclosure. Ten young militant Communist girls under the direction of a woman in charge made up the "salon" with ten native Carmelites, each of the girls taking charge of one of the Carmelites, with a smile on their lips, with consummate art bringing about a sociable atmosphere. After this the circle met several times a month in the exterior parlor so that the Carmelites did not have to leave their enclosure, but with Marxist books read and commented upon by Catholic women, they gained a reputation for "untiring concessions" that could not but erode the foundations of their religious spirit.[81]

Nevertheless, the community tried to continue leading a normal life. On 10 December 1950 the decision was made to proceed with the clothing of a novice. In 1951 Bishop Jantzen, under house arrest,

---

[81] "Relation de la fin du Carmel de Chung-King," 4–5 (AGOCD, sez. D, 58). For more information on the last months, November 1949 to the middle of 1951, of the community of Chongqing, see also the long circular letter of Sr. Jeanne de Jésus-Maria, 11 August 1951 (AGOCD, sez. D, 58; there are two copies, one with the title "Chungking—Récit de fermeture [Chine]—11 août 1951").

advised the European nuns to request exit visas. Following the resignation of Mother Marie-Élisabeth, Sr. Juliana, who was Chinese,
was appointed subprioress. In her memoirs Mother Marie-Élisabeth
wrote with emotion but also with a clear sense of what lay ahead:
"There were some tears when I was seen taking my place in the
choir according to my rank of profession, but very soon everything
calmed down, and Sr. Juliana assumed her new role with simplicity
and delicacy. At the next chapter I remarked that it was in fact better
to hear a Chinese speak to her sisters according to race and tongue
in a language already 'grammatically' incomparably better than ours,
but above all, in its substance, closer to their mentality."[82]

The monastery was officially suppressed on 31 July 1951, and in
August the European nuns finally left China. The Catholic information service Fides reported on their departure:

> Contemplative life too has been banished from red China, where
> there is no more room for those who dedicate themselves to
> prayer and penance. The most recent case is that of seven Belgian
> and French Carmelites who had to abandon their monastery of
> Chungking [Chongqing], opened thirty years ago. At any hour of
> day or night minor officials, students, and anyone at all claimed
> to have the right to inspect the enclosure, which for months
> and months the sisters vainly tried to defend. They wanted,
> but were not able, to force the sisters to leave the monastery to
> participate in Communist demonstrations in the streets, while
> inside the enclosure they were supported by a "comrade" charged
> with giving them courses of Marxist doctrine. In the end the
> poor cloistered sisters saw themselves morally obliged to leave
> China; ten native Carmelites remain to defend the existence of
> their monastery.[83]

Two of the seven sisters embarked for the Carmel of Goa, India,
where they later took part in the founding of several Carmelite monasteries.[84] Three returned to their original monasteries, namely,
Niort, Reims, and Nancy. One took up temporary residence in Hong

---

[82] Mère Élisabeth, *Partir*, 130.

[83] Report of the news agency Fides, 1 September 1951.

[84] Sr. Jeanne de Jésus-Maria, after having assisted in the founding of the Carmel of
Shembagamur, founded those of Soso (1969), Sitagarha (1975), and Jalpaigury (1977).
Sr. Marie du Sacré-Cœur participated in the founding of the Carmel of Bombay.

Kong and another moved to the Carmel of Singapore.[85] Upon the departure of the European nuns, the archives of the Carmel of Chongqing, along with library books and the Chinese translation of the rule, the constitutions, and the book of ceremonies, were burned to avoid causing problems for the Chinese nuns who remained in China. The nuns were thus unable to preserve any internal documents on the life of the Carmel of Chongqing. The property of the Carmelites in Chongqing was expropriated by the progressive committee, which sold the monastery to a state-owned factory. In 1952, the same progressive committee ordered the chaplain of the Carmelite community, who secretly continued to provide the sacraments and spiritual care for the nuns, to terminate all relations with them, making it necessary for the Chinese nuns who remained to attend the parish church for Mass.[86]

Thanks to the support of local people, the sisters were able to remain in the outer part of the old monastery for a few years. They made rag dolls for a living, until the rationing of goods made it impossible to obtain the material they needed for their work. At the end of the 1950s they were forced to move to the Church of St. Joseph, and they worked in a knitting factory. For a time the Chinese sisters managed to maintain some form of community life. However, with the outbreak of the Cultural Revolution, that was no longer possible. Some of the few remaining Chinese Carmelites returned to their own families; others were accused of being agents in the pay of foreign powers.[87]

As in the case of the Carmel of Shanghai, here too it is interesting to read what an official Chinese source, the *Chronicles of Chongqing*, had to say about the Carmel of Chongqing.

> The Carmelite Order, called also the "order of the holy habit,"
> is one of the mendicant [*sic*] Catholic orders. It was founded in
> the mid-twelfth century in Palestine, on Mount Carmel, from

[85] Cf. the typewritten document preserved in AGOCD, sez. D, 58. It is undated but presumably written shortly after the expulsion of the European nuns.

[86] According to *Contemplation et Apostolat*, in 1951–1952 "no more than ten Chinese nuns" remained in Chongqing. Cf. CA 17 (1952): 14.

[87] Cf. Wang, "An Account of My Journey," 13.

which it takes its name. In 1920 the bishop of the Chongqing diocese, Shu Fulong [Célestin Chouvellon], invited the nuns of the Shanghai Carmel to found a Carmel. On 18 May 1921 he sent to Yu[88] four foreign and three Chinese nuns, led by the French Anne [de Saint] Paul to found the monastery of Chongqing. They first resided temporarily on the property of a family of Catholic faithful [in the suburb of] Zengjiayan, then in 1925 the construction of the monastery at number 152–153 [in the suburb of] Longjiawan was completed and they transferred there. Later three Chinese sisters, among them Wan Xizhen,[89] entered. After the foundation of this order in Chongqing, all in all thirty Chinese and fifteen foreign sisters entered there, not counting those who died on account of sickness, or abandoned the monastic life and returned to the secular life. In December 1949 there were still thirteen Chinese and seven foreign sisters in the monastery. If before 1951 the prioresses were always foreigners, in 1951 the Chinese nun Wan Xizhen assumed the office of prioress. On 1 August 1951 seven foreign nuns left Yu and returned to their countries. In 1985 the nuns of this order, after the death of some sisters from old age or sickness, still numbered five, among them Wan Xizhen, and lived in a building next to the Church of St. Joseph.[90]

There was no news about the life of the sisters of this community from the years of the Cultural Revolution until the 1990s. The same is true of other Chinese Carmels, contacts with which were lost already in 1950: "What has happened to the Carmels under the new regime? Evidently, those in Macau and in Hong Kong have not been troubled at all. . . . We do not know the fate of the Carmels of Zikawei, Kiashing, Chungking, and Yunnanfu."[91]

By their prayer and community life, the Carmelite nuns of Chongqing were eloquent witnesses of the way of love modeled by St. Teresa. For thirty years they prayed the liturgical offices in Latin according to the same schedule and the same rubrics that were used in Europe, supporting themselves mainly through embroidery work

---

[88] Another name for Chongqing.

[89] See *infra*, p. 109, n. 166.

[90] *Chongqing shi shizhongqu zhi* [Chronicles of the city of Chongqing, central zone] (Chongqing: Chongqing chubanshe, 1997), 721.

[91] CA 14 (1950): 36.

and spinning and weaving flax. As one of the sisters wrote, their common life based on the Gospel created a community that overcame cultural differences: "Over the course of weeks, of months, of years, our little community has become unified, larger. No longer are there Europeans and Chinese, but . . . the Carmelites of Tsen-kia-gai [Zengjiayan]. The language, still poorly mastered—it will never be mastered perfectly—, is no longer an obstacle to joyous and profound relations between Europeans and Chinese."[92]

This life attracted a fair number of young Chinese women, who entered the novitiate at the Carmel of Chongqing over the years. Many of them, however, were unable to remain because they became victims of the epidemics of tuberculosis or malaria that were rampant in those years.[93] However, the clothing of postulants, temporary professions, and solemn professions took place with a certain regularity.[94] The community built a small library and stocked it with Christian books in Chinese: translations of the gospels, works of Christian spirituality and theology, the catechism, and several prayer books. Some of the European nuns made an effort to learn Chinese, so as to be able, above all, to form novices and postulants in the Carmelite way of life and to explain to them the Carmelite rule, constitutions, and ceremonial.[95] They also began translating materials into Chinese with the help of the Chinese sisters. Their commitment to the work of translation is attested to by two passages

---

[92] Mère Élisabeth, *Partir*, 42.

[93] "The climate is humid in the summer, fertile ground for tuberculosis, the cause of the death of more than a dozen sisters in less than thirty years." Carmel de Cherbourg, *Génèalogie des couvents de Carmélites*, 39.

[94] The chronicle of the monasteries contained in *Contemplation et Apostolat* reports on several occasions that the community "has had significant success recruiting Chinese girls" (CA 1 [1933]: 31) and that "numerous indigenous vocations have come knocking at the door of the monastery" (CA 5 [1935]: 205). Because of the destruction of the archives of the Chongqing Carmel it is not possible to provide exact information on the dates of entry, clothing, and profession of young Chinese nuns.

[95] In addition to the constitutions and the works of St. Teresa (primarily the rule), the ceremonial held an important place in the spiritual formation of French-speaking Carmelites. The work of the Barnabite Augustin Galice, the *Ceremonial* (1659; new ed. 1888) was a manual containing the rituals and rubrics to be observed in the monastery, as well as a description of the places where these ceremonies were to be celebrated.

in the letters of the prioress, Sr. Isabelle de Jésus, at the end of the 1930s.

> Having finished the translation into Chinese of our holy constitutions, we are now beginning the translation of the ceremonial. . . . Since our girls do not belong to the well-educated class, the translation has been made into the spoken tongue, the only one they understand. The text has been compared with the original by one of our Chinese fathers at the mission print shop, and he has made a few small corrections that were needed.[96]

> Please let me know if I can send you, on the first reliable occasion, the book of the rule and constitutions, which we have translated into Chinese and which should pass the censorship.[97]

Mention should be made of a special guest at the "Rock Carmel," the Christian philosopher John Wu Jingxiong (1899–1986). In the early 1940s, when he followed President Chiang Kai-shek (Jiang Jieshi) and his government to Chongqing, John Wu Jingxiong "liked to come and pray . . . when his other commitments left him time."[98] In fact, it was reading *The Story of a Soul*,[99] the autobiography of St. Therese of Lisieux, that led him to ask to be baptized in the Catholic Church in 1937. "There I found the living synthesis between all pairs of opposites, such as humility and audacity, freedom and discipline, joys and sorrows, duty and love, strength and tenderness, grace and nature, folly and wisdom, wealth and poverty, corporateness and individuality. She [St. Therese of Lisieux] seemed to me to combine the heart of the Buddha, the virtues of Confucius, and the philosophic detachment of Lao Tse [Laozi]. . . . It was through this book that I decided to become a Catholic. Grace had touched my heart."[100]

In 1940 John Wu wrote an article about his discovery of the spirituality of the Carmelite saint; this article was later converted into

---

[96] Letter of Sr. Isabelle de Jésus, 22 February 1938 (AGOCD, sez. D, 58).

[97] Letter of Sr. Isabelle de Jésus, 2 April 1939 (AGOCD, sez. D, 58).

[98] Mère Élisabeth, *Partir*, 79.

[99] The first Chinese translation of this book was made by Ma Xiangbo in 1928. In 1950 another translation was published in Hong Kong: *Yiduo xiao bai hua* [A little white flower], trans. Su Xuelin (Hong Kong: Zhenli xuehui chubanshe, 1950).

[100] Cf. John C. H. Wu, *Beyond East and West* (New York: Sheed and Ward, 1951), 243. John Wu had already been baptized in the Methodist Church in 1917.

a book and soon translated into many languages.[101] In it he wrote that the "little way" of Christian love, as presented by the Carmelite tradition and made to bloom by the "little flower" of Lisieux, is a fruitful point of encounter between Christian and Chinese spiritual traditions. "To me as a Chinese, the great thing about Christianity is that it combines the profound mysticism of Lao Tzu with the intense humanism of Confucius. . . . The Confucian idea of God is personal but narrow, while the Taoistic idea is broad but impersonal. . . . Only Christianity can satisfy my mind completely, because its idea of God is at once broad and personal. And it is Therese who has confirmed my faith in my religion, for her mind is as subtle and detached as that of Lao Tzu, while her heart is as affectionate and cordial as that of Confucius."[102]

The Carmel of Jiaxing

In 1927 the Carmelite community in Shanghai founded a new Carmel in Jiaxing (Kiashing or Kashing) in the Vicariate Apostolic of Hangzhou (Hangchow), Zhejiang province. The foundation was headed by Mother Thérèse Xavier de Saint Stanislas (Thérèse Élisabeth Ratel), who was already seventy years old. She was a nun of the Carmel of Tours who went to China in 1889 and died there in 1937. The initial community consisted of her and five other nuns.[103] It was supported financially by the propertied family of one of the Chinese nuns, Sr. Madeleine, whose mother (Sophie Song) was granted the privilege of being buried in the cloister of the monastery, clothed in a Carmelite habit. Four years after foundation, the community of the Carmel of Our Lady Mediatrix of Jiaxing numbered twelve nuns (six European and six Chinese), six novices, and three postulants,

---

[101] John C. H. Wu, *The Science of Love: A Study of the Teachings of Thérèse of Lisieux* (Hong Kong: Catholic Truth Society, 1941); available at http://www.ourgarden ofcarmel.org/wu.html, accessed 21 August 2013.

[102] Ibid. John Wu was for some years the Chinese ambassador to the Holy See. In addition to his autobiography, *Beyond East and West,* another important work is *Chinese Humanism and Christian Spirituality* (Jamaica, NY: St. John's University Press, 1965).

[103] Cf. news report of the foundation: "Jiaxing chuangshe shengyiyuan yi chengli" [The Carmelite monastery founded in Jiaxing is completed], YZB 32 (1928): 12.

all Chinese.[104] In 1937, because of the Sino-Japanese War, the community was forced to leave the monastery of Jiaxing and take refuge with the Sisters of the Good Shepherd in Shanghai. The last two superiors were Sr. Élisabeth de la Trinité and Sr. Claire, both nuns of the Reims Carmel.

From 1937 on the documentation available to us is incomplete, thus it is not possible to determine exactly what happened next. What can be surmised is that around 1938, through the intervention of the Congregation of Propaganda Fide, a Jesuit was appointed as visitator. He noted that the community was affected by an "original flaw" due to the influence of the benefactors who contributed to the founding of the Carmel. These benefactors had several relatives in the community and "had their own ideas of what needed to be done. They attempted to meddle in the internal affairs [of the community], with great damage to the enclosure and religious life." The visitator also found significant weaknesses in the way authority was exercised within the community, hence he asked Propaganda to issue an order to dissolve the community.[105] Published sources say that the community was suppressed because of the war, perhaps so as to "save the face of the founders,"[106] but some documents and letters kept in the General Archive of the Discalced Carmelites in Rome show that the real reason was because of serious internal problems.[107]

It was officially said that "because of the war, the nuns had to find refuge where they could in nearby monasteries."[108] Some nuns went

[104] Cf. *MCJ. Dixième année [1931–1932]*, 421.

[105] Cf. letter of Yves Henry, superior of the Jesuit mission of Shanghai, to the superior general of the Discalced Carmelites, 9 July 1938 (AGOCD, sez. D, 107: "Kiashing").

[106] Ibid.

[107] See especially the long letter of Sr. Marie-Xavier du Cœur de Jésus to the superior general of the Discalced Carmelites, undated, but most likely written at the end of 1945 or the beginning of 1946 (AGOCD, sez. D, 107). Cf. also extracts from the letters of some sisters of the Carmel of Jiaxing kept in AGOCD, sez. D, 184. It is significant that in a letter dated 16 November 1939 (or 1938?), the same superior general of the Discalced Carmelites says that he is "in the dark about the reasons that led ecclesiastical authority to suppress the monastery of Kashing" (AGOCD, sez. D, 107).

[108] Letter of the superior general of the Discalced Carmelites to Msgr. Carmelo Parisi, 9 January 1940 (AGOCD, sez. D, 107).

to the Carmel of Chongqing, others to Kunming, which had opened the previous year, and one to Manila in the Philippines. When the Carmel of Kunming was closed in 1951, three of the Chinese nuns returned to Shanghai, where they had to wait one year before the bishop gave permission to the Carmelite monastery to receive them. The worst consequence of this suppression appears to have been the dissolution of the vows of some Chinese nuns (possibly four), though they were allowed to continue to wear the Carmelite habit and live together in the building of the Carmel of Jiaxing. In 1945/1946 Sr. Marie-Xavier du Cœur de Jésus, who was of Portuguese origin, a nun of the Carmel of Shanghai for several years and subprioress of the Carmel of Jiaxing, wrote from Manila:

> My four Chinese companions who had returned to Kashing were waiting for me in the same house. . . . They are sisters and daughters of the mission's benefactors, released from their vows because Carmel has been dissolved, but according to what was ruled, they still continually wear the holy Carmelite habit. One of them, a choir sister, wrote to tell me that she had immediately repeated her vows, and not having any longer a prioress to obey, she obeys her confessor. But this is not a normal situation. These dear sisters keep our holy rule, even the fasts of the order. The superiors made them leave the enclosure because of the war. But they hope, together with me . . . to obtain this grace. . . . The last words of one of them as I was leaving were: "Return! For our Carmel!"[109]

In the same letter a request was made that these sisters be allowed to repeat their vows without having to redo their novitiate and that the father general intervene "so that . . . the four poor Chinese nuns may again live and die as Carmelites, in accord with their vocation." In his reply, the superior general claimed that he did not have authority over a Carmelite monastery that was not under his jurisdiction and therefore did not have the power to restore it.[110] His response and, even more, the political upheaval in China over

[109] Letter of Sr. Marie-Xavier du Cœur de Jésus to the superior general of the Discalced Carmelites (AGOCD, sez. D, 107).

[110] Cf. letter of the superior general of the Discalced Carmelites to Sr. Marie-Xavier du Cœur de Jésus, 25 February 1946 (AGOCD, sez. D, 107).

the following years, would eventually lead to a forced closure of the "Kashing dossier."

The Carmels of Canton / Hong Kong and Macau

In the 1930s three Carmelite monasteries were founded in southern China. In March 1931, a few months after the insistent appeal of the vicar apostolic of Canton to found a Carmel in that city, the Carmel of Saint-Michel in Bruges, Belgium, sent four nuns to China. In August 1930, in fact, Archbishop Antoine Fourquet had gone to Belgium and had spoken with the mother prioress of Bruges.

> —I have come to seek Carmelites for China. I need them at whatever cost!
>
> —For China! . . . But events in that country have taken a bad turn.
>
> —It's exactly because things are going badly that I am looking for a lightning rod, a fortress to defend us.
>
> —But we are not numerous . . . and also quite poor.
>
> —What's that before God? He doesn't need anything to make something come about. Pray and you will see: God wants it! And don't forget the Holy Spirit! I am leaving, I have to continue my trip, but I will be waiting for you in Canton.[111]

In 1933, not long after the foundation of the Carmel of the Sacred Hearts of Jesus and Mary in Guangzhou (Canton), three other nuns from Belgium joined its initial nucleus. At that time the community included also twelve Chinese sisters, some from humble backgrounds, some from the upper class.[112] These Chinese vocations

---

[111] "Le Carmel de Saint-Michel-lez-Bruges établit une fondation à Canton," CA 1 (1933): 41. Some years earlier, in 1926 or 1927, the same Archbishop Fourquet had written to *Contemplation et Apostolat* expressing his earnest request for help in establishing a contemplative presence in his vicariate: "I would very much like some contemplative order of men or women to make a foundation in the territory I am responsible for. Do what you can to help me bring that about." Cited in "L'œuvre 'Contemplation et Apostolat'," 9*.

[112] Cf. CA 1 (1933): 43–44, where it was said about these young Chinese women, "The divine artist chooses them from very different backgrounds. There were delicate

were regarded by the founders as the most beautiful flowers of the fledgling community. "Our little Chinese nuns are in no way inferior to our best European vocations; the firmness of their virtue is equal to the delicacy of their love."[113] Well regarded and loved by the local people, these Carmelite sisters were called "women who pray and do penance." The city authorities, however, soon created some problems for this "inactive" presence in the city, as they are described in a document in the archives.

> The city authorities are opposed to the establishment of a contemplative monastery, as something without any usefulness, so leaving Canton has become necessary for yet another reason. I say another, because a disguised persecutor was making their life morally impossible, and their small temporary house, without a garden, was ruining their health in this poor climate. They had endured as long as possible, then were obliged to leave suddenly. . . . In Hong Kong their health is getting better, and their life of prayer can follow its course in peace.[114]

The cryptic content of this letter indicates that the "persecutor" was most probably a clergyman, perhaps a missionary. The records kept in the General Archive of the Discalced Carmelites in Rome make it possible to identify him: the vicar apostolic of Canton, Archbishop Fourquet, who made false accusations against the foreign nuns recently arrived in Canton and created all sorts of impediments to their remaining in the city. The real reason for his opposition, however, is unclear.[115]

Because of this, that same year (1933) construction of a new Carmelite monastery was begun in Stanley, a suburb of Hong Kong, so

---

flowers of refined culture and wild flowers whose scent was no less fragrant; daughters of old Christian families and of newly converted families" (p. 43). Cf. also A. L., "Een Missie-Karmelietessen-Klooster in China," *Kerk en Missie* 17 (1937): 18–20.

[113] Cited in CA 1 (1933): 43.

[114] Note of Sr. Marie-Cécile to the superior general of the Discalced Carmelites, no date (around the mid-1930s), regarding the transfer of the Canton Carmel to Hong Kong (AGOCD, sez. D, 100).

[115] Cf. the documents collected by the superior general of the Discalced Carmelites and sent on 23 January 1934 to the prefect of the Congregation of Propaganda Fide, Cardinal Pietro Fumasoni Biondi, about the Canton Carmel and its transfer to Hong Kong (AGOCD, sez. D, 100).

that the group of five nuns coming from Belgium could be transferred to the British colony.[116] The inauguration ceremony of the new Carmel, dedicated to the Sacred Hearts of Jesus and Mary, took place in 1937. The chronicler of a Chinese Catholic magazine who reported the news expressed his doubts about its future: "One only doubt: how can such austere monastic life as that of the Carmelite nuns attract girls to enter?"[117]

On the contrary, a few months after this inaugural ceremony, the prioress, Mother Thérèse de l'Enfant-Jésus, could joyfully write that "vocations abound and some of them are excellent."[118] The letters sent in those years by the Carmel of Hong Kong to the father general of the Carmelites make constant reference to the abundance and quality of vocations. "We give thanks to God . . . for the growth of our little community. We are full, so to say; there is only one free place left, and many aspirants are asking for it. Our chapter already has ten members, and we have the intimate and sweet joy of forming only one spirit and one heart. The native vocations are steadfast and quite profound. . . . [God] has chosen beautiful souls here in southern China, in milieus that are often hostile to Catholicism. May our little community be truly a center of zeal, of love, and of holiness."[119]

Four years after its inauguration, the Carmel numbered twenty-five nuns, nineteen Chinese and six foreign, plus seven postulants.[120] In 1947 it became a fully Chinese Carmel, with a prioress, a sub-

[116] Cf. CA 7–8 (1937): 287–88 and CA 10 (1938): 27*; R. Gallagher, "The Contemplative Life: A New 'Carmel' in Hong Kong," *The Rock* (July 1937): 305–8; "Xianggang shengyihui xiunü qianju xinyuan" [The Carmelite nuns of Hong Kong take up residence in a new monastery], *Gongjiao funü* 3 (1937): 246–47.

[117] "Xianggang shengyihui yuanmen juxing fengsuo li" [Claustration ceremony celebrated at the Carmelite monastery of Hong Kong], YZB 26 (1937): 775.

[118] Letter of Sr. Thérèse de l'Enfant-Jésus to the superior general of the Discalced Carmelites, 9 March 1938 (AGOCD, sez. D, 100).

[119] Letter of Sr. Thérèse de l'Enfant-Jésus to the superior general of the Discalced Carmelites, 29 May 1938 (AGOCD, sez. D, 100). The constitutions of the Carmelite Order allow a community to be no larger than twenty-one members.

[120] Cf. Lazaristes du Pétang, *Les missions de Chine. Seizième année (1940–1941)*, 409–10. The bishop of Hong Kong, Enrico Valtorta, already wrote in the years 1928–1929 that he was hoping to establish a monastic foundation in his diocese *corde magno et animo volenti*. Cited in Édouard Neut, "Le Christ apôtre cherche des contemplatifs," BM 9 (1928–1929): 305.

prioress, and a mistress of novices all Chinese.[121] According to the directory of the Diocese of Hong Kong, today there are eleven sisters in the Hong Kong Carmel.[122]

The abundance of vocations soon led the monastery in the British colony to found a Carmel in the neighboring Portuguese colony of Macau in 1941. The sisters lived in temporary quarters until a Carmelite monastery was built in 1950. There were ten nuns, nine of whom were Chinese.[123] In 1993 the community of Macau moved to Edmonton, Canada.

The Carmel of Kunming

The Carmel of Kunming (Yunnanfu) was founded on 6 October 1936. Earlier that year the Carmel of Phnom Penh, the capital of what was then the protectorate of Cambodia in French Indochina, sent two groups of three nuns to China, the second group following the first by a few months.[124] The first prioress of the Carmel of Mary Immaculate and St. Therese of the Child Jesus in Kunming, inaugurated in 1938, was Mother Marie-Michelle du Saint Esprit, a nun of the Carmel of Courtrai and former prioress of the Carmel of Phnom Penh.

The desire of the vicar apostolic, Georges-Marie de Jonghe d'Ardoye, to have a Carmel in the ecclesiastical territory of his jurisdiction fulfilled the long-standing wish of his predecessor, Charles

---

[121] Cf. CA 12 (1947): 40.

[122] Cf. http://www.catholic.org.hk/v2/cath_db/search.php?search=carmelite, accessed 21 August 2013. In sec. 5 ("Mission Personnel") of the Diocesan Archives of Hong Kong, there are two boxes containing documents about the Carmelite nuns (nos. 41 and 42).

[123] Cf. Ilario G. Castellan, "Sorge un nuovo Carmelo a Macau (Indie portoghesi)," *Il Carmelo e le sue missioni all'estero* 49 (1950): 150–52.

[124] Cf. CA 7–8 (1936): 285–86. Cf. also Apis., "Il Carmelo di Yunnanfu-Yunnan," *Il Carmelo e le sue missioni all'estero* 38 (1939): 234–35; "Yunnan jianzhu shengyihui xiunüyuan" [A monastery of Carmelite nuns erected in Yunnan], *Gongjiao baihua bao* 18 (1936): 387–88; "Yunnan jiaoqu chengli shengyihui yinyuan" [A Carmelite monastery founded in the diocese of Yunnan], *Gongjiao baihua bao* 20 (1936): 433; "Yunnan jianzhu shengyihui xiunüyuan" [A monastery of Carmelite nuns erected in Yunnan], YZB 35 (1936): 908. The Carmel of Phnom Penh was founded by the monastery in Saigon in 1919.

de Gorostarzu, who corresponded with the Carmel of Hanoi in the decade between 1912 and 1922 and also visited it. In 1923, he sent the first three young Yunnan aspirants to Hanoi for their monastic formation. In the following years he devoted all his energy to looking for Carmelite monasteries that would be willing to make a foundation, and in 1927 he almost succeeded. In 1930 he even obtained a sum of money directly from Pope Pius XI as a personal contribution to a foundation in China.[125]

The desire to have a Carmel in his vicariate was voiced by Bishop de Jonghe in a letter sent to *Contemplation et Apostolat*: "During my travels on horseback I had long meditated on the need to have a contemplative order in my diocese; in addition, I have just founded the major seminary of Yunnanfu, under the direction of the Sulpicians, a very delicate project. . . . I find it indispensable to have in front of it a spiritual lightning rod. I am therefore asking for an immediate foundation of a Carmel in the city of Yunnanfu (China)."[126]

The delay in the actual foundation seems to have been due, among other reasons, to opposition expressed by missionary personnel in the vicariate. In 1946 the prioress of the Carmel of Kunming, the Dutch Marie-Agnès du Bon Pasteur, wrote about this: "The missionaries here never wanted a Carmel. Our founder fought for twenty years against their opposition before bringing about his heart's desire. Afterward not much changed. There are, nevertheless, now a few fathers who appreciate the contemplative life. Last Christmas, however, our present bishop pronounced words that pierced our heart: 'You're no longer useful. Works are more necessary.'"[127]

In January 1939 the Carmelite community of Kunming grew with the arrival of three new Chinese sisters from the Carmel of Jiaxing. In 1940 the community numbered ten nuns: four Europeans, three Vietnamese, and three Chinese.[128] During the war the Carmel was

---

[125] Cf. C. de Y. (Carmelites of Yunnanfu), "Yunnanfu (Chine). Origine de la Fondation du Carmel," *Le Carmel. Bulletin mensuel du Carmel de France et son Tiers-Ordre* 25 (1938–1939): 280–82; CA 11 (1939): 44*–45*.

[126] CA 7–8 (1936): 285.

[127] Letter of Sr. Marie-Agnès du Bon Pasteur to the superior general of the Discalced Carmelites, 6 July 1946 (AGOCD, sez. D, 111).

[128] Cf. Lazaristes du Pétang, *Les missions de Chine. Seizième année (1940–1941)*, 457.

bombed by the Japanese and the bishop ordered the nuns to leave the monastery and take refuge in a mission house a five-day walk from the city. They returned in 1943 to find the monastery looted and occupied by the Chinese Army. After being housed for ten months at the school of the Franciscan Missionaries of Mary, they went to live in a private home, where they built a small chapel, a choir, the turn, and a parlor.[129]

In 1945 the monastery was finally returned to the nuns, thanks to the intervention of the wife of Chiang Kai-shek. In 1946 the community was still composed of twelve cloistered sisters (eight choir nuns, four French, one Dutch, and three Chinese; two lay sisters, one French and one Chinese; and two lay sister postulants) and four extern sisters (a professed Vietnamese, one novice, and two Chinese postulants). That same year the prioress noted, with a hint of bitterness, that "in ten years we have gotten only one vocation from Yunnnanfu,"[130] that is, one local vocation. They gained their livelihood from a herd of cows.

Because of the worsening political situation, in 1949 the authorities of the order insisted that the Carmel of Kunming send its young sisters to Macau.[131] A part of the monastery was soon occupied by the police and then used as a place for political meetings. "Our large chapter room, occupied for a year by the police, from the beginning of August served as the room for the meetings. We had bricked up the doors so as to preserve enclosure, but we heard everything that went on there. . . . Our souls were broken! And these infernal meetings are taking place in our so peaceful chapter, where our sisters had pronounced their holy vows . . . what sorrow!"[132]

---

[129] Cf. letter of Sr. Marie-Agnès du Bon Pasteur to the superior general of the Discalced Carmelites, 6 October 1944 (AGOCD, sez. D, 111).

[130] Letter of Sr. Marie-Agnès du Bon Pasteur to the superior general of the Discalced Carmelites, 6 July 1946 (AGOCD, sez. D, 111).

[131] Cf. telegram of the superior general of the Discalced Carmelites to the prioress of the Kunming Carmel, 17 June 1949 (AGOCD, sez. D, 111).

[132] Page 6 of a typewritten account of the last month at the Carmel of Kunming, most likely written by the prioress, Mother Marie-Madeleine de Jésus, who was French (AGOCD, sez. D, 111). For more on the last months of the Carmel, see "Nouvelles du carmel de Kunming (Chine)" (AGOCD, sez. D, 111); letter of Mother Marie-Madeleine de Jésus, 16 December 1951 (AGOCD, sez. D, 111).

Questioning of the nuns and searches of the monastery intensified. Finally, the Carmel was canonically suppressed on 13 July 1951. Three of the European sisters went to Shanghai, while the others were forced to leave the country between August and November that year. They were able to choose to return to their monastery of origin or to go to another Carmel in mission. Three chose Saigon, and three Calcutta.[133] The building of the former convent became the property of the government. In 1958 it was largely demolished and a hospital built in its place.[134]

The young nuns who remained in China soon felt like "orphans without [their] mother,"[135] as Sr. Johanna de Marie Immaculée, a Chinese lay sister, wrote in a letter to the father general of the Discalced Carmelites, giving him a vivid picture of the pain of separation.

The two sisters who were from Saigon were prevented from returning to their country; hence they remained in Kunming. One of them was able to make a living by taking care of a child.[136] Three choir nuns who had come from Shanghai in October 1951 returned there and were received back in their original monastery.[137] When it was closed, they worked for a living. Of these Sr. Anna de Sainte Thérèse de l'Enfant-Jésus died in 1957, and Sr. Marie des Anges died

---

[133] Cf. "La situation du Carmel de Kunming" (AGOCD, sez. D, 111). A little later Mother Marie-Agnès du Bon Pasteur would be transferred to the Carmel of Bangkok, where she became the prioress.

[134] Cf. Wang, "An Account of My Journey," 7.

[135] Letter of Sr. Johanna de Marie Immaculée to the father general of the Discalced Carmelites, 29 September 1951 (AGOCD, sez. D, 111). There are two copies: the original manuscript, which is difficult to read because of many spelling mistakes, and a typewritten copy.

[136] Cf. "Sœurs du Carmel de Kunming (Prov. de Yunnan) restées en Chine lors de l'expulsion des 7 Carmelites Européennes" and "Copie d'une lettre de Sœur Marie de Saint-Jean-Baptiste, du Carmel (dispersé) de Kunming (Yunnan)" (AGOCD, sez. D, 111).

[137] This clarification is given in a letter of Sr. Thérèse de Jésus to the father general of the Carmelites, 5 September 1988 (AGOCD, sez. D, 184). Several letters written from the Carmel of Shanghai in the months following the arrival of three sisters from Kunming speak of the beautiful reception given to them and their valuable contribution to community life, especially by their labor and services. A description of the journey of the three nuns from Kunming to Shanghai is given by one of them: cf. letter of Sr. Marie-Thérèse de Jésus to Mother Marie-Agnès du Bon Pasteur, 10 November 1951 (AGOCD, sez. D, 111).

of starvation six years later, in 1963.[138] We have information about the third sister, Marie-Thérèse de Jésus (Wang Zhixiu), through 1958, thanks to the numerous letters she sent to Mother Marie-Agnès du Bon Pasteur, who had become prioress of the Carmel of Bangkok. Her letters testify to her daily struggle to keep the faith and to resist, no matter at what cost, the pressure of those who wanted her to join the independent church.

In August 1957 she wrote: "Things and life do not matter very much; however, what they are after is not life, but souls."[139] Her letters demonstrate her fidelity to a spiritual life nourished by daily prayer, the private and hidden recitation of the Divine Office, and the occasional secret reception of Communion from trusted priests who had not joined the independence movement. The letters also give evidence of absolute trust in the Providence of God in spite of the great difficulties she had making a living by tailoring and embroidery.

> Over the last two months I have done a lot of knitting and sewing, but right now I have no work. The good God, however, feeds the birds of the air, and if one day the good God asks us to die of hunger, what better thing can we offer him. It is not those who say "Lord, Lord" who please the good God, but those who do God's will.[140]

> I no longer work for the outside, but Divine Providence watches over the little bird that abandons itself to and trusts in its goodness. *Fiat* to everything that God might want. Now there is no longer any spiritual consolation, God's will is my daily nourishment. . . . I am very solitary, alone with God only.[141]

Using coded language to escape censure and so as not to endanger others, her letters also refer to the times she and her sisters were in re-education camps and prisons.

---

[138] Cf. letter of Sr. Marie-Agnès du Bon Pasteur, 10 June 1963, containing the necrology of Sr. Marie des Anges (AGOCD, sez. D, 111).

[139] Letter of Sr. Marie-Thérèse de Jésus to Mother Marie-Agnès du Bon Pasteur, 4 August 1957 (AGOCD, sez. D, 111).

[140] Letter of Sr. Marie-Thérèse de Jésus to Mother Marie-Agnès du Bon Pasteur, Christmas 1957 (AGOCD, sez. D, 111).

[141] Letter of Sr. Marie-Thérèse de Jésus to Mother Marie-Agnès du Bon Pasteur, Passion Sunday 1958 (AGOCD, sez. D, 111).

> I await God's will, I don't ask for anything, I don't refuse any-
> thing, whatever the good God wants is good. For union with God
> there is no better place than the "school." . . . [A]las, I don't
> merit this happiness. If the good God would again grant me this
> good fortune, what sacrifice could I refuse? I believe I would not
> refuse anything, with the grace of God. My dear mother, do not
> pray that I be spared from returning to the "school," pray rather
> that God's holy will be fulfilled in me.[142]

> For the time being I am not going to school, because I am not
> able to pass the exam. But when the "epidemic" will again break
> out, I will certainly be obliged to return to the "hospital."[143]

One of the last letters of hers that has been conserved speaks
in code and in the third person to say that her situation and that
of the other sisters has now become "desperate," but is accepted
with full confidence in God. "Dear mother, for the last two months
Marie-Thérèse and her sisters have all been studying at the house of
the Presentandines. . . . The great retreat is certain. Everyone is in
'good health.' The angels are guarding all the doors. Do not write to
us. . . . Pray for all. I don't forget anyone. To God through Mary."[144]

Three other Chinese sisters (two lay sisters and a novice) returned
to their families in the southern provinces of Yunnan and Guangxi.
We know that Sr. Thérèse Marguerite du Sacré-Cœur, after having
been with some religious in her home city of Nanning "to offer
support to the Christians in the bitter struggle they now have to
undergo," died in 1963.[145] Sr. Johanna de Marie Immaculée spent
fourteen months in a labor camp, then went to live with her family in

---

[142] Letter of Sr. Marie-Thérèse de Jésus to Mother Marie-Agnès du Bon Pasteur,
1956 (AGOCD, sez. D, 111). See the reproduction *infra*, p. 112. The "school," of
courses, means "re-education camp."

[143] Letter of Sr. Marie-Thérèse de Jésus to Mother Marie-Agnès du Bon Pasteur, 27
December 1956 (AGOCD, sez. D, 111). The "hospital," of course, means "prison."

[144] Letter of Sr. Marie-Thérèse de Jésus to Mother Marie-Agnès du Bon Pasteur,
15 June 1958 (AGOCD, sez. D, 111). The "studies" are courses of indoctrination,
the "great retreat" is prison, "good health" means remaining faithful, and "guardian
angels" are police guards. The Presentandines or Presentation Sisters, known in
China as *Shengmu xiantang hui* 聖母獻堂會, are officially the Society of the Presentation of the Blessed Virgin, the first Chinese women's religious congregation,
founded in 1869 in Shanghai.

[145] Cf. her necrology (AGOCD, sez. D, 111).

the mountains a two-day journey from Kunming, where she tended a herd of goats that provided milk for the family. In a letter written in December 1962, which may have been her last, she expressed her gratitude to the mother prioress and at the same time spoke about how terribly difficult it was to persevere in faith and in her vocation, given the situation in which she found herself.

> My dear mother,
> For several years now I have no letters from you. Are you in good health? I continually think of you. Although we were together only a few years, I will never forget you. My mother's sweet face and love have entered deeply into my heart. Your photo is in my prayer book and when I open it, I see your face. Once upon a time I used to receive advice when I saw my mother; now there is only the picture, which cannot speak or console. . . . Living in the midst of people who don't believe in God, I find it difficult to progress in the spiritual life. . . . Now many things are gone: it is like death. At one time I would never have believed that my happiness in Carmel would have disappeared thus and that we would have to separate. . . . My dear mother, you always remain my comfort. I know how many difficulties you had to deal with in Kunming. . . . Pray for me, that I may remain faithful to Jesus . . .
>
> 　　　　Your little daughter Johanna de Marie Immaculée[146]

The official Chinese report on the Carmel of Kunming, found in the *Chronicles of Kunming*, provides interesting and helpful information.

> The order of the holy habit is one of the mendicant [*sic*] Catholic orders, called also the "Carmelite Order." The branch of this order in Kunming was the women's. Since among the Catholic religious orders present in Kunming it was the most austere, it is known also as the "ascetic order" (*kuxiuhui* 苦修會). This order was founded in Kunming in 1936 by Sr. Jin [Marie-Michelle du Saint Esprit] of Belgian nationality and during the war of resistance it was transferred to Weize, [district of] Lu'nan. In 1942 [the nuns] returned to Kunming and first lived for a

---

[146] Letter of Sr. Johanna de Marie Immaculée, December 1962 (AGOCD, sez. D, 111, the original Chinese and a French translation).

time in Xingrenjie, then moved first to Shuanglongqiao, then to
Pingzhengjie. The Carmelite sisters, once they enter the monastery, leave society for good and devote themselves assiduously
to prayer, to ascetic discipline, to silence, and to other austere
disciplines. Even when their relatives come to visit them, the
nuns, with their faces covered by veils, receive them through a
window. To enter the order one has to make three vows: poverty,
chastity, and obedience. Only at the moment of death might they
cross the monastery's threshold. The nuns were for the most
part Vietnamese, and no girls from the Kunming diocese entered
the monastery. Before 1950 those responsible for this community were Li Mingde, Hao Huaxian, and Wang Zhixiu. Their
principal economic resources came from the sale of milk and of
embroidery work, and also from subsidies from the Carmelite
Order. After the founding of the People's Republic of China this
order dispersed by itself, and in 1953 the immoveable properties of Pingzhengjie were sold by the Catholic committee that
promoted the reform of the "Three Selfs" of the Kunming city
to the Honghui 紅會 hospital.[147]

The Proposal for a Carmel in Yangzhou
and Its Implementation in Taiwan

In 1946 the Jesuit priest Paul O'Brien, superior of the China mission of the Jesuit California province, wrote to the Carmel of Santa
Clara in California, inviting it to found a monastery in the Apostolic
Prefecture of Yangzhou (Yangchow). The response of the mother
prioress was positive, partly because one member of the community,
Sr. Therese, had long wished to go to China, and also because of the
possibility of attracting Chinese women to the Carmelite life. The
superior of the mission of Yangzhou, Msgr. Eugene Fahy, moved
quickly to locate a large plot of land and began work on remodeling

---

[147] *Kunming shi zhi* [Chronicles of the city of Kunming], vol. 10 (Beijing: Renmin
chubanshe, 2003), 93. A statement of 30 November 1950, drawn up by Fr. Matthias
Wang Liangzuo of Guangyuan, Sichuan province, following a meeting that was
attended by over five hundred Catholics, proposed a total break in relations with
the imperialist powers, among them the Vatican, and the establishment of a church
governed by the "Three Selfs": self-government (rejection of foreigners' influence on
church leadership), self-support (rejection of foreign financing), and self-propagation
(rejection of foreign missionaries).

the buildings to serve as a monastery and on erecting a high wall to guarantee enclosure. In 1948 the monastery was finished and the nuns were expected later that year. In January of the following year, however, the Communists took over Yangzhou, and the nuns were unable to leave the United States for China.[148] The building that had been intended for the future Yangzhou Carmel would soon become a prison. Earlier in that same year of 1949, however, two young Chinese had been sent to the Carmel of Santa Clara to begin their monastic formation.

It was hoped that the impossibility of going to China was only temporary, and in fact soon the same Msgr. Fahy wrote from Taiwan, where he had moved, and repeated his invitation to the Carmelites in California. In response, the Carmel of Santa Clara sent eight nuns (four Americans, including Sr. Therese, and four Chinese) to Taiwan in 1954, where they founded the first Taiwanese Carmelite community at Xinzhu (Hsinchu). Housed temporarily in a monastery at Ximenjie (Hsi Men Chieh), the sisters built a Carmel at Zhongzhengjie (Chung Cheng Chieh) in 1958. The quiet and peaceful environment was particularly well-suited for a secluded life of prayer and silence. Photos of this first Taiwanese Carmel show a building in pure Chinese architectural style, as desired, and also designed, by the prioress, Mother Therese, and constructed by a Chinese architect: upturned red roofs, stone and brick walls, and spacious interior patios.

Mother Therese resigned in 1966, firmly convinced that for the sake of communication with the sisters, a Chinese nun should succeed her. In the following years Chinese became the language of the house and later of its liturgical prayer as well. This may have been one of the reasons why young Chinese women began to enter the Carmel in greater numbers. Since the place where they lived was becoming less peaceful because of the encroachment of the city, in 1978 the nuns decided to build a new monastery in Xionglin (Chiung Lin), where they moved in 1981. The monastery was still in the

---

[148] Cf. "Shengyihui xiunü she xiuyuan" [Carmelite nuns establish a monastery], YZ 12 (1948). "An unexpected development. At the beginning of 1949 it was announced that nuns coming from Santa Clara (California) would be founding a new Carmelite monastery at Yangchow. Who would have believed it?" CA 14 (1950): 36.

same Diocese of Xinzhu, but now at a higher elevation. In 1996, after almost ten years of planning, the Carmel of Xionglin, which now had about twenty nuns, founded a new Carmel at Shenkeng (Shen Keng), a secluded area just outside Taipei.[149] Today the Carmel of Xionglin has twenty-three members and that of Xionglin Shenkeng thirteen; all are Chinese.[150]

The Carmelite Friars in China

The foundation of the only male Carmelite community in China was relatively late and lasted only a short time.[151] Letters sent to the superior general and preserved in the General Archive of the Discalced Carmelites in Rome express the desire of missionary nuns in China to have Carmelite priests near their convents. A letter of 1938 testifies to the desire of the order to make such a foundation: "We greatly desire to make a foundation of our fathers in the Far East, to provide for the spiritual needs of the Carmelite sisters. We have begun to work on this and we shall see the results, we hope, quite soon."[152]

It was only in 1946, however, that Propaganda Fide permitted the Veneto province of Italian Carmelites, assisted by Carmelite missionaries of the Lombardy and Tuscany provinces, to designate a small

---

[149] Cf. Fang Zhirong, "Taiwan shengyihui yinxiuyuan sishi zhounian" [The fortieth anniversary of the Carmel in Taiwan], *Shenxue lunji* (*Collectanea Theologica Universitatis Fu Jen*) 102 (1994): 580; The Discalced Carmelite Nuns of Chiung Lin, *It Is Good to Be Here: The Story of Our Foundation* ([Chiung Lin: Discalced Carmelite Monastery], 2004).

[150] Information furnished by Mother Paula of the Trinity, prioress of the Shenkeng Carmel, in a letter dated 16 November 2009.

[151] Six Carmelite missionaries had been present in China previously, but only for short periods of time and without the intention of establishing a monastic presence. They had been sent to that country in the eighteenth century by Propaganda Fide, four of them as papal legates or members of papal legations. Cf. Ambrosius a S. Teresia, *Bio-bibliographia Missionaria Ordinis Carmelitarum Discalceatorum (1584–1940)* (Rome: apud Curiam Generalitiam, 1940); Antonio Fortes, *Las Misiones del Carmelo Teresiano, 1584–1799. Documentos del Archivo General de Roma* (Rome: Teresianum, 1997).

[152] Letter from the curia of the Generalate of the Discalced Carmelites to the prioress of the Carmel in Hong Kong, 19 June 1938 (AGOCD, sez. D, 100).

group of religious for the Hubei (Hupeh) region, where Italian Friars Minor were already present. After studying Chinese for some months at the Carmelite seminary for missions in Rome, nine missionaries received their "licenses" for missionary work from the vicar general on 1 February 1947. In April they sailed from Marseille for China, where they opened a convent near Huangzhou (Hwangchow).[153]

Among the pioneers of the missions of Carmelite friars in East Asia was the superior of the first group, Fr. Ilario del Sacro Cuore e di Maria (Guglielmo Castellan), and Fr. Gioacchino di Maria Bambina (Virginio Guizzo). The latter arrived in China in early 1948, was soon imprisoned, then was expelled in 1950. When political turmoil forced the rest of the Carmelites to leave China, many of them moved to Japan, where they contributed to the establishment of a male Carmelite presence in that country.[154] Also deserving of mention is Fr. Giovanni Maria della Croce (Enrico Chin Ah Phen). He was of Chinese origin and was already working in the mission of Malabar when he joined the group of Italians. He was also expelled from mainland China. In the early 1980s he introduced male Carmelite life to Taiwan, where he became the provincial delegate.[155] A student house in Taipei was later added to the first Carmelite community of Xinzhu, and a few years ago the provincial house and novitiate were opened in Singapore. It now has several candidates from Southeast Asian countries.[156]

---

[153] Cf. "Nova Missio in Sinarum imperio," *Analecta Ordinis Carmelitarum Discalceatorum* 19 (1947): 65–66. The members of the group were Ilario del Sacro Cuore e di Maria (Guglielmo Castellan), Gioacchino di Maria Bambina (Virginio Guizzo), Atanasio di San Brocardo (Ernesto Danieletti), Ermanno del Santissimo Sacramento (Narciso Cagnin) and Giuseppe di Sant'Elia (Giuseppe Faotto) of the Veneto province; Roderico di Santa Teresa (Santo Bonaldo) and Pietro Giuseppe di San Luigi (Luigi Teruzzi) of the Lombardy province; Tommaso di Gesù (Francesco Pammolli) and Elia della Vergine del Carmelo (Aquilino Santori) of the Tuscany province.

[154] Carmelite nuns had been in Japan since 1933. After spending some years in Japan and Italy, Fr. Guizzo was invited to South Korea in 1974, where he contributed to the founding of a Carmel.

[155] Cf. P. D'Souza, "Unforgettable Carmelite Missionaries on Asian Soil," http://www.ocd.pcn.net/mission/News17Congr4.htm, accessed 21 August 2013.

[156] Cf. Discalced Carmelite Nuns of Chiung Lin, *It Is Good to Be Here*, 203–7.

In the Fidelity of Love

There is very little data about the Chinese Carmelite nuns between the last days of the Carmelite monasteries in China and the present. One of the few sources of information is *Contemplation et Apostolat*, where reference is made to the last Carmelites in Shanghai at the end of 1955. "Four Carmelites of Canadian and French nationality have been expelled from the country. Of the eighteen Chinese sisters of Carmel, five are in prison. The others undergo continual interrogations: three or four hours at a time per day for each. The sisters are deprived of Holy Communion, having refused the services of a priest who had participated in the campaign against Bishop Kiong [Gong Pinmei]."[157]

Some letters did reach their foreign destinations in the first months after these events. "Their letters are edifying and moving; you sense how much they suffer, but you sense as well their faithful love. They remain standing in the darkness that surrounds them. . . . The danger is great, terrible. The protection proclaimed aloud of all religious cults, of the *patriotic Catholic* cult in particular, creates a dangerous environment, where only God's grace can protect one."[158]

Dispersion and silence followed. The last words of some of the Chinese Carmelites just before the Bamboo Curtain fell on China were a beacon of light illuminating the dark years that followed: "We will remain daughters of the Roman Catholic Church."[159]

Only a few decades later, in the 1990s, a Carmelite of the Carmel of Indianapolis of Chinese origin was able to visit the sites of the former Carmelite monasteries and meet some of the older sisters who suffered the torments of the previous years.[160] She was able to have contact especially with some of the nuns of the Shanghai Carmel. The brief reference to some of them in these pages is an expression of gratitude for their fidelity to their monastic vocation in the midst of great difficulty. May their perseverance be a source of inspiration and edification for many.

---

[157] CA 24 (1956): 11.

[158] "Le carmel de Tou-se-wei (Shanghai) du 8 septembre au 26 décembre 1955," 15.

[159] Ibid., 7.

[160] Sr. Helen Wang's typewritten, unpublished account of her journey is the source of what follows. Cf. Wang, "An Account of My Journey."

Cécile de la Vierge (Deng Jinde), one of the last novices, entered the Carmel of Shanghai in 1951, received the habit on 9 January 1955, then after the tragic events of 8 September of that year, privately and conditionally professed her solemn vows to the prioress on 10 December. For her firm opposition to the "Three Selfs" movement, which aimed to establish a national church independent of Rome and completely cut off from the universal church, she was sentenced to several years of imprisonment in labor camps. According to the report of the nun whom she met in 1993, "Cécile said that while she was in prison she often recalled in her memory our primitive rule that was read in the refectory every Friday, and she renewed her vows in her heart every day. She said pensively: 'I don't even know if my profession is valid anymore, but it is deep in my heart.'"[161]

Once freed, she returned to Nanchang (Jiangxi province), the city she was from, and became active in the underground Catholic community. For this she was again arrested in 1983 and imprisoned for three years. In the late 1980s, Sr. Cécile began training young diocesan catechists, first in Shanghai and then in Nanchang. During the day, she never removed the crucifix of her monastic profession from the pillow of her bed.

Thérèse Élie de l'Enfant-Jésus (Zhou Shuying, 1909–1999) entered the Carmel of St. Joseph in Shanghai in 1933 and received the habit the following year. She pronounced her first vows in 1935 and became a fully professed nun in 1940. Sentenced in 1958 to imprisonment in a labor camp, she was "ideologically re-educated" for thirty years. In 1987, upon release from the detention camp in Anhui province, to which she had been transferred in 1970 and where many other religious from Shanghai were interned, she chose to remain there to share the life of people who were still confined to the camp and by whom she was much loved. She lived in a small house that was also home to other workers on what she called her "Carmel farm." Even in the last years of her life she prayed the psalms she had memorized in French, claiming that she didn't care for their Chinese translation. She wore a vest made from her old Carmelite habit, which had survived the Cultural Revolution and the house searches of the Red

---

[161] Ibid., 25.

Guards. She said that she had never left the Carmel because she always kept it in her heart: "I've always carried Carmel in my heart. I've never left Carmel in my heart. When I was in the detention center, the detention center was my Carmel. When I was in the labor camp, the labor camp was my Carmel. And now, *this* is my Carmel. . . . If ever there is the possibility of returning to the monastery, even if I am a hundred years old, I will still want to return."[162]

Shortly before her death she wrote to a nun who was living outside China: "During the past year I have felt my energy diminishing daily. But this is normal with old folks, so please do not worry. I only pray that our Blessed Mother of Mount Carmel will help me to remain faithful to God's love and to complete joyfully my final journey. I have no other needs. I only ask that you pray for me."[163]

Some of the other Chinese nuns of the Carmel of Shanghai, who in the early nineties were still radiant in their old age, should at least be mentioned. Marie du Carmel (Chen Meiying) entered Carmel in 1921 and received the habit the following year. She pronounced her first vows in 1923 and made solemn profession in 1927.[164] Marie du Rosaire (Cai Xingzhen) was born in 1906 and entered Carmel at an early age. She regretted that she had to leave before making solemn vows, but she was able to make her solemn profession in 1993, at the age of eighty-seven, before the clandestine bishop of Shanghai, Fan Zhongliang, and using the old formula of profession that a Chinese Carmelite, who was also still living, translated from French into Chinese for her. Lucie des Anges (Pan Sujing, 1909–2004) entered Carmel in 1937 and made profession in the forties. After the forced abandonment of Carmel in 1954 she moved to Peking, where she led a simple life, working at home and in a garment factory. In the early 1980s she was received by the official bishop of Peking, and in 1986 went to live in the recently reopened convent of the Sisters of

---

[162] Ibid., 45.

[163] Cited in Tripod Staff, "Faithful Daughter of the Church," *Tripod* 110 (1999): 46.

[164] The one who gave these dates, which are based on a document of the same Sr. Marie, suspected that they should be understood in terms of the "Republican" system of calculation that is still in use in Taiwan today. If this is the case, the corresponding years would then be, respectively, 1932, 1934, and 1938 (cf. Wang, "An Account of My Journey," 34).

St. Joseph. While maintaining her independence, she continued, as a nun, to have an intense prayer life, to embroider liturgical vestments, and to regard the Carmelite rule as her rule of life. She even sent some liturgical vestments she had made to Pope John Paul II, who, in return, sent her a new Carmelite habit, of which she was very proud.[165]

In 1993, four elderly Carmelite nuns were still living in Chongqing. They were staying in the residence of the bishop at the Church of St. Joseph. They no longer lived a community life, but they continued to be women of prayer and models of Christian life for the faithful who knew them as Carmelite nuns.[166]

We can make the following comment our own. "We give thanks to God for the courage of these Carmelite sisters and for the innumerable martyrs of the Catholic faith in China. After more than forty years, after the dispersal of the few Carmelite sisters in China, our Chinese sisters continue to hope in the faithfulness of love and in silent prayer. We await the day when contemplative Carmel can be officially reestablished on mainland China, the day when the Carmelite nuns will be able to live openly their prayer and their mode of life. . . . There is no need to say how much these sisters have suffered. . . . There is no trace of bitterness, only a few silent tears every once in a while during prayer and the Eucharist."[167]

By the same token, we recognize that "the history of Carmel in China shows that . . . this love for each other, this mutual esteem [between Carmel and the Chinese people], this longing for communion have not been denied for a single moment."[168] It appears

---

[165] Cf. Li Qingmei, "Pan Sujing xiunü" [Sister Pan Sujing], *Xinde*, 1 July 2004, 3. In addition to these recollections, following her death an obituary appeared in the Peking Catholic newspaper *Tianguang* 天光.

[166] These four sisters were Zhou Chengyu (Sr. Marie-Paule du Saint-Sacrement), who was responsible for the formation of a group of young sisters belonging to the new diocesan congregation of the Immaculate Heart of Mary, Deng Yufang (Sr. Thérèse de l'Enfant-Jésus), Wan Xizhen (Sr. Juliana du Sacré-Cœur), and Xie Zhixian (Sr. Marguerite du Sacré-Cœur); Xie Zhibin (Agnès), the cousin of Wan Xizhen, who had been an extern sister of the Carmel of Chongqing, was also part of this group.

[167] Cited in Étienne Ducornet, *L'Église et la Chine. Histoire et défis* (Paris: Cerf, 2003), 81.

[168] Molnar, "Recherches," 59.

that out of these still smoldering ashes of the Chinese Carmelite communities new flames of Carmelite monastic life in China are beginning to spring up. In 2002 some Indonesian Carmelite nuns who were visiting the People's Republic of China were able to meet a group of nineteen young Chinese women who in their desire to live according to the Carmelite charism had led a common life for five years.[169] The contacts of this and other groups of young Chinese women with Carmelite communities in other countries may be a sign that the Carmelite way of life will one day return to China, in spite of the many restrictions that are still in place.

---

[169] Cf. *Carmelite Missions* (January 2005), http://www.carmelitemissions.org/saint /saint2005-01.pdf, accessed 21 August 2013.

Se Carmel et l' Orphelinat de T'ou-sè-wè.

Shanghai, suburb of Tushanwan (T'ousèwè), before 1900. The Carmelite monastery of St. Joseph (left) and the orphanage (right). Sketch in August M. Colombel, *Histoire de la mission du Kiang-nan (1840–1899)*, vol. 3/2: *L'épiscopat de mgr Languillat, 1865–1878* ([T'ousèwè]: n.p., 1900), 253.

Shanghai, Carmelite monastery of St. Joseph.
The monastery church can be seen on the right. Undated photo, probably taken in the first years of the twentieth century.

Letter of the Carmelite nun Marie-Thérèse de Jésus (Wang Zhixiu) to Mother Marie-Agnès du Bon Pasteur, 1956. Two photos are attached to the letter. The one on the left shows Sr. Marie-Thérèse in the Carmelite habit she wore when she was in the monastery; on the right, she is in the secular dress she wore "under the red regime" (written in the margin of the photo).

1954. Four Chinese Carmelite nuns on the ship that will take them and four American sisters from California to Taiwan.

Taipei, 1954. Shortly after their arrival in Taiwan, the Carmelite nuns visiting the American Benedictine sisters, who also went to Taiwan when they left China.

Xinzhu (Hsinchu, Taiwan).
The Carmelite monastery, built in the Chinese architectural style, of Zhongzhengjie (Chung Cheng Chieh), where the nuns resided from 1958 to 1981. Undated photo, probably taken in the 1970s.

Chapter 3

||||||||||||||||||||||||||||||||||||||||||

The Trappists

The Trappist Monastery of Our Lady of Consolation (Yangjiaping)

Of all the monastic communities that were present in China the Trappists are certainly the best known, thanks to several monographs and articles dedicated to them. Even though many of these publications are now outdated or difficult to find, those that are accessible make it fairly easy to reconstruct Trappist life in mainland China between 1883 and the 1950s and in Hong Kong and Taiwan from 1950 to the present time. In particular, the history of the Abbey of Our Lady of Consolation in Yangjiaping, which for decades was the most significant monastic community in East Asia, has been carefully documented.[1] Moreover, the martyrdom of thirty-three of its monks by the Communists between the years 1947 and 1953 has given this abbey a special aura within the church by the witness of its

---

[1] The two principal sources that make it possible to reconstruct the history of the Trappists' first fifty years in China and on which my summary of that history is based (unless otherwise indicated) are A. Limagne, *Les Trappistes en Chine* (Paris: J. de Gigord, 1911); and Alphonse Hubrecht, *Une trappe en Chine* (Peking: Imprimerie des Lazaristes, 1933). The work edited by Paolino Beltrame Quattrocchi, *Monaci nella tormenta. La "passio" dei monaci trappisti di Yan-Kia-Ping e di Liesse, testimoni della fede nella Cina di Mao-Tze-Tung* (Cîteaux: n.p., 1991), is equally valuable in that it includes rare archival materials that have not been published. The work of Ren Dayi, *Yangjiaping Shengmu shenweiyuan shi* (*The History of Our Lady of Consolation Yang Kia Ping*) (Hong Kong: n.p., 1978), contains numerous photographs of great historical value. For a work in Chinese, see *Xiduhui jianshi* [A short history of the Cistercian Order] (Taipei: Huaming shuju, 1964), 176–84 (app. 1).

monks to the Christian faith with the gift of their lives. In his 1949 book *The Waters of Siloe,* Thomas Merton made their martyrdom known to the world.[2]

Preparations

Perhaps the first indication of a desire for Trappist monks in China is found in a letter that the Jesuit Adrien-Hippolyte Languillat, vicar apostolic of Southeastern Zhili (1856–1864), sent to the Jesuit provincial of Paris in 1862: "I think that a religious order that would unite work and contemplation could be established very easily, at least with time and perseverance, in this northern land. I have, therefore, thought of the Trappists. . . . It is a purely contemplative order, which doesn't, I believe, occupy itself with evangelization and which, hence, could be useful. Their virtues, their austerity, their prayers and mortifications would preach eloquently, even though silently, to the Chinese."[3]

The true beginnings of the presence of the Trappists in China, who are known there as the "Order of Cîteaux" (*Xiduhui* 熙篤會) or the "Order of severe asceticism" (*Kuxiuhui* 苦修會),[4] however, are due, as has already been noted, to the difficulty the Carmelites had in sending nuns to the Vicariate of Peking.[5] In 1870, Countess Sophie de Stolberg, who was preparing to enter the Uccle Carmel in Brussels,

---

[2] Cf. Thomas Merton, *The Waters of Siloe* (New York: Harcourt Brace, 1949), 249–61. A French translation of Merton's description of the martyrdom of the monks is given in Thomas Merton, "Et les trappistes allèrent au martyre," *Digeste Catholique* 8 (1950): 48–55. In Chinese we have a work by Lin Da, "Xunfang Yangjiaping" [In search of Yangjiaping], in *Zai bianyuan kan shijie* [Looking at the world from the edges] (Kunming: Yunnan renmin chubanshe, 2001), 152–67.

[3] Letter of A.-H. Languillat, 26 April 1862, in *Lettres des nouvelles missions de la Chine*, vol. 4: *1861–1862* ([Paris]: n.p., 1862?), 217–21. A few years later Languillat would contact the Carmelites about making a foundation (cf. *supra*, pp. 64ff.).

[4] An official Chinese historical source explains the reasons for this way of referring to the order as follows: "This order is called 'of severe asceticism' (*kuxiu* 苦修), because of its many rules, such as the prohibition to speak at will, sleeping with a brick for a pillow, self-flagellation, etc." *Hebei sheng zhi. Zongjiao zhi* [Chronicles of the province of Hebei. Chronicles about religion] (Beijing: Zhongguo shuji chubanshe, 1995), 265.

[5] Cf. *supra*, pp. 78–79.

met Louis-Gabriel Delaplace, vicar apostolic of Peking (1870–1884), in Rome and gave him sixty thousand francs to construct a monastery for the Carmelites or another monastic order in his vicariate.[6] When plans to establish a Carmelite foundation came to naught in 1878, Bishop Delaplace decided to consult the Order of Cistercians of the Strict Observance, also called "Trappists." He drew inspiration from the synod of vicars apostolic of the first ecclesiastical region of China (North China) held in Peking in 1880, which formally expressed "the desire to have in China a Trappist house or a house of any other institute devoted to penitential austerity, so that authentic monastic life may be known in this region and at the same time the salvation of all may be advanced through the prayers and example of the religious."[7] Consulted on the advisability of such an undertaking, Cardinal Giovanni Simeoni, prefect of the Congregation of Propaganda Fide, wrote encouraging words to Bishop Delaplace in 1882: "I praise your project of introducing, if it is possible, the Trappists in your vicariate. This corresponds exactly with the wishes of the Sacred Congregation, which is of the view that the zeal with which these religious give themselves to prayer and to rigorous penance is of the kind to exercise a real and beneficial influence, as opposed to the austerities feigned by the bonzes and lamas."[8]

According to Limagne, the first author to write a history of the beginnings of the Trappist community in China, the foundation did not arise by chance. "The founding of the Trappist monastery of Yang-Kia-Pinn [Yangjiaping] was not due to one man's whim or to a chance concurrence of events. It came from a profound conception of Bishop Delaplace of Peking and the persevering efforts of his successors. The goal of these missionary bishops was twofold: (1) to ensure spiritual help to their priests; (2) to oppose Catholic religious to the Chinese bonzes."[9]

---

[6] Cf. "Le Cinquantenaire," in Hubrecht, *Une trappe en Chine*, 118.

[7] Cited in A. Thomas, "Projet d'une Trappe à Pékin. Approbations reçues," in *Histoire de la mission de Pékin*, vol. 2: *Depuis l'arrivée des Lazaristes jusqu'à la révolte des Boxeurs* (Paris: Vald. Rasmussen, 1933), 565.

[8] Letter of G. Simeoni to L.-G. Delaplace, 23 September 1882, cited in Thomas, *Histoire de la mission de Pékin*, 2:566.

[9] Limagne, *Les Trappistes en Chine*, 11.

According to this same early twentieth-century historian, the proposal to have a contemplative foundation in the Vicariate of Peking was "a beautiful dream of an apostolate without words, an apostolate by example, manual labor, mortification, and prayer,"[10] a proposal, in short, aimed at implantation of the church in the local social context, with the intention of showing a new face of Christianity in China, one that would be more authentic and "lovable," one that could "gain their deep confidence," because it would finally be separated from the colonialism that had done so much harm to the church since the mid-nineteenth century.

> A Trappist monastery, with its acres of cultivated lands, its heavy masonry structures, its customs of hospitality and of work, becomes established in a desert place, which blooms at its breath; a monastery that incessantly disseminates its benefits throughout the district, enrolls natives in its numbers, and transforms them into other persons, such a Trappist monastery incorporated in the Celestial Kingdom, penetrated into its life, such a *truly Chinese monastery* will not be suspected of spying or of commercial calculations. People will not see in it the advance guard of an army on the march. The Chinese will be able to tolerate it, even to love it, and little by little to allow themselves to be conducted by it, by the action of its prayers and its example, to the feet of the missionary who together with the monk will enter into the confidence of the inhabitants.[11]

That very year, 1882, Bishop Delaplace began to contact the Trappist Order, which since the mid-nineteenth century was expanding into mission lands outside Europe. The Cistercian Order had "blanketed" Europe with monasteries, but, with the exception of Cyprus and Syria, it had never made a foundation outside the continent. Following the French Revolution, however, and especially after the Revolution of 1848, the Cistercians (Trappists) began to found monastic communities in America, then in Africa, Asia, and Oceania. A significant influx of new vocations, the political circumstances of the moment, and a mounting missionary spirit contributed to this expansion.[12]

[10] Ibid., 15.
[11] Ibid., 14–15 (emphasis added).
[12] Cf. Jean de la Croix Bouton, *Histoire de l'ordre de Cîteaux*, vol. 3 (Westmalle: n.p., 1968), 461–68.

Despite this burgeoning apostolic dynamism among the Trappists, however, the first inquiries Bishop Delaplace addressed to Trappist monasteries were not well received. In September 1882 the Trappist monastery of Staoueli, Algeria, then known throughout Europe for its important contribution to the development of agriculture, turned down the request of Bishop Delaplace, saying that it was "impossible, for a number of reasons." The initiatives of Dom Alphonse Favier, a Lazarist missionary in Peking, who was commissioned to continue negotiations in France, were also unsuccessful at first. The Trappist monasteries of both Orne and Aiguebelle declined his request to make a foundation in China. The following year, however, Jérôme Guénat, the abbot of the Trappist monastery of Sept-Fons near Dompierre-sur-Besbre, accepted the proposal of Dom Favier, despite the recent trials undergone by his community. "In February 1883 [Alphonse Favier] stopped at the Abbey of Sept-Fons and recounted to the abbot his bishop's project, Rome's blessings, the countess's donations, the unanimous wish of the Peking synod. The abbot listened and the more he heard, the more he felt that God wanted this. He promised, therefore, to seek and, if possible, to find volunteers for this distant foundation."[13]

On 21 February 1883 Dom Favier and Abbot Guénat signed a provisional contract, which set out the main conditions of the proposed foundation. A few months later, on 11 June 1883, the founding document of the Trappist monastery of Our Lady of Consolation (*Shengmu shenweiyuan* 聖母神慰院) was endorsed.[14]

Abbot Guénat then sent a letter to Dom Éphrem (Louis Seignol, 1837–1893), prior of Tamié in Savoy since 1875, asking him to accept an assignment to the new foundation in China. Even though it was not an easy time for his community,[15] Dom Éphrem accepted

---

[13] Hubrecht, *Une trappe en Chine*, 7.

[14] Cf. "Acte de fondation du Monastère de N.-D. de la Consolation au Tchély Septentrional," in Thomas, *Histoire de la mission de Pékin*, 2:568–70.

[15] The situation of the priory after its restoration in 1861 was precarious for several years because of a lack of financial resources and vocations. The situation worsened after the antireligious decrees of 1879. The community was dispersed until 1881, when it resumed monastic life at Tamié, even though it was still under a decree of suppression issued by the Congregation for Religious. Cf. Bruno-Jean

the assignment and on 27 February 1883 left for China along with
Marie-Joseph Pavin, a lay brother of Notre-Dame du Désert who had
been at Tamié since 1880. They arrived in Peking on 7 May and in
Yangjiaping on 16 June. Before leaving Marseille for China, Dom
Éphrem went to Turin to pay a visit to his friend, Don Giovanni
Bosco.

> —"What name do you advise me to give to my little foundation
> in China?" he asked him.

> —"Our Lady of Consolation," the man of God replied and wrote
> on a little image of the Consolata of Turin, piously conserved
> at the Trappist monastery of Yang-Kia-Pinn [Yangjiaping]: "May
> God bless you, your work, and may the Holy Virgin always
> protect you!"[16]

As stated in article 7 of the decree for the foundation, "since the
Very Rev. Dom Abbot Jérôme [Guénat] has pledged to send some
monks to Peking by the end of this year [1883], the mission, counting
on this promise, asks the Rev. Dom Éphrem, who has accepted an
invitation to participate in this new foundation, to hasten the implementation of that promise."[17] And so he did. On 14 December of
that year he found three other monks to join the two pioneers of the
Trappist mission in China: Dom Marie-Bernard Favre (1854–1900),
a monk of Grâce-Dieu, Dom Fortunat Marechal, also of Grâce-Dieu
but residing in Tamié, and Br. François Jorgan, a solemnly professed
monk of Tamié.[18]

The Foundation and Its Development

The first article of the decree establishing the Trappist monastery
of Our Lady of Consolation reads as follows:

Martin, *Histoire des moines de Tamié et de quelques autres* (Saint-Étienne: Action
graphique, 1991), 115–19.

[16] Limagne, *Les Trappistes en Chine*, 50. The image of the Consolata, with the
words written by Don Bosco, was lost when the monastery was burned in 1947 (cf.
Ren Dayi, *Yangjiaping Shengmu shenweiyuan shi*, 2).

[17] Thomas, "Acte de fondation," 570.

[18] Cf. Beltrame Quattrocchi, *Monaci nella tormenta*, 27–28.

In the name and to the glory of the Most Holy Trinity, to the honor of the immaculate Mary, consoler of the afflicted and help of Christians, under the protection and with the help of the just Joseph, husband of the Blessed Virgin, of St. Benedict, of St. Vincent de Paul, a monastery of the Order of Cîteaux, Congregation of Our Lady of the Trappe, is established in the Peking and North Tchély [Northern Zhili] mission, prefecture of Suen-hoa fou [Xuanhuafu], in the place called Yang-kia-keou [Yangjiagu]. This monastery will be called Our Lady of Consolation.[19]

The location of the foundation had not been chosen at random. In fact, a short time before, some Christians had offered the bishop some land in the hope of getting a resident priest in the Yangjiagu ("the throat of the Yang family") region. A Chinese priest had already been sent to this remote area, pending the arrival of the first Trappists, and the Peking mission, taking advantage of favorable conditions, had purchased the mountain adjacent to the residence, all planted with apricot trees, as well as other adjoining lands. Yangjiagu, an open gorge between the mountains, which are about nine hundred meters high, is one hundred and fifty kilometers northwest of Peking, about a three-day walk from the capital. "Far removed from the noise of the world," the place appeared to be, to use the words of the description that was given on the fiftieth anniversary of its foundation, "a true Thebaid, where it is hard to nourish bodies, but where souls can peacefully dedicate themselves to contemplation."[20]

The first monks began to till this land, which was only marginally suitable for cultivation because it was mostly rocky and wooded. The work of clearing the land took a long time but resulted in the best possible use of it. Most of the land was planted with apricot trees and grape vines, the latter brought from Burgundy by Dom Marie-Bernard. Because of the terracing done by the monks, the name of the place was eventually changed to Yangjiaping, "the flatlands of

---

[19] Thomas, "Acte de fondation," 569.

[20] "Le Cinquantenaire," 119. The Thebaid is a region of ancient Egypt whose capital was Thebes. During the first centuries of Christianity many hermits lived there, hence the use of the word to refer to a quiet and peaceful place where one can live in solitude and tranquility.

the Yang family."²¹ A Western visitor described the area of the Trappist monastery in the early years of the twentieth century: "This is Trappe: a circle of mountains forty kilometers in diameter, which form a gigantic wall; within these natural confines a rippled plateau, similar to sea waves suddenly immobilized; across the plateau a deep ravine, which becomes an impetuous torrent during the rainy season and the rest of the time a thin brook; sterile and desolate soil on the peaks, and on the plateau rows of trees, some neat cultivated plots, an effort evident everywhere of obtaining rich harvests where poor briars grow with difficulty."²²

At the same time, using half of the money offered by the Countess de Stolberg, the monks began to put up some buildings to provide the minimal spaces that were needed for monastic life. On 16 June 1884, they dedicated the first rooms of the monastery, "the first stage of a monastery built in Chinese style, that is, on one level."²³

In order for the community to take root in this place and grow, it was necessary to receive Chinese vocations. A "studium" was opened to welcome Chinese postulants, who began arriving already in 1885. According to monastic practice in Europe at the time, the most intellectually gifted postulants were destined for the priesthood and followed a formation program that included the study of Latin. The others, who would become lay brothers, were offered an educational program that was less demanding. Among those who entered during these early years of the community were Stephen Tian, John Baptist Tian, Gerard Zhang, and Joseph Wen, a priest of Peking, together with his brothers Gabriel and Raphael.

Bishop Delaplace died in 1884, a great loss for the monks of the fledgling community, who considered him a co-founder and a father. His successor as vicar apostolic of Peking, François Tagliabue (1884–1890), continued to support the development of the community, visiting it just a year after he took office. Noting that Dom

²¹ Cf. Jean-Marie Struyven, "Martyre d'un monastère chinois. N.-D. de Consolation à Yang-Kia-Ping [codex C]" (unpublished typewritten manuscript, AGOCSO, fondo postulazione generale, D.7, 1953), 7.

²² Limagne, *Les Trappistes en Chine*, 33.

²³ Letter of a monk of the Trappist monastery of Our Lady of Consolation to a priest of the Diocese of Clermont, in MC 21 (1889): 353.

Éphrem's direction of the community, which at the time was made up of fifteen members, left something to be desired, Bishop Tagliabue advised him to send Dom Marie-Bernard, recently arrived in China, back to France to meet and take counsel with the chapter of Sept-Fons, which he did in 1886. When he returned to China the following year with two new monks, Dom Maur Veychard (1854–1919) and Br. Laurent, he brought the news that the Abbey of Tamié had handed over the guardianship of Our Lady of Consolation to the Abbey of Sept-Fons, that the general chapter had elevated Yangjiaping to the rank of a priory on 10 August 1886, that Dom Éphrem was removed from his position as superior, and that Dom Marie-Bernard Favre was assigned to take his place, becoming the first prior of Yangjiaping. Even though Éphrem Seignol had received permission to return to Tamié, he chose to remain faithful to his vocation as a missionary monk in China until his death in 1893.[24]

Within a few years the community became more stable and grew larger, thanks to a surprisingly large number of Chinese candidates to the monastic life.

> As concerns vocations, [the situation] is very encouraging. We are at the moment [1891] forty-two religious, professed and novices, thirty-eight of which are Chinese, among them a number of priests. I should add that the number of Chinese could easily be doubled or even tripled if we had the necessary resources for admitting them. Requests come to us from all parts, and the missionaries say that it is enough for them to mention our existence and to explain our manner of life to prompt vocations in the Christian communities. Add to this that our native religious write to their relatives, their friends, their acquaintances; . . . they like to praise the cloister's union and peace. In this way a very useful apostolate is carried out. . . . You can easily understand, hence, that we have many vocations.[25]

[24] Cf. his necrology in Seraphin Lenssen, *Hagiologium cisterciense*, vol. 2 (Tilburg: n.p., 1949), pp. 363–64, no. 733.

[25] J. Lemire, *Une trappe en Chine* (Paris: Sécretariat de la Société d'économie sociale, 1892), 13–14. In 1927, a missionary in Peking wrote as follows about vocations to the Trappist monastery: "As for vocations, fortunately, the Cistercians have plenty of choices. Ever since the opening of the monastery, they have been receiving a multitude of requests to join, mainly from the Vicariate of Peking." M. V. W.,

When the number of monks in the community reached more than forty, the Trappist Order did not delay in making the monastery of Yangjiaping an abbey. Its first abbot was Dom Marie-Bernard Favre. He went to Europe in 1891 to participate in the general chapter of the Trappists, which was held in Rome. While there, he received the abbatial blessing at Sept-Fons from the hands of the bishop of Moulins. He was abbot for nine years, and under his competent and charismatic leadership monastic life was built up at Yangjiaping, and new Chinese brothers entered the community. "Rev. Fr. Dom Bernard, young, intelligent, resourceful, who loved the Chinese, possessed everything for being successful in his undertaking. . . . He knew how to attract vocations, and, in spite of some chaff, he soon had a considerable number. . . . As postulants arrived, Dom Bernard had his community undertake all the observances of the rule, with some exceptions on account of the youth of the postulants and novices."[26]

In the last years of the nineteenth century, the community of Yangjiaping numbered sixty monks, including eight Europeans.[27] To provide better accommodation for this growing community Dom Bernard had to construct new buildings (the so-called cloister of the Sacred Heart). The high cost of this construction, plus the expenses related to the ordinary maintenance of the community, meant that the monks were under heavy financial constraints for several years. There were also pressing problems regarding the community. Only three of

---

"La Trappe de Notre Dame de la Consolation," BCP 14 (1927): 74. A Jesuit priest who visited the Trappist monastery during those same years noted: "Recruiting is mainly done in the province of Tchely [Zhili], especially in the vicariates of Peking and Suanhoafou [Xuanhuafu]; exceptionally some candidates come from the South of China." Philippe Leurent, "À la Trappe de Yang kia p'ing," *Chine, Ceylan, Madagascar* 19 (1930–1931): 187.

[26] "Le Cinquantenaire," 121.

[27] The data contained in the *Registro della casa generalizia* (Registry of the Generalate) of the Trappist Order are as follows: in 1885 the community was composed of sixty-seven members. Choir monks numbered twenty-one professed, three novices, and two postulants. Lay brothers numbered twenty-eight professed, nine novices, and four postulants. In 1899, when Our Lady of Consolation began the foundation of Our Lady of the Lighthouse in Japan, there were fifty-nine monks in Yangjiaping. Choir monks numbered fifteen professed, five novices, and six postulants. Lay brothers numbered twenty-one professed, eight novices, and four postulants (cf. fiche "Consolation," in AGOCSO, fondo postulazione generale, B.2/1).

the monks who had arrived from Europe were still in the community: the abbot, Dom Éphrem, and Dom Maur. For various reasons, the others had all returned to France. The abbot was thus obliged to return to Europe in search of recruits, but he was only able to bring three back with him, all very young: Dom Irénée; Albéric Achte, a novice from Mont-des-Cats; and Léon Janssens, a Dutch postulant.

Despite the shortage of missionary monks and financial resources, the apostolic zeal of Dom Bernard led him to respond to requests from several bishops. He traveled to other parts of China and other East Asian countries (Korea, Japan, Indochina), wishing to establish other monastic communities. Of all his dreams, only one was realized. In 1896 he founded the Trappist monastery of Our Lady of the Lighthouse near Tobetsu, in the Vicariate of Hakodate, Hokkaido, the northernmost of the major islands forming the Japanese archipelago. Because of the limited number of European monks in Yangjiaping and the young age of many of the Chinese monks, the community could send only one monk to Japan, Dom Irénée. Dom Bernard made one last trip to Europe, with visits to France, Belgium, and the Netherlands, to seek monks for the mission in the Far East and was able to recruit eight young monks for Japan. Soon after their arrival one of them died and another left the monastery. Additionally, in 1896, when the Trappist monastery of Our Lady of the Lighthouse was founded, Dom Bernard negotiated with Bishop Alexandre Berlioz, vicar apostolic of Hakodate, to found a Trappist monastery for women. In 1898 a group of eight French Trappist nuns of Ubexy established the monastery of Our Lady of the Angels, also in Hokkaido, not far from Our Lady of the Lighthouse. In the following decades it founded three other Trappist communities in Japan.[28]

Dom Marie-Bernard Favre "not only sowed the seed of Cistercian life in the Far East, he also established the principles of its development: all races, by the very fact that they have become Christian, are suited to this way of life. Cistercian life must, therefore, be so rooted

---

[28] Cf. Ren Dayi, *Yangjiaping Shengmu shenweiyuan shi*, 165–83 (app. 2: "The Monasteries of Japan"); "Le Cinquantenaire," 128–38 ("L'ordre cistercien au Japon"). See also the work of a Trappist monk of Our Lady of the Lighthouse: Frère Ignace, *Au Japon. Mes premières années. Souvenirs et impressions* (Alençon: Imprimerie alençonnaise, 1907).

in a country that everything that is needed for its vitality, including the abbot, comes from that country."[29] This echoes what Dom Bernard himself repeated insistently: "I will say my *Nunc dimittis* when the Chinese Trappists are capable of governing themselves. I don't despair of seeing that day, because already I have under my orders a Chinese novice master, who carries out his task to his honor and to my great satisfaction. The Rule of St. Benedict will be observed, and the superior, whoever he is, will draw from the prayers of his native subjects new strength to govern them."[30]

The first major ordeal that the young Trappist community had to face came less than twenty years after it had been founded. The xenophobic Boxer Rebellion (1899–1901) was particularly virulent against Chinese Christians, who were considered to be allies of foreign powers, hence traitors. Initially, thanks to their secluded location far from Peking, the center of the insurgency, the monks of Yangjiaping were safe. Their situation became precarious, however, when the rebels moved out of the city during the summer and laid siege to the area around the abbey. In addition to having to defend themselves, the monks soon found that they had to give shelter to hundreds of Christians in the area. Thanks to the fortifications they built, the trenches they dug, and other means of defense, along with the protection of St. Joseph, their patron, the community escaped major harm. In mid-July the Boxer troops withdrew, leaving the buildings of the abbey practically intact.[31] However, the danger was not over, since the rebels did not abandon the surrounding areas and the Christians living there were still coming to the abbey to seek refuge. In August Dom Maur, who after the death of Abbot Bernard in July had assumed interim leadership of the monastic community of three Europeans and fifty Chinese, wrote to the abbot of Sept-Fons, who was their father immediate:[32] "It is probable, hence, that our

[29] "Le Cinquantenaire," 124.

[30] Cited in Lemire, *Une trappe en Chine*, 23.

[31] Dom Maur kept a daily record of what the community went through between May and December 1900. It can be found in Limagne, *Les Trappistes en Chine*, 57–77.

[32] "Father Immediate" is the title of the abbot of a Trappist monastery (the "motherhouse") that has made a foundation (a "daughter house"). He is charged

last hour has arrived! Even though we cannot avoid feeling a certain emotion, quite natural under such circumstances, we are nevertheless tranquil and resigned to God's will and we even feel happy to have been judged worthy, in spite of our abject misery, to shed our blood for the faith and to give new martyrs to our order."[33]

In the following months the situation gradually improved. The Boxer troops withdrew completely from the region, which then enjoyed a stable peace for nearly forty years. The task then was to resume and strengthen community life. The vicar apostolic of Peking offered his spiritual and material support and encouraged Dom Maur to visit Sept-Fons to report on the new situation of the community to the general chapter.

Returning from Europe, Dom Maur brought the encouragement of Abbot Chautard and five new monks from Sept-Fons. Thanks to the financial support the abbey had received from the Vicariate of Peking, he was able to begin building a new church. The project, which had been put on hold until then for various reasons, was given to a famous architect who had already built several churches in China, Dom Alphonse de Moerloose of the Belgian missionary congregation of Scheut (CICM, Congregation of the Immaculate Heart of Mary). He considered himself "more monk than missionary"[34] and after the construction of the church in 1904 lived in a hermitage near the abbey until 1927.

The architect chose to imitate the Gothic architectural style of the thirteenth century for the new church, believing that neo-Gothic was best suited to a Cistercian monastery and would hark back to Cîteaux and the origins of the order. A vivid description of the church a few years after its construction is offered by Limagne:

> On granite foundations dug deeply rises an imposing mass in stone and brick. From the outside one can already see that there is a central nave dominating all the others, crowned by a small belfry with slender spires, and four side naves, the roofs of which

---

with watching over the daughter house, usually through visitations, and offering it counsel, but does not have jurisdiction over it.

[33] Limagne, *Les Trappistes en Chine*, 65.

[34] Ren Dayi, *Yangjiaping Shengmu shenweiyuan shi*, 59.

descend by steps. The church has four *pignons*: that of the main façade is supported at the corners by small and slender octagonal towers; that of the sanctuary, in which is mounted a window; and two small *pignons*, which cut the monotonous length of the church and imitate a transept. The interior is like that of all Cistercian churches: a large nave divided, from the door to the main altar, by: the inferior choir of the domestics; below the guests' tribune the choir of the lay brothers; the choir of the sick below the *jubé*; the fathers' choir; and finally the sanctuary. On each side two small naves are for circulation. Beyond there are two lower naves: the one on the west side has nine small chapels and opens on the cemetery; the one on the east side, contiguous with the cloistered buildings, forms the cloister of the Way of the Cross and opens to the church by three large doors. The sacristies embellish the sides of the sanctuary for all its length. The total length of the chapel is fifty meters. The granite is of a spotted gray, the bricks are blue, all the woodwork is carved from elmwood, the vaults are of a brownish hue, the painting in green and blue gives the monument an exceptionally delicious exotic color.[35]

The community invited Fr. Jean-Baptiste Chautard, abbot of Sept-Fons and father immediate of Yangjiaping (1899–1935), to preside at the consecration of the new church. Actually, the main reason for inviting him was so that he could preside at the election of the new abbot. However, he was unable to come at that time, and the community was allowed to proceed with the election of a new abbot without his presence. On 2 July 1904 Dom Maur Veychard was elected second abbot of Our Lady of Consolation. The election was presided over and ratified by the bishop of Peking. The new abbot was blessed a few months later in the cathedral of Peking by the new vicar apostolic, Bishop Stanislas Jarlin. In May 1906 Abbot Chautard was able to travel to China to embrace his "daughter." Warmly welcomed, Dom Chautard presided over the blessing of the new church and was able to experience firsthand the vitality of the Chinese community. As someone wrote, the "daughter of China was able to do justice to its name: it gave consolation" to the father immediate.[36]

---

[35] Limagne, *Les Trappistes en Chine*, 80–81.
[36] Cf. Hubrecht, *Une trappe en Chine*, 30.

During the fifteen years Dom Maur was abbot (1904–1919) the community continued to grow. According to the data given in the yearbook of the missions in China, in 1916 the abbey had ninety members, twelve of them Europeans. There were twenty-five professed choir monks (fourteen priests), five novices (four priests), and fifteen postulants. There were thirty professed lay brothers, a novice, and seven postulants.[37]

Because there was insufficient accommodation, young people who aspired to the monastic life could not always be received, as a member of the community noted in 1911: "Why should this Trappist oasis, on account of insufficient buildings and resources, be obliged to refuse the numerous postulants that come to it?"[38]

The decision was therefore made to expand. In a short time, the cloister was enlarged, the area next to the church was landscaped for a new cemetery, and two granges were built. The granges were typical Cistercian buildings, used to house the brothers who worked out in the fields and returned to the monastery only on Sundays and feast days. One of them, the Xinzhuang (Hsinchuang, Sintchouang) grange was located about two kilometers northwest of the monastery. It was described as "an elegant Chinese building of ash-colored bricks, built next to the hill and surrounded on three sides by other buildings and terraced gardens." It provided quarters for twenty to thirty brothers. A priest came to celebrate Mass daily, and each week the master of the lay brothers came to hold classes. The brothers raised goats for milking and operated a kiln to fire bricks.[39] About the same distance from the abbey, but in the northeast, the Beigou (Peikou) grange was built. It was smaller than the other, and the brothers lived there for a shorter period of time.

---

[37] Cf. *MCJ. Deuxième année [1916]*, 52. On p. 53 there is a list with the names of the priest-monks of the abbey (eleven Europeans and six Chinese). The *Registro della casa generalizia* of the Trappist Order reports that in 1922 Yangjiaping had eighty-six monks: thirty-six choir monks (twenty-nine professed and seven novices) and fifty lay brothers (forty-two professed, seven novices, and one postulant), cf. fiche "Consolation," in AGOCSO, fondo postulazione generale, B.2/1.

[38] "Providentielle conversion d'un jeune lama," MC 43 (1911): 164.

[39] Cf. Ren Dayi, *Yangjiaping Shengmu shenweiyuan shi*, 43.

In those years other major construction projects were completed: a three-kilometer-long canal was built, a root cellar was dug into the mountain, other smaller caves were made for the production and storage of cheese, and in 1909 a chapel was built for the Sunday Mass of Christians in the region. As a visitor reported a few years later, "everywhere the industrious ingenuity of the monks is manifest."[40]

Limagne provides an interesting description of the appearance of the monastery of Yangjiaping in those years. He emphasizes that the complex looked like "a bit of France" transplanted in Chinese soil: "The edifices of the monastery rise before us. We had expected to see a Chinese village, like those we had passed through, and instead we gradually perceive a monastery almost like a monastery in France with its three parallelograms of interior courtyards, its numerous dependencies dominated by the three slender spires of God's house."[41]

A few years later another visitor wrote that he had the same impression, but unlike Limagne, he expressed regret: "As for the buildings, some of them are in Chinese style, others in 'European' style; the European influence, alas, is dominant."[42] The principle of uniformity of architectural standards, based on European models, was applied to every nook and cranny of the monastery. For example, Limagne notes that the chapter room was very similar to those in other countries of the world, since "the chapter rooms are no different in Sept-Fons or in China or Brazil or Japan."[43] Some proponents for the inculturation of Christian architecture in China could not

[40] Ildephonse [Brandstetter], "A Pilgrimage to the Trappist Monastery of Yang Chia Ping," BCUP 2 (1927): 29.

[41] Limagne, *Les Trappistes en Chine*, 35–36. On pp. 37–48 the same author gives a graphic description of the monastic spaces of the Trappist monastery he visited in the early years of the nineteenth century. Two helpful plans of the monastery, in addition to numerous photographs from that period, are to be found in Ren Dayi, *Yangjiaping Shengmu shenweiyuan shi*, 63–64. A description of the layout of the monastery is also given in Li Dongming, "Zhili Zhuolu xian dongnan baisishi li Yangjiaping kuxiuyuan zhi" [Chronicle of the Trappist monastery of Yangjiaping, 140 *li* southeast of Zhuolu, Zhili], SZ 6 (1917): 252–56.

[42] Raymond Lei, "En promenade à la trappe de Yang-Kia-P'ing," *Jeunesse chinoise. Bulletin de la Jeunesse catholique chinoise* 85 (1932): 336.

[43] Limagne, *Les Trappistes en Chine*, 43.

resist asking some questions: "Once again we find the neo-Gothic style. . . . Faced with this, first of all a series of questions arise. Is such standardizing of all the churches in the world necessary? Are there not particularities proper to each people, local colors that are to be respected? Do Chinese souls, in order to become Christian, have to pass through the European mold?"[44]

This principle of uniformity was also extended to the liturgy; "the liturgy of France" was transplanted on Chinese soil. "At the hour of the Divine Office, whether that of the day or of the night, one seemed to be no longer in China: it is the liturgy of France and the glorious Salve Regina of the best monastic singers. . . . We feel better than in France, we feel we are in the Catholic Church."[45]

In those times, Catholicity was synonymous with uniformity. The instruction of the Sacred Congregation of Propaganda Fide in 1659 had made little impression. "What is more absurd than to bring France, Spain, Italy, or another part of Europe to China? You are not introducing these nations, but the faith, which neither rejects nor injures the rites or customs of a people, as long as they are not evil, but on the contrary wants to preserve them in all their vigor. . . . For this reason never compare the customs of those peoples with European customs, but rather accustom yourselves to them with the greatest diligence."[46]

During his long tenure as abbot Dom Maur saw not only the completion of material works but also the flourishing of a life of prayer that became the "pride" of the Vicariate of Peking and of all China. As he said in a letter to Jean-Baptiste de Guébriant, vicar apostolic of Guangzhou (Canton), "There is a great current of sympathy of Catholic China for the monastery [of Our Lady of Consolation]."[47] For this reason, several other vicars apostolic in China not only urged the monks to pray for the Christian communities entrusted to them, but also expressed their desire to have new monastic foundations

---

[44] Struyven, "Martyre d'un monastère chinois," 5.

[45] Limagne, *Les Trappistes en Chine*, 48.

[46] Sacred Congregation of Propaganda Fide, *Instruction to the Apostolic Vicars of Eastern Asia* (1659), in *Collectanea sacrae congregationis de Propaganda fide*, vol. 1 (Rome: Typographia polyglotta, 1907), p. 42, no. 135.

[47] Cited in Hubrecht, *Une trappe en Chine*, 47.

in their vicariates. One source speaks of twenty requests in all.[48] To respond to such requests for prayerful intercession with even greater fervor Dom Maur began planning for what would later become the *Pium opus messarum et precum* for the conversion of China.[49]

The rapid and remarkable development of the community under the guidance of Dom Maur Veychard in the first two decades of the twentieth century was summarized by Alphonse Hubrecht.

> The government of Dom Veychard lasted almost twenty years: twenty years of growth, of vigor, of prosperity. After a harsh tempest, suddenly everything bloomed, like a tree planted in arid soil, shaken by a hurricane, but which resists, becomes stronger, rises, gives out roots, and gives fruit. Wasn't it in the middle of the [Boxer] rebellion that Dom Veychard was invested with authority? Cruel hour! . . . To judge rightly the efforts of these twenty years it is necessary to know both the start and the results. The result is now this community of ninety-five religious, an enlarged monastery, an elegant and vast church, more numerous fields, vineyards, and in place of debts, some savings. Ten priests have been ordained, among them seven natives. In these results, for those who are able to see and understand, there was something of the miraculous.[50]

When Dom Maur died in 1919 the prior, Dom Albéric Achte, temporarily assumed the leadership of the community until a new abbot

[48] "The archives of Our Lady of Consolation contain letters from thirteen different vicariates, some more eloquent than others, all urging the reverend father abbot to establish a Trappist abbey in their vicariate as soon as possible. They offer land and all necessary assistance. Above all, they guarantee that the new foundation will be able to receive vocations. Do you want to know from where these requests come? From India, Siam, Annam, Burma, and China (Kantung [Shangdong], Honan [Henan], Hopei [Hebei], Kweitchow [Guizhou], Yunnan, Koangson [Guangxi], Setchoan [Sichuan], Koangtung [Guangdong]). In addition to letters, oral requests were also made during various encounters. Some individuals were authorized to let the reverend father Dom Louis know that the Trappists would be most welcome to make a foundation in Korea, Manchuria, Malacca, Hong Kong, Canton, Ningpo [Ningbo], Lanchow [Lanzhou], Sienhsien [Xianxian]. In all, there were more than twenty requests for foundation. The only one that was accepted was the request from the Apostolic Vicariate of Cheng-ting-fu [Zhengdingfu]." "Notre apostolat missionnaire monastique. Sa légitimité," COCR 6 (1939): 227–28.

[49] Cf. "Introduction," *supra*, pp. 9–15.

[50] Hubrecht, *Une trappe en Chine*, 49.

could be elected. Because of the length and difficulty of the journey from Europe to China, it would be two years before the election took place. In February 1921 Dom Bernard Delauze, the abbot of Dombes, arrived in Yangjiaping. He had been delegated by the abbot of Sept-Fons to conduct a canonical visitation and to preside over the election, in which Dom Louis Brun (1876–1942), the subprior, was chosen as the third abbot of Our Lady of Consolation. Before entering Yangjiaping in 1911 he had been a priest of the Paris Foreign Missions Society and its procurator in Hong Kong and Shanghai from 1901 to 1911. On 27 February 1921 Fr. Louis received the abbatial blessing from Bishop Jean de Vienne, coadjutor of Bishop Stanislas Jarlin of Peking.[51]

The golden age and further flowering in many aspects of community life continued for fifteen years, until 1937. Thanks to the unstinting efforts of the new abbot, who "loved the Chinese and was loved by them,"[52] and his trip to Rome to visit the motherhouse of the Trappist Order, the Congregation of Propaganda Fide, and the Vatican, "the work [that is, the *Pium opus messarum et precum*] timidly launched a few years earlier became a general mobilization, a large-scale campaign."[53] The restructuring of some areas of the monastery and the rearrangement of various monastic spaces involved additional construction. These works were directed by Dom de Moerloose and paid for by benefactors.

> [Our Lady of] Consolation, restored in this way, appeared as a monumental abbey in the arena of its valley, in the midst of its rocky rampart: majestic façades, airy porticos, corridors carefully paved, the chapels decorated with beautiful altars, decent apartments for visitors, large rooms inundated with light for the monks, colonnades of trees with dense foliage, gurgling waters, foamy cascades, the whiff of the breeze, the coolness of the mountaintops, the scent of the wood, in a word, all the advantages of virgin nature combined with the efforts of art and

---

[51] Cf. "Une élection abbatiale à la Trappe de Yang-Kia-Ping," MC 53 (1921): 247; "Yangjiaping kuxiuyuan xin yuanzhang Wang siduo dangxuan" [Dom Brun elected the new abbot of the Trappist monastery of Yangjiaping], SZ 4 (1921): 182; "Yangjiaping kuxiuyuan xin yuanzhang zhusheng jilüe" [A brief account of the blessing of the new abbot of the Trappist monastery of Yangjiaping], SZ 5 (1921): 228.

[52] Struyven, "Martyre d'un monastère chinois," 7.

[53] Hubrecht, *Une trappe en Chine*, 57.

of work. . . . The abbey, especially when seen from afar and from a height, gives today the impression of opulence, but it does not recount its difficult beginnings, or rather, it recounts them, but to those who are able to see, who are able to guess, who are able to understand the sum of the accumulated efforts in this transfigured desert.[54]

This was the magnificent sight that greeted the visitator, Bernard Delauze, abbot of Aiguebelle, when he came for the regular visitation of Yangjiaping in early 1926. He could see for himself the latest evidence of the spiritual and material progress of the abbey and he confirmed that the community was now mature enough to sow the seeds of Trappist life in other regions by making a foundation.[55]

A little later construction work was begun again with the extension of the wall around the monastery, the construction of a new chapel for Christians in the area, and the construction of a house at Beigou for future aspirants to the monastic life. Fr. Louis had long desired to have a school (a "probatorium") to receive and prepare candidates for monastic life. Something similar had been established at first and had existed for a number of years, but was then closed, one of the reasons being the opposition of the community. Once elected abbot in 1921, Fr. Louis lost no time in carrying out his plan to reopen this school near the Beigou grange, where it would not disturb the community. The St. Stanislaus Beigou School was built in 1928 and opened the following year.[56] It was large enough to accommodate up to twenty boys between the ages of twelve and fourteen. Three Chinese Marist brothers were hired as teachers. A chapel was built on this site in 1936, the year in which the house was enlarged to accommodate even more aspirants. Between the years 1929 and 1947 many candidates were introduced to the monastic life here, fifteen becoming priests and twenty brothers.[57]

[54] Ibid., 62.

[55] This came about two years later with the foundation of the Trappist monastery of Our Lady of Joy at Zhengding (cf. *infra*, pp. 148–53).

[56] This name was chosen in honor of the vicar apostolic of Peking, Bishop Stanislas Jarlin, a major benefactor of the monastery.

[57] Cf. Ren Dayi, *Yangjiaping Shengmu shenweiyuan shi*, 13, 79–81.

The Beigou school was created to solve the problem of how best to organize a formation program for the large number of young candidates who were coming to the monastery. From the very beginning of the community it was clear that presenting Christian monastic life in a language and with concepts that would be intelligible to the Chinese was going to be a major challenge. In addition to the necessity of learning Chinese well, a necessity that does not seem to have occurred to many of the foreign monks in Yangjiaping, there was also the urgent need to prepare materials for the intellectual and spiritual formation of aspiring Chinese monks. "The Europeans, in spite of their good will, had not been able to learn Chinese perfectly; . . . not only was it necessary to give the required orders for the good administration of the house, but it should have been necessary also to nourish the young souls full of good will with doctrine and the rule, which was all the more indispensible since there was no ascetic literature in Chinese at this time. A Christian language needed to be created, a task that only masters could have undertaken with success."[58]

Since the days of Abbot Maur the Trappist monastery of Our Lady of Consolation was aware that it had to offer a spiritual and intellectual training to its postulants and novices. For this reason, the formation program was carefully thought out.

> At [Our Lady of] Consolation the intellectual life every year received new vigor, with all the levels of ecclesiastical schooling. At the time of Dom Maur it was decided that the postulants destined to the choir would be oblates for one year, novices for three years, then would make simple vows during five years, and finally would be admitted to solemn profession. During all this time they would be occupied by a cycle of studies that included Chinese and Latin languages, philosophy, theology, and related sciences. . . . The Chinese abbey . . . wants to give its choir monks all the knowledge useful for their profession. To achieve this better it takes in young aspirants and keeps them at school desks until they are admitted. In Dom Maur's time these youngsters had their classes and courses within the monastery enclosure and at certain hours took their place in choir. . . .

---

[58] "Le Cinquantenaire," 122.

Recently they have been brought together in a neighboring valley, where they study, pray, play, and work under the supervision and vigilance of two Marist fathers, their teachers.[59]

When Dom Louis became abbot, formation was consciously aimed at preparing future monks to govern the abbey and render it independent. Such farsighted and commendable vision was not yet common in many church circles, nor in many religious communities in China, where the Chinese were relegated to a second-class position.

> We are to give on principle to our Chinese religious, especially to the choir brothers, who are the true monks and who form, as it were, the skeleton of our monasteries, the best religious, ascetic, philosophical, theological formation, with all the connected church subjects, and Chinese and French. This is not only justice and charity toward our Chinese religious: it is also, we believe, wisdom to prepare them to render to their monastery all possible service as professors, confessors, masters of novices, and superiors. We do not know the future, which remains in God's hands, but in the present circumstances we would be guilty not to prepare for it. . . . We are so convinced of the importance of this question, the education of our young religious, that we have already discussed the project, without yet being able to resolve it practically, of a monastery that at the same time would be a higher school of dogmatic and mystical theology, where our young professed Chinese might perfect their monastic education in an appropriate setting with professors selected in their own country, without the inconvenience of a trip and a stay abroad.[60]

Life at the monastery consisted of an austere round of prayer and work. The austerity of monastic discipline was even harsher in Yangjiaping, because the winters were particularly cold in that region of China. The daily routine was demanding.

> Rising is at 2:00 a.m. on weekdays, at 1:30 a.m. on Sundays. The Cistercian sleeps fully dressed; a few minutes after the sound of the bell he is already in church, which is illuminated by oil lamps. Matins and Lauds of the day with the great Office of

---

[59] Hubrecht, *Une trappe en Chine*, 39–40.
[60] Louis Brun, "La vie contemplative en Chine," in Hubrecht, *Une trappe en Chine*, 95–96.

the Blessed Virgin are alternately chanted or recited. The lay
brothers remain in the choir until 3:00 a.m., then they attend
to kitchen tasks. Masses are at 4:00 a.m., followed by breakfast
for the lay brothers. The choir monks still have Prime, then the
chapter, with the daily exhortation on the rule. After a very light
breakfast the conventual Mass is sung, then Office and manual
work. Dinner is toward noon, followed by an hour's siesta in
the summer, free time in the winter, then again manual work. In
the evening there is Vespers, spiritual reading, a quarter-hour of
meditation, supper, Compline, and the solemn chanting of Salve
Regina. Bedtime is at 7:00 p.m., at 8:00 p.m. in the summer.[61]

The harshness of life in Yangjiaping remained so even after the
expansion of the monastery buildings. An added difficulty was learning the Chinese language, as described in a diary of a Trappist monk
who arrived in 1938 and remained until 1946.

My beginnings there [at Yangjiaping] were extremely difficult. . . . The general living conditions at Yang Kia Ping [Yangjia-
ping] were extremely difficult for a foreigner. I did more penance
during my few years in this abbey than throughout the whole
of my life. . . . The standard of cleanliness was very far from
ours. . . . The sleeping conditions were a severe trial. . . . The
house was not provided with . . . central heating. . . . The food
was that of the peasants and coolies.[62] . . . To begin to learn Chinese at forty is difficult enough under the best of conditions. It
was made more difficult by the dearth of good study books. . . .
By dint of constant application, I managed to learn enough to
make my way along, though I never became a fluent speaker.[63]

The main work of the monks was the cultivation of cereals, fruit,
and vegetables, the raising of pigs, and the production of cheese from
the milk of cows and goats, which they also raised. The chief crop
was apricots; the pits were sold, mostly abroad, for the production
of oil. Monks were also involved in a variety of other occupations: as
blacksmiths, tinsmiths, masons, weavers, cobblers, millers, bakers.

[61] Leurent, "À la Trappe de Yang kia p'ing," 185–86.
[62] A term used in Asian colonies by Europeans to designate an indigenous worker
who earned a wage or was paid for a service performed.
[63] Patrick J. Scanlan, *Stars in the Sky* (Hong Kong: Trappist Publications, 1984),
75–77.

The Trappist monks had much communication with their neighbors, but within the bounds of monastic decorum. In addition to occasional visitors, priests and religious came to the Trappist monastery for their retreats, some of them from very distant areas. In the 1920s the monastery offered three thousand free meals a year. Ministry to local Christians was mainly in the form of catechism classes and the celebration of Mass, which was attended by about fifty people from nearby villages. As a testimony to their good will toward the monks, the local people gave them some panels inscribed with expressions of their gratitude. One of them hung at the main entrance of the monastic enclosure and reproduced a traditional Chinese expression of thanks: "The burden of [our] gratitude [to you] weighs as much as a mountain" (*en zhong ru shan* 恩重如山).[64]

From Consolation to Desolation

The development of the Trappist community of Yangjiaping was gradual and steady during the first three decades of the twentieth century and reached its peak in the early forties, when the community of Our Lady of Consolation counted between 110 and 120 monks, including those in formation.[65] After a long period of prosperity and peace, the abbey was afflicted with such terrible trials that in the course of a decade the community was completely wiped out.

War between China and Japan broke out in 1937. From 1938 on, the monastery found itself not only in the region occupied by Japanese troops, but it was regularly "visited" by Communist troops. In those

[64] Cf. Marcel Raymond, *Trappists, the Reds, and You* (n.p.: Abbey of Gethsemani, 1949), p. [9]; Ren Dayi, *Yangjiaping Shengmu shenweiyuan shi*, 95.

[65] The 1930 yearbook of Catholic missions in China lists 111 monks, of whom fifty-nine were choir monks and fifty-two lay brothers (cf. *MCJ. Neuvième année [1930]*, 55); in 1931–1932 it gives 101 monks, of whom thirty-nine were choir monks and sixty-two lay brothers, in addition to nineteen students in the school (cf. *MCJ. Dixième année [1931–1932]*, 56); in 1940–1941 it gives 106 monks, of whom fifty-three were choir monks (thirty-one professed, four novices, and eighteen postulants) and fifty-three lay brothers (forty-six professed, seven novices, and postulants), plus nineteen students in the school (cf. Lazaristes du Pétang, *Les missions de Chine. Seizième année [1940–1941]*, 92). These figures are confirmed, with some slight variations, by the *Registro della casa generalizia* of the Trappist Order (cf. fiche "Consolation," in AGOCSO, fondo postulazione generale, B.2/1).

years some of the foreign monks were even temporarily interned by the Japanese in a concentration camp in Weixian (Weihsien).[66] After the resignation of Dom Louis Brun in June 1941, Alexis Baillon was elected abbot. He remained in office until 1946, when he went to France for the general chapter, at which the Chinese monk Michael Xu (Xu Zongmin, 1901–1947), one of the future martyrs, was appointed administrator, that is, superior with full authority.[67]

The monks had become friends with the local people over the course of the previous decades. This slowed down the political action of the Communists, which, along with military action, was intended to raise the social consciousness of the farmers, especially the poorest among them, in order to create a reliable base of rural support. Because they were friends with the monks, the farmers in the areas surrounding the monastery were reluctant to take possession of the monastic estates and cultivate them for their own use. The situation changed in mid-1947. The combination of political unrest, fears arising from insecurity, and the program of re-education, which had always painted the monks as feudal oppressors who usurped the rights of the peasantry to the land, began to bear fruit. The farmers began to take the produce of monastic lands. The control of the peasantry by the Communist authorities became virtually all-encompassing, foreshadowing the start of what would be one of the most dramatic stories of persecution in Communist China. "This is a story, which on account of its brutality and violence undoubtedly constitutes a *unicum* in the vast scenario of anti-Catholic persecution. . . . On account of both the killers' cruelty and especially the extraordinary witness to the faith given by the monks who suffered this cruelty, it is a paradigm of the many stories of suffering that were written with blood in the following years."[68]

The story of the "terrible yet glorious holocaust of Yangjiaping"[69] can be reconstructed, because documentation about it is abundant

---

[66] Cf. Scanlan, *Stars in the Sky*, 143–83.

[67] A brief portrait of Micheal Xu is found in Struyven, "Martyre d'un monastère chinois," 15–16.

[68] Gerolamo Fazzini, introduction to "La 'via crucis' dei monaci trappisti di Yangjiaping," in *Il libro rosso dei martiri cinesi. Testimonianze e resoconti autobiografici,* ed. Gerolamo Fazzini (Cinisello Balsamo: San Paolo, 2006), 219–20.

[69] Beltrame Quattrocchi, *Monaci nella tormenta,* 14.

and varied. Much of the Trappist Order's collection of personal testimonies of those who suffered and of eyewitnesses has not been published. That documentation is the basis for the incomplete reconstruction of events that follows.[70]

July 1947 marked the beginning of the odyssey of the Trappists of Yangjiaping. In that month the monastery was devastated by repeated looting and then set on fire by revolutionary troops.[71] The monks were all arrested, subjected to repeated and tumultuous public trials, grueling interrogations, and inhumane physical and moral torture. During the course of the public trials, the monks had to answer accusations that were all blatantly false. Their accusers were the same peasants with whom they had established bonds of friendship and mutual support over many years. For that reason their martyrdom has also been described as a "martyrdom of ingratitude." The only person who remained loyal to the monks was Mary Zhang, a devout Christian and a catechist in one of the surrounding villages. She came to their defense by publicly denying the crimes they were unjustly

---

[70] The precious material collected by Dom Paolino Beltrame Quattrocchi, postulator of the cause of beatification of the thirty-three Trappist martyrs in China, is held in the General Archive of the Trappist Order in Rome. A selection of this large number of documents was first pulled together in Postulatio Generalis OCSO, *Dossier "China" pro capitulo generali 1980* (Montecistello: n.p., 1980), an expanded version of which was published in 1990 (cf. Beltrame Quattrocchi, *Monaci nella tormenta*). See also the documentation published in Ren Dayi, *Yangjiaping Shengmu shenweiyuan shi*, 93–122; Seraphin Lenssen, *Hagiologium cisterciense*, vol. 1 (Tilburg: n.p., 1948), 405–8; Seraphin Lenssen, *Supplementum ad hagiologium cisterciense* (Tilburg: n.p., 1951); "A Story of Communist Terror in China," *Catholic Missions* 25 (October–November 1948): 6, 11–13, 15; Charles J. McCarthy, "Trappist Tragedy: The Truth about the 'Land Reformers' in Action," *Catholic Review* (January 1948): 20–21, 34; (February 1948), 71–74; Raymond, *Trappists, the Reds, and You*; Struyven, "Martyre d'un monastère chinois," 17–38; Eusebio Arnáiz Álvarez, "Los monjes blancos," in *Religiosos mártires. Persecución comunista en China* (Hong Kong: n.p., 1960), 330–464; Scanlan, *Stars in the Sky*. In Chinese, in addition to various news articles that have appeared in the Catholic press and are given in the bibliography below (under "Trappists"), a book that provides a particularly rich source of information about the thirty-three martyrs is that of Ren Dayi, *Zhongguo xiduhui xundaozhe zhuanji* (*The Lives of the Martyrs of O. L. of Consolation Yang Kia Ping, 1947–1953*) (Hong Kong: Dayushan Shengmu shenleyuan, 1985).

[71] It is not certain that the monastery was burned by Communists. Nationalists may have set fire to it to keep it from being turned into a Communist stronghold.

accused of. This act of courage cost her dearly. She was savagely beaten and then imprisoned as she lay dying.

Shortly afterward the monks began their way of the cross. Deported en masse, they were ruthlessly coerced to undertake a long death march that went nowhere. For months they were forced to walk along the winding and steep mountainous trails of northern China. Hands tied behind their backs with handcuffs or iron wire, shoulders crushed by heavy loads, subjected to brutality and unspeakable torture, the monks saw their confreres die one after the other and often had to leave their bodies unburied. Six were executed.[72] In all, the number of monks who died on the "long march" between August 1947 and April 1948 was thirty-three: fourteen priests and nineteen brothers. The news of the tragedy was widely reported in the international press.[73]

Of those who died, only five were foreigners: Augustine Faure, Stéphan Maury, and Guillaume Cambourieu from France; Aelred Drost from Holland; and Alphonse L'Heureux from Canada. The last had been a Jesuit and had received permission from the Society of Jesus to spend the rest of his life at Our Lady of Consolation.[74] It may have been his Jesuit education and the force and clarity with which he defended the faith and criticized his captors' mistreatment of his confreres that singled him out for especially severe abuse. According to the account of an eyewitness, when the guard, who most likely had previously been at the Abbey of Yangjiaping and had contemplated the crucifix in the church, went to tell the other monks that Fr. Alphonse had died, he said: "That man died very

---

[72] In 1950 some inhabitants of the area took their remains to Peking, where Fr. Jean-Marie Struyven had them buried in the old Catholic cemetery of Zhalan. The identities of the six monks are not clear; the sources give different names. Cf. Struyven, "Martyre d'un monastère chinois," 35–36; Beltrame Quattrocchi, *Monaci nella tormenta*, 261–63.

[73] See, e.g., the report by the international news agency Fides on 28 November 1947: "La destruction de l'abbaye des trappistes de Yangkiaping par les communistes et la mort tragique de plusieurs religieux. August–October 1947," *Fides documentazione* 10 (1947): 78–82.

[74] For more about him, see Prosper Durand, "Le père Alphonse, trappiste (Albert L'Heureux)," *Prêtre et Missions* 10 (1949): 132–36.

peacefully. He looks like the other man on the figure-ten frame in the Yang Kia Ping [Yangjiaping] chapel. The figure 'ten' is written as 十 in Chinese, and the 'figure-ten frame' [*shizijia* 十字架] is the Chinese word for a crucifix."[75]

The only foreigner who survived was Dom Maur Bougon. He had been a key mediator between the various forces in the vicinity of the monastery during the turbulent years of the Sino-Japanese conflict, but in January 1947 he left the community of Yangjiaping with the permission of his superiors to become pastor in a Christian village south of Peking. He returned to France in 1952.[76]

Between mid-October and mid-December 1947 a dozen young monks were released from prison and went to Peking.[77] Fortunately, it was at that very time that Paulinus Lee, prior of Our Lady of Joy, the foundation made by Our Lady of Consolation in Zhengding in 1928,[78] also arrived in Peking, along with some members of his community.

Initially, they were all housed in the Benedictine monastery, but it soon became clear that they would need to find a place in Peking to accommodate the newly arriving Trappist monks who had escaped imprisonment and martyrdom. In January 1948 the number of monks who were released and found their way to Peking rose to thirty-eight; by November they were forty-one.[79] Dom Paulinus looked everywhere for a possible solution, then, unexpectedly, made

---

[75] Cited in Scanlan, *Stars in the Sky*, 295.

[76] Cf. Beltrame Quattrocchi, *Monaci nella tormenta*, 264–70.

[77] According to the diary of Fr. Patrick J. Scanlan, a first group of five was released with orders to return to their home, a week later another group of seven were released and, finally, another seven (nineteen in all). The last group consisted of choir monks who were candidates for the priesthood. Before their release, the Communist guard is said to have told them: "We have your photos and your fingerprints. We will take all of North China soon, and if we come to some city and find that you have relapsed and made yourselves priests, we will kill you." Cf. Scanlan, *Stars in the Sky*, 300. In his *Chronologies*, Dom Maur Bougon speaks of twenty-four refugees (cf. Beltrame Quattrocchi, *Monaci nella tormenta*, 320). A photo of thirteen of them along with their names can be found in Ren Dayi, *Yangjiaping Shengmu shenweiyuan shi*, 124–25.

[78] Cf. *infra*, pp. 147–62.

[79] Information given by Maur Bougon in his *Chronologies*. Cf. Beltrame Quattrocchi, *Monaci nella tormenta*, 320.

contact with a Russian immigrant who was preparing to leave China and wanted to sell his cheese factory in Peking, two pieces of land, and two hundred head of dairy cows. The price was good, and thanks to a loan from Archbishop Antonio Riberi, nuncio to China, the cheese factory was purchased and gradually all the employees were replaced with monks who had been released from prison.[80] The two properties, located in the area of the city's eastern gate (Dongzhimen) and a kilometer away from each other, were confiscated by the Communists in 1953. The community was then dispersed, the brothers returning to their places of origin. No further news about them appears in published sources.

After this purchase was made, Dom Paulinus was able to return to his community in Sichuan. Dom Stanislaus Ren, also of Our Lady of Joy, was in charge of the cheese factory for several months. At the beginning of 1948 he was replaced by Dom Jean-Marie Struyven.[81] In the years immediately following, the Peking community did surprisingly well, given the conditions, even attracting postulants and novices. In 1950, one of the houses connected to the cheese factory was transformed into a novitiate for ten novices. Moreover, in 1949 five of the monks were ordained priests, and it appears that seven others were ordained in 1952.

Community life was gradually reestablished. At first, because the monks were few, their day was almost totally occupied by work. When other monks were released from prison and the community grew to around sixty members, including novices and postulants, it became possible to follow the normal monastic horarium. The

---

[80] In 1948 there were forty-five monks in the Peking community. In 1950, when the community of Our Lady of Joy, which was in exile in Sichuan, had to return to Peking once again, the number had increased to sixty, of whom twenty were priests and ten novices. Cf. Ren Dayi, *Shengmu shenleyuan cangsang wushi nian huashi* (*Pictorial History of Our Lady of Joy [Liesse] Written for Its Golden Jubilee of Foundation, 1928–1978*) (Hong Kong: Catholic Truth Society, 1978), 15.

[81] Jean-Marie Struyven (1897–1959) went to China in 1934. After he was expelled from the country in 1953, he transferred to the Trappist Abbey of Scourmont in Belgium, where he died in 1959. Cf. Vincent Hermans, "Dans le feu de la lutte. Le trappiste belge Jean-Marie Struyven en Chine (1934–1953)," *Courrier Verbiest* 23 (December 2010): 17–19.

monks, however, did not wear the habit.[82] We have an horarium of daily life on the Trappist farm in Peking between 1947 and 1954.[83]

2 a.m.: Rising, Divine Office, meditation.

3 a.m.: Work (milking cows).

4 a.m.: Mass, Lauds, breakfast, work (preparing for the delivery of the milk).

5:30 a.m.: A group of brothers (12/16) rode their bicycles to deliver milk to their customers in different parts of Peking. . . . The monks remaining in the dairy performed other works, such as making cheese, cream, butter, looking after the cows.

9–10 a.m.: The delivery brothers returned home (dairy), took a rest, read, and prayed.

11 a.m.: Common prayer, lunch, rest.

1 p.m.: Work (milking cows, pasteurizing, bottling for the next day's delivery).

5:30 p.m.: Common prayer, supper, reading.

7:30 p.m.: Compline.

If overtime work was required, they had to finish the work before going to bed.[84]

This relatively peaceful period ended with the expulsion from China and return to Belgium of Fr. Struyven, who had been appointed superior *ad nutum* in March 1953. Benedict Wang assumed his post as superior of the Peking community, which at that time numbered forty monks. On 16 June 1953 the community still had the audacity to celebrate the seventieth anniversary of the founding of Our Lady of

[82] "The monastic habit, resumed after the canonical visitation the previous year [1947], was again abandoned, this time definitively. After all, I did not want by any means to provoke the Communists. I had a clear responsibility toward the monastery and the religious and I was ready to make concessions in everything on the social plane, on condition that we might remain in community." Struyven, "Martyre d'un monastère chinois," 43–44.

[83] More details about the life at the Trappist farm in Peking are found in the report of the superior, Dom Struyven (cf. Struyven, "Martyre d'un monastère chinois," 38–56).

[84] Ren Dayi, *Yangjiaping Shengmu shenweiyuan shi*, 133.

Consolation, going so far as to print memorial cards and brochures for the occasion.[85] Some months later, in early March 1954, the dairy was confiscated and fifteen priest-monks were arrested, imprisoned, and after lengthy interrogations sentenced to *laogai* 劳改, re-education labor camps. In 1961 Jean Pasqualini met one of them, Benedict Labre Hou (Hou Shi'en), when the two were together for a year in a labor camp. Pasqualini described him as "a little old man who in the camps stubbornly kept alive the passion of Western missionaries."[86]

The thirty lay brothers were allowed to stay and work on the farm under the supervision and direction of Communist supervisors, an arrangement that actually made the farm little different from a work camp. The last news of their presence in the cheese factory comes from 1957. It is possible that they too were transferred and dispersed at that time, a fate they had sadly anticipated for several years. In fact, when the monastery was looted in July 1947, it became clear to the monks that they would be dispersed and that the future of the lay brothers would be especially bleak.

> The older fathers tried to console them. One of them said, "You have the priesthood, which cannot be taken from you. But when we will no longer have Yangjiaping, how will we be able to approach the altar? How will we be able to live our life as Trappists?" They felt oppressed by a profound sense of uncertainty. Fr. Michael [Xu Zongmin], the prior [abbot administrator], then wrote a small note for each of them recommending them to the charity of any bishop they might encounter once they were dispersed. That simple document written in pencil on wrinkled paper was a great comfort to the students. Many succeeded in keeping that scrap of paper hidden in their clothing during the following three months of trials.[87]

The monastery was destroyed and the monks dispersed, but outside of China the hope remained alive that all was not lost and that one day something would again spring up. In the following years

---

[85] Cf. ibid., 139.

[86] Cf. Jean Pasqualini, "The Christmas Mass of Father Hsia," *Reader's Digest*, Hong Kong ed. (February 1970): 70–74; Jean Pasqualini, *Prisonnier de Mao. Sept ans dans un champ de travail en Chine* (Paris: Gallimard, 1975), 245–47, 256, 271–72.

[87] "La 'via crucis' dei monaci trappisti di Yangjiaping," 228–29.

very little information about the dozens of monks interned in camps or in prison made its way out of China. Each year until 1963 the *Registro della casa generalizia* (Registry of the Generalate) of the Trappist Order provided data on the composition of the community of Our Lady of Consolation, each year stating that there were forty-three monks, fifteen of whom were professed choir monks and twenty-eight professed choir lay brothers.[88] The real situation was noted in 1960 in the Trappist journal *Collectanea Ordinis Cisterciensium Reformatorum*: "There is no notice of our brothers in China. They are suffering and are silent. They are suffering for Christ and for his church. Ten years have already passed since our separation. May the good God grant them to be reunited soon, *ut tristitia nostra convertatur in gaudio.*"[89]

In 1978 the historian of the community of Our Lady of Joy in Lantau (Hong Kong) wrote the following.

> [About] the monks who remain in China, everybody has to work for the government, no exception at all. Some monks work in factories; one of them, our youngest brother, works as a veterinarian in Inner Mongolia. We do not know much about them; they are the silenced monks suffering with the silent Christ, but their life and silent suffering is of inestimable value before God and the church. The monks from Our Lady of Consolation who lived in Peking from 1949 to 1953, and worked in their dairy farm, were unable to follow the fixed structures of the order, nor follow the rules and the constitutions. . . . But what of that! They were and still are the faithful monks, followers of Christ, living in absolute poverty and perfect giving-of-self to God as Christ offered himself naked on the cross. We, monks in Lantau, have good reason to be proud of our dear brothers we have left behind.[90]

Beginning in the 1980s, with progressive reforms accompanying China's opening, Christian life could be resumed in China, and the monks who had been dispersed and sentenced to labor camps were

---

[88] From 1956 on, however, the data were accompanied by a question mark (cf. fiche "Consolation," in AGOCSO, fondo postulazione generale, B.2/1).

[89] Cited in Beltrame Quattrocchi, *Monaci nella tormenta*, 325.

[90] Ren Dayi, *Shengmu shenleyuan*, 42.

eventually freed.[91] Some of those who had been ordained returned to exercise their priestly ministry clandestinely.[92] And, surprisingly, there were some who again began to welcome young aspirants to the monastic life, as the abbot general of the order, Dom Ambrose Southey, wrote in a circular dated 6 January 1990: "An interesting fact has recently drawn my attention. A letter written by one of the monks of Our Lady of Consolation (China) mentions a certain number of youths and girls who aspire to the monastic life whom he is training to live our life. Outwardly, they work in a factory, but they also pray together. It seems there are about twenty persons, or perhaps more. Permission is also asked for their profession, since they have been living this kind of life for a number of years!"[93]

After the fire of 1947 nothing remained of the old and flourishing Trappist monastery of Yangjiaping but ruins that were still visible and recognizable more than fifty years later. In 2004 a visitor discerned the remains, "all in excellent condition" and from which "you could feel the imposing dimensions" of the original complex, of the church, the residence of the monks, the cemetery, the cellars, and the vineyard. However, the situation changed in the years immediately following, as the government began to tear down or remodel the old buildings still standing in order to transform the site into a recreational area for vacationers. The kitchen and the monastic refectory

---

[91] A list compiled around 1987 gives twenty-one members of the community of Our Lady of Consolation and nine members of the community of Our Lady of Joy who were still living in China at that time (cf. AGOCSO, fondo postulazione generale, F.12).

[92] A case we know about is that of Fr. Placidus Pei Ronggui, arrested on 3 September 1989, when he was about fifty years old, for refusing to join the Chinese Catholic Patriotic Association. Cf. *Asia News* 59 (1989): 473. A Chinese blog has also recently published a photograph of four of the last Trappist priests who, after the destruction of Yangjiaping, exercised their ministry in mainland China and died between 1989 and 2007: Romanus Mao Yonghui (died in 1989 at the age of sixty-five in the Diocese of Xuanhua), Joachim Liu Yajing (died in 1998 at the age of seventy-five in the Diocese of Xianxian), Nicesius Zhang Depu (died in 2005 at the age of eighty in Changping), and Benjamin Zhao Zhenfu (died in 2007 at the age of eighty-five in Weixian). Cf. "Yizhang zhengui de Yangjiaping Shenweihui xiushi zuihou de heying" [A final precious photograph of the monks of Consolation at Yangjiaping], http://blog.sina.com.cn/s/blog_5eaa27e8010017h2.html, accessed 21 August 2013.

[93] Cited in Beltrame Quattrocchi, *Monaci nella tormenta*, 342.

on the east side of the old monastery were completely demolished, the church was turned into a cafeteria. Some Gothic-style arches inside are all that remains to indicate that it was a church. Two of the three old cellars were destroyed to build a large new building. The residence of the monks was remodeled into a conference room and a pavilion housing several specimens of pheasants. The original style of the facade was fortunately preserved.[94] The remark of someone who observed these sudden transformations comments on the operation that led to the almost total loss of this historical, artistic, and religious patrimony: "It is really distressing that the oldest and largest Trappist monastery in Asia has been transformed, in just five years, into a recreational area."[95]

The Trappist Monastery of Our Lady of Joy

As we have seen, the flowering of monastic life at Our Lady of Consolation allowed it to make foundations and spread Trappist monastic life to other parts of China. The requests of vicars apostolic were numerous, but the abbot of Yangjiaping judged that only two could be given serious consideration, since these foundations would not be far removed from Yangjiaping, making it easier to be in communication with them.

In 1926 Dom Brun and two brothers were sent out to assess these two offers. One was from the vicar apostolic of Weihui (southern Henan), Bishop Martino Chiolino, the other from the vicar apostolic

---

[94] Cf. the information and pictures published in the Chinese blog *Beijing Zebra*: "Zai dao Yangjiaping" [Again at Yangjiaping], http://blog.sina.com.cn/s/blog_5eaa27e 80100cjx3.html, accessed 21 August 2013; "Wunian nei sifang Yangjiaping Shen-weiyuan yougan" [The emotions resulting from four visits over the course of five years to the monastery of Consolation at Yangjiaping], http://blog.sina.com.cn/s /blog_5eaa27e80100d5xu.html, accessed 21 August 2013; "2011 nian de Yangjiaping Shenweiyuan yizhi" [The ruins of the monastery of the Consolation at Yangjiaping in 2011], http://blog.sina.com.cn/s/blog_5eaa27e80100oi5n.html, accessed 21 August 2013. Some photos of the site showing the ruins of the monastic buildings can be seen on the blog http://blog.voc.com.cn/blog.php?do=showone&uid=2359& type=blog&itemid=454097, accessed 21 August 2013. A collection of photos showing the ruins of Yangjiaping, presumably taken in the 1990s, can also be found in AGOCSO, fondo postulazione generale, F.12.

[95] "Wunian nei sifang Yangjiaping Shenweiyuan yougan."

of Zhengding (Zhengdingfu, Chengtingfu, or Tchengtingfou, in the region of southern Hebei), Bishop Frans Hubert Schraven. The meeting with Bishop Schraven and his vicar general, Fr. Nicolas Baroudi, proved to be decisive for making a foundation.

The Foundation in Zhengding

Of the three pieces of land offered by the Vincentian mission, the choice fell on the large property, about 120 hectares (approx. 300 acres), called Hetan ("quay of the river"), because it was located between the two arms of the Putuo River, about five kilometers southwest of the city of Zhengding. Since it was a floodplain, the ground was fertile and had already been cultivated for some years. The fact that Zhengding was only about three hundred kilometers from Peking and near a railway junction, where there was a thriving Catholic population, and that the seminary was a short distance from the property offered by the vicar apostolic, were further decisive factors that led Dom Brun to decide to make a foundation on the site. It was called Our Lady of Joy (*Shengmu shenleyuan* 聖母神樂院).[96]

The construction of the first buildings of what would soon become "the most beautiful jewel in the works of the vicariate"[97] of Zhengding, was initiated by Fr. Baroudi at the end of 1926. By the beginning of 1928 most of the work was done, and the new monastic foundation could count a chapel, a scriptorium, a refectory, and a dormitory.

Three "precursors" had already arrived in Zhengding in September 1927. In 1928 abbot Dom Louis and another brother arrived, and finally, a few days apart in April of that year, two groups of seven monks chosen by the abbot for the new foundation. The feast of St. Robert of Molesmes, founder of Cîteaux, 29 April 1928, was chosen as the day when the nineteen members of the new community of Our

---

[96] The history of Our Lady of Joy is given in Hubrecht, *Une trappe en Chine*, 66–72; Ren Dayi, *Shengmu shenleyuan*; Beltrame Quattrocchi, *Monaci nella tormenta*, 68–77, 281–96. For an account in Chinese, see *Xiduhui jianshi*, 185–99 (apps. 2 and 3).

[97] A. Morelli, "Les Trappistes (N. D. de Liesse)," in *Notes d'histoire sur le vicariat de Tcheng-ting-fou. 1858–1933* (Peking: Imprimerie des Lazaristes, 1934), 171.

Lady of Joy would begin regular monastic life. The official inauguration and blessing of the chapel took place on 9 May in the presence of the bishop, the priests of the diocese, and many benefactors.

During the thirteen years that the community of Our Lady of Joy was a dependent foundation of Our Lady of Consolation, hence under the direct guidance of its abbot, there were four local superiors. From 1928 to 1930 Dom Anthony Fan, who was Chinese, led the community. He was followed by François Rols, a monk from Timadeuc, who was superior for only six months in late 1930 and early 1931. From 1931 to 1934 the superior was Albéric Achte, who came to China when he was still a novice at Mont-des-Cats and who had been prior at Yangjiaping for twenty-seven years. From 1934 to 1941 the superior was Laurent Gérardin, a monk from Sept-Fons. The community maintained itself by growing crops and raising cattle. The work of land reclamation attracted the notice of the official chronicler, who was charged with drawing up a brief report on the presence of the monks in Zhengding and who was obviously more interested in their material than their spiritual works. "This order is known in Europe for its rural mission. Similarly, also in China it adopted agricultural activity as a form of mission. So, for example, the Trappist community . . . in Zhengding, founded in the sixteenth year of the Republic [1927], through the work of land reclamation carried on for over twenty years by the monks, has transformed more than 2000 *mu* [approx. 133 hectares or 329 acres] of sandy banks into 1253 *mu* [approx. eighty-four hectares or 208 acres] of cultivated land, eighty [approx. five hectares or twelve acres] of which are occupied by an orchard."[98]

Because of the difficult climate, especially the hot and humid summers, the life of the community in those early years was very hard. The reluctance to adapt the rules of monastic life, based on French customs, caused weakness, illness, and even death among the brothers in the early 1930s. Only when faced with this emergency

[98] *Hebei sheng zhi. Zongjiao zhi*, 265. The chronicler immediately adds, "Today the land belongs to the Fruit Tree Research Institute of the Hebei Academy of Agricultural Sciences. In 1989, some parts of the real estate were designated for the Catholic seminary of the province of Hebei" (ibid.). One *mu* is equal to 0.0667 hectares.

situation did the chapter of Our Lady of Consolation rule that some practices could be mitigated:

1. During the summer, as regards the diet, no fast is to be observed;

2. As regards the schedule, no one is to work in the fields between 9:00 a.m. and 4:00 p.m.;

3. During the night the monks are to be dressed more lightly;

4. For the Divine Office the monks are not to wear the cowl.

After the early years, when the difficulties of the life kept several young persons away, a good number of newcomers entered the community, especially as lay brothers. Since it was not possible to provide formation for choir monks on site, for the first twelve years almost all postulants were sent to Yangjiaping for their formation. Between 1930 and 1940 at least a dozen went there. It was only in 1940 that the decision was made to open a novitiate for choir novices. To ensure their formation, five monks were sent from Yangjiaping. The opening of the novitiate gave fresh impetus and new vitality to the community of Our Lady of Joy. In a few months the number of novices rose to twenty. Another remarkable development was that shortly after its foundation Christians from various regions around the monastery formed a village in its vicinity and called it "Benduzhuang," "[St.] Benedict village."

The community of Our Lady of Joy in Zhengding was affected by the Sino-Japanese War (1937–1945) from its very beginning. On the evening of 9 October 1937 a squadron of the Japanese army, actually made up of Koreans and Manchurians, burst into the bishop's house in Zhengding, where some of the sick and older monks of the Trappist monastery had taken refuge. Among the nine Europeans massacred and burned that night were Bishop Schraven and the Trappist Emmanuel Robial, who was the nurse and sacristan at Our Lady of Joy.[99]

---

[99] Cf. the accounts of the massacre compiled by the Trappist fathers Laurent Gérardin, superior of Our Lady of Joy, and Denis Van Leeuw, which are contained in Beltrame Quattrocchi, *Monaci nella tormenta*, 80–98 ("The Massacre of Cheng-Ting-Fu"). Regarding Emmanuel Robial, see "Une première victime sanglante de

Because of the continuous raids made by the Communists in the early years of the Sino-Japanese War, monastic life became impossible even at Yangjiaping. In particular, the young monks were prevented from continuing their studies and their formation. In 1940, hence, the community of Our Lady of Consolation decided to send its novices elsewhere. Twelve postulants were transferred to the Marist Brothers in Peking, and later thirty monks, novices, simply professed, and young priests were sent to Our Lady of Joy in Zhengding. For a few months the community of Zhengding was particularly large and lively. Deceived by the promises of security made by the Communists stationed in Yangjiaping, the Peking and Zhengding groups returned to Our Lady of Consolation in 1941, unaware of the persecution that awaited them in the following years.

The Sino-Japanese War and the illness of Abbot Louis Brun accelerated the process of granting autonomy to Yangjiaping's daughter house. Following the resignation of Dom Brun in 1940, the general chapter decided to elevate Our Lady of Joy to the rank of an independent priory (*sui iuris*). The monks from Our Lady of Consolation transferred their stability to Our Lady of Joy on 22 May 1941, and on 31 May the community proceeded to elect its first prior. The election was held by the visitator, Fr. Benoît Morvan, abbot of Our Lady of the Lighthouse in Japan. The official installation of Dom Paulinus Lee (Li Bolan, 1906–1980), a Chinese monk who until then had been novice master, took place on 30 November 1941, the feast of St. Andrew.[100] A member of the community of Zhengding described the significance of this event for the Trappist Order and the church: "Our reverend father [prior] is the first superior of Cîteaux not of the European race. His presence at the general chapter will reinforce the essentially Catholic character of this venerable assembly, just as it pleased our holy father, the pope, to create recently a Chinese cardinal so as to affirm the Catholicity of the church. These facts show the

---

notre apostolat missionnaire en Extrême Orient," COCR 5 (1938): 40; Anne-Marie Robial, *Père Emmanuel Robial. Une vie consacrée* (Jouaville: Scripta, 2005).

[100] Cf. his necrology in *Sunday Examiner* (Hong Kong), 8 August 1980.

progress made by Catholicism in our regions. Let us hope that this is only a prelude to even more rapid progress in the near future."[101]

The composition of the community during its first two decades shows significant growth. In 1931 the community consisted of thirty to forty members, ten years later the number was in the fifties, and in 1947, prior to evacuation, there were sixty-five, including novices and postulants.[102] A summary of the life of the community in these years was given by a Trappist monk in 1946. He first describes the trials undergone by the community, then he speaks of the positive side.

> The tangible protection of the good God has shown us . . . that he wanted the foundation and the growth of our dear Order of Cîteaux in the Far East. What happened to the real religious life of the community amidst all these perturbations? Thanks to God, we have not felt the counterblow of outside events. Divine Office has been celebrated without interruption and the daily efforts of everyone have aimed at realizing better and better the Cistercian ideal of union with God and immolation of self. This intimate life of prayer and sacrifice, however, does not lend itself to long descriptions.[103]

Immediately after independence, the monks began to think of expanding their living quarters and building a new chapel. These

---

[101] Cited in Beltrame Quattrocchi, *Monaci nella tormenta*, 115. The first Chinese cardinal was the archbishop of Peking, Thomas Tian Gengxin (1890–1967), who was made a cardinal on 18 February 1946.

[102] Cf. "Trappistes et Trappistines en Extrême-Orient," BCP 16 (1929): 269; *MCJ. Dixième année [1931–1932]*, 34–35; Lazaristes du Pétang, *Les missions de Chine. Seizième année (1940–1941)*, 63; Ren Dayi, *Shengmu shenleyuan*, 10 (on pp. 50–73 there are numerous photos of the places and of the members of the community during this first period of life at Zhengding, i.e., between 1928 and 1947). A report appearing in the journal *Collectanea Ordinis Cisterciensium Reformatorum* gives the following composition of the community: in 1938 there were thirty-two members (twelve professed and one postulant for the choir monks; eleven professed, four novices, and four postulants for the lay brothers). By 1946, the number had almost doubled. The sixty-two members were twenty-three professed, five novices, and one postulant for the choir monks; twenty-four professed, six novices, and three postulants for the lay brothers. Cf. COCR 7 (1940–1945), 116–18. These figures are confirmed by further data given in the *Registro della casa generalizia* of the Trappist Order, which make it clear that the number of the community reached its high point in the 1940s. Cf. fiche "Liesse," in AGOCSO, fondo postulazione generale, B.2/2.

[103] Cited in Beltrame Quattrocchi, *Monaci nella tormenta*, 115.

projects would never be realized, however, because within a few years Communist attacks brought an end to the expansion of Our Lady of Joy. The 1945 victory of China in the Sino-Japanese War did not lead to peace within the country. On the contrary, the civil war between the Nationalists and the Communists intensified. The monks were soon separated from each other and wandered from place to place for a few years before reestablishing their monastery in Hong Kong.

The Refuge in Chengdu

The story of the "wandering" of the community of Our Lady of Joy between their evacuation from Zhengding in 1947 and the arrival later that year of some of them on the island of Lantau in the territory of the British colony of Hong Kong to reestablish the community is, in fact, the "most complicated [page] in the history of Our Lady of Joy."[104] Nevertheless, it will be summarized here briefly.

The first attack was launched by the Communists in April 1947. Some of the monks fled to the nearby city of Shijiazhuang but returned to the monastery shortly afterward. Two other monks (Laurent Gérardin, subprior, and Ivo You) fled to Shanghai, where the community would gather a few months later. Taking advantage of their momentary escape from the Communists, but recognizing that troops would soon return to the city to occupy it definitively, the community lost no time preparing to go to southern China, which was still untouched by the turmoil of war. The whole community came together to discuss the difficulties involved. "The members agreed in principle to the evacuation, but the manner, the means, where and how, were hard to detail. It had to be decided according to the circumstances, which were not under their control. All they could do was to give themselves to God's Providence. Nine old fathers and brothers of the community would remain in the monastery with one dying novice in the infirmary. . . . None of the monks could give any decisive solution to so many problems."[105]

[104] Ren Dayi, *Shengmu shenleyuan*, 16. The map at p. 75 in that volume is helpful.
[105] Ibid., 12.

A large majority of the community chose to flee to the South. "They considered, it was not a question of life or death, but a question of the future of monastic life in China. It was not the time to show how firm one was. Since Our Lady of Consolation was completely destroyed and the monks were all in jail or had died, the fate [of the community] was unknown. The only remaining monks were those of Our Lady of Joy. They would try their best to save monastic life in China. Therefore the community decided to move to South China."[106]

Prior Paulinus then had the idea of contacting Bishop Jacques Rouchouse of Chengdu (1924–1948). More than two decades earlier, he had expressed a keen interest in having Trappists in his diocese, which was located in the southern province of Sichuan. The positive response of the elderly bishop of the Paris Foreign Missions Society came without delay: "I welcome you to my diocese. The house, prepared twenty-six years ago, is still there kept for you, as well as the land, about two hundred acres. Everything is ready for your accommodation."[107]

Heartened by these words of welcome, the community decided to send two "precursors," Fr. Victor Zhu, treasurer, and Fr. Jean-Marie Struyven, a Belgian, to Sichuan to see the place and prepare for the reception of the refugees.

In September many of the community traveled by plane to Peking, where they stayed for a few days with the Benedictines. They then proceeded to the port of Tianjin and sailed to Shanghai. From there they took a boat on the Yangzi River to Chongqing, the capital of Sichuan, and on 22 October they made their way to Chengdu. Three days later, on 25 October 1947, they finally arrived at the house in Weijiahexin that had been offered them by the bishop. It was located about twenty kilometers from the city, near the village of Nibatuo, in the district of Xindu.[108]

The house and the fields were surrounded by rivers that formed a natural enclosure around the monastery. Thanks to the presence of plentiful water, the land was suitable for the cultivation of rice,

[106] Ibid., 42.
[107] Ibid., 12. Two hundred acres corresponds to around eighty hectares.
[108] Consult the map and the many photos of the place contained in Ren Dayi, *Shengmu shenleyuan*, 89–97.

vegetables, and bamboo. In the year they settled there, a Benedictine wrote: "Really, the Trappist farmers could not have chosen a better place."[109] However, the climate, mild in the winter but like a sauna in the summer, initially proved unbearable to this group of Chinese from the North, who were not accustomed to such humidity. The above-mentioned Benedictine, a member of the Xishan community, which had recently taken refuge in Chengdu, who wrote an account of his visit to the Trappist community of Nibatuo in 1948, expressed great joy at the presence of these brother monks and admiration for their "regular" life.

> The Benedictines are happy to have at their side their Cistercian brothers. . . . A visitor who knows our European Trappist monasteries, transported suddenly to Gnipato [Nibatuo], would certainly say: "I am here in a Trappist monastery!" Undoubtedly, it is a matter of the atmosphere of a Cistercian monastery, of a regular life with its rhythm of prayer and work, the alternation of which maintains the equilibrium of body and spirit and supports the continual union of the soul with God. . . . Work in the fields alternates with sung Mass and the Divine Office, with spiritual reading and meals, with conferences or courses of philosophy and theology for the clerics. In fact, the community consists of eight priests, four theologians, two philosophers, a novice of Sichuan, and twenty-two lay brothers, of whom two are novices.[110]

He noted, however, that not all the monks who had been driven from Zhengding immediately reached the South. The last three monks who were preparing to leave Peking, after a short stay in Shijiazhuang, were detained for a few more weeks because of an unexpected development: the arrival of six confreres from Yangjiaping who had just been released from prison. After making arrangements for the lodging of his confreres in Peking, Prior Paulinus was able to rejoin his community in Sichuan, leaving Fr. Stanislaus Ren to run the dairy. In 1948 he too was able to make his way to the South, having handed over his position to Fr. Jean-Marie Struyven. The exiled community of Our Lady of Joy was thus finally complete, now

---

[109] Raphaël Vinciarelli, "Les trappistes de Gni-pa-to," CSA 19 (1949): 17.
[110] Ibid., 18–20.

comprising forty-nine members. Having found refuge in southern China, it was finally able to live a peaceful, joyful, and happy monastic life.

Dispersion and "Vagrancy"

The political events that followed, however, did not allow the community to continue to live in this relative tranquility. The Communist forces, having taken over all the northern and central regions of China, headed south in 1949, making the communities in Sichuan fear for the worst. Prior Paulinus and his confreres once again had to start looking for escape routes. It now becomes even more difficult to follow the movements of the Trappist community during the following months, between mid-1949 and 1951, when the first group reached the island of Lantau, Hong Kong, than it has been up to this point, because the community split up into different groups and only came together again in Hong Kong in 1953. What follows is a very sketchy summary of their peregrinations.

Nine monks stayed on in Zhengding, some at the monastery, now transformed into a government farm, others in St. Benedict village. One of these nine was Hilary Shen, who died in 1958 and was briefly referred to in the journal of the Trappist Order: "Our dear Fr. Hilary, so attached 'to the rule and to the place' that he never wanted to leave Chengtingfu [Zhengdingfu], at the arrival of the Reds went about the streets wearing the habit of lay brothers and a large crucifix on his breast. He even made a hat with this writing: 'Brave soldier of Christ.' They took him for a madman. Mad with the folly of the cross."[111]

Twelve monks remained in Nibatuo (Sichuan) after the confiscation of the monastery, living in extreme poverty.[112] Among them were the first two martyrs of the Trappist community of Our Lady of Joy. One of them, Vincent Shi (1904–1951) from Shijiazhuang

---

[111] Cf. Beltrame Quattrocchi, *Monaci nella tormenta*, 278.

[112] The journal *Collectanea Ordinis Cisterciensium Reformatorum* reports that because of extreme poverty four lay brothers were forced to leave their dwelling in Nibatuo. They returned to their families in 1953. Two priests, a choir monk, and two lay brothers stayed behind. Cf. COCR 16 (1954): 229–30.

(Hebei), had entered the monastery of Our Lady of Consolation in Yangjiaping in 1926, was ordained priest in 1937, and then transferred to Our Lady of Joy, where he held the positions of guest master, novice master, and subprior. Subjected to terrible torture to induce him to deny his faith in God, Fr. Vincent died in prison on 7 August 1951.[113] The Chinese Benedictine Pierre Zhou Bangjiu described the last hours of Fr. Vincent:

> Fr. She [Shi], subprior of the Trappist monastery of Our Lady of Joy at Nibatuo, near the village of Tianhui, Sichuan Province, was incarcerated in spring 1951 after being accused of irresponsibility in paying the grain tax for the monastery farmlands, a sum of money too huge to pay. He was also blamed for refusing to hand over firearms allegedly hidden in the monastery. When he held firmly to the truth during study sessions of prisoners in the Chengdu Prison that man was created by God, and when he bravely recited the Creed in public, he was severely criticized, beaten and handcuffed. On August 7, 1951, shortly after many tortures, he heroically sacrificed his life in witness of the true faith.[114]

The second martyr was Albert Wei, who was accused of antirevolutionary crimes because of his leading role in the Legion of Mary.[115] During his eight months in prison he was tortured and

---

[113] The most detailed account of the martyrdom of Vincent Shi is found in a letter of 16 August 1952 from Br. Xavier Sun, published in Beltrame Quattrocchi, *Monaci nella tormenta*, 297–301. News of his heroic death was also reported by the *China Missionary Bulletin* 4 (1952): 230.

[114] Peter Zhou Bangjiu, *Dawn Breaks in the East: One Spiritual Warrior's Thirty-Three Year Struggle in Defense of the Church* (Upland, CA: Serenity, 1992), 10.

[115] The Legion of Mary, founded by Frank Duff in Ireland, was introduced into the Diocese of Hanyang (Hubei) in the late 1930s by an Irish priest, Fr. W. Aedan McGrath. The Legion was guided by a set of strict rules that described its function as "sanctification of its members through prayer and active co-operation under the leadership of the church in the work of Mary and the church to trample the head of the serpent and advance the reign of Christ." Invited by the internuncio Riberi in 1948, the Legion grew rapidly under the guidance of Fr. McGrath, and many groups, called *praesidia*, were established in Chinese cities. After the Communist takeover in 1949, the work of the Legion became increasingly important in the face of growing persecution of the church. When the movements and activities of foreign and Chinese religious began to be restricted, and especially when missionaries began to be expelled from China, it fell to the legionaries to carry out the work of catechesis, visit the sick, and perform other services previously performed by priests and nuns.

then, on the point of death, turned over to his confreres. He died in the monastery on 27 November 1951.[116]

Seven monks from Sichuan moved immediately to Peking. Ten monks went to Hong Kong and then to Canada, where they lived for three years at the Trappist monastery of Our Lady of the Prairies. Fourteen monks, divided into several groups, wandered from southern to northern China, from Sichuan to Canton, and from there to Peking, and then again from the North to the South, from Peking to Canton.[117] Eight of them found a way to reach Hong Kong where, together with two monks who already lived there and Prior Paulinus, they began to rebuild the community on the island of Lantau. Some of the Chinese brothers returned to live with their families.[118]

Reunification and Installation in Hong Kong

In the mid-1950s both the government and the bishop of Hong Kong expressed willingness to accept the refugee monks and to provide them with the land they needed.[119] Bishop Enrico Valtorta had

---

In many places the Legion became especially important in holding together the Catholic community. For these reasons, and especially because of the influence that the Legion exercised on young Catholics, it became the target of perhaps the most ruthless attacks organized by the government against the Catholic Church. Cf. James T. Myers, *Enemies Without Guns: The Catholic Church in the People's Republic of China* (New York: Paragon House, 1991), 98–103.

[116] News of the two deaths was also given in 1952 in *Collectanea Ordinis Cisterciensium Reformatorum*. Cf. COCR 14 (1952): 301–4.

[117] Stanislaus Jen (Ren Dayi) reported how much the monks suffered because of the sudden changes and contradictory decisions of superiors regarding their destination. "They had passed through a difficult and dangerous journey to Canton, then back to Peking, and just settled down, when they had to leave again. This contradictory order made them suffer and did not help them. The double-edged sword separated not only their bodies, but also their hearts. It was tragic and sad. It would be hard to heal in the future. The superiors concerned did not know the situation and the sufferings of the community in such circumstances. They did not realize they were giving such an unwise order." Ren Dayi, *Shengmu shenleyuan*, 27.

[118] The details of their adventures can be read in Ren Dayi, *Shengmu shenleyuan*, 16–32.

[119] The history to 1978 of Our Lady of Joy in Hong Kong, together with many photos, is recounted by Ren Dayi in *Shengmu shenleyuan*, 33–42. A summary of the community's experiences up to the present day is given by Ng Ka Chai, "Pax Intrantibus: The Cistercian Monks and Monastery," in *History of the Catholic Religious*

already indicated in the 1940s that he would like a Trappist monastic presence in his diocese and had taken steps to bring this about. A first attempt came to naught, however. A 1946 letter from the abbot of Our Lady of Gethsemani (Kentucky, United States) declined the invitation of Bishop Valtorta to found a monastery in Hong Kong.[120]

In April 1951, after living for several months in a house made available by the Little Sisters of the Poor in Ngau Chi Wan (Niuchiwan), eleven Trappists landed on the deserted island of Lantau (Lantou, Lantao), the ancient name of the island that today is called Dayushan. Here they immediately began working to make the site habitable. First of all, they cleared paths and then built a wooden shelter divided into four rooms: chapel, refectory, dormitory, and space for the workers who helped them with the construction. When that was finished, they built a masonry building with eight rooms: two for the chapel, two for the scriptorium, three for the dormitory, and one for guests; it was completed in early 1952. The new abbot general of the Trappist Order, Dom Gabriel Sortais, came to Hong Kong that same year and encouraged the community to continue its work. In June two Chinese monks were recalled from Canada to reinforce the community, but one died of malaria shortly after his arrival.

Thanks to the support of many Catholics in Hong Kong and benefactors from abroad, several other works were completed in the following years, including farm buildings, the monastic residence, and, in 1954, a building for guests, described by Prior Paulinus Lee as "a project for the benefit . . . of future generations of Catholics in Hong Kong."[121] The most significant event was the completion of the church, on which work had begun in February 1955. The official opening ceremony of the monastery on 19 February 1956 took place

---

Orders and Missionary Congregations in Hong Kong, vol. 2: *Research Papers*, ed. Louis Ha and Patrick Taveirne (Hong Kong: Centre for Catholic Studies, Chinese University of Hong Kong, 2009), 700–739. See also *The Ninth Centenary of Foundation of Cîteaux and the Seventieth Anniversary of Foundation of the Monastery of Our Lady of Joy* (Hong Kong: n.p., 1999).

[120] Cf. the letter of the abbot of Our Lady of Gethsemani to Enrico Valtorta, 4 November 1946 (Diocesan Archives of Hong Kong).

[121] An unsigned open letter written in 1952, probably by Paulinus Lee (Diocesan Archives of Hong Kong).

in the presence of the abbot general, Gabriel Sortais, who read the indult issued by Pius XII for the canonical establishment of a Trappist monastery in the Diocese of Hong Kong.

Over time, the Trappist community became a reference point for the spiritual needs of the local Christian community, to which the monastic community became ever closer in the years following. The Trappists remained a spiritual point of reference for many, exercising a ministry that is properly monastic: organizing retreats and seminars, offering spiritual direction, and publishing books and articles on spirituality in Chinese.[122] The hope of welcoming local vocations was supported by several initiatives of the prior, who, in an open letter in 1959, expressed the desire soon to receive aspirants from among the young people of Hong Kong. "I know that our hope for the future depends most of all on our local youth. I note that even in the materialistic city of Hong Kong we can find some souls in search of perfection in the contemplative life and who do not fear the austerities of our life."[123]

He was not as optimistic a few years later. As he was leaving the office of prior, he wrote: "I am not as enthusiastic as I used to be when, as a young man, I encouraged young people to enter the Cistercian Order; I have seen too many failures."[124]

If the decade of the 1950s was the period of the founding of the Trappist community in Hong Kong, the 1960s and 1970s were the time of consolidation and transformation. The *aggiornamento* of the church called for by the Second Vatican Council (1962–1965) affirmed the deliberations of the 1959 general chapter of the Trappist Order, which called for a partial rethinking of the lifestyle of Trappist communities throughout the world. It invited communities to adapt themselves to the local social and cultural context in order to be better able to meet the spiritual needs of contemporary men and women.[125]

---

[122] Among the Trappists of Hong Kong, Stanislaus Jen (Ren Dayi) was the most prolific author. He published three volumes on the history of the Trappist monks in China and translated several books on Cistercian history and monastic tradition, as well as some works by ancient monastic authors, primarily St. Bernard. Cf. Ng Ka Chai, "Pax Intrantibus," 727–31.

[123] Open letter of Paulinus Lee, 17 February 1959 (Diocesan Archives of Hong Kong).

[124] Letter of Paulinus Lee to friends, 1965 (Diocesan Archives of Hong Kong).

[125] Cf. M. Basil Pennington, *The Cistercians* (Collegeville, MN: Liturgical Press, 1992), 61–64, 70–74; M. Basil Pennington, "Cistercians," in *A Dictionary of Asian*

Given the difficulties that the Trappist monastery of Sept-Fons had expressed about making regular visits to China, in 1960 the Trappist monastery of Our Lady of New Clairvaux (California, United States) became the new mother house of the Trappist monastery in Hong Kong. To strengthen the community, New Clairvaux sent four volunteer monks from the Trappist monasteries of New Clairvaux, Guadalupe, and Gethsemani to Lantau, raising the number of that community to twenty-two members and renewing its vitality. Larger numbers made possible a gradual replacement of the Latin liturgy with a newly created Chinese Liturgy of the Hours, as well as a significant expansion of the farm.

In the late 1960s the Trappists of Hong Kong began the arduous work of inculturating the liturgy by adding some liturgical texts in Chinese. Some were taken from the Breviary (*Suoben rike jing* 縮本日課經), translated by the Franciscan Antoninus Lee (Li Shiyu) for the Carmelites of Taiwan in 1969, and others were added. The musical settings were mainly the work of one of the monks, Clemens Kong (Jiang Keman), who arranged some Gregorian melodies and composed new tunes that were suitable for the texts recently translated into Chinese for the Liturgy of the Hours.[126]

In 1965, upon the resignation of Paulinus Lee, Simon Chang (Zhang Ximo) was elected prior; he remained in office until 1974. Benedict Chao (Zhao Bendu) was then chosen as prior; and he led the community until 1998. Although the community failed to attract many young recruits from Hong Kong, some older priests who were retiring from active ministry entered. In recent years some young men from mainland China have joined the community of Hong Kong, though they had to overcome many obstacles to do so.[127]

In 1986 the abbey founded the small priory of the Holy Mother of God in Shuili, district of Nantou, Taiwan. In 1998, the seventieth anniversary of the founding of the Trappist monastery of Our Lady of Joy in Zhengding on the mainland, Maurus Pei (Pei Maolu)

Christianity, ed. Scott W. Sunquist (Grand Rapids, MI/Cambridge, UK: Eerdmans, 2001), 180–82.

[126] Cf. Ng Ka Chai, "Pax Intrantibus," 720–27.

[127] In 2010 the community numbered seventeen monks (nine priests and eight brothers). Cf. "I trappisti di Hong Kong festeggiano, dopo tanti anni, i voti perpetui di due monaci," a notice published by the news agency Fides on 4 February 2010.

was elected superior of the community. A year after celebrating this important anniversary and electing a new superior, the joy of the community was further enhanced by the elevation of the priory to an abbey on 5 September 1999.[128] On the same day Clemens Kong was elected first abbot of the Trappist monastery of Our Lady of Joy in Lantau, Hong Kong, and received the abbatial blessing on 15 January 2000. Four years later his deteriorating health forced him to resign, and the young Anastasius Lee (Li Daxiu) was elected abbot and blessed on 22 January 2005. Since 2011 the community of around fifteen monks has had Paul Kao (Gao Hao) as its new superior *ad nutum*.

The Trappist monks in Hong Kong continue to be faithful followers of the monastic way of life in China, the intention they already expressed at the time of their installation on Lantau: "We are aware of our responsibility to fulfill our *pensum servitutis*, because we represent the existence of Cistercian life in China."[129] Since Christian monastic life is still outlawed in the People's Republic of China, they are also the visible representatives of those monastic communities that, in the face of great difficulty, are forced to live clandestinely in order to remain faithful to their vocation.

In mid-2009 a small group of nuns from the Trappist Abbey of Gedono in Indonesia began preparing to found a monastery in Macau, which will be located on the island of Coloane, at the gates of greater China.[130]

[128] To be made an abbey, a monastery needs to have more than twenty professed monks and to be able to support itself.

[129] Cited in Beltrame Quattrocchi, *Monaci nella tormenta*, 274.

[130] Cf. the news reported by UCANews, 19 January 2010, and by *Églises d'Asie* 522 (2010): 5–6.

Yangjiaping. The Trappist monastery of Our Lady of Consolation in its early years.
Undated photo, probably taken in the 1890s.

Yangjiaping, 1890.
The Trappist community of Our Lady of Consolation.

Yangjiaping, 1904 (?).
The priests and Chinese brothers of the Trappist community of Our Lady of
Consolation.

Yangjiaping, 1912.
The Trappist community of Our Lady of Consolation. The photo was taken on the
occasion of the visit of Edmond Obrecht, abbot of Our Lady of Gethsemani, United
States. He is shown in the center, alongside Maur Veychard, second abbot
of Yangjiaping.

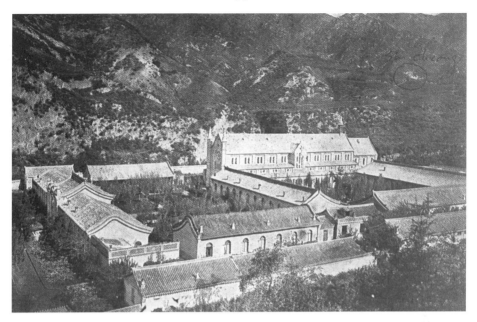

Yangjiaping, Trappist Abbey of Our Lady of Consolation. The abbatial church, constructed in 1904, is prominent. On the right, the Xinzhuang grange can be seen on the slope of the mountain. Undated photo, probably taken in the 1920s.

Yangjiaping, 1929. The Trappist community of Our Lady of Consolation. The photo was taken on the occasion of the second visit of Abbot Jean-Baptiste Chautard, the father immediate of Our Lady of Consolation.

Yangjiaping, 1930. The Trappist Abbey of Our Lady of Consolation after new buildings were added.

Yangjiaping, 1933. Chinese monks at work in the Trappist Abbey of Our Lady of Consolation.

Peking, house of the Benedictines, October 1947. The first group of monks of the Trappist Abbey of Our Lady of Consolation, having survived persecution and then been released from prison, at their meeting with Paulinus Lee, prior of Our Lady of Joy, and some other monks of that community.

Zhengding, 1930.
The Trappist monastery of Our Lady of Joy. The chapel with a small belfry is visible on the right.

Peking, September 1947. The forty monks of the community of Our Lady of Joy in the capital, where they have taken refuge.

Nibatuo. The monastery where the community of Our Lady of Joy took refuge. Undated photo, taken between 1948 and 1950.

Zhengding, 1942 (?).
Paulinus Lee, prior of Our Lady of
Joy (center) with three brothers.

Nibatuo. Monks of the community of Our
Lady of Joy at work in the monastery where
they had taken refuge. Undated photo,
taken between 1948 and 1950.

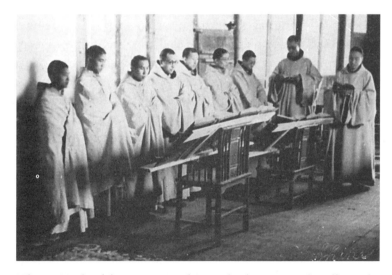

Nibatuo. Monks of the community of Our Lady of Joy singing the Office in the
monastery where they had taken refuge. Note the makeshift lecterns for the
choir books. Undated photo, taken between 1948 and 1950.

Chapter 4

The Benedictines

During the third decade of the twentieth century, three different congregations of Benedictine monks (the American Cassinese Congregation, the Belgian Congregation of the Annunciation, and the German Congregation of Saint Ottilien) and two different families of Benedictine nuns (the American Benedictine sisters and the Swiss Olivetan Benedictine sisters) made monastic foundations in China. Different "styles" of monastic presence, different forms of ministry, and different geographical areas characterized the monastic mission of the followers of St. Benedict in China, where their order is known as the "Order of Benedict" (*Benduhui* 本篤會).[1]

As the following pages will show, each of these Benedictine congregations responded to the "Chinese challenge" according to its peculiar form of mission, but all sowed the seeds of Christian monastic life on Chinese soil with courage and determination. Violently wiped out a few decades after being sown, the plants that grew during that time have nevertheless continued to produce fruit. Although Chinese fields could no longer be sown with the seeds of Benedictine monastic life after 1949, Benedictine monasticism had taken root in China. From the 1990s onward, various congregations of the Benedictine and Trappist orders have not ceased to till the field they have loved so much, implementing different kinds of projects and

[1] An informative overview of the Benedictine mission in China is given by Jeremias Schröder, "The Benedictines in China," *AIM Bulletin* 98 (2010): 15–28; repr. in *Courrier Verbiest* 28 (December 2010): 15–17. See also "I benedettini in Cina," *San Benedetto* 4 (1997): 34–38.

offering partnerships in support of the church in China.[2] In 1996 a special Benedictine China Commission was established to help coordinate and implement the different contributions of those who, within the Benedictine world, continue to give concrete expressions of their love for the Chinese church.[3]

The Difficult Mission of American Benedictine Men and Women

Interest in China by St. Vincent's Archabbey (Latrobe, Pennsylvania), the first Benedictine monastery in the United States, dates back to the early twentieth century. Missionaries returning from China visited the monastery, and their stories and exhortations moved some of the novices as well as some students in the seminary attached to the abbey to volunteer as missionaries to China.[4] It was only in 1920, however, that direct contact regarding a mission in China was made, by the visit to that country of George Barry O'Toole, a diocesan priest and Benedictine oblate, who in 1917 became professor of philosophy at the seminary run by the abbey.

During a visit to Peking in October 1920, O'Toole met Vincent Ying Lianzhi (1866–1926), a prominent Catholic intellectual who

---

[2] Cf. Notker Wolf, "An Experience of Cooperation with Chinese Church Institutions," in *Papers and Materials of the European Catholic China Meeting "Prospects of Catholic Cooperation with China in the Present International Context" (Verona, December 12–14, 1992)*, ed. China-Zentrum (Sankt Augustin: China-Zentrum, 1994), 84–87; Notker Wolf, "Mission als Partnerschaft. Die Mitwirkung der Benedektinerkongregation von St. Ottilien in der Diözese Jilin," in *"Fallbeispiel" China. Ökumenische Beiträge zu Religion, Theologie und Kirche im chinesischen Kontext*, ed. Roman Malek (Sankt Augustin: China-Zentrum / Nettetal: Steyler, 1996), 665–76; Notker Wolf, "In Geduld Ängste abbauen—Das Engagement der Benedektiner in heutigen China," *Forum Weltkirche* 1 (2003): 20–23; Joseph Wong, "Teaching in China," *AIM Bulletin* 70 (2000): 107–9.

[3] Cf. Nicholas Koss, "The Benedictine Commission for China," *AIM Bulletin* 70 (2000): 101–4.

[4] A well-documented presentation of the mission of St. Vincent's Archabbey is given by Jerome Oetgen, *Mission to America: A History of Saint Vincent Archabbey, the First Benedictine Monastery in the United States* (Washington, DC: The Catholic University of America Press, 2000), 281–331 (chap. 6: "Mission to China [1918–1930]"), and 332–406 (chap. 7: "Depression and Judgment [1930–1940]"). Unless otherwise indicated, the material presented here is taken from this source.

for some years had been trying to find a way to establish a Catholic university in Peking. Already in 1913 he had founded the Academy of Chinese Studies "Furen she" 輔仁社 in Peking, with the aim of forming a group of young and well-educated Catholic intellectuals. For lack of funds, however, the academy had to suspend its operations in 1918.[5] Vincent Ying presented his plan to Fr. O'Toole, asking for the support and collaboration of the American Benedictines. A few years later, when he became rector of the newly formed Catholic University in Peking, he formally expressed what his intuition had been: "The zeal and energy of the American Benedictines . . . may renew in the East the former glories of the monks of the West, becoming the builders of New China even as the monks of a thousand years ago were the builders of modern Europe."[6]

Passing through Europe on his way back to America, O'Toole presented the proposal to Abbot Primate Fidelis von Stotzingen and Pope Benedict XV, both of whom encouraged him. Once back in the United States, however, he was not met with the same enthusiasm from either the abbot president of the American Cassinese Congregation, Ernest Helmstetter, or by the abbot of St. Vincent, Aurelius Stehle (1877–1930).

Soon, however, they were urged to take charge of the enterprise by the Congregation of Propaganda Fide, which, first through its secretary, Archbishop Pietro Fumasoni Biondi, and then through its prefect, Cardinal Willem Van Rossum, contacted von Stotzingen, Helmstetter, and Stehle, pressing them to respond positively to the request of the Holy See. In a letter that Cardinal Van Rossum sent to Archabbot Stehle in June 1922 he explained why the Holy See chose to ask the Benedictines to found a Catholic university in Peking. The disintegration and weakening of Chinese culture following the collapse of the empire, he wrote, was very similar to the situation of the Roman Empire in the dark ages. At that time Benedictine

[5] Cf. Donald Paragon, "Ying Lien-chih (1866–1926) and the Rise of Fu Jen, The Catholic University of Peking," *Monumenta Serica* 20 (1961): 165–225; "The MacManus Academy of Chinese Study," BCUP 1 (1926): 40; "Chronicle of Events Connected with the Origin of the Catholic University of Peking," BCUP 1 (1926): 63.

[6] George Barry O'Toole, "The Spiritual Lineage of the Catholic University of Peking," BCUP 1 (1926): 22.

monks were able to preserve Christian faith and classical culture, thus bringing about a renaissance of European culture. The Holy See therefore believed that the Benedictines were in the best position to establish and administer a high-level intellectual and educational apostolate in China. "It is the most intense desire of this Sacred Congregation of the Propaganda that the Order of Saint Benedict, which during the Middle Ages saved Latin and Greek literature from certain destruction, should found in the city of Peking an institute of higher Chinese studies as the most apt means of fostering a more vigorous growth of our Holy Religion in the vast territory of China."[7] Pope Pius XI personally offered further encouragement when at the beginning of 1923 he donated money to start a foundation in China.[8]

When the general chapter of the American Cassinese Congregation met in August 1923, it could hardly say no to the Holy See, which had so insisted on the project. At the same time, many expressed reservations because of the enormity of the challenge. The chapter entrusted the project to St. Vincent's Abbey, "with the promise of support, both moral and physical, on the part of all the other abbeys of the congregation."[9] A few weeks later Abbot Stehle presented the project to the chapter of St. Vincent's Abbey, explaining that although he was at first reluctant to take charge of the enterprise, he now thought that the community was obliged to accept it, not only because the Congregation of Propaganda Fide had requested it, but also because the other abbots of the American Cassinese Congregation trusted in the ability of St. Vincent to respond to a proposal that came from the pope himself. After a heated debate, the chapter voted by a very small margin to "accede to the request of the Roman authorities to establish a foundation in Peking, China."[10]

In response to the direct request of the Holy See, Abbot Stehle chose the first two candidates to be sent to China: Fr. Ildephonse

---

[7] Letter of W. Van Rossum to E. Helmstetter, 22 June 1922, cited in BCUP 1 (1926): 17.

[8] Cf. "Chronicle of Events," 64.

[9] Ibid.

[10] Minutes of the chapter of 5 October 1923, cited in Oetgen, *Mission to America*, 287. Word of this decision was quickly picked up in China. Cf. "Bendu huishi yu gaihua huaren" [Benedictine monks want to convert the Chinese], SB 8 (1924): 248–49.

Brandstetter, subprior, and Fr. Placidus Rattenberger, both of German origin. "To them has been commissioned the difficult and laborious, yet, withal, glorious task of being the pioneers of Benedictine life in China."[11] In his speech on the day of their departure, 10 June 1924, the abbot offered his encouragement, asked for prayers for the success of the undertaking, and expressed his personal hope that the new foundation of St. Vincent would generate numerous vocations for the Benedictine Order. Once in Peking, the two monks were guests for six months at the residence of the apostolic delegate, Archbishop Celso Costantini, who advised them to move with caution.

The Foundation of the Catholic University of Peking

Meanwhile the Holy See had issued a double rescript, dated 27 June 1924, that established the Catholic University of Peking as a pontifical university and gave full powers to the archabbot of St. Vincent to appoint professors and to organize the academic life of the institution, and that allowed the Benedictines to erect a public oratory within the university and gave them pastoral rights for English-speaking Catholics in Peking.[12]

In October of that year Abbot Stehle issued a "call to arms" to the abbots and monks of the American Cassinese Congregation. He confessed that it was impossible to carry out the mission to China, which, according to the Holy See, was a "great work" (*magnum opus*) and "undoubtedly difficult" (*sane difficile*), with the resources of his community alone, even though it was the largest and most prosperous, and asked for the cooperation of the other eleven monasteries of the congregation. The cooperation he sought for the intellectual task entrusted to St. Vincent was financial support and volunteers for the mission in China, if possible "young and educated volunteers." An arduous task lay ahead, but the abbot concluded his appeal with an expression of hope:

> Solemn and momentous is the charge, which the Holy See has confided to our congregation and to Saint Vincent Archabbey.

---

[11] *Saint Vincent College Journal* 33 (1923–1924): 313. Cited in Oetgen, *Mission to America*, 287.

[12] Cf. "Chronicle of Events," 65.

Rome bids us to do for China what the first members of our order did for Europe during the Middle Ages. This means that we must *preserve* and *christianize* Chinese literature, art, and philosophy. This means that we must place before the eyes of the Chinese people an ideal exemplar of truly Christian civilization. The monks of Saint Vincent will do their best to prove worthy of this trust, and in their effort to do so, they are consoled and heartened by the encouraging pledge of the general chapter: *"Ceteris monasteriis nostrae congregationis pro viribus co-operantibus."*[13]

In January 1925 Abbot Stehle appointed George Barry O'Toole as rector of the newly established Catholic university and a month later accompanied him to China. In Peking he authorized the purchase of the palace that had belonged to Prince Tao Beile and its adjacent properties, located a short distance from the headquarters of the apostolic delegation, as the site of the future university. In a short time the work of restoring and adapting the premises began. "All the buildings of the former palace have been renovated. Chinese artists were engaged to restore the various structures to their original splendor. The result has exceeded expectations. Those who visit the place are invariably captivated by its beauty, and carry away with them a never-to-be-forgotten impression of the artistic genius of the Chinese people."[14]

Meanwhile, Fr. O'Toole was organizing the structure and academic programs of the nascent university. The first item on the agenda was the reopening of "Furen she," the Academy of Chinese Studies founded a few years earlier by Vincent Ying, as the initial nucleus of the Catholic university. To solve the financial problems that had been the cause of its closure in 1918, O'Toole turned to an American benefactor, Theodore MacManus. O'Toole appointed Vincent Ying dean of the academy and involved some prominent Chinese intellectuals as teachers.[15] The aims of the academy are expressed in a

---

[13] "With the cooperation of the other monasteries of our congregation." "Archabbot Aurelius Stehle to the Monks of the American Cassinese Congregation on the Founding of the Catholic University of Peking. October 5, 1924," in Oetgen, *Mission to America*, 536 (emphasis added).

[14] "Buildings and Grounds," BCUP 1 (1926): 12.

[15] An introduction to them can be found in "The MacManus Academy of Chinese Study," 45–49.

letter Vincent Ying sent to the vicars apostolic and to the clergy of
the church in China on 17 August 1925:

> 1. To preserve and elevate the religious sentiments and Catholic
> ideals of the students.
>
> 2. To provide for their intellectual improvement and perfection
> through the medium of literary studies and pursuits.
>
> 3. To impart to them a liberal education in useful knowledge,
> including the canons of good breeding and Chinese etiquette.[16]

On 1 October 1925 "Furen she," that is, the MacManus Academy
of Chinese Studies at the Catholic University of Peking, was inaugurated to prepare young Catholic students for Chinese studies at
the university level. Twenty-three students, mostly Catholics, were
accepted on the basis of merit. Despite the untimely death of Vincent
Ying in January 1926, the academy was soon on a solid footing with
a well-stocked library and also an office for translating and publishing
short but significant works of various kinds.[17]

The establishment of the MacManus Academy of Chinese Studies
was the Benedictines' first step toward the creation of a full Catholic
university in China. The project was ambitious, but clearly conceived, as demonstrated by the name chosen for the university and
its appropriate translation into Chinese (*Beijing Gongjiao daxue* 北
京公教大學). By choosing the term *Gongjiao* (literally, "universal
teaching") to translate the adjective "Catholic," Vincent Ying wished
to echo the idea of the chancellor of the university, Abbot Stehle, who
was "determined that everything connected with the new institution
should give expression to the universalism of the Catholic ideal."[18]

> The monks of Saint Benedict were to function as disinterested
> administrators of an educational institution dedicated wholly
> and exclusively to the service of the Catholic missions in China.
> Instead of reserving for their own the prerogative of teaching,

[16] Ibid., 41.

[17] Cf. Francis Clougherty, "The Publications of the Catholic University of Peking,"
BCUP 6 (1929): 67–91.

[18] "'Pei-ching Kung Chiao Ta Hsüeh'. The Chinese Name of the Catholic University of Peking," BCUP 1 (1926): 7.

they would associate with themselves in this office not only their European confreres but also members of the secular clergy and of other religious orders, as well as prominent Chinese literateurs and scholars from among the laity. . . . They would do all in their power to hasten the day when both the university and their own community in China would become indigenous institutions. . . . They would welcome the day when the Catholic religion would cease to be an exotic plant in Chinese soil, and when they themselves might be able to hand over to native successors the task of continuing in China the educational mission recently confided to them by the Holy See.[19]

This expression of the Catholicity of the church was also what Rome wanted of a Benedictine institution in China: "In the coming of the Benedictine fathers from America to teach sacred and profane studies to the inhabitants of China, it will once more be made manifest that the Catholic Church knows no territorial or national limits, and is universal not only in name but in very truth."[20]

The university, as it was conceived in the initial academic prospectus, was "not intended to be primarily a professional school, but rather . . . to lay special emphasis on general culture and learning."[21] As a missionary in China in those years wrote, "The future Catholic University of Peking should aim first of all to furnish what China lacks most: leaders"[22] able to assume positions of responsibility in Chinese society. At the heart of the university was the faculty of Chinese studies, which gave the institution "a national Chinese character."[23] Its dean was Chen Yuan, a renowned historian and former deputy minister of education. The project involved the establishment of five university faculties (theology, philosophy, arts and letters, sciences, and Chinese studies), various departments, and two secondary schools (a Chinese preparatory school and a general

---

[19] Ibid.

[20] W. Van Rossum, protocol dated 18 June 1924, in which the prefect of Propaganda Fide recommends the foundation of the Benedictines in Peking to the generosity of the bishops and the faithful, especially those in America. In BCUP 1 (1926): 7.

[21] "A General Prospectus of the Institution," BCUP 1 (1926): 13.

[22] "The Catholic University of Peking," BCUP 2 (1927): 31–32.

[23] "A General Prospectus of the Institution," 13.

preparatory school).[24] Some courses were taught in Chinese, which was not the case in other institutions of higher education run by missionaries in China. Jehan Joliet, a Benedictine who taught French at the Catholic University of Peking for a short time in 1927 before going to Sichuan, where he founded a Chinese-style Benedictine monastery, emphasized this: "If Catholics do not furnish the Chinese with a complete education in their language and adapted to their mentality, others are working on this and will do it against the church and to China's misfortune. . . . How wonderful it is to imagine young Chinese discussing in Chinese the great questions of Catholic philosophy and theology!"[25]

The university soon became known as Furen University, taking the same name as the preparatory school. After gaining accreditation from the Chinese government in 1927, it was able to begin its third academic year with an increase in students (155, of whom sixty were Catholics) and professors (twelve of whom were Chinese laymen and eleven American and European priests). The numbers grew in the 1928 academic year, when there were 190 students and two new American professors, a Benedictine priest and a Passionist priest. It soon became clear that the university would need more space to accommodate its growing student body.

For this expansion, property adjacent to the university was purchased, and the prior, Ildephonse Brandstetter, commissioned the construction of a new university complex in Chinese style that would include a library, an auditorium, classrooms, laboratories, offices, and dormitories to accommodate four hundred students. The buildings were designed by Fr. Adalbert Gresnigt, a Belgian Benedictine monk from Maredsous who belonged to the Beuronese architectural school.

---

[24] See also the summaries given in Hubert Vanderhoven, "L'Université Catholique Chinoise de Péking," BM 8 (1926–1927): 174–79; Hubert Vanderhoven, "L'Université Catholique de Péking," BM 8 (1926–1927): 207–12; Wu Xiaoxin, "A Case Study of the Catholic University of Peking during the Benedictine Period (1927–1933)" (PhD diss., University of San Francisco, 1993); John Chen Shujie, *The Rise and Fall of the Fu Ren University, Beijing; Catholic Higher Education in China* (New York: Routledge, 2004).

[25] Jehan Joliet, "L'avenir du haut enseignement catholique en Chine," BM 9 (1928–1929): 38.

He arrived in China the previous year at the request of Celso Costantini, who intended to commission him to design several Catholic churches and schools in the Chinese style, thus making him an early contributor to the "Sino-Christian" architectural style so desired by the apostolic delegate.[26] His plans for the Catholic University of Peking embodied "the characteristic spirit of Benedictinism, inasmuch as it reconciles the old with the new, adapting the traditional Chinese forms to the needs of modern school architecture."[27] The plans were already completed in March 1929, and construction began in September. Two months later, on 13 November, Archbishop Costantini, in the presence of Chinese education officials and members of the Catholic hierarchy in China, presided over the laying of the foundation stone and delivered a speech that expressed appreciation for the work of the Benedictines in Peking.[28] The completed university complex now offered "visible proof . . . that its mission is to idealize and purify what is already dear to them [i.e., the Chinese students], and not to deaden their taste for the culture of their native land by overemphasizing that of other countries."[29]

In the same year, 1929, the Holy See authorized St. Vincent's Archabbey to establish a faculty of theology and philosophy at the university to prepare Chinese students for the priesthood. In a brief of 29 August 1929, addressed to the abbot of Saint Vincent, Pius XI entrusted this new mission to the Benedictines, praising them for "not only how much . . . they have achieved in so short a time, but also how much in the near and distant future they are prepared to accomplish for the glory of God and the welfare of the Chinese people."[30]

In spite of difficult relations with the Chinese Ministry of Education, the academic year 1929–1930 saw a further increase of students

---

[26] Cf. Thomas Coomans, "La création d'un style architectural sino-chrétien. L'œuvre d'Adalbert Gresnigt, moine-artiste bénédictin en Chine (1927–1932)," *Revue Bénédictine* 123, no. 1 (2013): 128–70.

[27] Sylvester Healy, "The Plans of the New University Building," BCUP 6 (1929): 3.

[28] Cf. Gregory Schramm, "The Laying of the Corner Stone," BCUP 7 (1930): 19–30.

[29] Healy, "The Plans of the New University Building," 9.

[30] *Saint Vincent College Journal* 42 (1932–1933): 158. Cited in Oetgen, *Mission to America*, 322.

(three hundred). There were forty professors, twenty-eight of them Chinese laymen, and twelve Benedictines from abroad. Most of the students were not Christians, and although the government forbade teaching Christianity to Chinese students, the Benedictines offered private catechism classes. A chaplain saw to the spiritual needs of the students, giving conferences and preaching at the Sunday student Mass. A small number of students were baptized each year in the chapel of the Benedictine priory at the university.[31]

Surprisingly, the number of students doubled to 705 the next academic year, 1930–1931, 155 of whom were Catholics. To the faculty were added several new professors, Benedictine priests and brothers, as well as secular priests sent by Benedictine monasteries in America, Europe, and Asia. The number again increased significantly in the academic year of 1931–1932, when there were one thousand students, 20 percent of whom were Catholic. With these increased resources, academic research and publications also increased in number and quality.

On 25 September 1930 six Benedictine nuns from St. Benedict's Monastery (St. Joseph, Minnesota) arrived in Peking.[32] Invited the previous year by Fr. Francis X. Clougherty, the sisters of Saint Benedict's Monastery welcomed the proposal with such enthusiasm that 109 sisters volunteered to go to China.[33] The prioress chose six, and

---

[31] Cf. W. O'Donnell, "Progress at the Catholic University of Peking," BCUP 7 (1930): 115.

[32] For the history of the mission of the American Benedictine sisters in China, see M. Wibora Muehlenbein, *Benedictine Mission to China* (St. Joseph, MN: Saint Benedict's Convent, 1980); M. Grace McDonald, *With Lamps Burning* (St. Joseph, MN: Saint Benedict's Convent, 1957), 267–86 ("Foreign Missions"). Rare images can be seen in a video on the Benedictine mission in Peking and Kaifeng, *Mission to China, 1930–1949*, http://cdm.csbsju.edu/u?/SBM,1167, accessed 21 August 2013. Archival materials at Saint Benedict's Monastery (St. Joseph, MN) are described in Archie R. Crouch et al., *Christianity in China: A Scholars' Guide to Resources in the Libraries and Archives of the United States* (Armonk, NY: M. E. Sharpe, 1989), 196–97. Especially interesting is the typewritten manuscript of Wibora Muehlenbein, "China Memoirs: The Sisters of Saint Benedict's Mission to China, 1930–1950" (n.p., preface 1962).

[33] Cf. the minutes of the 1 September 1929 chapter that approved the resolution to make a foundation in China. In Muehlenbein, *Benedictine Mission to China*, "Introduction," [p. x].

they arrived in Peking at the end of September 1930: Francetta Vetter (superior), Regia Zens, Ronayne Gergen, Rachel Loulan, Donalda Terhaar, and Wibora Muehlenbein. The sisters dedicated their first two years in China to the study of Chinese and to preparing themselves for the mission that was taking shape with some difficulty and not a few misunderstandings. Fr. Clougherty and the departments of the institution had decided on a very challenging role for the Benedictine sisters. They wanted them to establish, manage, and fund a women's college at the university run by the Benedictines. Although uncertain about their responsibilities, the sisters rented a suitable building to house the school, and in the fall of 1932 a secondary school began its first year with twenty students.[34] The idea was to add a class each year so as to have graduates ready to begin university studies in 1935.

The academic program was flourishing, but diverse and increasingly serious problems threatened a continuing Benedictine presence in the Catholic University of Peking. There was significant disagreement between the rector, Fr. George Barry O'Toole, and the prior of the Benedictine community in Peking, Fr. Ildephonse Brandstetter, about their respective jurisdictions. The main problem, however, was financial, and the situation worsened over the years because St. Vincent's Archabbey and the American Cassinese Congregation could no longer support a university in China, partly because of the United States' economic crisis of the early 1930s.

Even though the abbot president of the American Cassinese Congregation, Alcuin Deutsch, continued to the very end to explain that "the reasons for our failure to do more lay rather in the manner of its development and in unfavorable conditions than in our lack of good-will,"[35] at the beginning of 1933 the Holy See decided to entrust the management of the Catholic University of Peking to another religious order and accepted Costantini's recommendation that the missionaries of the Society of the Divine Word (SVD) be chosen. Even though the apostolic delegate expressed his desire that

---

[34] Cf. "Statuta scholae puellarum, dictae 'P'ei-Kenn', in municipio Peiping privatim erectae," *Collectanea Commissionis Synodalis* 5 (1932): 224–31.

[35] Letter of A. Deutsch to the abbots of the American Cassinese Congregation, 10 May 1933, cited in Oetgen, *Mission to America*, 347.

the Benedictines continue to have a monastic community in China, Abbot Alfred Koch (1879–1951) ordered his monks to return from China and advised the other abbots who had monks there to do the same.

The most concise explanation of the failure of the Benedictines at the Catholic University in Peking was given by Francis Clougherty, chancellor of the university, who wrote to the prior of St. Vincent that the mission was "too much for us."[36]

Benedictine Monastic Life in Peking, Kaifeng, and Taiwan

From the very beginning of their stay in China the Benedictines were aware that if their mission was to succeed they needed to have monastic vocations from among young Chinese. From past experience they knew that such vocations would come primarily through a secondary school run by monks. They believed that such a school was also needed in Peking to ensure a solid future for a Benedictine presence in China. Without it they would continue to depend on missionary monks from the United States. The two American Benedictines who arrived in China received the approval of the apostolic delegate and the bishop of Peking for this proposal. As they put it in a letter, "Our work therefore is twofold: the erection of a monastery with a religious training school and the erection of a university."[37]

A part of the palace that once belonged to Prince Tao Beile was converted into a monastery that was able to accommodate a community of thirty monks. By a few months after the opening of the Academy of Chinese Studies at the university, "some of the students [had] already applied for admission into the prospective novitiate of the Benedictine fathers at Peking."[38] In 1930 there were two candidates for the Benedictine monastic life, raising the hope that the order

[36] Letter of F. Clougherty to F. Fellner, 25 November 1933, cited in Oetgen, *Mission to America*, 348.

[37] Letter of I. Brandstetter and P. Rattenberger to A. Stehle, 17 July 1924, cited in Oetgen, *Mission to America*, 289.

[38] "The MacManus Academy of Chinese Study," 49. The anonymous author adds, "From their number, it is hoped, will arise future Benedictine scholars whose literary productions and historical research will reflect credit on the Catholic religion and uphold its intellectual prestige in China."

would gradually take root in Chinese soil. "The aim of the order has ever been to strike root as quickly as possible in native soil so that the faith will bloom, not as a foreign flower but will flourish because it draws its life under God from its surroundings—the faith that is indigenous to every clime."[39]

The new community grew. From late 1927 to early 1928 three American diocesan priests who had worked for several years at the American School of Kaifeng (Henan)—Francis Clougherty, Sylvester Healy, and Carl Rauth—became novices at the Benedictine monastery of Peking. In subsequent years, other monks from the United States, in small groups of two or three volunteers each, arrived in Peking, consolidating the community and the teaching staff of the university. All had to deal immediately with the difficult task of learning Chinese, aware, as Fr. Callistus Stehle wrote shortly after his arrival in China in 1927, that the American Benedictines would have to become "thoroughly conversant with [the] written and spoken language [of China], a highly difficult task."[40] They were also aware that this immersion in Chinese culture involved an "emptying" if they were really to take on the culture and language of the other. As Br. Hugh Wilt wrote to his confreres at St. Vincent in 1930: "China has a culture of its own. . . . Its history and literature antedate our own by centuries. To a mind westernly trained, however, the cultural element seems to be a minus quality at first for the simple reason that we set up [as] standards of judgment our own ideas and occidental customs, forgetful of the fact that China has her own *li* 禮 (meaning 'rite' or 'etiquette' in English) and her own standards, some of which existed for centuries before ours began to exist. It is not fair, therefore, to maintain that ours is the only worthwhile culture."[41]

Although the plan to establish a faculty of theology and philosophy at the Catholic University of Peking was never realized, a small seminary did come into being in 1930, when two Benedictine clerics from the United States arrived in Peking. They had to complete

---

[39] O'Donnell, "Progress at the Catholic University of Peking," 119.

[40] Callistus Stehle, "The Catholic University of Peking," *The Call of the Mission*, 20 October 1929, 1–2. Cited in Oetgen, *Mission to America*, 295.

[41] Cited in Oetgen, *Mission to America*, 295, 297.

their theological studies before ordination and were joined by some Chinese seminarians. The American Benedictines, who were eager to foster vocations to the monastic life among young Chinese, were extremely happy when one of the Chinese seminarians, Thaddeus Wang, completed his theology studies at that small seminary and, just prior to his ordination in February 1932, became a Benedictine postulant. Seven months later, Aloysius Ching and Joseph Wang, who had recently completed their secondary education at the preparatory school of the Catholic University and had begun their university studies, received the habit as Benedictine postulants.[42] Unfortunately, the American Benedictines left China before these candidates for monastic life were able to enter the novitiate.

The observance of monastic life in the Benedictine priory of Peking was very precarious and difficult. During his canonical visitation to Peking in 1932 the new abbot of St. Vincent, Alfred Koch, recognized that the greatest obstacle to monastic observance in the Peking community was the absence of a proper monastery. The living quarters of monastic community, which at that time numbered fifteen priests, a deacon, three clerics, and two oblates, were scattered in different places on the property, while the monks waited for the financial resources that would allow them to construct a monastery.[43] The new prior, Fr. Basil Stegmann, who arrived in the middle of 1932 to succeed Fr. Ildephonse, remained in China too short a time for the proposed reform of monastic observance at the priory to be implemented.

Following Fr. Basil's departure from China, a reorientation of the monastic life of the Benedictine communities of men and women was made obligatory. Of the monks who were present when the university was transferred to the Divine Word Missionaries, only Ildephonse Brandstetter, the first monk of St. Vincent to arrive in China in 1924, and Francis Clougherty, who had worked in China since the early 1920s and had taken vows as a Benedictine monk in 1928, expressed a desire to remain in China and continue their

[42] Cf. *Fu Jen Magazine* 2 (1932): 28–29; 5 (1932): 25.
[43] Cf. [A. Koch], "Promemoria de Prioratu S. Benedicti in urbe Pekino necnon de Universitate Catholica Benedictinorum Pekinensi," 5 July 1932, cited in Oetgen, *Mission to America*, 342–43.

mission. In December 1934 they, along with Oswald Baker, another monk of St. Vincent who had been a missionary in Peking, founded a Benedictine priory in Kaifeng (Henan) at the request of the local bishop, Noè Giuseppe Tacconi.

The archabbot of St. Vincent did not consider these three monks competent to make the new monastic foundation in Kaifeng. He did not recommend the project, and the monastic chapter voted it down. In 1936 the Abbey of St. Procopius (Lisle, Illinois) accepted the proposal to adopt the monastery of Kaifeng as a dependent priory. The three monks of St. Vincent transferred their stability to St. Procopius and were soon joined by three monks from St. Procopius: Cosmas Veseley, who was appointed prior, Richard Shonka, and Gerard Mach.[44] The first two, however, returned to the United States in 1938 because of the war and also for health reasons.[45] A little later Sylvester Healy, another diocesan priest who had become a Benedictine in Peking, returned to China and was appointed prior of the community of Kaifeng.

Together with the Benedictine sisters, who had also moved to the capital of Henan province in July 1935, the priests served the Catholic community of Kaifeng until the Communists took over.[46] The relocation of the sisters was not easy, as Sr. Wibora wrote: "The change from Peiping [Peking] to Kaifeng was almost as big a change as had been our transplanting from the States to Peiping in the first place."[47] "Our move to Kaifeng had not automatically solved the problem of what our work for the future was to be. What work were we capable of? What work did His Excellency [the local bishop] wish done in his vicariate? What work was our motherhouse willing to finance? All these points had to be considered. But above all these

[44] Cf. Vitus Buresh, *The Procopian Chronicle: Saint Procopius Abbey, 1885–1985* (Lisle, IL: Saint Procopius Abbey, 1985), 95–98.

[45] Cf. the account of their trip from Kaifeng to Hong Kong, where they embarked for the United States, in James Flint, "A Benedictine Missionary's Journey Out of Wartime China," *American Benedictine Review* 46, no. 4 (1995): 367–87.

[46] Cf. "Benduhui xiunü dao Kaifeng" [The Benedictine sisters arrive in Kaifeng], *Gongjiao funü* 1 (1937): 75. Of the six founding sisters, one of them, Donalda Terhaar, returned to the United States in 1935 because of ill health.

[47] Muehlenbein, *Benedictine Mission to China*, 7.

questions was the need of the people. What work could we do that would most fully meet those needs?"[48]

While the priests taught at a local junior high school, the sisters, joined by Srs. Annelda Wahl and Ursuline Venne in 1936, ran a clinic for poor patients and also devoted themselves to the education of catechumens. One of them taught English at the University of Henan. They soon had Chinese vocations[49] and built a monastery, St. Benedict's Monastery, with room for about twenty sisters.[50]

A recent discovery and cataloging of a book collection at the Kaifeng cathedral brought to light some volumes that had belonged to the library of the Benedictine sisters, many of which were transferred from the library of the women's college the sisters had established at the Catholic University of Peking. A significant part of the collection consists of monastic liturgical books (such as the *Breviarium Monasticum* and the *Missale Monasticum*) and spiritual books (such as the *Benedictine Martyrology* and the Rule of St. Benedict in English) that were used by the American Benedictine monks and sisters in China.[51]

The work was promising and rewarding, but when the Sino-Japanese War broke out the sisters dedicated themselves exclusively to the care of the wounded. Since their work was carried out under the auspices of an international aid committee, whose local president was Fr. Francis Clougherty, their dispensary assumed a public character, which made it better known and appreciated. In 1939 two more sisters came from the United States, Flora Goebel and Vestina Bursken, and in 1940 Sr. Felicia Stager arrived. Although regular monastic life

---

[48] Muehlenbein, "China Memoirs," 40.

[49] Cf. "Diyiwei guoji benduhui xiunü" [The first Chinese Benedictine sister], *Gongjiao funü* 2 (1937): 148–49.

[50] Cf. "Kaifeng xinjian benduhui xiunüyuan" [A monastery for Benedictine women recently built in Kaifeng], SB 4 (1941): 131.

[51] For a description of the project that led to the recovery of the library holdings in the Kaifeng cathedral in the years 2008–2010, see Laura Denaro, "La storia dei libri 'dimenticati' di Kaifeng. Un progetto di promozione di beni culturali in Cina," *Quaderni asiatici* 93 (2011): 5–20. For the first cataloguing of the 1,138 volumes in the collection, see "Catalogo del fondo librario presso la cattedrale di Kaifeng (Henan, Repubblica popolare cinese)," unpublished typewritten manuscript (Centro missionario PIME, Milan, 2011).

was virtually impossible in these circumstances, the dedication of the sisters was so great that they decided not to leave, as witnessed by a source: "Please, do not recall us from China; it would break our hearts, for there are so many chances here of doing good. It is a dangerous work but the good God will care for us."[52]

Interned by the Japanese in concentration camps, first in Kaifeng from December 1941 to March 1943 and then in Weixian (Weihsien) from March to August 1943, the sisters offered many forms of assistance to the inmates and the sick, all the while continuing their Benedictine community life. They were allowed to make use of their prayer books, and a space was made available to them where they could pray the Liturgy of the Hours. From August 1943 to August 1945 they were forced to stay in Peking at the Christ the King Monastery of the Daughters of Jesus, a Spanish religious order. When they were released in August 1945 and returned to Kaifeng, they found their monastery and the dispensary severely damaged. Joined by Mariette Pitz, another sister from the United States, they devoted themselves to the reacquisition and reconstruction of their facilities. At the end of 1947, after having been in China for seventeen years, they were visited for the first time by the mother superior of St. Benedict's Monastery in Minnesota. A few months later, the invasion of Communist troops forced the sisters to leave Kaifeng and then, in 1949, to say goodbye forever to mainland China.

Two of the sisters returned to America, while the rest remained in the Far East. After moving to Taiwan, three of them made their way to Japan in 1950 and began a Benedictine presence in Tokyo, while the others remained in Taiwan. After initially settling in Tainan, in 1952 they founded a monastery in Danshui (Tanshui), not far from Taipei. In 1975 the monastery was made a dependent priory. It became independent in 1988 with a community of fourteen sisters and is still in existence. The sisters have been involved in various activities—in particular, teaching, pastoral ministry to students in schools of various kinds and levels, the management of a home for

---

[52] Letter of W. Muehlenbein to R. Pratschner, 9 May 1938, cited in McDonald, *With Lamps Burning*, 274.

orphans and troubled youth, and the running of a retreat center.[53]
Today the sisters, all Chinese, still have a dream: "Our project for the
future is hoping to be able to reestablish Benedictine life in mainland
China. . . . We are preparing for this by deepening our monastic life,
strengthening our community life, listening attentively to the Holy
Spirit, and praying that one day we may return there. This is what
we aim at as we prepare to work on the mainland and carry on our
apostolate here in Taiwan."[54]

The story of the Benedictine monks after 1945, when they were
freed from house arrest at the Franciscan house of studies in Peking,
is not easily reconstructed on the basis of published documents.
One of the most accessible sources, though providing little data for
historical reconstruction, is the monthly *Benedictine Orient*, published since 1936 by the Abbey of St. Procopius, the motherhouse
of the Benedictine priory in China. In addition to letters sent by
missionaries from China, the monthly occasionally featured news
about the community.[55] After the death of Ildephonse Brandstetter
in 1945, the pioneer of the Benedictine mission in China, the other
three monks from St. Vincent returned to the United States. The few
remaining Benedictines were divided between Kaifeng and Peking,
where Fr. Sylvester Healy and Br. Alphonse Keprta bought a house
in 1947. For some months they were "busy repairing and remodeling their new home in Peiping [Peking] to make it serviceable as
a house of studies."[56] They had "great hopes that they will be able
to establish a community of monks living according to the mind of
Saint Benedict."[57] There is a passing comment about the monks even
"waiting patiently and making plans for the monastic foundation

---

[53] The events that befell the Benedictine community between its last months
in Kaifeng and its settlement in Taiwan are recounted in Sisters of Saint Benedict,
Beyond the Horizon (n.p.: n.p., 1980).

[54] Lucas Chin, "Benedictines in Taiwan," *AIM Bulletin* 98 (2010): 13.

[55] Particularly valuable are the serialized chronicles entitled "Turning Back the
Pages," published in the journal in the 1960s.

[56] "News from Peiping," BO 6 (1947): 1. Peiping was the Chinese name of Peking
(Beijing) in those years.

[57] "House of Studies, Peiping," BO 4 (1947): 1. For a map of the Benedictine
property in Peking, see: "News from Peiping," BO 5 (1947): 1.

in Chowtsun [Zhoucun, Shandong province]."⁵⁸ In mid-1947 Fr. Gerard Mach returned to Peking, reinforcing the small community there, as witnessed by a member of it: "Father Gerard has recently returned from Kaifeng. Now there are more of us, and we can better carry out our liturgy. His voice added to ours makes a difference in our chanting of the Divine Office. The authorities in Honan [Henan] University begged him to be back for the Fall term, but I am afraid we won't be able to comply with their wishes."⁵⁹

In 1948, after making his novitiate and profession at St. Procopius Abbey in Lisle, the first Chinese Benedictine, Fr. Ambrose Wang, joined the American monks in Peking.⁶⁰

The monastic project that the monks had in mind was clear and simple, perhaps refined by lessons learned from past experience. It envisaged a small and economically productive foundation, "tied into the social and economic life of the people." On this basis, the monks were sure that "Benedictines can do much for China, but only on one condition: that they carry out the real Benedictine life," that is, a life of study and manual labor. For this reason they began some agriculture in Peking, crops and cattle, hoping to "apply them in proper proportions to our [future] monastic foundations."⁶¹ They were aided by the Trappist monks who had fled to Peking and had been offered shelter by the Benedictines. After a few months they also acquired a residence in Peking. In October 1948, one year after the founding of the People's Republic of China, Fr. Sylvester still painted a hopeful picture of the future of Benedictine monasticism in China: "Monasticism is the prototype by which the Chinese family can be brought to live a full Christian life. Here young boys can be steeped in solid Christian culture which a properly organized monastery almost alone among Catholic institutions can give. The need is

---

⁵⁸ "News from Peiping," BO 6 (1947): 1. Cf. also "Benduhui jiang zai Shandong Zhoucun liyuan" [The Benedictines will found a monastery at Zhoucun in Shandong], SB 5 (1946): 138.
⁵⁹ "The Empty Bottle Is Full Again," BO 7 (1947): 1. Gerard Mach had taught English at the University of Henan in Kaifeng.
⁶⁰ Cf. BO 1 (1948): 4.
⁶¹ [Sylvester Healy], "China Letter. Back to Benedict—in China," BO 1 (1948): 3.

extremely great; even serious we might say. This is then the golden opportunity for the Benedictines."[62]

Political developments prevented the Benedictines from taking advantage of this opportunity. Like many other missionaries who were forced to leave China, they made their way to Taiwan, where they acquired property in Jiayi (Chiayi) and then founded a monastery in 1967. "With the dedication of the buildings, a new phase will begin for our priory on Formosa [Taiwan]. The work of retreats, conferences and other spiritual exercises will have to be organized and developed. Native vocations must be promoted to perpetuate the work and to establish Benedictine monasticism on a firm basis in the Far East. . . . From our humble and small monastic seed on Formosa, Benedictine monasticism may some day be spread throughout the mainland of China."[63]

That day still lies in the future. In the meantime the Benedictines have continued their life in Taiwan in the small Wimmer priory, dependent on St. Vincent's Archabbey, and at the Furen Catholic University of Taipei, where, as teachers, they continue to be involved in higher education, for which mission Benedictines had come to China several decades earlier.

The Belgian Benedictines: Prophets of a Chinese Monasticism

The Chinese Dream of Jehan Joliet

Had it not been for Jehan Joliet (1870–1937), no one would have conceived, awaited, and finally realized an authentic, at least as proposed, Chinese Benedictine monastery, which, even though founded by foreigners, would be "with its prominent Chinese character . . . in every aspect a Chinese house."[64] When the founder of the

---

[62] Sylvester Healy, "China Letter. No Need for 'Setting Up' Exercises—Grain Mill Does It," BO 6 (1948): 1.

[63] BO 10–11 (1967): 1.

[64] Jehan Joliet, "A Project for a Chinese Monastery (1922)." See app. 2, p. 325. On the person of Jehan Joliet, see esp. the biography of Henri-Philippe Delcourt, *Dom Jehan Joliet (1870–1937). Un projet de monachisme bénédictin chinois* (Paris: Cerf, 1988). See also Un moine de Saint-André, "Dom Jehan Joliet," CSA 1 (1938): 30–52 (also republished as a pamphlet); Raphaël Vinciarelli, "Dom Jehan Joliet et son

monastery of Xishan died, its prior, Raphaël Vinciarelli, summed up the essential character of this man and his work. "Dom Joliet's personality was full of energy, entirely at the service of an idea that had matured over thirty years and that he was able to bring to life. To introduce in China a monastic life whose roots would seek the original currents of Chinese civilization: this was his aim, this is Si-Shan [Xishan]."[65]

While it is true that "China gave him his monastic vocation,"[66] it is important to trace, however briefly, the dual path that led Jehan Joliet, through China, to the monastery and that through his continuous interest in the Chinese world led China to the monastery.

This young French naval officer was born in Dijon in 1870. It seems that his first contact with the Chinese Empire dated back to 1892, the year of his second stay in the Far East. He began to study Chinese in Shanghai and to admire Chinese culture and thought. In a letter to his sister Ida there is an almost clairvoyant hint of the two basic guidelines regarding a monastic presence in China that Joliet would hold on to and develop over time, namely, the need to "become Chinese" and to break the despicable alliance between evangelization and colonization: "I would be very happy to see monks in China, and it would be well for Solesmes to come there one day. At least, the monks will not arouse jealousy, because, once planted in China, they will become Chinese, so to say, and they will not be the ones to summon vice-ridden armies and odious functionaries to avenge Christ's cause. . . . When Solesmes will have sent monks and nuns to China, it will perhaps be so much the worse for the West, but so much the better for the church and for the world."[67]

œuvre monastique en Chine," CA 10 (1938): 6*–11*; "Dom Jehan Joliet," *Bulletin M.E.P.* (1938): 245–47; Henri-Philippe Delcourt, "Dom Jehan Joliet (1870–1937). Un projet de monachisme bénédictin chinois," *Mélanges de science religieuse* 43, no. 1 (1986): 3–19; Henri-Philippe Delcourt, "The Grain Dies in China," *AIM Bulletin* 40 (1986): 44–55.

[65] Vinciarelli, "Dom Jehan Joliet et son œuvre monastique en Chine," 6*.

[66] Ibid.

[67] Letter of J. Joliet to I. Joliet, 14 October 1892, in Delcourt, *Dom Jehan Joliet*, 32–33.

In a passage in his *Note on the Origins of Xishan*, written in 1937, Joliet testified that while he was in China in May 1892, he suddenly experienced what he described as "a strange and powerful attraction to China, along with an obscure sense that I belonged there. Almost at the same time, the thought that China would be converted by monasteries took possession of me, even before I dreamt that I might be part of this apostolate. Immediately the main lines, which would remain substantially the same, fixed themselves in my mind."[68]

The monastic vocation of young Jehan was meanwhile becoming clearer. The choice of the place for his future Benedictine life was not difficult to make, since his older brother was already a monk of Solesmes and his sister a nun at the Abbey of Sainte-Cécile. At the end of 1895 Joliet decided to enter the Benedictine Abbey of Solesmes. As he recalls in his *Note*, it was not long before he spoke to Abbot Paul Delatte about his idea for monastic life in China: "In December 1895 I entered Solesmes. Dom Delatte knew my thoughts, neither disapproving nor encouraging me, not asking me to give them up but to confide everything to God, to my present monastic life. This is what I did for thirty years, seeking to remain ready, taking advantage of the rare occasions to prepare myself more positively. No detailed plan, no conditions or requests *sine qua non*, but always the Chinese monastery. . . . And more and more I saw this dwelling Chinese in character and in 'sap,' not French or European or even Latin, but developing along the lines and with the resources of the national culture."[69]

Joliet made his monastic profession in June 1897 and was ordained priest three years later, never giving up his dream of a mission to China. While leading his "ordinary" monastic life, he continued to prepare for this possibility by studying the language, history, religion, and philosophy of China. As he wrote in 1935, "Then as now I dreamt of myself as both monk and Chinese. At Solesmes I became the first, and I handed myself over to God so that the second might come true as well."[70] The intellectual and spiritual will to make him-

---

[68] Cited in Vinciarelli, "Dom Jehan Joliet et son œuvre monastique en Chine," 6*.
[69] Ibid., 7*.
[70] Letter of J. Joliet to C. Rey, 4 July 1935, in Delcourt, *Dom Jehan Joliet*, 39.

self Chinese in order to bring about a Chinese monasticism shines
through in what he wrote in 1907: "If God leads me [to China], with
what joy I'd become Chinese, not just in dress or language, that's
just the beginning, but in the depths of my soul, in order to make
[the Chinese] monks."[71]

The years from 1917 to 1926 were a period of slow incubation.
During that time what was happening in Joliet's personal life and
in the church brought about a maturation of his China project, but
his vision remained basically the same: "[My project] is the foundation of a monastery in China with the same orientation of life as at
Solesmes, that is, first of all the Divine Office and prayer, normally
without a ministry or travels, and intellectual work as the principal
work. But there is no monastery without monks, and naturally what
will be necessary in the end will be Chinese monks, and to have true
Chinese monks, it is necessary that the foundation, made entirely
by Europeans, adopt resolutely and clearly everything from China
except sin."[72]

A leading figure at this stage was the commanding officer Charles
Rey, a fellow student at the naval academy of Brest and a faithful
friend of Joliet, who kept in touch with him over the years. Rey
shared Joliet's idea of founding a monastery in China, and thanks to
him and to his work behind the scenes, Joliet could make contacts
outside the monastery and build relations with some key figures for
the development of the project.

The church atmosphere at that time had become receptive to a
missionary project in accordance with the "new" ideas of Vincent
Lebbe and Antoine Cotta, which Joliet shared. Missionaries in China
were becoming increasingly sensitive to and eager for a monastic
presence on Chinese soil. The encyclical of Benedict XV on missionary activity, *Maximum Illud*, made Rome's position on mission
reform explicit and official.

[71] Letter of J. Joliet to C. Rey, 1 November 1907, in Delcourt, *Dom Jehan Joliet*,
42. In a letter written in 1926, Joliet wrote to Fr. É. Licent: "If I go to China . . . it
will be for the sole purpose of learning the language and the customs. I will have to
work hard to make myself Chinese, since I am getting such a late start," in Delcourt,
Dom Jehan Joliet, 93.
[72] Letter of J. Joliet to C. Rey, 30 August 1917, in Delcourt, *Dom Jehan Joliet*, 69.

In Cherbourg in 1917, Commander in Chief Rey had met Gabriel Maujay, a Jesuit who had been a missionary in China, and presented Joliet's ideas to him. This first contact led to a series of negotiations with Jesuits in France and in China in order to identify an appropriate place for a foundation and a bishop who would support missionary monks. Already in 1921 the Jesuit vicar apostolic of Xianxian (Hebei), Henri Lécroart, having been informed of the intentions of Joliet, contacted Solesmes, asking it to send monks, and also the Congregation of Propaganda Fide to seek its support. Even though the pope himself, when informed of the proposal, wrote to Abbot Germain Cozien of Solesmes to express his enthusiasm about the Chinese character of the proposed monastery, the abbot replied that he was not in a position to undertake such a project. The reason, he said, was not only lack of resources and personnel. The kind of missionary monasticism promoted by Saint-André was far removed from the monasticism observed by the monks at Solesmes, who were formed according to the spirit of Prosper Guéranger. A few months later, however, when he was in Rome, he assured the cardinal prefect he would at least consider Jehan Joliet to be at his disposal. In 1922 the abbot of the Trappist monastery of Our Lady of Consolation in Yangjiaping, Louis Brun, visited Solesmes in the course of his travels in Europe to convince the abbot of the usefulness of a Benedictine foundation in China and to assure him that it would be successful.

Efforts to form a group of Benedictines to leave for China proceeded at a leisurely but steady pace over the following years. Repeated applications were submitted to the Congregation of Propaganda Fide and efforts were made to find a community willing to be involved and an abbot who would assume responsibility for the foundation.

In the light of subsequent developments, mention should be made of the contact Charles Rey and a Chinese student had with Abbot Nève of the Belgian Abbey of Saint-André at the beginning of 1924. Since it was not possible for Saint-André to take charge of the foundation at that time, Pope Pius XI advised Rey to get in touch with the abbot primate of the Benedictines, Fidelis von Stotzingen, who "played a decisive but always discreet role in the realization of the foundation in China,"[73] since he never ceased looking for a Benedic-

---

[73] Delcourt, *Dom Jehan Joliet*, 85.

tine abbot who would be willing to take on the China project. To the abbot primate's search for an abbot and a community Joliet gave his full collaboration, stipulating only that the monastery to be founded be Chinese. There should be no predetermined form. Rather, once the monks arrived, they should adapt to the local setting.

> I see that the primate is still not discouraged after a lack of success once or twice. . . . It is encouraging that he tries to profit from every occasion. . . . As for the character more or less of Solesmes of the foundation, you are beginning to know well the different Benedictines, and I told you enough three weeks ago of the breadth of my ideas (at least in intention). For the rest, I have never thought that I would have a green light for a foundation made according to my ideas. Except for two points: *monastery*, that is, a stable life in a group, with abundant space for prayer, and *Chinese* monastery; my dream would be to go there with the fewest possible precise projects for or against a form or a work. . . . What I hope is that there be no haste, that decisions aren't made before living there. . . . In short, if a *Chinese monastery* is faithfully admitted, I believe I can get along with any congregation.[74]

Regarding the formation of the first group, Joliet's idea was to start out with at least two other monks, but he did not give up the idea of setting out alone if this was the only way he could accomplish what he wanted to do: "My firm intention is to start from the beginning with two or three. . . . Only in view of the impossibility of finding someone for the beginning, and rather than putting it off indefinitely, would I leave alone, if I am permitted to do so."[75]

In another missionary encyclical, *Rerum Ecclesiae*, promulgated on 28 February 1926, Pope Pius XI urged the monastic orders to create foundations in mission lands. The encyclical offered further encouragement to Joliet for the fulfillment of his dream. A decisive step was his visit to Théodore Nève in August 1926. Abbot Nève assured him that Saint-André was still open to cooperation, thus making the Belgian abbey the focus of further attempts.

---

[74] Letter of J. Joliet to C. Rey, 3 August 1924, in Delcourt, *Dom Jehan Joliet*, 88.
[75] Letter of J. Joliet to É. Licent, 27 April 1926, in Delcourt, *Dom Jehan Joliet*, 98.

Saint-André and the Foundation of Xishan

Joliet's dream about China would not have come true if he had not found a monastic community willing to carry out his plan on Chinese soil and to provide the necessary personnel and means. In Belgium the Abbey of Saint-André was the monastery most naturally suited to the monastic missionary project that Joliet had cultivated and refined over the years. Canonically established in Bruges in 1901, it was marked from the very beginning by the apostolic spirit of its founder, Gérard Van Caloen (1853–1912), a spirit that continued to be fostered by Théodore Nève (1879–1963), who was abbot from 1912 to 1958.

The abbey's interest in China was enkindled by its contacts with the most famous and creative missionary in China at the time, Vincent Lebbe. His initial visit to Saint-André was in August 1913, when, on his first home visit, he spent two days at the abbey with his brother Bède, a monk of Maredsous. From their first meeting, the contacts between Abbot Nève and Fr. Lebbe "were particularly warm and cordial: both had something in common and understood each other."[76] The relationship between the abbey and the Chinese mission grew over the years through various kinds of collaboration. In addition to a stimulating conference on the missions in the Far East that Lebbe gave at Saint-André in 1921 and an inspiring retreat that he preached in August 1923 to the monks and students of the abbey, there was the significant presence of Chinese students whom Fr. Lebbe sent to Europe from the early 1920s on and who were welcomed at Saint-André and offered support by the "Foyer catholique chinois," an association founded in 1927 that had Abbot Nève as its president and Édouard Neut, a monk of Saint-André, as its secretary. For several years Fr. Neut was an important link between the abbey and the "Lebbe-style" Chinese mission because, as editor of the missionary magazine of Saint-André, the *Bulletin des Missions*, he supported and always gave ample space to the appeals of Lebbe

---

[76] Christian Papeians de Morchoven, "The China Mission of the Benedictine Abbey of Sint-Andries (Bruges)," in *Historiography of the Chinese Catholic Church: Nineteenth and Twentieth Centuries*, ed. Jeroom Heyndrickx (Leuven: Ferdinand Verbiest Foundation, K. U. Leuven, 1994), 306.

for a church detached from European nationalism and governed by a native clergy.[77]

The decisive event that led to the realization of Joliet's dream was Abbot Nève's invitation to Joliet to spend Christmas 1926 in Bruges. Visiting Saint-André were two of the first six Chinese bishops, who had been consecrated in Rome on 28 October: Joseph Hu Ruoshan, bishop of Taizhou (Zhejiang), and Melchior Sun Dezhen, bishop of Anguo (Hebei). This was the second meeting between Joliet and Abbot Nève. The first had taken place during the visit of Joliet to Saint-André in late August 1926, during which the abbot had indicated the possibility of making a foundation in China in the future. The opportunity to reconsider the project came only four months later, but these positive signs had been nurtured by a climate of openness to China in previous years. "The *Bulletin des Missions*, a great defender of Fr. Lebbe; papal encyclicals that staked much on China; the numerous and always eagerly awaited visits of Fr. Lebbe; and the longer or shorter stays of Chinese students at the monastery—all these had created a climate favorable to an opening toward China."[78]

In preparation for the visit of Chinese bishops and in response to the continued urging of Charles Rey and Vincent Lebbe, Abbot Nève decided to assume Joliet's project after the first visit of Joliet to Saint-André at the end of August 1926. Toward Christmas that year Nève wrote a letter to the abbot of Solesmes, wondering "what is the will of God concerning the participation of the Abbey of Saint-André in the foundation" and asking that Joliet be given permission to spend a few months at Saint-André so he, Nève, could determine "the form of patronage and support" prior to Joliet's spending some time in China. With regard to the canonical responsibilities for the project, Nève spoke plainly: "I am for an immediate solution. Saint-André would take responsibility for Dom Joliet's activity in China. Solesmes would keep Dom Joliet among its members canonically until the

[77] Cf. Louis Wei Tsing-sing, "Le Père Lebbe et l'Abbaye de Saint-André-lez-Bruges (1877–1940)," *Rythmes du monde* 34 (1960): 218–24.

[78] Christian Papeians de Morchoven, *L'abbaye de Saint-André Zevenkerken*, 2 vols. (Tielt: Lannoo, 1998–2002), 2:192.

day when Providence will have confirmed by its blessings the work undertaken; then Dom Joliet and his collaborators, whom we will have given him, would be in the same stability under the jurisdiction of Saint-André."[79]

Although the Abbey of Saint-André had made a sizable contribution to the revival of Brazilian monasteries, which was the first aim of its foundation, and had sent monks for apostolic activity in the Katanga prefecture in Congo, the foundation of the priory of Xishan would be the first monastery the abbey itself founded in mission lands.[80] If the abbey and its abbot were enthusiastic about this foundation, the monks who had been sent to Katanga some years before were not favorable toward the idea. For them, this new venture would come at the expense of their work in Africa. But Théodore Nève, a few months after the decision to begin the adventure of China, responded firmly to this grumbling in September 1927: "We are founding in China, so that the Chinese can have the benefits of monastic life. All missionaries, even those in Katanga, should have a wide enough spirit and heart to understand the timeliness of a work of this kind."[81]

With the consent of the abbot of Solesmes, Joliet's dream became a reality. Since joining the monastery, he had spent almost thirty years silently waiting and praying for this day, and now events followed one another very rapidly. Théodore Nève first informed Celso Costantini, the apostolic delegate in China, of the decision with a letter that is worth citing, since it shows that in this first phase Nève and Joliet had a substantially similar vision. It also demonstrates consonance with the missionary ideal of Costantini. "We would like to bring Benedictine monastic life to the Chinese and to found a monastery in a native vicariate. . . . We would like this monastery to adapt itself as well as possible to Chinese customs. The Rule of St. Benedict is sufficiently broad to permit this adaptation naturally. . . . The Lord will indicate the time when we can send Fr. Joliet the help that he will need . . . so as to allow him to form quickly a local community

[79] Letter of T. Nève to G. Cozien, 18 December 1926, in Delcourt, *Dom Jehan Joliet*, 103.

[80] For the history of the Abbey of Saint-André/Sint-Andries in Bruges, see Papeians de Morchoven, *L'abbaye de Saint-André Zevenkerken.*

[81] Papeians de Morchoven, *L'abbaye de Saint-André Zevenkerken*, 2:193.

in which the European fathers will have no other desire but to be Chinese with the Chinese."[82]

The response of the apostolic delegate was immediate and positive. He recommended that Joliet first go to Peking, where he could continue to study Chinese. As for the location of the future foundation, Costantini recommended one of the three vicariates of the Sichuan region that would soon be created and entrusted to the care of the local clergy. This suggestion corresponded with what Joliet was thinking. He believed that the "temperate climate and charm of the landscape" of the central provinces of Zhejiang and Sichuan favored "a stable monastery with fixed intellectual pursuits." These areas were also sufficiently far removed from the "large concentrations of Europeans" and "ministers and general consuls," thus facilitating a "sincere and gradually complete adaptation to the life and culture of China."[83] Costantini also advised him to embark with one or more companions.[84]

Joliet unsuccessfully tried to have Émile Butruille of the Abbey of Oosterout, who had shown interest in the project, join him. Abbot Nève appointed a monk of Saint-André and former missionary in Africa, Pie de Cocquéau (1882–1961), to be a pioneer along with Jehan Joliet on his expedition to China. Setting sail from Marseille on 20 May 1927, they arrived in China about a month later. At the age of fifty-seven, Jehan Joliet once again set foot on Chinese soil, thirty-five years after his last visit.

Their preparatory stay in Peking lasted about a year, from July 1927 to April 1928. Hosted by the American Benedictines who had recently arrived to found and administer a university, they devoted themselves to the study of Chinese. They also made contacts with missionaries who were present there, but they kept their distance from diplomatic circles. Jehan Joliet was asked to teach French at the university. Even though there were some disagreements between the

[82] Letter of T. Nève to C. Costantini, 15 February 1927, in Papeians de Morchoven, *L'abbaye de Saint-André Zevenkerken*, 2:192.

[83] Letter of J. Joliet to É. Licent, 27 April 1926, in Delcourt, *Dom Jehan Joliet*, 98–99.

[84] Cf. letter of J. Joliet to A. Joliet, March 1927, in Delcourt, *Dom Jehan Joliet*, 112–13.

two pioneers of the Benedictine mission in China, in February 1928 Abbot Nève formally appointed Jehan Joliet superior. In addition to the poor health of Dom Pie, the different temperaments and the different levels of enthusiasm of the two contributed to their *malentendu*. Joliet pushed ahead, was always in a hurry, burned bridges, all of which gave de Cocquéau the impression that he wanted to pursue his own interests rather than make a foundation of Saint-André.

At the end of their stay in Peking, the abbot of the monastery of Our Lady of Consolation in Yangjiaping invited Joliet and his confrere to spend some time at the Trappist monastery, kindly offering to share with the two the experience that Trappist monks had gained during their fifty years in China. "Since we have been in China for fifty years already, having done what you wish to do, how many things could you not learn from us! Even our faults or lack of prudence could be useful for you. . . . You and your fellow monk will be most welcome here. And you will remain with us not one or two weeks, but several weeks or several months. We will share our experience with you, and you will leave better prepared for the great mission that awaits you in Sze-Chwan [Sichuan]."[85]

Probably because he had a different idea about the kind of monastic presence there should be in China, Joliet did not respond to the Trappist abbot's invitation and therefore the visit to Yangjiaping was never made.

The invitation extended by the vicar apostolic of Chongqing, Louis-Gabriel-Xavier Jantzen, to make a foundation in his diocese, which was located in the northern region of Sichuan and would have a Chinese bishop as ordinary, convinced Fr. Jehan and Fr. Pie "to continue the journey they had begun toward the unknown monastery."[86] In April 1928 Fr. Jehan and Fr. Pie began traveling once again, much of the time on inland waterways, arriving six weeks later in Chongqing. Bishop Jantzen's welcome was not as warm as was expected, and they left the city a few days after arriving. In the

[85] Letter of L. Brun to J. Joliet, 5 February 1928, in Delcourt, *Dom Jehan Joliet*, 131.

[86] J. Joliet, *À la recherche d'un monastère*, cited in T. Nève, "Le Prieuré des SS. Pierre et André de Si Chan," BM 10 (1930), supp. no. 1: *Le Courrier Monastique Chinois*, 2*.

nearby city of Chengdu, on the contrary, the vicar apostolic, Jacques Rouchouse, who "has long wanted a monastic colony"[87] and was "still feeling disappointed that he had not been able to get a Trappist foundation in his diocese,"[88] "not only welcomed the monks from the moment they arrived in Szechwan [Sichuan], but thanks to his advice, his dedication, and his generosity Si-Shan [Xishan] became a monastic land."[89]

The two monks' exploration soon led them to a site that seemed suitable for the installation of a first group of monks. Xishan was in the part of the diocese that would become the new Apostolic Vicariate of Shunqing (Shunking) in 1930. It was just five kilometers west of the city.[90] Its pastor, Paul Wang Wencheng, the future bishop of Shunqing (1930–1961), "offered the newcomers the most amiable hospitality and, from day one, his enlightened solicitude and his faithful friendship meant for the monks a continual collaboration."[91] Already on 22 July 1928 Fr. Jehan informed Abbot Théodore of his and Fr. Pie's decision to buy the six hectares of gently sloping land that belonged to the church. In early September the abbot of Saint-André approved the choice by telegram.

As fate would have it, Joliet lost his first companion, Fr. Pie, who had to return to Belgium because of ill health. The abbot, however, was already preparing to send Hildebrand Marga (1888–1971) and Émile Butruille (1888–1965), a monk of Oosterhout, to the fledgling foundation. Fr. Émile "for several years, in the quiet of his cell, [had] poured over Chinese characters, teasing out their secrets and penetrating their meaning and beauty."[92] His abbot had accepted the wish of the abbot of Saint-André to assign him to Xishan and gave Fr. Émile permission to leave for China. On 4 November 1928 Abbot

[87] Nève, "Le Prieuré des SS. Pierre et André de Si Chan," 7*.

[88] "Notice sur la fondation du prieuré des SS. Pierre et André de Sischan, Shunking," *Bulletin M.E.P.* (1929): 486.

[89] Théodore Nève, "Le monastère des SS. Pierre et André de Si-Shan," BM 15 (1936), supp. no. 1: *Le Courrier de l'Apostolat Monastique*, 11*.

[90] Cf. "Sichuan jiang jian benduhui xiuyuan zhi didian" [The place where a Benedictine monastery will be constructed in Sichuan], YZB 32 (1928): 8.

[91] Un moine de Saint-André, "Dom Jehan Joliet," 10–11.

[92] Théodore Nève, "Le Monastère des SS. Pierre et André de Si Chan," BM 9 (1928–1929): 291.

Théodore presided at a liturgical service to bless the foundation cross of the new monastery to be built in China. "We have chosen for the foundation cross to be given to those leaving a crucifix that is particularly dear to us: that which from the beginnings of the abbey has been offered to the veneration of the community during the Good Friday ceremony, solemnly unveiled, adored and kissed by all. May it be in the first Chinese monastery a witness to the profound faith and love with which we wish to give to the church of China the best of what, without meriting it, we ourselves have received."[93]

Following monastic tradition, the abbot also gave those who were departing the Rule and the Psalter. On 1 November they embarked from Marseille, arriving in China three months later. The abbot exhorted them to "become Chinese with the Chinese. Try to adapt yourselves to the uses and customs of the country, doing so to the extent that you judge appropriate and prudent."[94]

Rome gave canonical approval for the development of the foundation, first by means of a rescript from the Congregation of Propaganda Fide that authorized the foundation (8 November 1928), then by a decree of the Congregation for Religious that erected the foundation as a simple priory with a canonical novitiate (3 January 1929), but kept it dependent on the Abbey of Saint-André, "until the day that its growth will allow it to become autonomous in accordance with the Rule of St. Benedict and the constitutions that interpret it."[95]

A Chinese Monastery in a European Cage

When Frs. Émile and Hildebrand arrived in Xishan on 24 February 1929, they found that work on the construction of the new monastery had already begun.[96] Fr. Jehan had already entrusted the

---

[93] Ibid., 291–92.

[94] Cited in Papeians de Morchoven, *L'abbaye de Saint-André Zevenkerken*, 2:203–4.

[95] Nève, "Le Prieuré des SS. Pierre et André de Si Chan," 1*.

[96] Valuable details about the first years of the foundation of Xishan (1927–1941) are provided by Hildebrand Marga in a typewritten manuscript, "Début de la fondation de Si Shan, Chine" (ASA, Chine 9), which I have drawn on for the account given here. Soon after the new foundation was made (1929?), an account of it was also put out in Chinese. It was published as a brochure and also as an article that appeared in two different Catholic magazines in China: *Xishan sheng bendu xiuyuan chuangli*

project to Dom Paul Wang as foreman. The building was intended to be modest and basic but sufficient for what was needed for monastic life. "[The monastery], the stone foundation of which supports a wooden building, includes, in a reduced measure, all the usual places: chapel, chapter room, library, refectory, novitiate, cells, rooms for guests, and so on. It can house about twenty religious, about a dozen guests, and some servants."[97]

So "nothing great, but in very good taste and completely in local style."[98] Photos show what was done at that time in Xishan.[99] The building, whose architecture was inspired by the layout of traditional Chinese houses, consisted of two rectangular buildings that were twenty meters long and had black tiled roofs. The first building was primarily for hospitality, with a reception hall, visiting rooms, and guest rooms. In the back was the chapel, with altars decorated in Chinese style, and the sacristy, where there was a reliquary of St. Therese of the Child Jesus, the design of which was also Chinese. The second building contained the various monastic areas: chapter hall, refectory, recreation room, and monastic cells. The surrounding land, enclosed by a wall, included a garden, a grove of fruit trees (oranges, tangerines, and peaches), and a vineyard.[100]

The three monks inaugurated monastic life at the monastery of Sts. Peter and Andrew in Xishan by singing the Mass of St. Benedict on his feast day, 21 March 1929, together with Bishop Wang and some local Christians. The decision to dedicate the monastery of

ji [Information on the foundation of a Benedictine monastery in Xishan] (Shanghai: Tushanwan yinshuguan, n.d.); Zhang Weibing, "Ji Zhonghua diyizuo sheng benduhui xiuyuan zhi yuanqi ji chengli" [Information on the origin of the foundation of the first Benedictine monastery in China], SZ 10 (1929): 419–24; "Sichuan Xishan sheng benduhui xiuyuan chuangli ji" [Information on the foundation of the Benedictine monastery in Xishan, Sichuan], YZB 6 (1935): 9–11; 7 (1935): 6–8.

[97] Nève, "Le Prieuré des SS. Pierre et André de Si Chan," 11*. Cf. also letter of J. Joliet to T. Nève, 7 September 1928, in Delcourt, *Dom Jehan Joliet*, 155–57.

[98] Un moine de Saint-André, "Dom Jehan Joliet," 11.

[99] See the images *infra*, pp. 253–55.

[100] Cf. Ma Wan Sang, "Le Monastère de Si shan en Chine," BM 13 (1934), supp. no. 1: *Le Courrier de l'Apostolat Monastique*, 4*–14* (with photograph); Nève, "Le monastère des SS. Pierre et André de Si-Shan."

Xishan to Sts. Peter and Andrew is explained in a note included in an article by Abbot Nève:

> The choice of Saints Peter and Andrew as patrons of the monastery of Si Chan [Xishan] was inspired, first of all, by the devotion of the entire Abbey of Saint-André for Peter's See and also in remembrance of the monastery of St. Andrew on the Caelian Hill, whose abbot, St. Gregory the Great, once he had ascended to the Roman See, opened the field of the apostolate to the Benedictines and sent St. Augustine of Canterbury to England to erect there the first monastic cloister in a mission land. The names of Sts. Peter and Andrew recall as well the two patrons of the abbatial church of Saint-André, and that of St. Peter expresses our acknowledgment of the Abbey of Saint-Pierre of Solesmes, which freely gave to the priory of Si Chan the first stone of this foundation.[101]

Work proceeded quickly, and toward the end of November most of the construction was completed, allowing the monks to hold the solemn blessing of the chapel. The ceremony took place on 15 December, presided over by Paul Wang, who had been appointed the new bishop of the vicariate of Shunqing a few days earlier. Jehan Joliet, who had been appointed prior on 10 June by Abbot Nève, blessed the monastic areas. The day before, the prior had also clothed the first postulant with the habit, in the presence of three other aspirants from the region of Yunnan.[102] Among the guests was the bonze of the Taoist temple in Xishan, who "seemed to be one of the most satisfied: he told us quietly that he worships God like we do, in his own way."[103] The next day one of the monks wrote: "Now that we are officially

---

[101] Nève, "Le Monastère des SS. Pierre et André de Si Chan," p. 292, n. 1. The "first stone" of the foundation is Jehan Joliet, a monk of Solesmes. The same motive, with some variations, for choosing the two patrons is given in a photograph caption accompanying an article, Nève, "Le Prieuré des SS. Pierre et André de Si Chan," 3*. The article notes that the Abbey of Solesmes gave "the first but not only stone" to the priory of Xishan. In 1930 Solesmes also sent Gabriel Roux to China.

[102] Cf. "Chengtu. Inauguration et Bénédiction de l'Oratoire du Monastère bénédictin de Sischan," *Bulletin M.E.P.* (1930): 161–63.

[103] [Jehan Joliet], "Bénédiction de l'oratoire et installation officielle du nouveau monastère des ss. Pierre et André de Sichan" (ASA, Chine, Joliet 4 [Personalia], manuscript dated 17 December 1929).

installed and resume monastic life, we feel very inadequate, three poor monks, with only one official postulant and three on trial, who came after a walk of twenty-one days, to take up all the observances of a monastery. We have one joy: the Chinese already form a majority among us!"[104]

On 10 January 1930 the novitiate was opened with Fr. Émile as novice master. The formation of postulants and novices was the key to achieving the kind of "Chinese-style" monasticism envisioned by Jehan Joliet.[105] From the time of his arrival in China, his main concern had been that the "door be wide open, from day one, to all those who *vere quaerunt Deum.*"[106] "If you want a Chinese monastery, . . . a Chinese novitiate is essential."[107] At the end of 1927 Joliet wrote to Abbot Nève, dwelling at length on the issue:

> How are [the postulants] to be received? Sending them to Saint-André, it seems to me, is impracticable under the present circumstances. . . . If I were to suggest to these postulants that they, or at least some of them, could go to make their novitiate in Belgium, I can see their profound dismay: "You too, you are like the others, you want to westernize us, you will not treat us as equals unless you form us in isolation outside China." . . . Suppose that this is ignored and that some will certainly come to Belgium . . . and that they return to China as excellent monks. Since the best were chosen to be sent and since they had a good formation, it is inevitable that they will be given positions of authority and will have influence, and this will confirm the others and the laypeople in their preconceptions, without calculating the division in the monastery itself. . . . To accept postulants *a novitiate is needed here,* and only with the assurance of having a novitiate open can we deal seriously with these budding vocations. . . . In sum, what we urgently demand is [for you]

[104] Hildebrand Marga, "Inauguration du monastère chinois," BM 10 (1930), supp. no. 1: *Le Courrier Monastique Chinois*, 29*.

[105] Cf. also *infra*, app. 2, pp. 328–33.

[106] Letter of J. Joliet to G. Aubourg, 3 July 1928, in Delcourt, *Dom Jehan Joliet*, 151. Joliet refers to the passage of the Rule of St. Benedict that asks that the candidate for monastic life be examined to determine if *revera Deum quaerit* ("he truly seeks God": RB 58.7).

[107] Letter of J. Joliet to T. Nève, 26 September 1928, in Delcourt, *Dom Jehan Joliet*, 158.

to press Rome for the opening of a novitiate as soon as we are established in Sze-Chwan [Sichuan], this very year.[108]

As has been mentioned, Rome gave permission to have a canonical novitiate on site. However, the kind of formation that would be given in this novitiate was a further source of misunderstanding between Joliet and Abbot Nève. According to canon law, it was not possible to begin studies for priestly ordination without being *inferioribus disciplinis rite instructi*,[109] that is, without having a basic knowledge of Latin. It was Joliet's firm conviction, gained over the years, that it was "difficult and disastrous to impose on the Chinese a European training as an essential preparation for the priesthood."[110] Even before the arrival of the first Chinese postulants, he proposed that monastic profession be separated from priestly ordination, and that those who demonstrated an aptitude for the monastic life, but were not suited for language studies and philosophy, be allowed to enter the novitiate and make monastic profession. Joliet was against the division of the community into two categories of monks, so he made a bold proposal: "My wish always has been to have only one category of monks, period. This is completely Chinese and it avoids the danger of two castes, those of the choir (Europeans with some rare Chinese) and the other, the mass of Chinese lay-brothers. . . . I am decided . . . in this sense. . . . From the beginning of their postulancy they would come to the choir with us, learning the psalms by heart or reading them transcribed phonetically in Chinese."[111]

The correspondence between Joliet and Nève shows how important this issue was. The attitude of the abbot of Saint-André was defensive, invoking canon law and church discipline rather than demonstrating an understanding of the real situation: "Your difficulties arise from a misunderstanding. It is not a matter of working for

---

[108] Letter of J. Joliet to T. Nève, 6 December 1927, in Delcourt, *Dom Jehan Joliet,* 126–27.

[109] *Codex Iuris Canonicis Pii X Pontificis Maximi* (n.p.: Typis Polyglottis Vaticanis, 1932), c. 589, p. 176.

[110] Letter of J. Joliet to T. Nève, 9 April 1930, in Delcourt, *Dom Jehan Joliet,* 191.

[111] Letter of J. Joliet to G. Aubourg, 8 October 1929, in Delcourt, *Dom Jehan Joliet,* 184.

the glory of Saint-André or of Saint-Pierre of Solesmes rather than following your own will. Rome has made me responsible for the foundation of Si-Shan [Xishan] and not for its prior. The foundation charter foresees this. Si-Shan is a simple priory dependent in everything on its mother abbey. As a result, it has to develop according to the spirit and the letter of the constitutions of Saint-André unless it has special privileges."[112]

His rigid position reflected that of Roman church authorities. Approached several times for an answer to these questions, their only response was silence. Joliet therefore decided to go his own way, no longer consulting the abbot regarding the acceptance of applications for entry into the novitiate and admission to first monastic profession. However, since he was unable to find persons able to ensure the formation of postulants and novices, all of them eventually left the monastery.[113] Then there was the question of learning French. Joliet asked that only the most talented be required to learn it. On this point Abbot Nève finally gave his consent.

The questions raised by Joliet were related to other issues regarding monastic life in the Chinese context. "The problem of adaptation remained unsolved, and the arrival of Chinese interested in the monastic life from the very beginning posed serious questions. . . . What clothes should one wear?[114] In the course of studies for the postulants

[112] Letter of T. Nève to J. Joliet, 21 February 1931, in Delcourt, *Dom Jehan Joliet*, 204.

[113] One of them, Vincent Chen, made his first profession in 1931 and received the tonsure in 1932 and minor orders in 1935. He then went to Saint-André. When he was told by Abbot Nève that his solemn profession would be postponed, he left the monastery.

[114] Joliet wrote about this matter: "With regard to the monastic habit, I never thought about making the least modification without getting your consent. We have adopted the Chinese form of dress (nothing special; it's what Chinese priests and missionaries wear) since it is used by everyone in the country, without exception. At the present time I do not have any suggestion to make about what might be possible in the future. It is my firm opinion that this is a matter (as is also true for points of discipline and observance) that should not be decided in advance. Once we have become established in the monastery, we will again use the traditional habit, just as, insofar as possible, we will follow the customs of Saint-André." Letter of J. Joliet to T. Nève, 26 September 1928, in Delcourt, *Dom Jehan Joliet*, 159. However, in 1930 Joliet's ideas had changed. "Everyone thinks that our monastic habit is Western, and

what place should be given to Latin and the European languages? Is it necessary to distinguish the choir monks from the lay brothers by two different habits? Is it also necessary to distinguish them . . . when distributing charges? Will it be admitted that one can be a full monk, hence choir monk, without demanding the priesthood?"[115]

In order to deal with all of these challenges, Jehan Joliet asked Abbot Nève to be flexible. "If you want a Chinese monastery . . . you have to be ready to experiment, try things out, innovate provisionally on site. It is only by putting something into practice that you will see what changes have a future."[116] He also shared the same conviction with his confrere Hildebrand Marga, who wrote: "A foundation in the Far East poses new problems, for the solution of which beneficial experience gives us possible answers only by analogy. . . . These conditions imposed on our foundation in China were to be first of all a way of approach, a work of discernment and of study. It was in fact a work requiring us to feel our way, which as yet does not let us see more than the general lines of the future construction. . . . It is futile to try to see what will be the physiognomy of Chinese monasteries."[117]

The issues faced by Joliet obviously went far beyond the specific inculturation of Christian monasticism in China. They had to do with the essence of monastic life, the way it was lived at that time in the West, and the European cultural forms that were imposed on nascent Christian monasticism in other cultural settings. It was not just a matter of an "institutional" abbot and a "prophetic" founder not agreeing on certain details. Rather, the problems they were dealing with brought to the surface deep differences in the way they understood monastic life. Christian Papeians de Morchoven, an historian and the archivist at Saint-André, sums up the situation: "Today, we

---

our Chinese postulants do not like it. . . . Thus I have come to the conclusion that the true Chinese monastic habit ought to draw inspiration from ordinary Chinese clothes, which are very decent and modest, and which they wear so well." Letter of J. Joliet to T. Nève, 30 January 1930, in Delcourt, *Dom Jehan Joliet*, 185.

[115] Delcourt, *Dom Jehan Joliet*, 188.

[116] Letter of J. Joliet to T. Nève, 9 October 1928, in Delcourt, *Dom Jehan Joliet*, 175.

[117] Ma Wan Sang, "Le Monastère de Si shan en Chine," 5*, 12*.

have to admit that the ideas of Dom Joliet were somewhat prophetic; being Chinese with the Chinese, adapting the Benedictine Rule to the Chinese mentality, accepting the Chinese ways and customs, preparing monk-priests to be ordained without any knowledge of Latin, all this was real 'inculturation,' long before the word began to be used. Neither Dom Nève nor Rome could be expected to acquiesce in this new understanding of the mission of the church; such ideas were quite unknown before Vatican II."[118]

To this we must add the strong, independent, and intransigent character of Jehan Joliet, who often gave the impression to those near him of following his own project and of not fitting into accepted limits diplomatically, at the same time being distant from concrete problems that were ever more complex and at times different from how they were seen at Saint-André.[119] "Dom Joliet has erred in wanting to do violence to an institution: he has imagined that Si-Shan [Xishan], which is part of the Belgian Benedictine congregation with its fixed rules for its foundations in mission lands, could take another direction and enter into the mind-set of his own vision."[120]

On 24 October 1930 two new members joined the community of Xishan: Gabriel Roux (1900–1936), a monk of Solesmes, who assumed the positions of subprior and librarian, and Dominique Van Rolleghem (1904–1995),[121] a monk of Saint-André, who would leave China just four years later for health reasons. With their arrival, a more structured common life was possible. Thanks to the support of many persons in China and abroad, the library was well stocked

---

[118] Papeians de Morchoven, "The China Mission of the Benedictine Abbey of Sint-Andries (Bruges)," 309.

[119] Cf. letter of J. Joliet to T. Nève, 10 February 1929, in Delcourt, *Dom Jehan Joliet*, 167–68.

[120] Letter of É. Butruille, 9 November 1933, in Papeians de Morchoven, *L'abbaye de Saint-André Zevenkerken*, 2:205.

[121] Dominique Van Rolleghem, after spending a brief "hard but good time" in China, had to return to Belgium because of poor health. After he recovered, he went to the Congo, where he worked from 1934 to 1949. From 1950 to 1995 he was in India, where he had close contact with Henri Le Saux. For a detailed account of Van Rolleghem, see Benoît Standaert, "P. Dominique Van Rolleghem (1904–1995). Un des pionniers sur la voie de la rencontre avec l'hindouisme?," *Dilatato Corde* 1 (2011): 117–31.

and various works were begun: a bookbindery, a laundry room, a chicken coop, and an apiary. All the European monks continued to take Chinese lessons. For the present and future welfare of the community the conflict between the prior of Xishan and the abbot of Saint-André would have to be dealt with and a decision taken. In mid-1931, after the happiness that accompanied the first months of the new foundation, things came to an impasse. Differences were too great to be resolved and positions too incompatible to prevent a breakdown. Joliet was an "idealist" with big dreams but with little common sense; Nève was a "realist" with a greater sense for the practical management of things but unable to be flexible because of his official position. However, their differences, deep as they were, were expressed without rancor or bitterness.

Given Joliet's rapidly deteriorating health and the "impossibility of working with such divergent visions,"[122] as he wrote to the abbot in September 1932, he left Xishan on 23 May 1933 to rest in a small hermitage not far from the village of Hebachang (Hopachang, Hopatch'ang) in the mountains north of Chengdu. Here, two months later, he received a letter from the abbot of Saint-André who ordered him to return to Belgium for "consultations" and assigned Gabriel Roux to take his place as prior.

The removal of Joliet as prior had wide repercussions for the community, particularly among the young Chinese monks in formation. With his departure they lost a European monk who was open to their way of life and who eagerly sought to convey the monastic tradition of the Rule of St. Benedict to them while respecting their cultural identity as Chinese. In his letter to Abbot Nève, Gabriel Roux made this point: "In August–September [1933] the tempest arrived that risked demolishing the monastery. Your Paternity's decision to recall Dom Joliet to Europe . . . provoked a rebellion, and I assure you that the word is not too strong, of our Chinese brothers. In the measure taken, which circumstances rendered more odious, they saw clear proof of what Dom Joliet had told them again and again:

---

[122] Letter of J. Joliet to T. Nève, 20 September 1932, in Delcourt, *Dom Jehan Joliet*, 218.

the incapacity of European superiors to govern a Chinese monastery from a distance."[123]

Given Joliet's poor health, which prevented him from making the long journey back to Belgium, the abbot of Saint-André authorized him to stay in China and lead the life of a hermit in the vicinity of Chengdu. He asked him to make a formal promise to live alone, not to interfere in the life of the Xishan community, and not to accept candidates to the cenobitic or eremitic monastic life, since to do so would give his confreres at Xishan the impression that he was founding a new monastery with other monks.[124] Having received authorization from the abbot of Solesmes, Joliet's monastery of origin, and from Rome, Fr. Jehan retreated to the hermitage of Hebachang, which consisted of five small rooms (oratory, refectory and library, cell, room for a possible domestic, kitchen), where he led a solitary life of prayer, study, reflection, and work in the garden until his death.

The new prior, Gabriel Roux, was able to guide the community through the difficult years following the departure of Jehan Joliet. He was, in fact, "the principal artisan of the development [of Xishan], as Dom Joliet had been of its foundation."[125] He too had been a monk of Solesmes, but he knew the Abbey of Saint-André better than Joliet. In fact, he had changed his stability to Saint-André and was therefore more willing to reconcile the broad directives bequeathed by the founder of Xishan with the missionary monastic style of Saint-André.

Continuing the line of inculturation tirelessly promoted by his predecessor, Roux was assiduously devoted to studying the Chinese language. His deep love of the culture of the country deepened his desire for a monastery that would look and feel Chinese. He made every effort to add interior decorations and furnishings that complemented the Chinese architectural style of the monastic buildings. To this end he commissioned a young sculptor to carve crosses and candelabra for the chapel in the best Chinese style from the stone of the surrounding

[123] Letter of G. Roux to T. Nève, 18 April 1934, in Papeians de Morchoven, *L'abbaye de Saint-André Zevenkerken*, 2:210.

[124] Cf. letter of T. Nève to J. Joliet, 4 August 1934, in Delcourt, *Dom Jehan Joliet*, 226–27.

[125] "In Memoriam Dom Gabriel Roux," BM 15 (1936), supp. no. 1: *Le Courrier de l'Apostolat Monastique*, 1*.

mountains. Jehan Joliet's insistence on giving monastic life in Xishan as much of a Chinese character as possible was now fully assimilated by the community. "The buildings are entirely Chinese—inside and outside. At Sishan [Xishan] even the church is decorated in the Chinese style, and the Gothic vestments, designed by one of the fathers, are made in Chinese embroidery. The monks wear Chinese dress, eat Chinese meals (with chopsticks), and, with the exception of the Holy Mass and the Divine Office, chant the prayers in Chinese."[126]

Fr. Gabriel followed the directions given by Saint-André regarding the monastic education of candidates. Between fall 1934 and spring 1935 Abbot Nève made proposals to the community of Xishan during his six-month-long visit to China. He was accompanied by two other monks assigned to the Xishan community, Raphaël Vinciarelli (1897–1972) and Thaddée Yang Anran (1905–1982).[127]

The chronicler of the bulletin *Contemplation et Apostolat* provides a snapshot of Abbot Nève's impressions of his visit to the community of Xishan: "The most reverend father was happily surprised by the look of the cloister constructions. They are simple and modest, but complete and perfectly proportioned. According to him, 'the chapel is a small masterpiece of good taste, the common rooms and the cells are arranged very well. Everything is Chinese, but practical Chinese and Chinese in the best taste.' The most reverend father's joy was even greater at seeing monastic life led there according to the rule. In spite of the small number, up till now the entire Office and the rigor of observances have been faithfully kept. As for monastic work, it has consisted principally in organizing the house, in forming the first postulants, in receiving guests, and in studies."[128]

---

[126] *Sketch of the Life of the Rev. Thaddeus Yang*, cited in David J. Endres, "The Legacy of Thaddeus Yang," *International Bulletin of Missionary Research* 34, no. 1 (2010): 24.

[127] Abbot Nève had a gift for narrative, and his accounts of this trip are filled with detail and commentary about Chinese culture and society, as well as about the situation of the church in China. See Théodore Nève, "À travers le Szechwan," BM 14 (1935), supp. no. 1: *Le Courrier de l'Apostolat Monastique*, 1*–9*; Théodore Nève, "En remontant le 'Yangtzekiang,'" BM 15 (1936): 31–46; Théodore Nève, "Vicariats européens et vicariats chinois au Szechwan," BM 16 (1937): 1–16.

[128] "Saints Pierre et André de Si-Shan, Shunking (Szechwan)," CA 5 (1935): 202.

During his visit to Xishan, Abbot Nève confirmed what had already been decided some months before with the bishop of Shunqing, Paul Wang, on the occasion of his visit to Belgium. A school for oblates dedicated to St. Placid was to be opened to provide a basic education to future monks and also to seminarians of the vicariate.[129] The monastic formation imparted in Xishan was now clearly formulated so as to be in line with the directions given by Saint-André. All the proposals made in previous years by Joliet were abandoned. The school, the foundation stone of which was blessed on 12 March 1937, would now offer a contribution to the local church, of which the Xishan monastery was part. In this regard it is worth citing the reflection that appeared in the *Cahiers de Saint-André* (the continuation, since 1938, of the *Bulletin des Missions*), which gives unequivocal support to the way candidates to the monastic life would be trained.

> The birth of monasticism in a church is a long and delicate work; it is often the fruit of its plenary development and presupposes before this long generations of elite Christians. If Szechwen [Sichuan] has been chosen for the introduction of Benedictine monasticism, it is just because Christianity has existed there for several centuries and Christian communities there are numerous. There is no doubt that the pure and simple religious life as it was practiced by the first monks will find in the generous souls of these Christians a terrain favorable for growth. It is not necessary therefore to seek elsewhere the causes that render recruitment difficult. Over the centuries Benedictine monasticism has undergone an evolution in the direction, so characteristic of the Christian West, of direct and sacerdotal action. It has become a clerical order, which requires, hence, of its recruits the intellectual qualities necessary for the acquisition of a theological culture and of the necessary judgment for governing souls. Transported to the Far East, these requirements have only become greater. The use of Latin in the Roman liturgy and in theological formation requires from the candidate to the Benedictine life the capacity

[129] In the years 1935 and 1936 Bishop Paul Wang often expressed the desire that the Benedictine mission sisters of Lophem (Sisters of Bethany) found a monastery for women near the men's monastery at Xishan. Cf. Papeians de Morchoven, *L'abbaye de Saint-André Zevenkerken*, 2: p. 320, n. 161.

to assimilate a culture completely different from his own. In fact, there young people capable of priestly functions are to be found only in the population of minor seminaries. Very few pupils of Chinese schools would find a means of adding to their national formation a real Latin formation that could allow them to undertake a productive priestly life, whether secular or religious. To remove this difficulty, the creation of a school of oblates at Si Shan [Xishan] has always been envisaged, where from an early age the children showing signs of a monastic vocation would receive a formation that responds to the requirements of clerical studies and to the needs of their natural milieu.[130]

During Abbot Nève's visit to China, another undertaking was slowly maturing in his mind, namely, a second foundation in China. The opportunity for such a venture presented itself before he left for China, when the notable Lu Baihong (Lo Pa Hong, 1875–1937) of Shanghai, president of Chinese Catholic Action, proposed to his friend Lu Zhengxiang, who had become a monk at Saint-André, his idea of purchasing land in Shanghai or Nanjing for a monastic foundation. During his time in China the abbot became convinced that it would be good to have a monastery closer to the coast, since it would be more accessible and thus facilitate relations between Saint-André and China. A monastery located there would also be able to "attract" more vocations, since the conditions for contacts would be better. In China everyone encouraged Abbot Nève to embark on this new adventure. The community of Saint-André was less enthusiastic, but finally it too was convinced. In May 1936 Lu Baihong announced the purchase of land in Nanjing and the intention to begin construction of a monastery the following year.

Meanwhile, Prior Gabriel Roux died of typhus on 9 April 1936. He was succeeded by Raphaël Vinciarelli, who remained at the helm of the community until his expulsion from China in 1952. Originally intended for the projected Benedictine foundation in Nanjing, he was appointed prior of Xishan by Abbot Nève, who was forced to set aside the Nanjing proposal, which never materialized. Although urged by Joliet to pursue his ideal of "monastic life alone," Vinciarelli continued to implement the Saint-André vision of "apostolic ministry"

---

[130] "L'année 1937 à Si Shan," CSA 1 (1938): 98–99.

by opening an elementary school, which was dedicated to St. Maur, and a dispensary for the inhabitants of the surrounding area, in a process of gradual adaptation to Chinese ways. "If an adaptation is to be made, let it be made slowly, naturally, in the course of experience. But let us not say: let us change, let us adapt. The Chinese are themselves occupied in adapting to European life. They are changing many things. Let them go on and let us wait. There is one adaptation necessary, to love them and to make them feel this."[131]

Putting aside Joliet's overly "contemplative" approach and adopting Saint-André's "apostolic" model demanded, among other things, an increase of personnel to carry out the various activities. Three new monks came to Xishan in November 1936: Eleuthère Winance (1909–2009), Wilfrid Weitz (1912–1991), and Vincent Martin (1912–1999). They immediately enrolled in an intensive Chinese language course in the city of Suining. Their arrival brought to ten the number of members in the small community, which now included six European monks, two Chinese monks, and two Chinese lay brothers, plus some postulants.[132]

With the death of Jehan Joliet on 23 December 1937, "a period in the history of Si-Shan [Xishan] closes."[133] A few months before his death Joliet shared with his confrere Raphaël Vinciarelli and his friend Charles Rey a summary of his Chinese experience and his confidence about the future of Xishan and monasticism in China: "For thirty years I desired China and the foundation of a monastery. Thanks to God, who has granted me to see the realization of my desires and to know that the monastery continues to live and to develop. The future is for us. Monasteries have their assured raison

---

[131] Letter of R. Vinciarelli, 19 April 1935, in Papeians de Morchoven, *L'abbaye de Saint-André Zevenkerken*, 2:220.

[132] Cf. "Les Bénédictins de Si-Shan," *CA* 7–8 (1936): 286.

[133] Letter of R. Vinciarelli to C. Rey, 6 February 1938, in Delcourt, *Dom Jehan Joliet*, 241. Cf. also "Sichuan Shunqing Xishan benduhui xiudaoyuan yuanzhang shishi" [The prior of the Benedictine monastery of Xishan, Shunqing, Sichuan has died], *SZ* 7 (1936): 441; "Shunqing Xishan benduhui chuangbanzhe ji diyi ren yuanzhang Yu siduo shishi" [The founder and first prior of the Benedictine monastery of Xishan, Shunqing, has died], *SZ* 3 (1938): 166.

d'être in the christianization of China. Let us give the time that is necessary. Neither monks nor Chinese are in a hurry."[134]

> What is extraordinary and consoling is to see [in the Xishan monks] sympathy for and understanding of my difficulties and approval of my conduct and the almost complete similarity . . . in our ideas and desires for Si-Shan [Xishan]. . . . Will [the monks] succeed?—I don't know, but it is great and rather curious that in the measure of what is possible there is much more future in the long run for Si-Shan and even for the prevalence of the ideas that guided me than when I was prior or Fr. Gabriel Roux after me. I inevitably appeared as a stranger, while the present prior is a child of the house (he was an oblate there); he will perhaps be able to obtain and carry out quietly quite a few things that from me provoked suspicion and resistance. It's not a question of being carried away or of triumphing, but of thanking God for the present results that have something of the marvelous. I wasn't sad, but this brings a note of joy to my hermitage.[135]

In his *Note on the Origins of Xishan* written the same year, he went into more detail regarding his thoughts on this subject: "This long-term work is not made with programs and rules or sanctions: it is made by carrying it out and living it, by bits and pieces, without the mirage of statistics, without praise; it is a work for which there is no gratitude or support. But whatever many may think and say, it is not an illusion of illuminated mystics. No! I am resolutely optimistic about the possibility and the reality of results."[136]

The years immediately following the death of Joliet saw the progressive loss of half of the European monks because of requests made to the community for assistance and the difficult political situation in China at that time. Thaddée Yang moved to Chongqing to assist Bishop Jantzen and to help edit the Catholic French-language weekly *Le correspondant chinois*. Published by the daily newspaper

[134] Cited in Vinciarelli, "Dom Jehan Joliet et son œuvre monastique en Chine," 9*–10*.

[135] Letter of J. Joliet to C. Rey, 17 October 1937, in Delcourt, *Dom Jehan Joliet*, 235.

[136] Cited in Vinciarelli, "Dom Jehan Joliet et son œuvre monastique en Chine," 10*.

Yishibao (*I-shih pao* 益世報), founded in 1915 by Vincent Lebbe, it later became the monthly English-language *China Correspondent*. Vincent Martin received the prior's permission to work with the Little Brothers of Fr. Vincent Lebbe on an ambulance team in northern China during the Sino-Japanese War. He was interned in 1941 and remained a prisoner of war until the end of the hostilities. Wilfrid Weitz was the French-language tutor of General Chiang Kai-shek's bride from 1939 to 1941. The absence of these brothers, wrote the prior, "is a very heavy sacrifice for Si Shan [Xishan], but a sacrifice we agreed to with joy," since it constituted "a participation in the joys and sufferings of the people" of China.[137]

The difficulties caused by the Second World War added to those brought about by the Sino-Japanese War. Despite this, two new monks arrived in Xishan, Werner Papeians de Morchoven (1914–2008) and Albéric de Crombrugghe de Looringhe (1911–1981). The community was able to live together, but 1941 brought a new exodus of some of its members, who moved elsewhere to find work and earn a living. Even Prior Raphaël left Xishan at the end of 1942 and moved to Chengdu in the service of Bishop Rouchouse. Vinciarelli was invited to teach at the university in the old capital of Sichuan, which had become a refuge for many intellectuals who fled from the eastern parts of China. It was in this setting that he began to think about the possibility of creating an institution that could offer students a way to learn about Chinese culture and Western Christianity, thus dispelling prejudices and providing a place for dialogue between Western and Chinese cultures. He reflected on the years the monks had spent in Xishan: "In the course of their long stay at Sishan [Xishan] the monks had the time to devote themselves to the study of the Chinese language and to have their first missionary experiences. There they learned to know the old China of the countryside, to open their minds and their hearts to it. This stay, hence, was extremely

---

[137] Raphaël Vinciarelli, "Au monastère de Si Shan," CSA 5 (1939): 158. In the official local chronicle, the few lines dedicated to the Benedictine community of Xishan are almost totally about the service of some of the monks to the cause of the liberation of China during the war against the Japanese aggressor. See *Nanchong shi zhi* [Chronicles of the city of Nanchong] (Chengdu: Sichuan kexue jishu chubanshe, 1994), 610.

useful for us; it imprinted on our monastery a Chinese orientation, which will remain as its characteristic note and will only become more accentuated in the coming years."[138]

Transfer to Chengdu and Expulsion

Because of the extreme difficulty in obtaining the means of subsistence, life in Xishan was no longer possible. Moving to Chengdu and offering the Benedictines teaching posts that would provide them with the possibility of exercising an influence in the Chinese intellectual world appeared as the best way to regroup them. Bishop Jacques Rouchouse encouraged the community to take this step by providing them with a large estate not far from his official residence.

In 1944 the prior, along with Frs. Werner, Albéric, and Eleuthère, moved into the house made available by the bishop. They were soon joined by Fr. Thaddée. Frs. Hildebrand, Émile, and Paul Wu (Ou K'i-in), who had made profession in 1939, remained at Xishan.

The Chinese and Western Cultural Research Institute soon began to operate. Recognized by the government, its purpose was to bring the two civilizations closer together by means of comparative studies and to prepare the groundwork for a future Catholic university in the provincial capital. The results of the research conducted at the institute, which focused mainly on the fields of religion, history, literature, and the arts, were published by the institute itself. A Catholic bookstore adjoining the institute was opened in 1948.[139]

One of the monks, Thaddée Yang, spoke of the high expectations, somewhat excessive, he thought, in view of the paucity of resources, that the church in Sichuan had of the new institution.

> Everybody was counting on us, Benedictine monks, to instill a new spirit, more dynamic, into the church of Szechwan [Sichuan], which a long, drawn-out war had more or less paralyzed. . . . I did not share their optimism. Our program was over-ambitious, and none among us had the necessary Chinese

[138] Raphaël Vinciarelli, "Témoin du Christ en Chine communiste. Le Prieuré de Saint-Benoît de Chengtu," BM 26 (1952): 192–93.

[139] With regard to the nature, range, and organization of the institute, see Vinciarelli, "Témoin du Christ en Chine communiste," 191–219.

intellectual training. . . . By experience I dare to say that it is impossible to prepare and teach college-level courses and study the Chinese language and culture at the same time. The Chinese language and culture are by far more difficult to learn. All the more so in our case, because as foreigners and Catholic priests, our fathers were not accepted by the better non-Christian society, guardians of the authentic Chinese tradition.[140]

The correspondence between Prior Vinciarelli and Abbot Nève reveals another basic question that such an institution posed to the larger Benedictine community. How could monastic life, with its requirements of community life and prayer, be reconciled with an academic institution created outside the monastic framework? Even if it was true, as Prior Vinciarelli put it, that "circumstances have given a new direction to the activities of the Benedictines in Sze-Chwan [Sichuan],"[141] Abbot Nève still urged his sons in China to integrate their new work into the framework of their monastic life, which continued to be the main purpose of the Benedictine presence in China.

For a long time I have thought that Si-Shan [Xishan] was not a good place for a monastery of great amplitude. I was convinced that one day we would transport our penates [*sic*] to Chung-king [Chongqing] or to Chengtu [Chengdu]. . . . Although you have found a solution to the financial situation by adding to the idea of a monastic foundation that of an institution of higher studies, you have given to the monastic foundation such a new orientation that I am somewhat disconcerted. . . . The danger was to see our monastic foundation commuted into a scientific enterprise or at least a monastic foundation only as a support to a scientific enterprise; this would end by eclipsing totally the former. . . . We are very happy about your fine initiative and we congratulate you for the results achieved so far, but . . . we would like to see assured the constitution of a true monastery such as it was intended at the beginning of our activity in China.[142]

[140] Thaddée Yang, "The Chinese Adventure of an Indonesian Monk," http://www.valyermo.com/monks/yang2.html, accessed 21 August 2013.
[141] Raphaël Vinciarelli, "Lettre du Szechwan," CSA 12 (1947): 54.
[142] Letter of T. Nève to R. Vinciarelli, 20 April 1945, in Papeians de Morchoven, *L'abbaye de Saint-André Zevenkerken*, 2:275–76.

Since Abbot Nève was assured that "the monastery was the foundation of the institute and ensured its continuity over time and in the way it was run"[143] and that the school and the monastery would move forward together, the foundation stone of the school was laid on 29 June 1948, and a year later, on 11 July 1949, the community took possession of the new building, which was acclaimed for its "architectural and artistic beauty" and to which were transferred more than ten thousand volumes from the library of Xishan.[144] A new monk from Saint-André, the last to be sent, arrived that year. He was Gaëtan Loriers (1915–1996), who before leaving for China had studied sinology in Paris for two years and now continued to deepen his knowledge of Chinese.

This educational project began to produce good results in terms of the number of students enrolled in courses offered by the institution, the quality of exchanges, and the number of baptisms in the student body. However, everything was sharply reduced and eventually brought to a halt when Communist troops invaded Chengdu on 25 December 1949. For nearly a year the courses at the institute were allowed to continue in the form of study circles, but the Communist pressure gradually intensified with the imposition of heavy taxes, rigid control of the activities and movements of the Benedictines, searches, and exhausting interrogations. Describing the situation of the community in those days, Pierre Zhou wrote: "Seeing confusion and division growing among the clergy and laity of Chengdu, Father Prior Raphaël Vinciarelli frequently explained to the community the real current situation of the local church and the monastery, asking us to prepare at any time for all eventualities. We tried to keep the usual schedule of our daily life in celebrating Masses, reciting collectively Vespers and Compline, teaching, studying and doing all the other works, in spite of living in a near panic under the tense atmosphere."[145]

[143] Vinciarelli, "Témoin du Christ en Chine communiste," 195.

[144] Cf. Thaddée Yang, "L'inauguration du Prieuré de Saint-Benoît à Chengtu," CSA 21 (1949): 127–30; Raphaël Vinciarelli, "Une réalisation," CSA 21 (1949): 131–37. Cf. also "Benduhui she Chengdu fenyuan" [The Benedictines establish the dependent monastery of Chengdu], YZ 23 (1947): 378.

[145] Zhou Bangjiu, *Dawn Breaks in the East: One Spiritual Warrior's Thirty-Three-Year Struggle in Defense of the Church* (Upland, CA: Serenity, 1992), 11.

Nevertheless, in October 1950 it appeared that everything was over. The Office for Foreign Affairs informed the Benedictines that they would have to leave Chengdu in two weeks. As a result of a counterorder, however, departure was changed to house arrest. Prior Vinciarelli was subjected to repeated interrogations in order to wring a confession out of him that he was an imperialist enemy of China and to obtain his support for reforming the church according to the principles of the "Three Selfs." In response to his firm refusal, Fr. Raphaël was imprisoned in November 1951 and three months later was brought before a people's court and together with Fr. Eleuthère Winance was sentenced to immediate expulsion from the People's Republic of China.[146]

In the month following, all the foreign monks were likewise sentenced to forced repatriation. The last monk to depart from China was the one who had most recently arrived in China, Gaëtan Loriers, who left on 12 March 1952. The only Benedictine seedlings left on Chinese soil were Fr. Paul Wu and the young Br. Pierre Zhou, who described their life in the early months of 1952 until the forced evacuation of everyone from the priory, its expropriation, and its occupation by the Communists in April. "During this period, all the foreign members of the community either left the country 'voluntarily' or were expelled. The monastic family was dispersed. Only two Chinese members, myself and Father Paul Wu, were left to take care of the solitary building. We were clearly aware that we would have to move out sooner or later. . . . We had no daily duties. After attending Father Paul Wu's early morning Mass . . . we stayed in our respective cells reciting the Divine Office and reading holy books or went out visiting some of the faithful laymen and sisters."[147]

More will be said of Br. Pierre Zhou below. All we know of Fr. Paul Wu is that he was ordained a priest in 1950 and that when his foreign confreres were expelled, he returned to his family, where he

---

[146] Cf. Raphaël Vinciarelli, "Jubilé du prieuré Saint-Benoît de Chengtu," CSA 31 (1952): 119–34; Eleuthère Winance, "Une séance de police," CSA 35 (1953): 82–89; Eleuthère Winance, *The Communist Persuasion: A Personal Experience of Brainwashing* (New York: P. J. Kenedy and Sons, 1959).

[147] Zhou Bangjiu, *Dawn Breaks in the East*, 23.

continued for some time to exercise priestly ministry, until he was prevented from leaving his home. He was sentenced to twenty years in prison and died tragically in 1960 at the age of forty-five in the same labor camp on the outskirts of Chengdu where his confrere Pierre Zhou was also held.[148]

As they waited for an opportune moment to return to their adopted country, the members of the Benedictine China mission quickly reconstituted their community in Valyermo, California, where the new priory of St. Andrew was canonically erected in 1955, became a conventual priory in 1965, and finally an abbey in 1992. They did not simply look backward nostalgically but were eager to bring their past experience in China to the work they would do in their new home, as Prior Raphaël put it in one of his reports: "Besides the entirely monastic context where the liturgy is given a prime place, it was necessary to preserve the missionary spirit, oriented above all toward China. It was not a question, however, of a monastery that lived only in the hope of returning to China: it had to have, on the contrary, an immediate usefulness where it was, as well as a concrete and immediate work for the Chinese."[149]

Among the monks of Valyermo who came from China, Vincent Martin was the one who in the last years of his life once again became directly and deeply interested in that country and its culture, returning to China for study and visits.[150]

As for the monastic complex at Xishan after its abandonment in the 1940s, the site was used for secular activities until 1985, when it was returned to the Diocese of Nanchong (Shunqing). Of the two buildings that were once the monastery, one was initially used as a hostel for tourists.[151] More recently the monastery was renovated and transformed into a retreat house and diocesan conference center. The building has a permanent exhibition on Catholic culture and

[148] Ibid., 47, where the author tells of the death of Paul Wu, who was asphyxiated by gas during the transport of a diesel engine. Cf. also Hildebrand Marga, "Historique de chaque moine de Chine" (ASA, Chine 9), typewritten source.

[149] Papeians de Morchoven, *L'abbaye de Saint-André Zevenkerken*, 2:284.

[150] Cf. Francis Benedict, "Valyermo and China," *AIM Bulletin* 70 (2000): 105–6.

[151] Cf. "Rinascita di un vecchio monastero," *Asia News* 8 (1999): 31.

opens onto a large square dominated by imposing statues of the twelve apostles.[152]

Three Chinese Benedictines: Thaddée Yang, Pierre-Célestin Lu, and Pierre Zhou

As has been noted, the visit of the Chinese bishops to Saint-André at the end of 1926 was propitious in many ways. It caused the abbot and the community to think about China and sped up the process that led to the departure of the first two missionary monks to that country in the following year. One of the indirect consequences of the bishops' visit was the arrival at Saint-André in 1927, within the space of a few months, of two Chinese candidates for the monastic life. What follows is a brief account of these two, whose monastic life began with the abbey's initial steps toward founding a monastery in China. There will then follow an account of a third Chinese monk, whose story begins when Saint-André's Chinese monastic venture was almost over, since he entered the novitiate in Xishan only a few years before its forced dissolution.

The first Chinese postulant to take the Benedictine habit was Thaddée Yang Anran (Yang An Yuen, Yong Ann Juen, 1905–1982).[153] Born to a family of Chinese immigrants on the island of Java in Indonesia, he was brought up as a Buddhist by his father, who led an austere, ascetic, quasi-monastic life. Following the advice of his mother and with a view to a future diplomatic career, he studied first in Hong Kong, then in England and in Germany, and finally

---

[152] Cf. Jean Charbonnier, "La vie de l'Église dans la province de Sichuan," *Églises d'Asie* 4 (2008): 62; Wang Huaimao and Yang Jun, "Xinian qingcong jin cheng qiaomu. Tianzhujiao Nanchong Xishan benduyuan" [The shrubs of the past have now become trees. The Catholic Benedictine monastery of Xishan, Nanchong], *Zhongguo zongjiao* (*China Religion*) 7 (2007): 51–53.

[153] The most documented biographical profile was recently given by Endres, "The Legacy of Thaddeus Yang," 23–27. Useful autobiographical sources are Thaddée Yang, "From Buddha to Benedict," http://www.valyermo.com/monks/yang1.html, accessed 21 August 2013; Thaddée Yang, "The Chinese Adventure of an Indonesian Monk." Unfortunately, I was not able to consult the sources in the archives of the Archdiocese of Cincinnati, OH, which include the autobiography *Chinese Bonzes and Catholic Priests* (4 January 1943), the transcript of an interview, *Sketch of the Life of the Rev. Thaddeus Yang* (15 May 1945), and a diary, *Across the Pacific* (March–April 1946).

in Belgium, where he studied French in preparation for university. There he met Vincent Lebbe, who offered him hospitality at the family of a sister and gave him a scholarship that allowed him to take courses in Thomistic philosophy and social and political sciences at the Catholic University of Louvain. Moved by the fervor of Fr. Lebbe and by the example of the faith life of the family with whom he was staying, he asked to become a Catholic and was baptized on 26 December 1923. Shortly thereafter, as he himself writes, he heard the call to monastic life: "Not long after my baptism, I made up my mind to become a monk. But my confessor and spiritual director, regarding my yearning for monastic and contemplative life as nothing but the fleeting enthusiasm of a new convert, advised me to wait a few more years until I had attained Christian maturity."[154]

His subsequent research led him to familiarize himself with the Belgian monastic world, as he himself tells us. It is interesting to note that as he became familiar with Christian monastic life, what came to the surface was the model of Buddhist monastic life with which he was familiar and which continued in some way to attract him.

> In my quest for "Christian maturity," I began to attend the Office of Vespers at the Benedictine Abbey of Mont-César, at the outskirts of the city. The spectacle of the blacked-robed monks singing in unison and by turns bowing, genuflecting, and kneeling together around the altar brought back to memory my early Buddhist ascetic-contemplative life, thus making my resolve to be a monk all the stronger. I talked several times with the guest master. He gave me Saint Benedict's Rule to read. The Benedictine Rule appealed to me very much. But written in the sixth century, could it still be followed to the letter in the twentieth century? According to the guest master, his abbey was composed mainly of scholars, writers and teachers. My conception of monasticism was still my Buddhist father's—that a monk is a pure contemplative. In the light of this conception, I could not figure out how a monk could be anything but a monk, that is to say, a man devoted exclusively to prayer and meditation.[155]

---

[154] Yang, "From Buddha to Benedict."
[155] Ibid.

At the same time the young Albert (his Christian name) heard people talking about Saint-André's plans for a monastic foundation in China and about Lu Zhengxiang, a Chinese diplomat who was considering becoming a monk at Saint-André. He interpreted this as a sign that the abbey in Bruges might be the place to begin his monastic life as a Chinese monk and therefore made a visit to Saint-André. He was warmly welcomed by the guest master and the abbot, who invited him to take part in the abbey's plans for China and also expressed the hope that he would agree to "take an active part in the new venture."[156]

Attracted by the project and receiving the permission of his parents,[157] Albert went to Saint-André and received the monastic habit from Abbot Nève on 22 April 1927. A few months later, on 4 October together with Lu Zhengxiang, the second Chinese postulant, he received the habit, beginning his novitiate with the monastic name of Thaddée. The reason for choosing this name is curious. It was selected in remembrance of and gratitude to Fr. Lebbe. The Hebrew name that seems to have been given to the apostle Thaddeus was Lebbeus, which recalled the last name of the Belgian missionary who had led the young novice to the Christian faith.[158] When he finished his novitiate, during which time he "did not have any trouble observing the rule and customary," thanks, in his own words, to his "early Buddhist ascetic training and the moral and spiritual support of the novice master,"[159] Br. Thaddée professed his first vows on 5 October 1928. After completing his studies in philosophy at Maredsous and in theology at Mont-César, he was ordained priest on 31 July 1932.[160]

---

[156] Ibid.

[157] The reaction of the Buddhist father to the news that his son was determined to become a Christian monk is noteworthy. According to his son, he said, "If your conscience tells you that you should become a Christian monk, then go ahead, follow the voice of your conscience. But go into it seriously and courageously. One needs courage to be a good monk." Yang, "From Buddha to Benedict."

[158] Cf. "Le premier bénédictin chinois," BM 9 (1928–1929): 239. In the same news story, on the same page, there is a photo of the clothing ceremony of Br. Thaddée. Abbot Nève is giving him the habit, assisted by Jehan Joliet and Pie de Cocquéau, who would leave for China a little later, on 20 May 1927.

[159] Yang, "From Buddha to Benedict."

[160] Cf. "Zhongguo diyiwei benduhui yinxiushi Yang Anran siduo xiaozhuan" [A brief biography of Dom Yang Anran, first Chinese Benedictine monk], SZ 2 (1933): 117–18.

The monastic education of Fr. Thaddée took place entirely in Belgium, but the time to make a contribution to the Chinese mission of Saint-André, the hope Abbot Nève had expressed some years earlier, was not long in coming. Two years after his ordination Fr. Thaddée saw himself in the role of a missionary in his ancestral "homeland." In 1934 Thaddée Yang and Raphaël Vinciarelli, accompanied by Abbot Nève, who was making a canonical visitation to the priory of Xishan, arrived in China and remained there as members of the Benedictine community of Xishan. They entered that community just as it was implementing its decision to make a considerable commitment to teaching monastic candidates, seminarians, and Christians of the Diocese of Nanchong. Fr. Thaddée immediately plunged into the study of classical Chinese, as well as the literary, philosophical, and religious culture of China.

Subsequent political and ecclesiastical developments meant that Fr. Thaddée had to become involved in a number of different occupations. At first, in 1936 and 1937, he took part, on behalf of Abbot Nève, in negotiations with the tycoon Lu Baihong and with Archbishop Paul Yu Bin (Yu Pin) regarding a second Benedictine foundation in China, in Nanjing, which was never made because of the Sino-Japanese War. Subsequently, after a year in Kunming, Fr. Yang moved to Chongqing in 1939 to contribute to the publication of the French-language weekly *Le correspondant chinois*, a periodical published in close collaboration with the Ministry of Information to inform mainly French-speaking missionaries of the war policies of the government, which had taken refuge in Chongqing. From December 1943 until it discontinued publication in September 1944 this newsletter became an English-language monthly that published articles of cultural, social, and religious interest, mainly for the benefit of the US military stationed in China. In addition to being its director, Thaddée Yang also wrote some articles.[161]

Meanwhile, as we have seen, the Benedictines were thinking of transferring their priory from its isolated location in Xishan to the city center of Chengdu, where it could invigorate a university-level cultural institute. Thaddée Yang was involved not only in negotia-

---

[161] Cf. Endres, "The Legacy of Thaddeus Yang," p. 26, n. 19.

tions with the bishop and with the government regarding this project, but also in raising funds for it. For ten months in 1945–1946 he traveled around the United States on a "loathsome begging expedition."[162]

Back in Chengdu, he simultaneously held the posts of subprior of the Benedictine community and vice president of the institute. Absolutely convinced that an effective intellectual mission among the Chinese cultural elite would require a deep immersion in Chinese culture, he took up his studies with a teacher once again. "I resumed as best I could my oft-interrupted study of Chinese literature and philosophy. . . . Two hours of lessons in the morning, and two hours of exercise in calligraphy in the afternoon."[163] The worsening of his health along with the final deterioration of the political situation in China forced him to leave the country. Later, along with many refugees from China, he took up residence in the new community of Valyermo in the United States, where he continued his Benedictine life until his death.

Regarding the particular contribution of Thaddée Yang Anran to the "Chinese Mission," David J. Endres observed that it "was twofold: to foster greater understanding of China by Westerners, and to interest the Chinese in Christianity and the Benedictine monastic life."[164] In order to break down the walls of misunderstanding and distrust between Chinese culture and Christian faith and to show the compatibility of the two and the possibility of a fruitful mutual enrichment, Thaddée Yang wrote numerous articles in various English-language and French-language periodicals in the 1940s and 1950s.[165] During his years in China in his role as intermediary between Chinese culture, his hereditary identity, and the Christian message, on which was grafted his new way of life as a Benedictine monk, Thaddée Yang also often tried to meet with influential Buddhist and Taoist masters—a practice certainly not common in

[162] Yang, "The Chinese Adventure of an Indonesian Monk."
[163] Ibid.
[164] Endres, "The Legacy of Thaddeus Yang," 25.
[165] Some of them were *America, American Ecclesiastical Review, Catholic Mind, Catholic World, Shield, Les Cahiers de Saint-André*. For a list—not exhaustive but still representative—of the articles of Thaddée Yang, cf. Endres, "The Legacy of Thaddeus Yang," p. 26, nn. 27 and 28.

those days—engaging them in a discussion of doctrinal and spiritual matters.[166]

The entrance of the first Chinese postulant at Saint-André in the spring of 1927 caused people in the Belgian monastic world to take notice, but the arrival of the second Chinese postulant produced an even greater reaction both inside and outside the Catholic world, and also gained wide press coverage. The person who asked to be clothed with the Benedictine habit was Lu Zhengxiang (Lou Tseng Tsiang, 1871–1949), a political figure and a high-ranking Chinese diplomat. He had been a prime minister and a minister of foreign affairs of the Republic of China and its representative to several foreign institutions.

Many studies have focused on his political and diplomatic activities, as well as his contribution to relations between the Catholic Church and the Chinese government. Future research on the abundant material kept in the archives of Saint-André and elsewhere will surely bring to light further aspects of the political, diplomatic, and spiritual life of this exceptional "Christian Confucian."[167] Here

---

[166] Cf., e.g., Thaddée Yang, "T'ai-K'oung Fa-Che. L'opinion d'un abbé bouddhiste," CSA 10 (1946): 213–16; Thaddée Yang, "Le thé chez les taoïstes," CSA 20 (1949): 67–73; Thaddée Yang, "Le paradis de l'abbé T'ai-K'ung," CSA 22 (1950): 191–95.

[167] Cf. Alphonse Monestier, "The Monk Lu Cheng-Hsiang: An Ex-Prime Minister of China Enters the Benedictine Order," BCUP 5 (1928): 11–21; Vincent Artus, "Hommage au révérendissime père dom Lou Tseng-tsiang," CSA 19 (1949): 24–36; Luo Guang, *Lu Zhengxiang zhuan* [A biography of Lu Zhengxiang] (Hong Kong: Zhenli xuehui, 1949); John Wu Ching-hioung, *Dom Lou. Sa vie spirituelle* (n.p.: DDB, 1949); Geneviève Duhamelet, *Dom Lou. Homme d'État, homme de Dieu* (Brussells: Foyer Notre-Dame, [1954]); Édouard Neut, *Jean-Jacques Lou, Dom Lou. Quelques ébauches d'un portrait, quelques aspects d'un monde* (Brussells: Synthèses, 1962); Fang Hao, "Lu Zhengxiang," in *Zhongguo tianzhujiao shi renwu zhuan* [Biographies of important figures in the history of Chinese Christianity], vol. 3 (Taizhong: Guangqi chubanshe, 1973), 326–29; Luke Dysinger, "Abbot Peter Celestine Lou Tseng-tsiang, O.S.B.: Chinese Diplomat and Benedictine Monk," *Valyermo Benedictine* 1, no. 4 (1990): 4–12; Anne Vansteelandt, "Lou Tseng-tsiang: zijn contactenen en zijn invloed als monnik in de Sint-Andriesabdij (1927–1949)," *Zevenkerken* 176 (1991): 5–23; Anne Vansteelandt, "Lu Zhengxiang (Lou Tseng Tsiang), a Benedictine Monk of the Abbey of Sint-Andries," in *Historiography of the Chinese Catholic Church*, 223–30; Claire Chang Shu-chin, "When Confucius Meets Benedictus: The Destiny of a Chinese Politician, Lou Tseng-tsiang (1871–1949)" (MA thesis, Katholieke Universiteit Leuven, 1994); Shi Jianguo, *Lu Zhengxiang zhuan* [A biography of Lu

consideration will be given primarily to his spiritual and monastic life, paying special attention to those of his writings that treat of the synthesis between Christian spirituality and Chinese culture and contain his reflections on the contribution of monasticism to the evangelization of China.[168]

Born in Shanghai in 1871, Lu Zhengxiang was baptized in the Protestant Church linked to the London Missionary Society, in which his father was a catechist. "Protestantism," he wrote, "has been for me a stage without which I think I should not have been able to reach Catholicism."[169] He studied foreign languages in Shanghai and Peking, where he excelled in the study of French language and literature. He was soon sent to be an interpreter for the Chinese legation in St. Petersburg, where he remained for fourteen years (1893–1906). There his diplomatic, but also human and spiritual, education was marked above all by the diplomat Xu Jingcheng (Hsü Ching-ch'eng, King Shu-shen, 1845–1900), of whom Lu Zhengxiang said: "This statesman, upright and clear-sighted, honored me with his confidence and his devotion. . . . Without him I would never have become a diplomat, and, ultimately, I would have not become

---

Zhengxiang] (Shijiazhuang: Hebei renmin chubanshe, 1999); Zhang Shujin (Claire Chang Shu-chin), "Tianzhu jiaohui de zai sikao. Cong Lu Zhengxiang de jiaohui yinxiang tanqi" [A new reflection on the Catholic Church. The repercussions (of the ideas) of Lu Zhengxiang on the church], in *Zhong Fan waijiao guanxi shi guoji xueshu yantaohui lunwenji* [Proceedings of the international scholarly meeting on the history of the diplomatic relations between China and the Vatican] (Taipei: Furen daxue lishi xuexi, 2002), 267–80; *Lou Tseng-Tsiang and His Contribution to China* = *Tripod* 152 (2009); Chen Fang-chung, "Lou Tseng-Tsiang, A Lover of His Church and of His Country," *Tripod* 153 (2009): 45–66.

[168] Among his writings, see esp. Pierre-Célestin Lou Tseng-Tsiang, *Ways of Confucius and of Christ* (London: Burns Oates, 1948), a collection of the conferences given to confreres of the Abbey of Saint-André; Pierre-Célestin Lou Tseng-Tsiang, *La rencontre entre humanités et la découverte de l'évangile* ([Bruges]: DDB, 1949); Association Relais France-Chine, ed., *Dom Pierre Célestin Lu. Une vie toute droite* (Mesnil-Saint-Loup: Le Livre ouvert, 1993), an anthology of writings. In Chinese: Lu Zhengxiang, *Benduhui shilüe* [Brief history of the Benedictine Order] (Shanghai: Shengjiao zazhi she, 1935); Lu Zhengxiang, *Benduhui xiushi Lu Zhengxiang zuijin yanlunji* [Collection of the most recent conferences of the Benedictine monk Lu Zhengxiang] (Shanghai: Guangqi xuehui, 1936).

[169] Lou Tseng-Tsiang, *Ways of Confucius and of Christ*, 3.

either a monk or a priest."[170] One day, as Lu recounts in his memoirs, this man spoke to him of Christianity, its spiritual force, and the role it would play in the life of the young diplomat. His words, Lu said, were "prophetic."

> In the course of your diplomatic career you will have occasion to study the Christian religion. It comprehends various branches and societies. Take the most ancient branch of that religion, that which goes back most nearly to its origin. Enter into it. Study its doctrine, practise its commandments, observe its government, closely follow all its works. And later on, when you have ended your career, perhaps you will have the opportunity to go still farther. In this most ancient branch, choose the most ancient society. If you can do this, enter into it also. Make yourself its follower, and study the interior life which must be the secret of it. When you have understood and won the secret of that life, when you have grasped the heart and the strength of the religion of Christ, bring them and give them to China.[171]

What Xu felt and desired for Lu Zhengxiang was, in fact, the trajectory of his life in the following decades. He moved to different countries: the Netherlands, back to Russia, and China, where he became the director of the Ministry for Foreign Affairs of the new republic from 1911 to 1920, and he served for two terms as prime minister. He then moved to Switzerland and finally to Belgium. He married a Belgian Catholic in 1899 and was conditionally baptized in the Catholic Church twelve years later, in 1911, taking the name René.

"Baptized a Protestant, . . . he became a Catholic, but he was and remained a Confucian."[172] The spiritual journey of Lu Zhengxiang can rightly be seen as a harmonious synthesis of the moral and ritual dimensions of Confucianism with the Christian faith. He lived with the conviction that his peculiar vocation was to be a Christian who had been formed in the school of Confucianism and whose life was focused on the fundamental dimension of "filial piety" (*xiao* 孝). As his friend Wu Jingxiong put it, "It was just in view of his vocation

---

[170] Ibid., 8.
[171] Cited ibid., 12.
[172] Duhamelet, *Dom Lou*, 7.

that God wanted for him a long formation at the school of Confucius, which indirectly predisposed him to accept and assimilate Christianity. . . . In the light of the Gospel and of the lives of saints, Dom Lou [Lu] truly made supernatural the natural doctrine of filial piety that Confucianism gives us."[173]

Some passages from the writings of Lu Zhengxiang are clear evidence of this journey.

> I am a Confucianist. . . . Confucianism, whose standards of moral life are so profound and so beneficial, finds in the Christian revelation and in the existence and life of the Catholic Church the most illustrious justification of all, human and immortal, that it possesses, and it finds there at the same time the fulfilment of moral light and moral strength, which solves the problems before which our sages have had the humility to draw back, understanding that it does not belong to man to penetrate the mystery of Heaven, and that it is necessary, in venerating the Providence of Heaven, to wait until, if he deigns to do so, the Creator himself reveals himself.[174]

> The Confucian tradition has determined the prescription of the law [of filial piety] and the duties derived from it toward our parents, our country, those close to us, and the entire human race and, in the first place, toward God, the Supreme, our Creator. These same duties Jesus Christ has divinely prescribed in revealing to us authentically the way of "our Father who is in heaven"; he has sent us the "Spirit of the Father," which is his own Spirit, the Spirit of Jesus, the Son of the eternal Father.[175]

> The Confucian spirit led me to see the evident superiority of Christianity, as three centuries ago it led the minister of state Paul Siu [Xu].[176]

In Paul Xu Guangqi (1562–1633), a Confucian scholar of the late Ming period converted to Christianity by Matteo Ricci (1552–1610), Lu Zhengxiang saw a prototype of his own life. "A Mandarin

---

[173] Wu Ching-hioung, *Dom Lou,* 29–30, 41.

[174] Lou Tseng-Tsiang, *Ways of Confucius and of Christ,* 51, 54.

[175] Lou Tseng-Tsiang, *La rencontre entre humanités,* 136–37. On the relationship between Chinese filial piety and Christian faith as interpreted by Lu Zhengxiang, cf. also Chang Shu-chin, "When Confucius Meets Benedictus," 299–311.

[176] Lou Tseng-Tsiang, *Ways of Confucius and of Christ,* 52.

Christian like his illustrious predecessor, the diplomat Paul Siu-Koang k'i [Xu Guangqi], he created the ideal of the wise man in all its humility and in all its grandeur."[177] Writing about Xu Guangqi, Lu Zhengxiang referred to him as this "great figure of a statesman and a Christian" for whom he harbored a "fervent admiration, . . . tried to follow in his footsteps,"[178] proposing him as an example of a successful encounter between Confucianism and Christianity.

The same Confucian spirit that had led him to accept the Christian message led him, after the untimely death of his wife in 1926, to embrace the next phase of his Christian-Confucian journey, "withdrawal from the world" to a monastery, there to live according to the Rule of St. Benedict, which was full of implicit references to Confucian ethics. "To summarize in one stroke [Dom Lu's] physiognomy, I would simply say that he was 'Benedictine' even before knowing the Rule of St. Benedict. The good God had formed Dom Lou [Lu] at the school of Confucius in the domain of the natural life and of culture, preparing him to embrace and to live fully the monastic life on the plane of grace and of the spirit. In his political career as in his family life he was inspired, as if naturally, by the principles of discretion and of strength that characterize the spirit of St. Benedict. In his monastic life he lived this spirit fully."[179]

If his wife's death was the immediate cause of his entrance into the monastery, as many biographers claim, the deeper reasons behind his decision were related to his spiritual persona, shaped by the multifaceted spirituality of China, and his political persona, formed by Confucian ethics. Lu's sense of "transcendent consciousness" drew him to pursue a spiritual life beyond the world's secularity and to withdraw from the political scene at a time when the conditions for proper and effective political action were no longer certain.[180]

Lu first thought of entering Maredsous, but then, having read the missionary magazine of Saint-André, the *Bulletin des Missions*, and having heard of the abbey's interest in China, he contacted Abbot

---

[177] Artus, "Hommage au révérendissime père dom Lou Tseng-tsiang," 25.

[178] Pierre-Célestin Lou Tseng-Tsiang, *La vie et les œuvres du grand chrétien chinois Paul Siu Koang-k'i* (Lophem-lez-Bruges: Abbaye de Saint-André, [1934]), 7, 19.

[179] Wu Ching-hioung, *Dom Lou*, 61–62.

[180] Cf. Chang Shu-chin, "When Confucius Meets Benedictus," 261–80.

Nève and made his first visit to Bruges in May 1927, with the intention of becoming a Benedictine oblate.[181] The abbot, however, made an alternate proposal, and a few months later, on 4 October 1927, at the age of fifty-six, René Lu Zhengxiang received the monastic habit. That simple but well-attended ceremony was the beginning of the monastic life of a man who immediately became "a glory of the abbey."[182] On 14 January 1928 he began his novitiate, receiving the monastic name of Pierre-Célestin. Like the pope in the Middle Ages who "made the great refusal," resigning the papacy to retire to a monastery, this Chinese diplomat was now leaving the political world for a secluded life in a monastery. In his wish to be an authentic follower of the way traced by Benedict, the years of his monastic formation were indeed characterized by withdrawal and humility, the monastic virtue par excellence. Two of his brother monks at Saint-André testified to this.

> The presence of Dom Lou [Lu] in the Saint-André cloister was a presence of humility and effacement. His perfect submission to the will of his superiors revealed how profound was his virtue of humility. All who knew him know to what an extent this virtue was incarnated in his person.[183]

> He was of an extraordinary docility for his age and experience. He accepted the monastic life as a whole, without voicing the least remark or criticism of an institution, the venerable character of which commanded his respect. . . . He was present with the other novices at the talks, where he enjoyed especially the commentaries on the holy Rule. He wanted to continue to be present at the instructions for novices even when his novitiate time was already ended.[184]

---

[181] When he was ordained to the priesthood in 1935, he said: "Eight years ago the only reason I came to Saint-André was to seek the silence and peace I needed. I aspired to nothing other than monastic life as a claustral oblate." Cited in Papeians de Morchoven, *L'abbaye de Saint-André Zevenkerken*, 2:200.

[182] Papeians de Morchoven, *L'abbaye de Saint-André Zevenkerken*, 2:199. A description of the ceremony, along with a photo of the group of postulants and novices, can be found in Monestier, "The Monk Lu Cheng-Hsiang," 11–13.

[183] Papeians de Morchoven, *L'abbaye de Saint-André Zevenkerken*, 2:199.

[184] Artus, "Hommage au révérendissime père dom Lou Tseng-tsiang," 29.

Despite this, and primarily thanks to Édouard Neut, the editor of the mission magazine of the abbey and also Lu's secretary at the time, from the day of his entrance into the monastery newspapers and magazines did not cease to draw attention to each of the stages of his monastic life. On 15 January 1929 Br. Pierre-Célestin made his first vows, then, on 15 January 1932 his solemn monastic profession, having received the tonsure a few days before. The most important and magnificent ceremony was his priestly ordination on 29 June 1935. It was presided over by Archbishop Celso Costantini, former apostolic delegate in China, and attended by numerous distinguished guests from the ecclesiastical, monastic, political, and diplomatic worlds.[185] The solemnity of the ceremony was repeated again a decade later, when Fr. Pierre-Célestin was blessed as the titular abbot of Saint-Pierre in Ghent.[186]

After his priestly ordination Fr. Pierre-Célestin accepted several invitations to lecture on his human and spiritual journey, on the church in China, and on the role of Christianity in its encounter with other civilizations. He sought various ways to strengthen relations between China and the Vatican and he continued to take an interest in the political, social, and moral situation of his homeland and of his new country, Belgium.[187] This is not surprising, given the prominence of the person who had entered the monastery and the resonance that his word could have in cultural, political, and diplomatic circles. What seems to be behind these public interventions, however, are the requests made by his superiors and his secretary more than his personal desire. That is the opinion of scholars who have carefully studied the written materials pertaining to Lu Zhengxiang. "When Lou [Lu] entered the monastery, he intended to lead a quiet life of prayer and meditation, but his social prestige and position had been so important and public that it would be difficult to expect people to respect his monastic seclusion. Even his superiors wanted him

[185] Cf. *Les solennités de l'ordination sacerdotale du r. p. dom Pierre-Célestin Lou Tseng-Tsiang O.S.B. Abbaye de Saint-André, le 29 juin 1935* (n.p.: n.p., [1935]).

[186] Cf. *La bénédiction abbatiale du révérendissime père dom Pierre-Célestin Lou Tseng-Tsiang, abbé titulaire de Saint-Pierre de Gand. Abbaye de Saint-André, le samedi 10 août 1946, fête de Saint Laurent* (n.p.: n.p., [1946]).

[187] Cf. Chang Shu-chin, "When Confucius Meets Benedictus," 321–37.

to maintain contact with all his former international acquaintances in political, diplomatic and cultural circles. In particular Lou's secretary Dom Édouard Neut stimulated Lou to maintain contact with his friends and resume his role in public life by giving lectures and speeches."[188]

All this activity, however, was not at the expense of his monastic life, to which he devoted himself faithfully for exactly two decades, until his death on 15 January 1949, the twentieth anniversary of his monastic profession.

The testimony of his Chinese confrere, Thaddée Yang, is especially significant. Immediately after his profession, Br. Pierre-Célestin opened his heart to Thaddée about the meaning of his monastic vocation.

> After his profession of vows, he confided to me that his sole ambition was to follow a centuries-old Chinese tradition. "You see, Brother Thaddée," he said, "In the past, when a public servant felt that he had fulfilled his obligations toward the state, he would retire to his native village or to some remote place to spend the rest of his life in contemplation or in communion with nature." . . . "Why then," I asked him, "Do you study Latin and scholastic philosophy and theology? At your venerable age, it must be hard on you." "Between you and me," he answered, "it is only because father abbot and Father Édouard, my spiritual counselor, have talked me into it. You see, Brother Thaddée," he went on after a short pause, "my Confucianist training has taught me never to disappoint people knowingly. I cannot shake off my Confucianist training any more than you can shake off your Buddhist training completely."[189]

Liturgy, specifically the *opus Dei* that is at the heart of the monastic life, must have played an important role in the monastic vocation of Lu Zhengxiang. That form of prayer would have been consonant with the ritual dimension of his Confucian education. "Dom Lu found true happiness in Catholic worship, centered on the self-offering of the Son to the Father and celebrated with all the beauty of the Benedictine liturgy. There he discovered the fulfillment of the

---

[188] Ibid., 321.
[189] Yang, "From Buddha to Benedict."

mystery of man's relation to God, a mystery that is foreshadowed in the Confucian ritual of sacrifice to Heaven. Ceremonies that carry such a depth of meaning do not become merely formal ritualism. Liturgical prayer is essentially an opening to God and to humanity."[190]

On this key issue of prayer, it is interesting to note that Dom Lu, in addition to *lectio divina* and liturgical prayer, practiced two forms of "meditation" that were typically Chinese. The first is known in Chinese as *jingzuo* 靜坐, "quiet sitting," a practice of Taoist origin but later also used by Buddhists and Confucians. It is oriented to interiority and the purification of mind and heart, and its goal is the fulfillment of one's true nature. That is what Lu Zhengxiang wrote in a notebook that is kept at the Abbey of Saint-André: "Doing *ching-tso* [*jingzuo*] can get rid of the factors that do not belong to God. Practicing *ching-tso* makes my mind pure. The man with a pure mind can keep in close contact with God. This is also said in Christianity. Christ insists on purity of heart, which means a capacity for seeing things in depth. 'Happy the pure of heart, they shall see God' (Matt 5:8). Thus the brightness of human nature can be indeed manifested. After we recognize our human nature clearly, we can gradually come closer to God and understand God. Man's first duty is to know Heaven, the root of our life."[191]

The second typically Chinese form of meditation that Dom Lu practiced is the daily discipline of introspection and discernment and involves a written record of one's good and bad deeds, called in Chinese *gongguo ge* 功過格, "record of merits and demerits." This practice of Taoist origin spread throughout China from late imperial times in various syncretic forms and became especially popular among the literati who were attracted by Buddhism. In the archives at Saint-André there is a Chinese paper notebook that belonged to Lu Zhengxiang in which he noted the times when he failed to acquire certain virtues.[192]

---

[190] Jean-Pierre Charbonnier, *Christians in China: A.D. 600 to 2000* (San Francisco, CA: Ignatius, 2007), 413. Cf. also the reflections of Lu Zhengxiang on the Catholic liturgy in Lou Tseng-Tsiang, *Ways of Confucius and of Christ*, 52ff.

[191] Cited in Chang Shu-chin, "When Confucius Meets Benedictus," 314.

[192] Cf. ibid., p. 318, esp. n. 100.

Apart from his numerous letters, which are yet to be studied, it is especially in his work about the history and characteristics of Benedictine monasticism, *A Brief History of the Benedictine Order*, written in Chinese, and in some pages of his *Souvenirs et pensées*, that we find reflections on monasticism's role in renewing the moral and spiritual life of the church and of European society. He had no hesitation in proposing the "monastic model" of the Rule of St. Benedict, which he never tired of sending to his many friends in China, and the spirituality of Benedictine monastic life as sources for the renewal of ancient Chinese culture: "I should like to invite my compatriots to make a brief stay in the guesthouse of the Abbey of Saint-André, and I should like to say to them: 'Read the Rule of St. Benedict, observe the family life which we lead, see how we conceive and organize prayer and work, and study how we Chinese might be able to adopt that Rule, which is a synthesis of Christianity, and to introduce it and to apply it among our people.' . . . The Rule of St. Benedict will not fail, in the hour chosen by Providence, to be understood by the East, to be admired and loved among our people and to be practised by them."[193]

In Lu Zhengxiang's mind, however, the biggest contribution that Benedictine monasticism could make to China was spreading Christianity in the land of his birth.

> What are the vocation and the function of Benedictine monasticism in developing the foundation of the church in China? . . . The Benedictine monastery is not a tomb. It is not even a hermitage. It is a family, a *"familia,"* and one of the most ancient and most characteristic institutions of the great family of God which is called the Catholic Church. For this reason it is particularly well qualified to give the hierarchy and diocesan clergy of China, and at the same time Chinese society, an active, *familiar* and religious assistance, a fraternal support, which will

[193] Lou Tseng-Tsiang, *Ways of Confucius and of Christ*, 92, 94. Regarding this similarity between life in a Benedictine monastery and life in a Chinese family guided by the principle of "filial piety," and regarding "Confucian" elements in the Rule of St. Benedict (such as modesty, honesty, self-discipline and ritual), see the first pages of Lu Zhengxiang, *Benduhui shilüe*, and Chang Shu-chin, "When Confucius Meets Benedictus," 284–87.

only be complete when Benedictine monasticism has gained within my country sufficient suitable recruits for the spirit of Saint Benedict to take root among the élite of our best minds and our greatest hearts.[194]

Fr. Lu takes his reflection a step further by comparing the respective spiritual paths of Buddhist and Christian monasticism, doing so with a bold reference to his own spiritual journey.

> At present Chinese monasticism is Buddhist. What would our country be today if that monasticism had been Benedictine? . . . In the seventh century of the Christian era, a Chinese Buddhist monk, wishing to give true monasticism to his country, left for the West and lived for seventeen years in the monasteries of India, fully acquainting himself with their doctrines and traditions, their observances and the whole of their life. After that he returned to China, assisting powerfully in giving to Buddhist monasticism an impulse which, [having] become irresistible, was to bring about the spread of Buddhism into all the provinces of the whole country. This monk was called Hsüan Tsang [Xuanzang, 602–644]. You may be assured that I have meditated long on the vocation of Hsüan Tsang; and today I cannot refrain from telling you the question which many are asking themselves about us in my country: "Is Benedictine monasticism inferior or superior to Buddhist monasticism?" One thing is certain, and that is that Buddhist monasticism in China has been the great instrument of the spread of Buddhism through the entire country. Is Benedictine monasticism in a position to take part on the same scale in spreading and establishing Christianity through the whole of China—to take a part of which the apostolic result would be incalculable. . . . I am not worthy to be a Benedictine Hsüan Tsang, but perhaps, during my lifetime or after my death, the Lord will cause his glory to shine so much the more because, among so many millions of Chinese, to help in bringing the Rule of St. Benedict to China, he has been willing to recruit one weak old man.[195]

---

[194] Lou Tseng-Tsiang, *Ways of Confucius and of Christ*, 91–92.

[195] Ibid., 92, 95–96. In a letter Lu Zhengxiang wrote to Archbishop Stanislaus Luo Guang, he stated that becoming a "Christian Xuanzang" was not his idea, but that of his secretary Édouard Neut (cf. the letter of 17 January 1944, cited in Chang Shu-chin, "When Confucius Meets Benedictus," 322–23). On his being identified as a

In one of his letters, Theodore Nève says that he asked Pierre-Célestin Lu if he thought Christian monasticism should undergo some modifications in China. The position of this "fundamentalist" Chinese monk seems to ignore, among other things, the fact that Buddhist monasticism took root in China and spread with surprising rapidity because of its willingness to change some of its forms. "I have consulted Br. Pierre-Célestin Lou about the possible modifications to be introduced into Benedictine life to adapt it to the needs of today's China. He told me not to introduce anything. He hopes that we will give monasticism to China as it exists in the West, except for some details. He says that China is trying much more to raise itself by adopting European customs than to remain fixed in ancestral ways."[196]

With a highly symbolic gesture, the city of Ghent offered Fr. Pierre-Célestin, at the time of his blessing as titular abbot of the Abbey of Saint-Pierre in 1946, a block of granite from the ancient cloister.

> The city of Ghent offered me a stone extracted from the foundations of the ancient Belgian abbey, so that it may become the first stone of the foundations of a new abbey, dedicated also to the prince of the apostles and built in our homeland. Circumstances so far have not permitted me to transport this foundation stone to China, which is destined to be laid most probably near Peking, on some hill that the Lord himself will indicate to us when the moment for building will have arrived. At the time when God called me to the monastic life, the Abbey of Saint-André-les-Bruges was founding in China, in the province of Setchwan [Sichuan], the first Benedictine cloister, the starting point of Benedictine monasticism in our country. This monastic hearth will bring a very efficacious fraternal cooperation when the providential hour arrives in which the thirteen-centuries-old Abbey of Saint-Pierre in Ghent will be reborn in China, of which a Chinese has become the titular eighty-first abbot.[197]

"Benedictine Xuanzang," cf. also a letter he wrote a month earlier to Pope Pius XI, 17 December 1943, cited in Chang Shu-chin, "When Confucius Meets Benedictus," 355.

[196] Letter of T. Nève to J. Joliet, 27 March 1931, in Delcourt, *Dom Jehan Joliet*, 207.

[197] Lou Tseng-Tsiang, *La rencontre entre humanités*, 151–52.

The story of a third Chinese Benedictine is one of unwavering fidelity to Christ and to his church during the first three decades of the People's Republic of China, when Chinese Christians were subjected to persecution.[198]

Br. Pierre Zhou Bangjiu was born in 1926 in Suining, Sichuan province. In August 1938, when he was twelve years old, he was received as a postulant at the monastery of Xishan. After more than a decade of study and spiritual formation he was admitted to the novitiate on 15 October 1949 and a year later, on 15 October 1950, he made his first monastic profession.

When the Communist storm struck, and the Benedictine community of Xishan moved to Chengdu, Br. Pierre proved his faithful adherence to the Catholic Church on more than one occasion, not hesitating to speak against and using whatever means he had to combat the "Three Selfs" movement, which aimed to establish a Chinese church independent of the universal church and free of all ties to papal authority. Br. Pierre gave his most courageous verbal and public testimony on 4 November 1951, when he was called to clarify his position in front of the "Three Selfs" committee and a popular assembly of a few hundred people. Accused of being a collaborator of the imperialists and, as a follower of the Christian religion, of possessing retrograde and reactionary thinking, this twenty-five-year-old man, with a "spirit completely serene" and a "soul imbued with the truth of Jesus and his inexhaustible goodness," testified to his absolute and unyielding faith in Jesus Christ and declared without hesitation his adherence to the Catholic Church.[199] The following is the essence of his impassioned profession:

---

[198] The main source for reconstructing the life of Br. Pierre Zhou is his autobiography: Zhou Bangjiu, *Dawn Breaks in the East*, which is also published in French and Chinese. Cf. also Zhou Bangjiu, "A Skiff Cuts through the Waves. A Discourse on October 15, 2000," http://www.valyermo.com/monks/peter.html, accessed 21 August 2013.

[199] The text of this declaration appears in a number of publications: cf. Raphaël Vinciarelli, "Profession de foi d'un jeune moine bénédictin chinois," CSA 31 (1952): 135–39; Vinciarelli, "Témoin du Christ en Chine communiste," 209–13; Pierre Zhou Bangjiu, *L'aube se lève à l'Est. Récit d'un moine bénédictin chinois emprisonné pendant 26 ans dans les camps de la Chine communiste au nom de la foi* (Paris: Pierre Téqui, 2000), 271–78 (with some variations from the text of 1952).

If you say that I have too much veneration for the "foreigners" and that I place too much trust in them, to the point of allowing myself to be deceived by them, then learn that these "foreigners" that you speak of for me are none other than Jesus Christ, a Jew, founder of the Catholic religion. I not only believe in him, but moreover I adore him and desire nothing else but to live thanks to him and for him. If you say that I am drugged by the "imperialist" to the point of making myself his "pack hound," then learn that this "imperialist" is none other than him, the Jew Jesus Christ, whom no one can overcome. Now my only regret is that I have not yet reached a full likeness to Christ and have not yet known the complete transformation to become a true "pack hound" of Christ.[200]

In April 1952, after all the European monks had been forced to leave the community, Br. Pierre returned to live in his father's house in Suining, helping him in his optical shop. A year later, in 1953, he returned to Chengdu to resume contact with the forces that opposed the independence movement. "I lived a hard life; however, I did not become discouraged, nor did my will weaken."[201] During those months he was still able to make a retreat at the Trappist monastery in Nibatuo and to look for ways, all of which proved unworkable, to flee to Hong Kong.[202]

The situation worsened further when in November 1955 Br. Pierre was arrested for counterrevolutionary crimes and held in prison in the same city of Chengdu. During that difficult time he kept his faith alive and nourished his spiritual life by praying the liturgical and devotional prayers he had learned in the monastery, as he wrote: "I began to draw on the firm foundation of my prayer life established during the years of my life in the monastery to console and strengthen my inner resolve. Each day I recited the necessary prayers which I had chosen by myself in the beginning of the fifties and had memorized—Compline and the daily fixed parts of Holy Mass. At different times, I raised my soul to Our Savior to adore and receive him spiritually in the sacrament of the Holy Eucharist. Whenever

[200] Zhou Bangjiu, *L'aube se lève à l'Est*, 277.
[201] Zhou Bangjiu, *Dawn Breaks in the East*, 29.
[202] Cf. Zhou Bangjiu, "Chine: une lettre émouvante," CSA 43–44 (1955): 165.

possible, I recited all the fifteen mysteries of the rosary in place of
the Divine Office. I used any opportunity or place to pray."[203]

In 1958 he was sentenced to twenty years in prison and transferred
to a re-education labor camp, known in Chinese as a *laogai*, on the
outskirts of Chengdu and forced to work in the local steel factory.
Two years later there was another transfer. From 1960 to 1971 he
was interned in the Nanchong Provincial Prison number 1, a maximum security prison for young criminals. Interrogation, torture,
and humiliation became more violent and more frequent, but the
steadfast resistance of Br. Pierre continued to be nourished by his
deep faith, fervent prayer, and the writing of poetry. The isolation
of his prison cell became for him a new monastic cell, as he wrote:
"With each day totally at my disposal in the peaceful and secluded
surroundings, I was offered an excellent opportunity for prayer and
meditation. Thus this prison cubicle became my monastic cell and
I enjoyed both peace and happiness. I gave no thought to life or
death, to good or bad fortune. I entrusted my destiny to the care of
my heavenly Father."[204]

In 1966, the beginning of the terrible "Great Proletarian Cultural
Revolution," he was sentenced to an additional five years in prison
and then transferred to the labor camp of Peng'an in 1971. Thanks
to the political changes that began to be implemented at the end
of 1978, the conditions of his life "began to change and improved
considerably,"[205] as he himself wrote. In this calmer climate he was
also able to resume his study of English and French.

Finally released in July 1981 after twenty-six years of detention, Br.
Pierre initially returned to live with his brother's family in Suining.
However, the hostility he experienced, especially from those in the
church who had joined the resurrected Chinese Catholic Patriotic
Association,[206] convinced him to seek a way to leave China as soon
as possible. He was able to resume contact with the rest of the com-

---

[203] Zhou Bangjiu, *Dawn Breaks in the East*, 37.

[204] Ibid., 62–63.

[205] Ibid., 92.

[206] The Chinese Catholic Patriotic Association, an organization created with
the aim of supporting the "Three-Selfs" policy of the Chinese government (self-
governance, self-support, self-propagation) and responsible for the management and

munity of Xishan-Chengdu who were exiled in the United States, and at the end of 1984 he was able to become part of the community of the priory of St. Andrew in Valyermo: "Thus the thirty-three-year struggle was ended. My long-cherished wish and fond dream of leaving China to rejoin my monastic community finally became a reality. I was beside myself with joy."[207]

The German Benedictines and the Mission of Yanji

In the same "axial age," if we may thus refer to the 1920s, that saw the beginning of the Benedictine presence on Chinese soil, German Benedictine missionaries also arrived in northern China. Their presence in that vast and promising field for the sowing of the Gospel that is China is not surprising.[208] Founded as the Missionary Institute of St. Joseph in Reichenbach-am-Regen, Bavaria, in 1884 by Andreas Amrhein (1844–1927), a Benedictine monk of the Abbey of Beuron with high missionary ideals, the institute moved to Emming in 1887, where the monastery took the name of the local chapel dedicated to St. Ottilia (or Odilia of Alsace, 660–720, foundress and first abbess of the Monastery of Hohenburg). The community grew rapidly, and in the same year, 1887, the first group of missionaries was sent to southeastern Africa. The missionary Benedictines of Saint Ottilien were recognized as a congregation in 1896 and were affiliated with the Benedictine Confederation in 1904. From the very beginning

---

control of the Catholic Church, was founded on 2 August 1957. Dismantled in the years of the Cultural Revolution, it was officially restored in May 1980.

[207] Zhou Bangjiu, *Dawn Breaks in the East*, 129.

[208] The sources I consulted for this brief account of the history of this Benedictine family in China are Theodor Breher, *Erntegarben vom Acker der Yenki-Mission, Mandschurei, den Wohltätern u. Freunden gebunden* (Yenki: Bischöfliche Missionsdruckerei, 1937); *Tatsachenbericht aus dem Missionsgebiet Yenki (Mandschurei)* (St. Ottilien: EOS, 1954); Adelhard Kaspar and Placidus Berger, eds., *Hwan gab. 60 Jahre Benediktinermission in Korea und in der Mandschurei* (Münsterschwarzach: Vier-Türme-Verlag, 1973), esp. chap. 3: "Yenki," 157–97; Johannes Mahr, *Aufgehobene Häuser. Missionsbenediktiner in Ostasien*, 3 vols. (Sankt Ottilien: EOS, 2009), esp. vol. 2: *Die Abteien Tokwon und Yenki*; Jeremias Schröder, "The Benedictines in China," 15–19. Occasional accounts of the Chinese mission can also be found in the congregation's periodical, *Missions-Blätter von St. Ottilien*.

their particular mission within the Benedictine Order was *pro missionibus exteris*.[209]

The Chinese mission of the Benedictines of Saint Ottilien is closely linked to their presence in Korea, where a first group of missionary monks had founded a monastery and opened a vocational school in Seoul in 1909. Soon the Holy See assigned them to evangelize the northern territory of the Korean Peninsula. The Apostolic Vicariate of Wonsan was created there in 1920, and in 1927 the Abbey of St. Benedict in Seoul was moved to Tokwon, near Wonsan. The abbey soon became the driving force of the mission, with its priests and brothers engaged in various activities: the care of the parish, the running of a seminary, a small hospital, various workshops.

In the following year the Benedictines of Wonsan were also entrusted with the mission and the pastoral care of southern Manchuria, a northeastern province of the Republic of China that today borders North Korea. This mission territory, whose area was almost three times that of the Vicariate of Wonsan, included two civil prefectures (administrative divisions of the Chinese state), Yanji (Yenki) and Yilan (Ilan). Most of the population of this region consisted of Koreans who had left Korea because of political turmoil or for economic reasons. Catholic communities of ethnic Chinese were still very few at this time and just beginning to develop. They were ministered to by some priests of the vicariate of neighboring Jilin (Kirin).[210]

Gradually the Benedictines founded mission stations in the territory assigned to them, but soon they realized that because of the

---

[209] The Latin name of the congregation is *Congregatio Ottiliensis OSB pro Missionibus Exteris*.

[210] The history of the Benedictine mission in Seoul and Wonsan is expertly told by Johannes Mahr, *Aufgehobene Häuser*, vol. 1: *Von Seoul zur Nordmission* (Sankt Ottilien: EOS, 2009). For the history of the Abbey of Tokwon see Johannes Mahr, *Aufgehobene Häuser*, vol. 2: *Die Abteien Tokwon und Yenki* (Sankt Ottilien: EOS, 2009), 11–347. In 1925 the Missionary Benedictines of Tutzing also came to Wonsan, where they founded a priory and received Korean women into their community. They remained in Wonsan until 1949. Cf. Johannes Mahr, "'Sie nähren sich wider ihrem eigentlichen Ideal'. Das Priorat der Missionsbenedektinerinnen in Wonsan," in *Aufgehobene Häuser*, 1:450–65; Johannes Mahr, "'Herz und Verstand machen uns zu Nonnen, nicht die Klausur und der Habit'. Die Flucht der Tutzinger Missionsschwestern aus Wonsan," in *Aufgehobene Häuser*, vol. 3: *Untergang und Neubeginnin Waegwan* (Sankt Ottilien: EOS, 2009), 406–23.

enormous distances it was almost impossible to care for the mission in Manchuria from the North Korean abbey. Consequently, in 1928 the Holy See decided to separate the part of their mission in Chinese territory from that in Korean territory. The first superior of the Chinese Benedictine mission was Theodor Breher (1889–1950), who had come to Yanji in December 1922. Fr. Theodor was prepared for the mission in the Far East: after having studied theology in Munich, his abbot, intending to send him to the mission in East Asia, had him study oriental languages at the University of Berlin, where he obtained his doctorate in sinology. In June 1921 Breher left for Korea with the intention of devoting three years to the study of Korean, but already the following year he was transferred to Yanji and appointed pastor of the Chinese Christians in that territory, in which the total number of Christians, Korean and Chinese, was 1,100. He was soon made superior of the mission, and in 1929 he was appointed apostolic prefect of Yanji and later vicar apostolic, hence bishop, when the prefecture was made a vicariate in 1937.[211]

Missionary work, which consisted mainly of the creation of mission stations for the organization and care of the Christian communities, developed intensely and rapidly, thanks to the gradual arrival in Manchuria of more European priests. Although the work was essentially pastoral, from the beginning Theodor Breher was intent on not neglecting the monastic character of the mission. He wrote as follows in 1929.

> Ever since I had the fortune, beginning last fall, to have three young fathers to whom I teach the [Chinese and Korean] language[s], we four fathers have prayed the entire Office every day just as in our homeland and have conformed our entire life as much as possible to that in our motherhouse. The common Office is a potent help in the mission, a great consolation and a great treasure for the missionary. This common prayer, the celebration of the liturgy, as far as it was possible for us, has made a deep impression on the somewhat lighthearted Koreans as also on the Chinese and has achieved good effects. Moreover,

---

[211] In 1933 the territory of Yilan was separated from that of Yanji and entrusted to the Capuchin province of Tyrol. For a portrait of Theodor Breher, see Lukas Ballweg, "Abt-Bischof Theodor Breher OSB," in Kaspar and Berger, *Hwan gab*, 159–70.

it makes easier for the fathers the transition from the strictly ordered community life of their home monastery to the independence of mission life without the previous obligations.[212]

The priests were soon assisted in their apostolic work by the Olivetan Benedictine sisters of the Holy Cross from the Heiligkreuz monastery in Cham, Switzerland. Four groups of missionaries, a total of twenty-one nuns, arrived in China between 1931 and 1939. They devoted themselves primarily to education and to the care of the sick and soon were accepting quite a few vocations from among young Korean Catholics. Fr. Breher, with the help of the Benedictine brothers, built a European-style monastery for the European nuns and a Korean-style house for the Korean sisters. In 1946 the European sisters returned to Switzerland, while the Korean sisters fled to South Korea, staying first in Sosa, southwest of Seoul, now part of the city of Bucheon, and then in Busan, where the congregation flourished. In recent years it has renewed contacts with the old mission.[213]

From the first years of his presence in Yanji it was Fr. Breher's desire that not only the priest-monks be actively involved in the mission but also the brothers who were not ordained. He therefore asked the superiors to send brothers to Yanji to build up the monastery and lead a communal monastic life. As he wrote in 1930: "I want [lay] brothers for my prefecture in order to offer the Gentiles a model of

[212] Letter of T. Breher to a confrere, 5 April 1929, in Mahr, *Aufgehobene Häuser,* 2:366.

[213] Cf. Heilig Kreuz Schwestern, *Aus Cham in Manchukuo* (Yenki: Bischöfliche Missionsdruckerei, n.d.); M. Consolatrix Germann, "Die Mission der Schwesternkongregation Heiligkreuz Cham in der Mandschurei," *Katholisches Missionsjahrbuch der Schweiz* 2 (1935): 82–84; M. Consolatrix Germann, "Die Schwestern von Heiligkreuz Cham in Mandschukuo," *Katholisches Missionsjahrbuch der Schweiz* 3 (1936): 94–95; M. Consolatrix Germann, "Die Missionstätigkeit der Schwestern von Heiligkreuz, Cham, in Mandschukuo," *Katholisches Missionsjahrbuch der Schweiz* 4 (1937): 132–34; M. Januaria Pfiffner, "Überblick über die Schwesterntätigkeit in der Yenki-Mission von 1931–1945," in Kaspar and Berger, *Hwan gab,* 194–97; Johannes Mahr, "Karger Beginn in der Rolle des armen Lazarus," in *Aufgehobene Häuser,* 2:397–410; Johannes Mahr, "'Der Boden unserer Heimat ist blutgetränkt'. Die Flucht der Chamer Olivetanerinnen aus Yenki (1946–1952)," in *Aufgehobene Häuser,* 3:375–405.

authentic Christian and monastic life; I need brothers so that, with their help, the material parts of the mission can be constructed."²¹⁴

The project that the documents refer to as the *Zentralkloster* (central monastery) of Yanji was initially very modest, in contrast to the model of a great abbey such as Tokwon. "For us [in Yanji], a Benedictine mission does not mean having a big abbey, but rather expressing the cenobitic life as well as possible, that is, with the most modest means."²¹⁵ The building that was finished in 1934 was actually quite respectable, as was described by the chronicler at the time.

> Thus the present abbey arose: a long building with a protruding part at each end and in the middle. . . . In the left wing the refectory is below and on the second and third stories the brothers' dormitories equal in size to it; on the north is the kitchen, above it the reading and study rooms for the brothers and the brothers' chapel; then to the west there is a part with twenty-three cells for the fathers. In the central part on the south is the entry and hallway, with parlors to the left and the right; over that is the fathers' reading room, and over that the father abbot's study; to the north is the stairway and toilets. In the next part to the west the procurator's office and bedroom is below, then a service room for the guests' refectory; on the second floor there are three large guestrooms; over that is the father abbot's parlor and bedroom and a large cell. In the same wing there are also the brothers' recreation room, a room for the superior of the house, and a large number of fathers' cells. In the westernmost wing a guests' refectory is below, the chapter room on the second floor, the vestry on the third floor. Construction began at the beginning of June 1933 and by 14 August the roof was completed. In 1934 the interiors were finished. We must be grateful to God that in these difficult times we have obtained a sufficiently large monastery for what is certainly a uniquely low price. In the houses that were bought together with the land we could install in one a print shop, workshops for bookbinding and for making shoes, and coal-powered generators and a battery room; the rest of the workshops were accommodated in the other houses.²¹⁶

²¹⁴ Letter of T. Breher to P. Vogel, 23 April 1930, in Mahr, *Aufgehobene Häuser,* 2:388.
²¹⁵ Letter of T. Breher to A. Mühlebach, 28 June 1929, in Mahr, *Aufgehobene Häuser,* 2:384.
²¹⁶ *Chronik Yenki bis 1934,* 5ff., in Mahr, *Aufgehobene Häuser,* 2:440–41.

In 1933 Fr. Theodor had to return to Europe to participate in the general chapter of the congregation. He remained there until 1935 for health reasons, and when he returned to Manchuria, he was an abbot. In May 1934 the Benedictine priory of Yanji had been canonically elevated to the Abbey of the Holy Cross,[217] and the following September Theodor Breher received the abbatial blessing at Sankt Ottilien.

Monastic life at the abbey still went hand in hand with missionary activity, which involved long absences from the cloister. Coming back to the monastery was looked on as a time to recuperate the bodily and spiritual energy necessary for apostolic activity. "[Since the construction of the abbey] it was possible to conduct a true Benedictine monastic life, that is, a life in which there is space for prayer in choir, for lectures, and for the other practices of the monastic life. About every four to six weeks the fathers who reside in districts outside [Yanji] came together [at the abbey] to be able to live as monks at least for a few days and to be able to dedicate themselves more to the interior life, to prayer, and to contemplation. . . . The abbey was to be a second homeland to which it was always possible to come again and be refreshed in body and spirit."[218]

The abbey, built by the tireless labor of European Benedictine brothers, included several workshops for a good number of the brothers. Particularly important was the print shop, where several dozen books were published in the 1930s and 1940s by the Benedictine abbeys of Yanji and Tokwon. They included missals and other liturgical books, various books for the Divine Office and other prayers, hymnals, catechisms, homiletic and pastoral materials, spiritual writings, and language manuals and dictionaries for learning Korean and Japanese. In most cases these books were the work of the monks themselves. They were published in German, Korean, and, in the years of the Japanese occupation of Korea and Manchuria, Japanese.

[217] "In oppido et praefectura apostolica de Yenki in Manciuria abbatia S. Crucis erigitur e congregatione ottiliensi ordinis sancti Benedicti," *Acta Apostolicae Sedis* 27 (1935): 365.

[218] Philipp Lenz, "Benediktiner-Mission Yenki—Mandschurei," in Kaspar and Berger, *Hwan gab*, 171–93, at 178–79.

It is significant, however, that nothing was produced or published in Chinese.[219]

The Abbey of Yanji also ran a high school and a seminary, from which came the first native priests at the end of the 1930s. These schools supported the missionary work of the Benedictine monks. In 1937, in anticipation of the episcopal consecration of Abbot Breher, a spacious new abbey church that also functioned as the cathedral was built in just six weeks. In 1938 the abbey received its first candidates for the monastic life, almost all of them ethnic Koreans.

This flourishing life of the local church was cut short by the Japanese persecution of Catholic missions in the region. Manchuria was being progressively invaded and occupied by the Japanese, who created the puppet state of Manzhouguo (Manchukuo) in 1932. In the early years of Japanese domination the government was rather well-intentioned toward the mission and Catholic schools were officially recognized. In the early forties, however, the occupying Japanese increased their stranglehold on the region, imposing, among other things, the use of the Japanese language in schools and the obligation of participating in Shinto rituals.

The subsequent capitulation of Japan in 1945 did not lead to the liberation of the mission, because the Russian troops that entered Yanji occupied the abbey. Even after the withdrawal of Soviet troops in May 1946, the situation did not improve. Indeed, 20 May 1946 was "the day the mission died."[220] Chinese Communists stormed the monastery and arrested the monks, exiling them to a concentration camp in Nanping (Namping) on the Korean border, where they remained until 1948.

When they returned to their damaged abbey, the monks found it occupied and its property confiscated. A school for young Communists, first installed in the monastery for nuns built by Breher in 1932, was transferred to the buildings of the Abbey of the Holy Cross and its adjacent workshops in 1949. The monks, who moved into a

[219] Cf. Adelhard Kaspar, "Die Veröffentlichungen der Benediktiner-Missionare in Tokwon und Yenki," *Zeitschrift für Missionswissenschaft und Religionswissenschaft* 42 (1958): 108–25.

[220] Lenz, "Benediktiner-Mission Yenki—Mandschurei," 183.

house of the sisters, experienced months of hardship, unable to carry out their mission because of tight security and oppressive measures by the Communists. At the other mission stations in the vicariate, too, the monks faced enormous difficulties and finally left the area.

To Bishop Breher the end of the mission that he had built was a traumatic experience. He became ill and after an intense internal struggle he finally decided on a gradual evacuation of the mission. He left China with the first group of missionaries in the winter of 1949. After several transfers, the last eight European missionaries were expelled from the country in August 1952.[221] Sometime later the monks who were forced to leave China settled in South Korea, where they founded what became the great Abbey of Waegwan.[222]

---

[221] Cf. Mahr, *Aufgehobene Häuser*, 3:13–172; Raymund Ackermann, "Der Untergang der Diözese Yenki und der Abtei Heilig Kreuz in der Stadt Yenki, Mandschurei. 1945–1952," in Kaspar and Berger, *Hwan gab*, 189–93. This last publication gives the statistics for 1946, which include the Benedictines who were in the Diocese of Yanji. In addition to the bishop, there were twenty German Benedictines, one Korean Benedictine choir monk, fourteen German Benedictine brothers, eighteen Swiss Olivetan Benedictine sisters and fourteen indigenous sisters (cf. Ackermann, "Der Untergang der Diözese Yenki," 193).

[222] The history of Waegwan is given in detail in Mahr, *Aufgehobene Häuser*, 3:525ff.

Peking, 1931.
The Catholic University founded by American Benedictines.

Peking, 1930.
The chapel of the Catholic University.

Peking, 1930 (?).
The Benedictine community in Peking at the foot of the circular pavilion of the Catholic University.

Peking, early 1930s.
The first group of American Benedictine sisters in front of their house on the campus of the Catholic University.

Kaifeng, 1940 (?).
Benedictine sisters caring for wounded Chinese soldiers in a railway station.

Xishan, 1932.
The Benedictine priory of Sts. Peter and Andrew, seen from the south. The entrance of the monastery is clearly visible, as are the monastery properties on the hill in the background.

Xishan, 1932. The Benedictine priory of Sts. Peter and Andrew, seen from the north. In the foreground, the rectangular building that housed the novitiate, monastic refectory, chapter room, cloakroom, library, and monastic cells. Behind it, the chapel (right) and guest parlors (left).

Xishan, 1932.
The Chinese-style chapel of the priory of Sts. Peter and Andrew.

Xishan, 1932.
The inner courtyard in front of the chapel of the priory of Sts. Peter and Andrew.

Xishan, 1932.
The exterior of the reception center for guests at the priory of Sts. Peter and Andrew.

Hebachang, mid-1930s.
Jehan Joliet, founder
and first prior of the
Benedictine monastery
of Xishan. Photo taken
during his sojourn in
the hermitage.

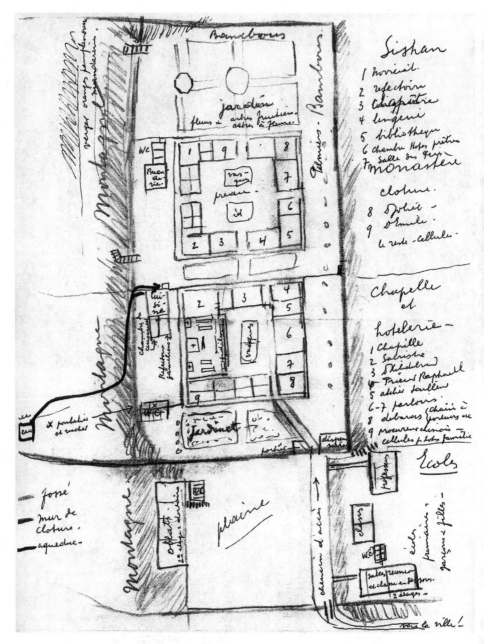

Plan of the priory of Sts. Peter and Andrew. Sketch in Hildebrand Marga, *Début de la fondation de Si Shan, Chine* (ASA, Chine 9).

Hebachang, major seminary, September 1937.
Jehan Joliet, center, with Raphaël Vinciarelli, third prior of Xishan (right), and Vincent Martin (left). This is the last photo of the founder of Xishan, taken two months before his death.

Chengdu.
The Cultural Institute of Sino-Western Research, founded by the Benedictines of Xishan and inaugurated in 1940.
Undated photo.

Bruges, Benedictine Abbey of Saint-André, July 1948. Pierre-Célestin Lu Zhengxiang, Benedictine monk and titular abbot. Photo taken in his study a few months before his death.

Yanji, mid-1930s.
The Benedictine Abbey of the Holy Cross in winter.

Yanji, 1930s.
Three German Benedictine brothers in the woodwork shop of the abbey.

Yanji, 1930s.
Two Olivetan
Benedictine
sisters of the
Holy Cross
providing
health care in
the clinic of
the mission.

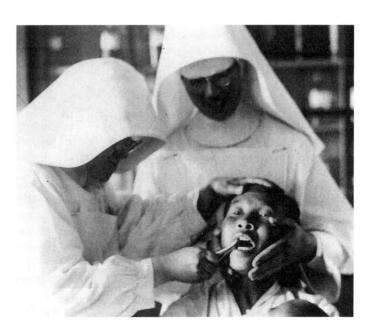

Chapter 5

|||||||||||||||||||||||||||||||||||||||||||||||

The Chinese Monastic Apostles

Shortly after the founding of *Contemplation et Apostolat* in 1926, Vincent Lebbe, a Belgian priest of the Congregation of the Mission (CM),[1] responded on behalf of his bishop, one of the first six Chinese bishops ordained that year, to its call for new monastic foundations in China. He affirmed the urgency of such an undertaking and insisted on one condition: that the monastery be "truly Chinese."[2]

Since the monastery that Fr. Lebbe founded in 1928 was actually the first monastic community to be made up entirely of Chinese brothers, he has been rightly called the "founder of Chinese monasticism."[3] Another person wrote: "A monastic life as has never before been seen is formed by his hands."[4] His unusual foundation, while undoubtedly the outcome of years of planning and the mature fruit of his "revolutionary" ideas, was also, as we shall see, the result of a number of contingent factors and inextricably linked to significant events in his own life.

Vincent Lebbe and His Monastic Spirituality

It is not my intention here to portray the unique and multifaceted figure of Frédéric Vincent Lebbe (1877–1940), "the apostle of mod-

---

[1] Its members are more commonly known as "Lazarists."

[2] Cited in Édouard Neut, "Le Christ apôtre cherche des contemplatifs," BM 9 (1928–1929): 304.

[3] Cf. Léopold Levaux, "Fondateur du monachisme chinois," in *Le père Lebbe, apôtre de la Chine moderne (1877–1940)* (Brussells / Paris: Éditions universitaires, 1948), 331–69.

[4] Jean Leclercq, *Vie du père Lebbe. Le tonnerre qui chante au loin* (Tournai / Paris: Casterman, 1955), 283.

ern China," as he has been called, or "the thunder that makes his voice heard afar," the meaning of his Chinese name (Lei Mingyuan), which well expresses his spirit, or "the man of words of light and of a heart of fire."[5] Several excellent biographies of him have been written.[6] There are also a number of scholarly works that show just how key a figure he was in changing the direction of missionary activity in China in the early twentieth century.[7] Here it will suffice to concentrate on the prophetic nature of his many-sided missionary activity. "In the crucible of action he prepares 'prophetically' the development of Christ's church in China, and well beyond China itself: an Asian and African episcopate, suppression of the foreign 'protectorate,' national emancipation, social questions, the sense of Scripture, liturgical reform, promotion of laypeople, activity as scholar and teacher, publications, esteem for non-Christian religions and ecumenism. In all this his spirit, which he himself liked

[5] Théodore Nève, "Moine et Abbé," in *Le Père Lebbe, missionnaire de Chine. Témoignages à l'occasion de sa mort* (Louvain: SAM, [impr. 1941]), 13.

[6] Cf. Raymond de Jaegher, *Father Lebbe: A Modern Apostle* (Louvain / New York: SAM, 1950); Leclercq, *Vie du père Lebbe*; Levaux, *Le père Lebbe*; Vincent Thoreau, *Le tonnerre qui chante au loin. Vie et mort du père Lebbe, apôtre des chinois (1877–1940)* (Brussells: D. Hatier, 1990). The most important biography of Lebbe in Chinese is that of Zhao Yabo, *Lei Mingyuan shenfu zhuan* [A biography of Fr. Vincent Lebbe], first published in 1963 and revised in 1977 and 1990 (Taizhong: Tianzhujiao Yaohan xiao xiongdi hui, 1990). In Italian there is a biography by Giovanni Barra, *Padre Lebbe. L'apostolo della Cina* (Brescia: Acqua Viva, 1955).

[7] For a brief introduction to the life of Vincent Lebbe, see Fang Hao, "Lei Mingyuan," in *Zhongguo tianzhujiao shi renwu zhuan* [Biographies of important figures in the history of Chinese Christianity], vol. 3 (Taizhong: Guangqi chubanshe, 1973), 314–21; Karl Josef Rivinius, "Lebbe, Frédéric Vincent," in *Biographisch-Bibliographisches Kirchenlexikon*, vol. 4 (Nordhausen: Traugott Bautz, 1992), 1291–96 (with a comprehensive bibliography); Peter Merten and Hugh O'Donnel, "Lebbe, Frederic Vincent," in *A Dictionary of Asian Christianity*, ed. Scott W. Sunquist (Grand Rapids, MI / Cambridge, UK: Eerdmans, 2001), 475–76. See also Pierre-Célestin Lou Tseng-Tsiang, "Hommage au Père Vincent Lebbe," BM 19 (1940–1945): 89–98; Frans Kuijlaars, "Ein Bahnbrecher der einheimischen Kirche Chinas: Vincent Lebbe—Lei Mingyuan (1877–1940)," *China heute* 51 (1990): 129–41; Claude Soetens, "Apôtre et chinois: Vincent Lebbe (Lei Mingyuan)," in *Historiography of the Chinese Catholic Church: Nineteenth and Twentieth Centuries*, ed. Jeroom Heyndrickx (Leuven: Ferdinand Verbiest Foundation, K. U. Leuven, 1994), 206–21; Jean-Paul Wiest, "The Legacy of Vincent Lebbe," *International Bulletin of Missionary Research* 23, no. 1 (1999): 33–37.

to call revolutionary, is also . . . tightly united to the church and to a tradition: that of the saints."[8]

In order to understand the principal themes of Fr. Lebbe's monastic spirituality and the characteristics of the two congregations he founded in 1928 and 1929, it is necessary to know something of his experience and contacts with European monks and liturgists.

His family, especially his mother, introduced the young Frédéric to the spiritual life. Above all, however, it was the visits he and his younger brother Adrien made to the monastery of Maredsous that instilled in him the monastic and liturgical spirituality that would mark his long life, even in the midst of lively missionary activities in China. In 1896 Adrien entered this Benedictine monastery, famous for the historical study of monasticism and known for its periodical *Revue bénédictine*, which Lebbe read and much appreciated during his years of study at the seminary of the Congregation of the Mission in Paris, which he entered in 1895. He always appreciated the Gregorian chant of Solesmes, which the Lazarists adopted in their liturgical celebrations. After his religious profession, when he took the name Vincent, Frédéric continued an intense epistolary relationship with his brother, who took the name Bède when he became a professed monk of Maredsous. His letters, which he continued to write after he left for China in 1901, show that his interest in monastic life never wavered, and they often reveal a nostalgia for contemplation. The following excerpt is an example: "I think of the great abbey, of the silent corridors where you walk with bowed head without being disturbed by anyone, the somber and poetic old church where you pray and chant every day alone with yourself, without having to think to distract yourself about ten or twenty thousand men, women, and children who await from you the salvation of their souls and often of their bodies, in such many and different circumstances that to think about it entangles the imagination in a kind of labyrinth of difficulties that appear inextricable."[9]

---

[8] Albert Sohier, "Profetismo e missioni: la figura di padre Lebbe," *Concilium* 4, no. 7 (1968): 132.

[9] Letter of V. Lebbe to B. Lebbe, 26 March 1907, in *Lettres du père Lebbe*, ed. Paul Goffart and Albert Sohier (Tournai / Paris: Casterman, 1980), p. 77, no. 32.

After Fr. Lebbe's death, a great Benedictine abbot acknowledged his monastic spirit: "From his youth he had frequent contacts with monks. A beloved brother had put on the Benedictine cowl, and he often visited him. . . . Doubtlessly, he came to like the things of the cloister: he loved its silence, its recollection, its isolation from the world. He felt the force that issues from continual contact with God, which leads to abnegation and to a complete spoliation."[10]

Beginning in 1906, Vincent Lebbe conferred with his brother Dom Bède, to whom in 1934 he referred as "my beloved monk, of whom I am more than ever brother in blood and in soul and in the [monastic] habit,"[11] about his plan to introduce Benedictine monasticism in China. He wanted to reflect with him on "what might be a useful role of the Benedictines here [in China] and the difficulties."[12] In a long letter he outlined the qualities that would have to characterize the presence of Benedictine monks in China in the early twentieth century. They would have to be "monastic apostles," involved above all in education and in fostering culture, totally assimilated and "kneaded" into the social condition of the people among whom they lived, acting as promoters of social development programs and agriculture and thus becoming the leaven for the Christian communities that would be formed around them. The example of the Trappists, present in China since 1883, did not seem to satisfy the monastic ideal that Lebbe had in mind, since they did not contribute, in his opinion, to the betterment of the miserable living conditions of the local people.

> Once upon a time you asked me whether it was opportune for orders such as the Benedictines to be in China. . . . These are serious questions, which I certainly would not dare to decide, but my humble opinion is that it would be magnificent and excellent if in coming to China you would become apostles, or at least would adopt the idea of active development of studies in a Christian sense, of making books, schools, in short, if you

[10] Nève, "Moine et Abbé," 14.

[11] Letter of V. Lebbe to his mother, 23 July 1934, in Goffart and Sohier, *Lettres du père Lebbe*, p. 293, no. 147.

[12] Letter of V. Lebbe to B. Lebbe, 6 December 1906, in Goffart and Sohier, *Lettres du père Lebbe*, p. 74, no. 29.

would again become in China the great Benedictines of past ages. . . . Between us, the Trappists who have settled here are not by any means making the "hit" (forgive the expression) they think they are making. In these poor mountains they are eating food about which they still complain, but which is a hundred times superior to that of the people that surround them. They rise . . . my faith!, like the peasants, except for the winter. . . . They are housed in palaces . . . and so on. The peasants say: these Europeans are rich for sure to be able to afford a good life like that! . . . It follows from this that such orders *simply from the point of view of example and of edification* are not practical here. Where they could do some good would be to settle some pagans on their lands, to teach them the latest methods of agriculture, and through the body to take gradually the soul, establishing thus Christian villages of which they would be the vivifying center . . . and it would be well, I think, to return to the original spirit.[13]

The simple transposition of the contemplative model of monasticism to China, without involvement in educational, social, or cultural activities, did not meet Fr. Lebbe's criteria. He feared that if there were no involvement in building up the local Christian communities, the Chinese would regard this kind of "useless" life as the domain of the privileged class. To Fr. Lebbe's way of thinking, the external forms of Trappist monastic life prevented the monks from having any involvement in the daily life of Chinese Christians, who already knew about an exclusively "contemplative" form of monastic

[13] Letter of V. Lebbe to B. Lebbe, 5 August 1906, in Goffart and Sohier, *Lettres du père Lebbe*, pp. 68–69, no. 27. In 1953 Jean-Marie Struyven, who had been prior of the Trappist community of Our Lady of Consolation when it was reconstituted in Peking in the years 1948–1952, developed similar ideas about the role of Cistercian abbeys (agricultural and social centers). Cf. Jean-Marie Struyven, "The Cistercian Trappist and the Rural Problem in China," *China Missionary* 1 (1949): 36–42. Elsewhere Vincent Lebbe will reiterate that "the Trappists in China are regarded with envy, not only by beggars, but also by farmers and people who live in mountain towns." Letter of V. Lebbe to A. Cotta, 13 July 1930, in Goffart and Sohier, *Lettres du père Lebbe*, p. 268, no. 138. Nevertheless, it seems that Lebbe, after founding the Little Brothers of John the Baptist in 1928, "would often send some Little Brothers to the Trappist monastery so that they could better understand what it means [to be] a 'Trappist-missionary.'" Petite sœur Louka, "Petites sœurs Thérésiennes," *Perspectives de catholicité* 15, no. 3 (1956): 82.

life in Buddhist monasticism: "As for the example of the contemplative life that is to be given here, the Chinese have one *externally* perfect in their monasteries of lamas and great bonzes, who lead a life fully monastic and according to rule, as if replicating that of European monks, and so truly edifying, chaste, and all the rest."[14]

A few years later, however, he seemed to have changed his mind and began to speak in favor of a Benedictine foundation in China, but one distinguished by the culture-shaping "primitive spirit" of *ora et labora*, which Lebbe saw as the best fruit of ancient and medieval Benedictine monasticism. He wrote to his brother Dom Bède in 1912: "I have a *great project to present to you*. Today's China is no longer what it was seven years ago. At that time you spoke to me about a Benedictine monastery here, and I dissuaded you. Right now you would be a salvation. *We need* a center of intensive Catholic studies and a school such as only you would be able to make."[15]

Fr. Lebbe recognized "the essential role favoring the coming of Benedictines to China."[16] For this reason, in the early 1920s he encouraged Jehan Joliet, a Benedictine monk of Solesmes, to pursue his project of founding a monastery in China, putting him in contact with the Abbey of Saint-André in Bruges and supporting the realization of the priory of Xishan in 1929.[17] Some letters of Jehan Joliet testify to his esteem for Fr. Lebbe, to whom he confided many of his key ideas about mission in China. In one of these letters he said he would be very happy to settle in the Diocese of Xuanhua,

---

[14] Letter of V. Lebbe to B. Lebbe, 5 August 1906, in Goffart and Sohier, *Lettres du père Lebbe*, p. 68.

[15] Letter of V. Lebbe to B. Lebbe, 1 September 1912, in Goffart and Sohier, *Lettres du père Lebbe*, p. 92, no. 40. Monks of the American Cassinese Congregation will go to China in 1923 with a mandate to run a Catholic university in Peking, but their involvement will last for only ten years (cf. *supra*, pp. 174–82).

[16] Sohier, "Profetismo e missioni," 148.

[17] Cf. Goffart and Sohier, *Lettres du père Lebbe*, p. 68, n. 11. On the monastery of Xishan see *supra*, pp. 190–218. Unfortunately, there is not much written on the relationship between Lebbe and Joliet. All we have are six letters Joliet sent to Lebbe between 1923 and 1926, which are conserved in the Vincent Lebbe Archives at the Université catholique de Louvain (Louvain-la-Neuve). Later correspondence most likely has been lost. Cf. Henri-Philippe Delcourt, *Dom Jehan Joliet (1870–1937). Un projet de monachisme bénédictin chinois* (Paris: Cerf, 1988), 12.

where Archbishop Philip Zhao Huaiyi was the ordinary and where Lebbe was stationed, and there establish a Benedictine monastic community that was really Chinese.[18]

The years Lebbe spent in "exile" in Europe (1920–1927), during which he oversaw the care of Chinese students in France and Belgium, gave him a further opportunity to renew contacts with monastic communities—Maredsous, first of all, then Saint-André in Bruges, where he became a friend of Abbot Théodore Nève, who invited him to preach the annual retreat to the monks of his community in 1923 and where in 1927 he founded, together with Abbot Nève, the "Foyer catholique chinois," an association to support the development of the Catholic Church in China.[19] After Lebbe returned to China and founded his two Chinese congregations, the *Bulletin des Missions*, the magazine published in Saint-André, followed their activities with regularity and great admiration. In several European Benedictine abbeys and priories Lebbe also managed to find accommodation for some of "his" Chinese students.[20] "Brother of a Benedictine monk, brother and uncle of canonesses of Saint Augustine, in contact with Dom Lambert Beauduin, who was very interested in the monasticism of the Orthodox Church, it was not surprising that [Lebbe] should become the initiator of a new style of Chinese monasticism."[21]

Thanks to his familiarity with the Belgian and French monastic world, where he believed the essence of primitive Christianity to have been preserved with freshness and intensity, Fr. Lebbe absorbed the spirit of radical Christianity, which, together with his missionary zeal, made him a remarkable apostle of the Gospel in China. "All

---

[18] "The new bishop, the most reverend Zhao, is his [Lebbe's] close friend . . . the prime consideration for me is not personalities or climate, but rather that I settle in the diocese of the first Chinese bishop." Letter of J. Joliet to C. Rey, 16 June 1926, in Delcourt, *Dom Jehan Joliet*, 101.

[19] Cf. Louis Wei Tsing-sing, "Le Père Lebbe et l'Abbaye de Saint-André-lez-Bruges (1877–1940)," *Rythmes du monde* 34 (1960): 218–24. In the same month of August 1923 Fr. Lebbe also preached a retreat to the Benedictine sisters of Bethany (Lophem). Notes taken by two participants are conserved in the Vincent Lebbe Archives and were consulted by Robert Guelluy for his article "La spiritualité du Père Lebbe," *Revue théologique de Louvain* 21, no. 4 (1990): 460–63.

[20] Cf. Leclercq, *Vie du père Lebbe*, 245.

[21] Guelluy, "La spiritualité du Père Lebbe," 459.

his reflections, all his initiatives were inspired by the radicalism and the concrete nature of his spirituality."[22] What he brought with him to China, therefore, was not only his missionary formation and his love for the Chinese but also a perception of the early church and of ancient monasticism that would nourish his ministry in modern China and give rise to a new form of monasticism, based on European Benedictine monasticism, but transformed by the needs of the apostolate in China. There can be no doubt that Lebbe was "a man faithful to events."[23]

The Little Brothers of John the Baptist

The History of the Foundation

We can trace the events that led to the founding of the Monastery of the Beatitudes on 16 December 1928, a day described by Lebbe as "an historic date, the date when Chinese monasticism was born— yes, Chinese totally,"[24] thanks primarily to what the founder of the Little Brothers of John the Baptist himself provided in some of his letters.[25] "Such a beautiful story," as he described it,[26] will also draw on the testimonies of those who lived there or had contact with that unique monastic experience,[27] as well as on reconstructions of that

---

[22] Ibid.

[23] Soetens, "Apôtre et chinois," 217.

[24] Vincent Lebbe, *En Chine, il y a du nouveau. Le Père Lebbe nous écrit...* (Liège: La Pensée Catholique, 1930), 171.

[25] Cf. ibid., 170–90 and 235; Goffart and Sohier, *Lettres du père Lebbe,* 264ff.; Vincent Lebbe, "Nova et vetera. Du vieux neuf," CA 9 (1937): 5–12; C. Renirkens, ed., *Les Monastères du Père Lebbe. Deux lettres du P. Lebbe* (Louvain: SAM, n.d.).

[26] Lebbe, *En Chine, il y a du nouveau,* 170.

[27] Cf. Clifford King, "Les Petits Frères de St Jean-Baptiste et les Petites Sœurs de Ste Thérèse," *Jeunesse chinoise. Bulletin de la Jeunesse catholique chinoise* 91–92 (1932): 482–92; 93–94 (1932): 514–20; 95–96 (1932): 550–56; Théodore Nève, "L'œuvre monastique du Père Lebbe," CA 9 (1937): 1–4; Un Bénédictin, "Huit jours au monastère des petits frères de St-Jean-Baptiste," *Société des Auxiliaires des Missions* 23 (1937): 11; Nève, "Moine et Abbé"; Raymond de Jaegher, "De vrais Moines et de vrais Chinois. Les petits Frères de Saint Jean Baptiste," *Église vivante* 1 (1949): 196–99; Frère Alexandre, "Petits Frères de Saint Jean-Baptiste," *Perspectives de catholicité* 15, no. 3 (1956): 73–79; Alexander Ts'ao, "Father Lebbe's Principles Live On," *Worldmission* 13, no. 3 (1962): 109–14.

history made by Lebbe's biographers, who also had access to these testimonies.[28]

Fr. Lebbe briefly described the germination of this newborn "living thing," this "growing plant" that was the Congregation of the Little Brothers of John the Baptist (in Chinese *Yaohan xiao xiongdi hui* 耀漢小兄弟會), when he wrote that it was born out of "a very practical concern: how to solve the distressing problem of the lay staff of the missions? How to obtain at the same time quantity, quality, and economize on expenses?"[29]

The way to a possible solution became clearer during a pastoral visit to the Apostolic Prefecture of Lixian (Lihsien) in the northern province of Hebei (Hopeh)[30] that he made with Bishop Melchior Sun Dezhen at the end of 1927 to administer the sacrament of confirmation. Listening to the complaints of the Chinese priests they met in the various mission stations about the difficulty of finding "educated and virtuous" teachers and catechists and not straining the limited financial resources of the church, Fr. Lebbe arrived at a proposal that would open the way for future fruitful developments.[31] "In my opinion, the only means of saving our missions from ruin and of preserving our independence is to transform our salaried personnel into non-salaried personnel. . . . Let us establish . . . a religious community whose particular aim would be to carry out everything with which our salaried dependents are charged."[32]

---

[28] Among them, those I have consulted are Théodore Nève, "S. Benoît et l'Action Catholique Chinoise," BM 9 (1928–1929): 419–20; T. T. E., "Une nouvelle congrégation religieuse en Chine," CA 2 (1933): 63–73; Levaux, "Fondateur du monachisme chinois"; "Les Petits Frères de Saint Jean-Baptiste," CA 13 (1949): 32–34; Paul Goffart, "Manuscrit définitif de la Vie du P. Lebbe" (unpublished typewritten manuscript, Vincent Lebbe Archives, Université catholique de Louvain), 565–72 and 577–99; Leclercq, *Vie du père Lebbe*, 282–304 and passim; Barra, *Padre Lebbe*, 141–80; Duoma xiongdi, "Yaohan xiao xiongdi hui de chuangli ji chuqi de huodong" [The foundation and the first activities of the Congregation of the Little Brothers of John the Baptist], *Lei Mingyuan shenfu zhuankan* 17 (1993): 21–26; Yaohan xiao xiongdi xiushi, "Yaohan xiao xiongdi hui jianshi" [A brief history of the Congregation of the Little Brothers of John the Baptist], *Shensi* (*Spirit*) 98 (2013): 81–99.

[29] Lebbe, "Nova et vetera," 5.

[30] The Apostolic Prefecture of Lixian was erected in 1924. It was made an apostolic vicariate, with the title of Anguo, in 1929 and a diocese in 1946.

[31] Lebbe, *En Chine, il y a du nouveau*, 171.

[32] Cited in King, "Les Petits Frères," 490.

In addition to the bishop's favorable reaction, two other factors made an attempt possible. "On the one hand a quite considerable number of good, of very good, Christians in the countryside remain celibate, most often out of fear of not being able to maintain and raise a family, sometimes also out of higher motives; love of continence is not rare among the young people. If these celibates do not become religious, it is certainly not because they are not prepared for it by their life and conduct and even more by their unconscious desires: it is only because they do not feel a vocation to enter one of the existing congregations. . . . We thought that there was here an entire category of reserve forces, unutilized until now."[33]

Fr. Lebbe discussed with the bishop some of the guidelines for this new religious community and the life within their communal home, which, he confessed, "we didn't even dream of calling a monastery." "The [religious] society to be founded by Bishop Sun would appeal to every adult celibate who desires to render service to the church under the protection of holy vows and community life. . . . Every skill can be used; everyone would be admitted. . . . One essential point: they would form a lay congregation, and all would be absolutely equal. They would have only one community house for the entire prefecture and would return to it whenever their work would not summon them outside."[34]

Presented with this proposal, Bishop Sun was "completely taken with it"[35] and instructed Fr. Lebbe to test the waters in the missionary districts they would later visit to see if there were candidates willing to form such a community. As Fr. Lebbe noted in retrospect, it was precisely through the adherence of possible candidates that God "marked the turning point" with regard to the nature of this new community: "Six young persons from six villages were found who agreed to enter in this new community with enthusiasm, but on condition that its rule be austere. I was surprised to find such agreement in their aspirations without their having been able to consult one another. Almost all had previously dreamed of entering the Trappist Order, which explains their desire for an austere life, but

[33] Lebbe, *En Chine, il y a du nouveau*, 171–72.
[34] Ibid., 172–73.
[35] King, "Les Petits Frères," 490.

had been impeded in this. I could not but admire the dispositions of Providence, which in this way prepared a nucleus for our new foundation and indicated to us the character to be given it."[36]

The austere character of the foundation would be strictly *monastic*, that is, his "tendency toward monasticism,"[37] as Lebbe put it, would be realized, while the possibility of outside apostolic ministries would also be considered: "When the foundation of a religious society completely indigenous was announced, all six [young Chinese] felt called, but they placed a condition: they would not be catechists who make vows, but *monks, authentic monks*, like the Trappists, only with apostolic works added, as in the formula dear to St. Vincent [de Paul], 'Carthusians in the house, apostles outside.'"[38]

In the spring of 1928 the first group of postulants began to construct the original nucleus of the Monastery of the Beatitudes in the western suburb of Anguo (Ankwo), on land generously donated by a benefactor from Peking. On 16 December 1928 Bishop Sun blessed the simple and poor new monastery and presided over the liturgy of clothing of the first fifteen novices.[39] A habit similar to that of the Trappists was chosen for them; it consisted of a robe of coarse gray cloth, a leather belt, and the traditional black Benedictine scapular.[40] On the scapular, at chest height, was embroidered a small cross, green for the simply professed and red for the solemnly professed (cf. RLB 20). Fr. Lebbe received his first scapular from his brother Bède, a Benedictine monk at Maredsous. The monastic habit would always be considered by the Little Brothers of John the Baptist as a clear outward sign of their monastic identity. Although there was almost universal objection to the choice of this dress on the grounds that it interfered with free movement, Lebbe and his Little Brothers always

---

[36] Ibid., 490–91.

[37] Lebbe, "Nova et vetera," 5.

[38] Lebbe, *En Chine, il y a du nouveau*, 173–74 (emphasis added).

[39] A description of the ceremony can be found in Lebbe, *En Chine, il y a du nouveau*, 177–79. On 28 November Vincent Lebbe wrote to his brother Robert: "The Monastery of the Beatitudes is certainly very well named because it has already attained a high degree of the first of the eight [beatitudes], that of blessed poverty!" Goffart and Sohier, *Lettres du père Lebbe*, p. 264, no. 137.

[40] These scapulars were generously offered by a businessman from Vervier, who was a benefactor of Fr. Lebbe.

held on to it. For them the habit was a sign of their identity, namely, that they were "a species of the genus monk."[41]

> I would prefer to dissolve [the Little Brothers] rather than transform them into "catechists with vows." What was desired above all was that they be *monks* and popularize in China, in local Chinese color, the *monastic habit* of St. Benedict. . . . Pagan men and even pagan women receive us with a kind of veneration. Never, absolutely never, have they been insulted on account of their holy livery, nor has it in the least embarrassed them on their journeys.[42]

> We have found it prudent to adapt ourselves to certain traditional rules in the church concerning the habit and the hair style of monks and religious. According to the impressions that we have gathered here, we have nothing to repent of. Of course, curious looks are fixed on our monks and sisters when they are working in the country, but there is nothing malevolent in the comments on their unusual appearance. On the contrary, when the people learn what all this means, ample testimonies of respect and deference follow. . . . The Little Brothers and Little Sisters are enthusiastic about their habit; the postulants await the day of their clothing, which marks a turning point in their lives, with impatient ardor.[43]

The monastic name given to most of them was that of one of the Chinese martyrs, whose lives would soon be painted on the walls of the chapel and whose biographies would be read during the meals of the community.[44] The reason for this was clear: to show their

[41] Letter of V. Lebbe to A. Cotta, 13 July 1930, in Goffart and Sohier, *Lettres du père Lebbe*, p. 268.
[42] Ibid., p. 269 (emphasis added).
[43] Cited in King, "Les Petits Frères," 550–51.
[44] Cf. Cao Lishan, "Zhongguoren neng chengsheng ma?" 中國人能成聖嗎? [Can the Chinese become saints?], in *Chunfeng shinian* [Ten years of spring breeze] (Taizhong: Tianzhujiao Yaohan xiao xiongdi hui, 1977), 62–64. In the history of the church in China, there have been numerous Catholic martyrs. Many of them were among the 30,000 killed in 1900 during the Boxer Rebellion. The church has promoted the cause of these martyrs on several occasions. The first were beatified in 1900, the largest group was beatified in 1946, and others were beatified in 1951 and 1955. On 1 October 2000, John Paul II canonized 120 martyrs of China, eighty-seven of whom were Chinese (laity, priests, and seminarians) and the rest missionaries.

willingness to hand their lives over to God without reserve, even to the point of martyrdom, and to show that they were Chinese Christian monks among their Chinese brothers. The Chinese martyrs were also chosen by Bishop Sun and Fr. Lebbe as secondary patrons of the congregation along with John the Baptist, the principal patron. "Saint John the Baptist has been chosen as the special patron of our brothers because his task, like theirs, is to prepare the way for Christ. Just as the Baptist prepared himself for the work of his whole life by a long retreat of prayer and mortification in the desert, so our brothers prepare for their apostolic task, the evangelization of the pagans, by leading in their monastery a life of prayer, of mortification, and of silence."[45]

In his explanation of the first article of the *Rule of the Little Brothers*, Lebbe explains how the choice of these patrons for the new congregation relates to its intended inculturation in the sociopolitical context of the new China.[46]

> The initial motive for the choice of St. John [the Baptist] (Ruohan 若翰) as patron of our little family was because the Little Brothers must open for the priests the way of mission, just as St. John was the precursor of Jesus. Later, the more we meditated on the saint's words and actions as the work of our little family was developing day by day, the better we understood the profound meaning of the choice of this great figure as the patron that God had made for us. He wanted us to imitate his ascetic (*kugan* 苦幹) and tenacious (*qiangying* 强硬) spirit and, by following his way, to retire first into the desert in order to later throw ourselves among the masses, intrepid and stable in announcing [the Gospel] to the very death. In addition, because of our desire to participate in the rebirth of the [Chinese] people, we have changed the phonetic translation [into Chinese of the name John] into "Yaohan" (耀漢) to show our desire that the Chinese people (*hanzu* 漢族) be our splendor (*guangyao* 光耀).[47]

[45] King, "Les Petits Frères," 516.

[46] Art. 1 reads, "This congregation is called the Congregation of the Little Brothers of John [the Baptist], who is its principal patron. The blessed Chinese martyrs are its secondary patrons."

[47] In the original manuscript, reproduced in RPF, p. 104, there is a marginal note written by Lebbe: "The glory of his people (Luke 2:31)" (should be Luke 2:32).

Because carrying out the patriotic implications of the Catholic religion (*Gongjiao* 公教) is a great desire of the Little Brothers, we have also wanted the first host of canonized saints of our country as our models and protectors in heaven.[48]

In a letter of 16 January 1929, Fr. Lebbe could not refrain from heartfelt exaltation. He had no doubt that his times represented the dawn of Chinese monasticism and its insertion into universal Christian monasticism. He saw the foundation of his "blessed monastery" as "the latest shoot emerging from the ancient yet still hardy trunk of the great order of St. Benedict."[49] "Oh, how beautiful they appear! . . . What then is this grace that immediately seems to make them participate in the monastic spirit of all ages, of the eternal Catholic monk? I assure you that they would not be out of place in Maredsous, in Saint-André, or in Forges, in the midst of their European brothers."[50]

Théodore Nève, abbot of Saint-André, recognized the monastic quality of "this 'spontaneous generation' that finds refuge under the mantle of St. Benedict,"[51] of this "authentic monastic institution" whose "character is distinctly Chinese."[52] Lebbe recalled that when Nève came to China in 1935 and visited the Monastery of the Beatitudes, he was convinced of the monastic spirit of the foundation: "He repeated to us that he feels at home among us, that we were really *true monks* and in the *authentic tradition of the ancient Benedictines*. He condescended to be present in the choir at our Chinese Office; one day he even put on our poor habit of rough cloth and took it away with him as a souvenir. This approval from one so eminent was for us a precious encouragement."[53]

---

[48] Vincent Lebbe, *Huigui shiyi*, pp. 1–2; cf. RPF, pp. 5–6, and Vincent Lebbe, "Petits Frères," *Église vivante* 17 (1965): 439–40.

[49] Lebbe, *En Chine, il y a du nouveau*, 181.

[50] Ibid., 179.

[51] Nève, "S. Benoît et l'Action Catholique Chinoise," 420.

[52] T. T. E., "Une nouvelle congrégation religieuse en Chine," 64, 63.

[53] Lebbe, "Nova et vetera," 12. Cf. also the talks given by Abbot Nève to the community of the Little Brothers during the days of his visit, which are reported in Chinese in "Nan yuanzhang zai Anguo Zhenfuyuan sanri zhong zhi jiayan shanbiao" [Words of praise from Abbot Nève during his three days at the Monastery of the Beatitudes in Anguo], in YZB 17 (1935): 1–3.

In the months following the founding of the monastery the number of novices grew. In March 1929 an unforeseen event led to a
reshaping of the exclusively lay nature of this new congregation. On
the eve of his ordination to the priesthood, a seminarian, "very young,
as is fitting for the undertaking that is just germinating here,"[54] asked
to be admitted to the novitiate. On 19 March the bishop ordained
him in the chapel of the Monastery of the Beatitudes, and that same
evening, along with four other novices, he received the monastic
habit. "This day of 19 March 1929, hence, is written in golden letters
in the monastery's chronicle; it is the second great date of its life,
after the unforgettable day of its foundation. The foundations have
now been laid of this Chinese society of Jesus' friends, in the form
that it has pleased Divine Providence to make us adopt here. . . .
The state of the monastery at present is: nineteen novices, one of
them a priest, and about twenty postulants, twelve of whom are in
probation in outside Christian communities."[55]

There was to be no difference between those brothers who were
priests, whose number would be limited to what was necessary to
meet the community's needs, and the other brothers. All would lead
the same life. "Those who are destined to the priesthood will be Little
Brothers like the others. They will not be distinguished in any way,
unless by the example of humility, of amiability, and of a mortified
life that they will give their brothers with God's help. Their external
life will be that of the Little Brothers. . . . It is our desire that the
Little Brothers who will be in the clerical state burn with a holy zeal
to become good priests, nothing less than saints, and that they have a
deeply rooted conviction that what China needs above all is this type."[56]

Great stress was placed on "the strictest equality" between the
brothers, abolishing the distinction in preconciliar monasteries between choir monks and lay brothers. "Going back to the sources (the
first Benedictines . . . the first Franciscans), we do not admit and
never want *at any price* two classes [of monks] in our monastery."[57]

---

[54] Lebbe, *En Chine, il y a du nouveau*, 181.

[55] Ibid., 181–82.

[56] King, "Les Petits Frères," 553.

[57] Letter of V. Lebbe to A. Cotta, 13 July 1930, in Goffart and Sohier, *Lettres du
père Lebbe*, p. 268.

This equality would also be evident in the rule of the congregation, at the very beginning of the section dealing with its members (RLB 6), and be particularly emphasized in Fr. Lebbe's commentary.

> *All the Little Brothers will be treated the same way, without classes, without distinctions based on social status, on function, on education.*
>
> This article is needed especially because among the brothers there are some who before or after entering the congregation have received a higher education or been ordained or have received something else. These brothers must watch that this not be a reason for being treated differently; such a thing is forbidden with the greatest severity by the rule. Outside the choir, where their post is closest to that of the father, in all other places order depends on precedence in vocation. It is absolutely forbidden that [brothers who are priests] receive material service from the other brothers; when they go out for mission they must provide for these material services with their own hands, on the example of St. [Francis] Xavier, and the brothers who go out with him will be his equal companions, his witnesses.[58]

Despite the austerity of the life and the number of postulants who discontinued, by the end of 1930 forty novices had been clothed with the monastic habit and there were ten postulants preparing to enter the novitiate.[59] With every corner occupied, "the number of the brothers is at the limit; even the small infirmary is occupied."[60]

The seeds had been planted, and now a small community of brothers and their work of evangelization might finally present a different face of Christianity, no longer aggressive and hostile, but brotherly and friendly. "By founding a totally Chinese monasticism,

---

[58] Lebbe, *Huigui shiyi*, p. 7; cf. RPF, p. 9, and Lebbe, "Petits Frères," 443–44. Cf. also article 11 of the rule (V. Lebbe, *Huigui shiyi*, p. 11; RPF, p. 13; Lebbe, "Petits Frères," 447). The RLB also provides that the Little Brother who is about to receive holy orders speak and sign a statement in which he affirms his total submission to the rule of the community and to his superior and his renunciation of any privilege (for the text of that statement, organized in eight questions and answers, cf. Lebbe, *Huigui shiyi*, pp. 7–9; RPF, p. 10).

[59] Cf. Leclercq, *Vie du père Lebbe*, 287.

[60] Letter of V. Lebbe to B. Lebbe, 26 January 1931, in Goffart and Sohier, *Lettres du père Lebbe*, p. 275, no. 140.

Fr. Lebbe wanted . . . a true manifestation of true Christianity to shine forth."[61] As a Benedictine monk reported after a visit to the Monastery of the Beatitudes of Anguo, Fr. Lebbe desired a Chinese Christianity lived by the Chinese in order to show that "a Chinese could carry out the full ideal of religious life while remaining himself."[62] What we now refer to as the inculturation of Christianity began to be realized. "Preserving the good customs of the country while rendering them Christian: this is what has been accomplished at the Monastery of the Beatitudes."[63]

The firstfruits of these seeds were seen in a short time. The people of Anguo recognized the Little Brothers as "real monks," confessing that "here are true bonzes, the ideal bonze that we have never seen among the Buddhists except in paintings; here they are shown us in flesh and blood." Fr. Lebbe, for his part, was happy to note that "in the city we are met with what is like a great wave of friendship. All-powerful grace has opened the hearts of all and at the same time the faces, which suddenly became pleasant, smiling, friendly."[64] Numerous reports in the Chinese Catholic press indicate that the number of guests, even from remote areas, increased over the years, as the lives of the Little Brothers came to be known.[65]

In the first four years of its existence the community of the Little Brothers grew quickly, and the members began to think of a possible presence in other parts of China. For the time being, however, they simply welcomed to the monastery of Anguo candidates from various regions of China. In the future it would be through them that the "movement of the Beatitudes" could be extended to their vicariates of origin. In 1932 Vincent Lebbe wrote as follows.

---

[61] Levaux, *Le père Lebbe*, 356.

[62] Un Bénédictin, "Huit jours au monastère des petits frères de St-Jean-Baptiste," 11.

[63] Ibid.

[64] Lebbe, *En Chine, il y a du nouveau*, 188–89.

[65] See, e.g., Liu Lingyun, "Zhenfuyuan de kuxiu shenghuo" [The ascetic life at the Monastery of the Beatitudes], *Gongjiao yuekan* 14 (1934): 18–19; 15 (1934): 25–26; 16 (1934): 21–22; Hu Yu, "Anguo Zhenfuyuan canguan hou zhi jianwen ji" [An account of what was seen and heard during a visit to the Monastery of the Beatitudes in Anguo], YZB 21 (1934): 8–10; Chen Ganfu, "Dao Zhenfuyuan hou" [After having been at the Monastery of the Beatitudes], YZB 36 (1936): 946–48.

We have not yet thought of the possibility of spreading into other parts of China. For the present, however, indications are not lacking that such a development might well be in the views of Divine Providence. In the two communities there are members from other vicariates, and more are being accepted; moreover, in some neighboring vicariates the authorities have already expressed a wish to see our religious undertake activities among them. All that we have been able to answer to these cordial invitations is that many workers are lacking in our own mission and that our present religious are not yet sufficiently advanced in their spiritual formation as to be able to found new undertakings in other vicariates. Nevertheless, to show our ardor in spreading the good toil, we have declared that we are ready to receive in each of our communities a group of candidates of any vicariate whatever of China; we will educate them according to the spirit of our communities so that they might be able in the future to render service in their original vicariate.[66]

By the middle of 1933 the number of the community reached 110, including postulants,[67] and "the comings and goings, the habit, the appearance" of the Little Brothers "were attracting more and more attention" among Christians and non-Christians.[68] They finally accepted the invitation to found other monasteries in different vicariates. A small monastery was established at Bushi (Pushih, Pou Che), in the Vicariate of Fenyang, Shanxi (Shansi) province. In a letter, Fr. Lebbe described it as "hidden in a corner of the mountains, isolated, and not very accessible."[69]

> You, and my dear Bède too, should see this place ideal for meditation and retreat: difficult to access, in real solitude. . . . On the southern slope of the mountain, facing a crown of mountains with woods very near, below a stream that is never dry, of abundant flow, which becomes a small torrent in the rainy season (just now), to the west a hamlet of sixteen families, all fervent Christians . . . and peace! There, in this church property

[66] King, "Les Petits Frères," 554–55.
[67] Cf. letter of V. Lebbe to P. Staes, 28 June 1933, in Goffart and Sohier, *Lettres du père Lebbe*, p. 290, no. 146.
[68] Lebbe, "Nova et vetera," 6.
[69] Ibid., 7.

belonging to Bishop Liou [Liu],[70] Chinese, at his invitation our
Little Brothers have come to build the poorest monastery in the
world, after those of St. Francis (I mean, of the Franciscans of
the heroic age).[71]

In Lebbe's "ideal Monastery of the Beatitudes" two essential principles were to be put into practice: economic autonomy and "workers
helping workers," that is, the provision of real and direct help to the
rural population by having the Little Brothers share the agricultural
work of the people among whom they lived.[72]

Another monastery was founded in the Apostolic Prefecture of
Zhouzhi (Chowchih), Shaanxi (Shensi), one of the poorest regions of
inland China. Requests for the presence of the Little Brothers came
from the provinces of Henan (Honan) and Chahar.[73] Bishop Joseph
Fan Heng'an of the Diocese of Jining (Tsining), in today's region of
Inner Mongolia, invited the Little Brothers to administer, together
with the Little Sisters, an institute for the blind. Spacious grounds
in the vicinity of Peking were offered to them to tend and on which
to build a future monastery. Catholics in Peking and Tianjin offered
them an entire mountain for their use.[74]

In 1933 Vincent Lebbe, with the consent of the local bishop, the
approval of his superiors, and the encouragement of Rome, left the
Congregation of the Mission, became a Little Brother, and formally
assumed the office of superior of the monastery.[75] Shortly thereafter
Rome, through the apostolic delegate in China, gave further encouragement to Fr. Lebbe by expressing appreciation for the vitality and

---

[70] Francis Liu Jinwen was vicar apostolic of Fenyang from 1930 to 1948. Fenyang
was made a diocese in 1946.
[71] Letter of V. Lebbe to his mother, 23 July 1934, in Goffart and Sohier, *Lettres
du père Lebbe*, p. 291.
[72] Cf. Lei Mingyuan, "Bushi. Wo lixiang zhong de Zhenfuyuan" [Bushi. My ideal
Monastery of the Beatitudes], YZB 39 (1936): 1028–30.
[73] A province of China that existed between 1912 and 1936. Its territory covered
the eastern part of what is today the autonomous region of Inner Mongolia.
[74] Cf. Leclercq, *Vie du père Lebbe*, 288.
[75] Cf. Levaux, *Le père Lebbe*, 343–46. Lebbe made solemn vows as a Little Brother
of John the Baptist at the hands of Bishop Sun on 24 December 1933, in the cathedral of Anguo. Three days later Rome confirmed his being named the first superior
of the Little Brothers.

the good fruits of the community he had begun. "What has especially filled me with joy in all that [the delegate] saw fit to say to me is this: that the Holy Father and the Sacred Congregation of the Propaganda follow the progress of the Little Brothers with great interest (he has paid me compliments that in fact we don't merit, except in intention). They are very content with us and place great hopes on us; they believe that our foundation is entirely of a providential order and for this they bless us and ask God to have us quickly grow to a great number."[76]

The war of resistance against the Japanese occupation led Fr. Lebbe to have his Little Brothers become active witnesses of the patriotism of the Catholic Church in China. Following a line of political commitment that had marked him since his early years as a missionary in China, Fr. Lebbe made his monks available for service in the Chinese Army as aides to the medical corps, in particular as stretcher bearers, for the first time in 1933, when the Japanese invaded Manchuria and North China, then again in 1937, when the Japanese resumed their assault.[77] Through this ministry of charity the Little Brothers witnessed to the Gospel and offered material and spiritual assistance to thousands of people.

In the midst of the turmoil of the war, the Little Brothers, who in 1938 were counted between 150 and 200, always sought to preserve the fundamental elements of their monastic life: prayer, meditation, silence, poverty, work. A letter of Fr. Lebbe from the front, dated 3 July 1938, depicts the life of this "monastery at the front" with the usual spiritual fervor that characterized him; "continuing to take care of his Little Brothers was one of his great concerns."[78]

> I am not sad or unhappy, but full of joy at the great work under the sun of the good God; I have with me forty Little Brothers, two of them novices (who have received the habit in our camps, I no longer know where . . . but it's in my diary), five postulants (received between two battles, one even during a battle).

[76] Letter of V. Lebbe to his mother, 23 July 1934, in Goffart and Sohier, *Lettres du père Lebbe*, p. 292.
[77] Fr. Lebbe and some ten or so brothers had taken a first aid course at the Protestant hospital of Anguo some time earlier.
[78] Vincent Martin, "Mes souvenirs sur le Père Lebbe," CSA 14 (1947): 158.

Because it is necessary to say that there is a Monastery of the Beatitudes of the 3rd Army, 12th Division. . . . It is a flying monastery like Moses' tabernacle in the desert, on the road to the Promised Land, which is the China of tomorrow. We have thrown ourselves into the midst of fire, in the front lines, with our holy habit, *all* our rules, our choir Office (and it is quite rare for us not to recite or *chant* it in common), our silence, our talks, and our work in [the spirit of] *gaudete semper.* . . . All this is nothing very extraordinary, but the atmosphere of joy and of enthusiasm for God and the good that accompanies it make it into so many monastic exercises. . . . You should see and hear this: besides those whose service takes them more or less far away, there always remain at the section, with me, at least a dozen brothers. This is the permanence of the Beatitudes, the Monastery, the Family. . . . Under the shells exploding thirty meters away, you would see the family gather together chanting Vespers. . . . The Beatitudes of Ankwo [Anguo] work in peace . . . the same for the Beatitudes of Peking. Also a new large monastery (about sixty brothers) in Shensi [Shaanxi] in a Chinese prefecture also sends me consoling news, and everywhere there is intense work.[79]

The life of the brothers in the "monastery at the front" is described in more detail in another letter, published in Belgium.

The Monastery at the Front.

The greatest problem to be resolved was maintaining rigorously the brothers' religious character, religious fervor. To obtain this, the fullest possible religious monastic life was transported to the front, in the midst of the camp: thus, following the army, when we arrive in a place, we transform a part of the lodgings assigned to us into a monastery, making true miracles in contriving to organize refectory, dormitory, chapel, common room, classes, chapter. No need to say that most often the same room has different uses at different hours of the day. Once the lodging is organized—and after a year of practice we can organize very quickly—the rule of the Monastery of the Beatitudes enters into vigor and, thanks to God, our good little monks observe it admirably.

---

[79] Letter of V. Lebbe to B. Lebbe, 3 July 1938, in Goffart and Sohier, *Lettres du père Lebbe*, pp. 300–301, no. 152.

Rising, according to the season, is at 3:30, 4:00, or 4:30; ablutions in abundant water (if there is a river or a large stream we go there); then Chinese gymnastics; then chanting of the Office, most often in the open air; meditation; Holy Mass, at which all the Catholic soldiers participate, more than half of them communicating every day. Daily preaching. Then our monks have free time, in silence. The postulants and novices (about thirty) have an hour of instruction. The first meal with reading at table, followed by a short period for recreation.

9:00 Terce. Then everyone goes to his work; for those who work within the "monastery," this work is done in great silence. According to how much time the doctors have after aiding the wounded and sick, they give one or two courses to the nurses and apprentice nurses every day.

Noon: Sext. Then siesta in the summer (work permitting).

2:00 Instruction to novices and candidates.

3:00 None. Work.

5:00 Second meal, followed by a period for recreation in common for all those whose work permits them this leisure.

6:00 Chanting of Vespers, followed by a spiritual talk, where each monk by turns gives a report about his work, his apostolate, successes, failures. Those who have transported the wounded, visited the Christians or the sick of the region, or have gone out of the camp for whatever charge, give an account of their journey. Afterward there is Compline and the great silence, except for those who at this time go to give catechism to the Catholic soldiers.[80]

At the end of 1938 another monk, Vincent Martin, who came to the monastery of Xishan (Sichuan) two years earlier from Belgium, received his prior's permission to join the medical corps organized by Fr. Lebbe and his Little Brothers.[81] While this service at the front made "the brothers' habit become exceedingly popular in the army,"[82] it cost the lives of twelve Little Brothers, who early in 1940

[80] Renirkens, *Les Monastères du Père Lebbe*, 29–30. Cf. the daily horarium as given in RLB 48–56.
[81] V. Martin recounts his experience in the battlefield alongside Vincent Lebbe in "Mes souvenirs sur le Père Lebbe."
[82] Renirkens, *Les Monastères du Père Lebbe*, 30.

were arrested and then shot by Communist soldiers while they were traveling to reach their superior. Two years earlier, at the monastery of Anguo, another brother had been beheaded by Japanese soldiers.

On 9 March 1940 Vincent Lebbe and seven other monks were captured by a gang of Communists. Released on 13 April in response to public outcry and the intervention of high-level representatives of the Nationalist government, Fr. Lebbe died shortly after, on 24 June 1940, the feast of St. John the Baptist, the patron saint of his monastic family.

Victory over Japan in 1945 did not mean the end of war. The Communist advance threw the country into a prolonged civil war. The Monastery of the Beatitudes of Anguo was forced to move to the Monastery of the Beatitudes that had been established in the 1930s in the neighborhood of Peking, Qinghe (Tsing Ho, Tsinghou), where the commanding general of the 29th Armored Division in which the Little Brothers had served in 1933, made available to them the buildings of an abandoned hospital. With the support of Cardinal Thomas Tian Gengxin, archbishop of Peking, the Little Brothers undertook social work and agricultural education, ran a school, and had some workshops for weaving. A brother assumed the post of director of the newspaper *Yishibao* in Tianjin.[83]

Since all the territories in which there were Little Brothers were occupied by the Communists, thirteen of the brothers chose to take refuge in Hong Kong, where the motherhouse had been moved, and for a time served in a refugee camp for people fleeing from mainland China. Most of them, however, remained in their regions, dispersing among the villages and continuing their apostolic work as far as possible, even though they were forced to abandon their monastic habit.[84] In 1956 the superior, Alexander Cao, wrote that "there are still two priests and more than fifty brothers behind the bamboo

---

[83] Cf. "Les Petits Frères de Saint Jean-Baptiste," 32–33; Ts'ao, "Father Lebbe's Principles Live On," 113; "Laodong shengchan de Zhenfuyuan" [The Monastery of the Beatitudes that produces by working], *Shiguang zazhi* 3–4 (1943); Yang Di, "Zhenfuyuan canguan ji" [Notes after a visit to the Monastery of the Beatitudes], *Gongjiao baihua bao* 11–12 (1944): 152; Chen Hui, "Qinghe Zhenfuyuan sumao" [Sketch of the Monastery of the Beatitudes at Qinghe], YZ 11 (1948): 172.

[84] Cf. Jaegher, "De vrais Moines et de vrais Chinois," 199.

curtain. Of these, many are in jail and several have been killed by the Communists."[85]

In 1954 the motherhouse was moved to Taiwan, where in 1957 the novitiate of the congregation was opened in Taizhong (Taichung). Today the congregation is present in several countries of East Asia (Taiwan, Vietnam, the Philippines) and in America, devoting itself mainly to pastoral work and education.

Life at the Monastery of the Beatitudes

According to the rule drafted by Fr. Lebbe for his Little Brothers, "each monastery of the congregation bears the name of 'Monastery of the Beatitudes' of the place or the diocese [where it is located]" (RLB 2). Lebbe explains this in his commentary on the rule.

> The name "Monastery of the Beatitudes" has two meanings: (1) the holy monastery has the Chinese blesseds for its patrons; (2) the holy monastery lives by practicing the eight beatitudes. For this reason the eight beatitudes occupy an important place in formation, in the rule, and in the customs of our family. The holy teaching of our Lord on the mountain constitutes the goal of the brothers' striving for perfection throughout their lives.[86]

According to the founder, this name, in Chinese *Zhenfuyuan* 真福院, literally "monastery of true happiness," helped him "always to remind the monks how much they should value the grace of their religious vocation and how unbecoming is all grumbling and lack of charity to these true 'sons of God.'"[87]

It was the founder's intention that the monastery be modeled on the image of the home, and community life within it on the image of the family. It was to be an environment where members live as brothers in Christ, in chaste intimacy devoid of any institutional coldness. That, in fact, is what is stated in article 3 of the rule and the commentary on it by Lebbe.

---

[85] Ts'ao, "Father Lebbe's Principles Live On," 114.
[86] Lebbe, *Huigui shiyi*, p. 2; cf. RPF, p. 6, and Lebbe, "Petits Frères," 440.
[87] Cited in King, "Les Petits Frères," 517.

> *The members of the congregation will be called "Little Brothers,"*
> *the superior of the monastery will be called "head of the family"*
> *(jiazhang 家長), the vice-prior of the monastery will be called*
> *"brother servant" (gongpu xiongdi 公僕兄弟), and the Little*
> *Brothers will call the Monastery of the Beatitudes "our home."*
> The nature of our congregation demands that each monastery
> become a real and true family, that every effort be made to avoid
> an institutional style. Through the above appellations we desire
> to create a family environment and cultivate the customs of life
> of a holy family. The Little Brothers should consider the Mon-
> astery of the Beatitudes their own home, respectfully love the
> head of the family and depend on him like a father in their new
> life. Among them they will consider themselves brothers in this
> holy family and will be bound by mutual affection closer than
> between hands and feet. To the name "brother" will be added
> "little" to show the degree of humility that the Little Brother
> ought to strive to reach.[88]

The new fraternal relations, expressed by calling one another
"brother," established a new community, made possible by severing
the ties of blood to their family of origin. This newness was also to
be expressed by the religious name that the Little Brothers receive
on entering the novitiate. Articles 7 and 8 of the rule speak clearly
of the need to abandon one's family, giving as examples Jesus, John
the Baptist, and, interestingly, Buddhist monks.

> *Apart from the postulants, who are called "companions" (bao-*
> *shou 保守), all the Little Brothers will be called "brothers"*
> *(xiongdi 兄弟). The head of the family too will call himself*
> *brother and will sign himself and affix his seal as such, but the*
> *brothers will call him "head of the family" (jiazhang 家長). The*
> *servant (gongpu 公僕) too will be so called.*
> *From the moment that a Little Brother receives his religious*
> *name, he abandons completely his name and the surname of*
> *his family and his native place; he assumes his religious name as*
> *his only name and the Monastery of the Beatitudes as his home.*
> Whenever the Little Brothers will be asked for their name and
> surname, they will answer: "Since the Little Brothers have aban-
> doned their families, it is not good to ask them their surname;
> since my humble name is X, I am to be called Brother X." In

---

[88] Lebbe, *Huigui shiyi*, pp. 2–3; cf. RPF, pp. 6–7, and Lebbe, "Petits Frères," 440–41.

China there is the expression: "A bonze hides his own name."
We who imitate the example of the radical abandonment of the
family of our Lord and of St. John should be ashamed of not
being the equals of Buddhist monks![89]

Words Fr. Lebbe wrote at the beginning of 1929, just a few months
after the beginning of the community, set out the broad guidelines
for life at the Monastery of the Beatitudes:

> We will try to begin again in China what St. Benedict had done
> in Europe. In the first place monastic life, a life of austerity, of
> prayer, of silence, all this not by halves, but "all the way," like
> the Trappists, even more severe than the Trappists on account of
> the food, which will be that of the poorest peasants of our coun-
> tryside. . . . Because they were truly monks and their house a
> monastery, the thought came that the best common prayer for
> them would be the Office. . . . The rest of the day will be divided
> among work, manual or intellectual, according to the aptitudes of
> each and according to the abbot's orders. At present, since all of
> them are novices, they have moreover several hours of spiritual
> instruction and the like. All day long we have the great silence,
> except for about half an hour after the noon and evening meals.
> Much time is left for prayer and meditation, because we have
> to prepare apostles for everything, *absolutely, without reserve.*
> We have constantly before our eyes the Benedictines who made
> Europe Christian and who had begun, with St. Benedict, with
> a group of lay monks, just like the *Minimi* of St. Francis (from
> whom our brothers have taken the name "Little Brothers").[90]

The intention to offer China the same tool for the rebuilding of
society that brought "Christian Europe" into being, that is, the monastic life, is evident in what Fr. Lebbe wrote a few years after the
foundation of the Little Brothers of John the Baptist:

[89] Lebbe, *Huigui shiyi*, pp. 9–10; cf. RPF, pp. 9–12, and Lebbe, "Petits Frères,"
444–47. It should be noted that here the Chinese word for abandoning the world and
deciding to become a monk is the Buddhist term *chujia* 出家, lit., "leaving home."

[90] Lebbe, *En Chine, il y a du nouveau*, 174–75. A visitor to the community of the
Little Brothers in 1932 recognized that this spirit had been achieved. He wrote: "I
had examined an undertaking at an early stage of its development, which resembled
greatly the great monastic orders that had made such a remarkable contribution to
the conversion of Europe by manifesting themselves as the guardians of the best
Christian traditions." King, "Les Petits Frères," 555–56.

The simplicity of [the monks'] life and the wealth of their spirit would enable the people in our country [China] to be reborn; the success of agricultural aid would need the spirit of Catholic monks. The Congregation of the Little Brothers of John the Baptist was born for this; its foundation has for its end to begin [in China] the work of St. Benedict and thus to save China in the same way that in his time St. Benedict had saved Europe. For this reason its way of life is strictly ascetic and [the Little Brothers], through a spiritual formation of two and a half years, aim above all to become men who are "universal, dispossessed of themselves," who can be defined as evangelized men, who come to serve society with the spirit of Jesus.[91]

The monastery of Anguo consisted of a chapel, painted by a non-Christian artist with Christian frescoes of the patron saints and scenes of the blessed Chinese martyrs, a Chinese-style altar, a very austere dormitory, a refectory, a room for reading and study, and several workshops in which the brothers composed, printed, and bound books, wove, sewed and mended, made shoes, and did carpentry. In addition, the brothers took care of all community services and cultivated the garden. The simple buildings "resemble the houses of the farmers around them; the roofs are flat and the walls made of bricks. . . . Even during the harshest winter cold there is no heating, for economy's sake."[92]

The austerity that reigned in the house was a dignified simplicity that had nothing to do with abject poverty. Great attention was given to the care and cleaning of the living spaces, which were to be "in good taste so as to provide a model for the construction of new villages" (RLB 28). "The good taste of the dwelling . . . indicates only the orderliness with which the monastery is furnished and the great care taken in planting the trees, in taking care of the vegetable garden, and in caring for the flower garden, so that the peasants can take this good taste as a humble example."[93]

[91] Lei Mingyuan, "Bushi," 1028.
[92] King, "Les Petits Frères," 488.
[93] V. Lebbe's interpretation of art. 28 of the RLB (Lebbe, *Huigui shiyi*, pp. 24–25; cf. RPF, p. 24). The Chinese word for "good taste" is *yishu* 藝術, a strong expression meaning "artful, artistic."

A visitor from abroad described the poverty of the monastery and the way of life of the community:

> From the material aspect, everything is poor, extremely poor. The monastic buildings are not pretentious, not even architecturally! Although cleanliness—meticulous cleanliness—reigns there, every comfort is excluded. In the dormitory there is a bed of boards and a pillow of three bricks; in the refectory there is a table of white wood and a tureen of the poorest of the poor. In the oratory the decoration is entirely Chinese, and the furnishings are as modest as everywhere else. In the alimentary regime of the monks there is nothing to flatter the palate, even that of the least demanding. Their table does not see meat or fish or eggs or dairy products. Cereals, legumes, and fruit compose all their menus.[94]

Through poverty of goods and of spirit the Little Brothers wanted to show the Chinese people a Catholic Church stripped of the opaqueness that comes from power and economic well-being. The Little Brothers were deeply convinced that only in this way could there be an encounter that was truly evangelical.

> We believe that a radical change in how we act is being forced upon us, not only under the aspect of economics, but above all to convince Christians and pagans of something that they have not come to understand: *that we are poor.* Once this change is realized, people will willingly share with us their bowl of rice or their wheat biscuit, according as they wish to keep our presence, or rather, our services. For this end, however difficult it may appear, we believe that there is a very effective means, maybe the only means, which is "to renounce ourselves and carry our cross every day" *in all truth.*[95]

A non-Christian intellectual who visited the monastery recognized the value in the Little Brothers' way of life, remarking, "Your strength lies in the poverty of your life."[96]

Work was considered an essential dimension of the life of the Little Brothers: "Without a job to be done," writes Fr. Lebbe, "the brothers would be like the flies, and a community of workers, which is what

[94] Nève, "L'œuvre monastique du Père Lebbe," 3.
[95] King, "Les Petits Frères," 517–18.
[96] Cited in Lebbe, "Nova et vetera," 11.

our family is, cannot accept that."[97] According to the rule, a good disposition toward work is the second of the two qualities necessary to enter the congregation: "There are two qualities necessary to enter the congregation: (1) a lofty intention; (2) sufficient ability to fulfill one of the works of the congregation" (RLB 12).[98] Work is to be carried out in charity and completed for the sake of charity; it is to be disciplined work that does not leave room for laxity and worldliness, as stated in article 13.2 of the rule: "In work, the prominent exercise of charity transcends all mechanical norms. Nevertheless, the Little Brother must guard against adducing charity so as to refuse work, contravene the holy rule, and pursue his own carnal desires or worldly habits."[99]

One of the Little Brothers, in witness to the centrality of useful work in the life of the Little Brothers, states that the life of the Monastery of the Beatitudes revolved around two main "movements," the second of which is the "movement of practical work" (*shiji gongzuo yundong* 實際工作運動).[100]

At first, work consisted of cultivating a large vegetable garden, which was to provide for the whole year, and some small crafts: binding, lithography, and fabrication of office glue.[101] In 1932, when the community numbered eighty brothers (thirty professed, thirty-one novices, and nineteen postulants), external tasks were divided as follows: twelve brothers devoted themselves to teaching in parishes, four were catechists, two were inspectors of the residences (their work involved supervision of the workers, the business office, the sacristy), one was in charge of the material affairs of the seminary, one was secretary of Catholic Action for the vicariate, another ran a medical dispensary, two worked at the bishop's residence, and three in the kitchen.[102] Their ministry soon also extended to prisoners.[103]

---

[97] Lebbe, *Huigui shiyi*, p. 12; cf. RPF, p. 13, and Lebbe, "Petits Frères," 448.

[98] Lebbe, *Huigui shiyi*, p. 11; cf. RPF, p. 13, and Lebbe, "Petits Frères," 448.

[99] Lebbe, *Huigui shiyi*, p. 13; cf. RPF, p. 14, and Lebbe, "Petits Frères," 448–49.

[100] Cf. Yilu xiongdi, "Wo suo renshi de Zhenfuyuan" [The Monastery of the Beatitudes that I know], YZB 5 (1937): 123–25.

[101] Cf. Lebbe, *En Chine, il y a du nouveau*, 182.

[102] Cf. King, "Les Petits Frères," 519.

[103] For several years Vincent Lebbe and another Little Brother offered spiritual assistance to prisoners in Baoding (Paoting). Cf. Levaux, *Le père Lebbe*, 361–62.

[Wherever the Little Brother works, he] lives in one of the sheds close to the chapel and maintains himself by his manual work. He is the soul of the Christian community, he directs Catholic Action, leads common prayers, presides at the Sunday meetings, explains Christian doctrine to adults and to children, and has a particular predilection for spreading the faith among the pagans. His austere life, his invincible and indefatigable charity (the gift of himself to all): this is his principal preaching, best suited to incite those who surround him to ask him to teach them.[104]

A missionary apostolate of this kind, however, was not to remove the Little Brother from his "family of origin" permanently. So "at least once a year the brother must return to the monastery, which throughout his life will remain the center of his affections. He will remain there at least two consecutive months to refresh himself in community life and to concentrate his spiritual energies."[105] "The apostolate exercised by the brothers will be less the fruit of personal action than the diffusion of the monastery. And when they set off in groups to offer their work where the needs of the apostolate are most urgent, they will spend in the service of the church the spiritual energies that they accumulated in the monastery."[106]

Work was carried out for about seven hours a day and in a climate of silence (cf. RLB 56) "as rigorous as that in a Trappist monastery."[107] The aim was self-sufficiency. "It is absolutely necessary that we be able to live by our work, without being a burden on the mission or public charity."[108] The pastoral ministries carried out in different places offered the local church an unsalaried "labor force," which was a primary requirement when this new Chinese congregation was formed.

What we wanted was to relieve the missions of the financial burden. We wanted to provide an army of zealous workers, trustworthy, well-disciplined, unsalaried, capable of carrying out

[104] Cited in King, "Les Petits Frères," 518.
[105] Cited ibid.
[106] T. T. E., "Une nouvelle congrégation religieuse en Chine," 70.
[107] Nève, "L'œuvre monastique du Père Lebbe," 3.
[108] Letter of V. Lebbe to A. Cotta, 13 July 1930, in Goffart and Sohier, *Lettres du père Lebbe*, p. 268.

everything that is done now by salaried personnel. We receive
for each of our Little Brothers a sum greatly inferior to what
had been paid until now. We aim at reducing expenses more
and more, at the same time furnishing more work and work of
better quality. We wish to live from our own means, hence we
are led to reduce more and more our expenses. . . . Our discipline has tended naturally toward an austere and parsimonious
life. Are not mortification and abnegation the conditions for
fruitful work?[109]

The wages of a Little Brother were not to be considered his personal property but were given to the community for its needs. As the
rule says, "All the money or goods a Little Brother earns thanks to
the work he has done or the position he occupies should be considered the property of the congregation" (RLB 96).[110] The prohibition
to possess even the least personal property is considered one of the
pillars of the life of the Little Brothers, and sharing is the one and
only principle in the management of assets (cf. RLB 100).

Genuine poverty in order to share in the life of the poverty-stricken
Chinese among whom the Little Brothers lived is certainly a hall-
mark of their rule and can rightly be seen to have been inspired
by the Franciscan ideal of "holy poverty." In a farewell letter to his
Little Brothers, a sort of abridged last will and testament, Fr. Lebbe
recommends: "Your level of life should be perpetually that of poor
workers in the region. What I recommend to you most insistently,
my dear ones, . . . is *true poverty without any artfulness*, a real
and unlimited charity, which will manifest itself by the courage of
assiduous work."[111]

Even the Communists were impressed that the Little Brothers
worked with their hands and for this the brothers were highly thought
of by the local people. Fr. Lebbe reports the observation made by a

[109] Cited in King, "Les Petits Frères," 492.
[110] Lebbe, *Huigui shiyi*, p. 67; cf. RPF, p. 60.
[111] Goffart and Sohier, *Lettres du père Lebbe*, pp. 295–96, no. 148 (emphasis
added). On 2 August 1937, Fr. Lebbe wrote two last will and testament letters in
Chinese, one to the Little Brothers and one to the Little Sisters. Translated into
French, the first was published in Goffart and Sohier, *Lettres du père Lebbe*, and the
second in *Perspectives de catholicité* 15, no. 3 (1956): 68–69.

Communist combatant to a fellow soldier: "[The Little Brothers] are not capitalists. . . . They themselves work. . . . They don't have servants. . . . And then, they are productive, and finally, the people are for them. If we persecute them, we will look as if we were going against our own principles and we will not please the simple working people."[112]

According to the rule (cf. RLB 57–121), the person aspiring to be a Little Brother spent a few days at the monastery as a guest. He was then admitted to the community as a postulant and received his religious name. During the six-month period of the postulancy he received a basic introduction to Christian doctrine if he needed it, along with an introduction to community life according to the rule.

The time of novitiate began with the ceremony of receiving the habit and lasted two years. "Under the guidance of the novice master, [the novitiate] is intended to form the soul of the novice through the study of the rules and the constitutions, through meditation and assiduous prayer, through teachings about the vows and the virtues, through exercises designed to eradicate vices, to direct the movements of the soul, and to acquire virtues" (RLB 80.1). At the end of the first year of novitiate the Little Brother "during a ceremony expresses before the whole community his desire to belong to the congregation" (RLB 87), and after the second year he makes temporary vows before the bishop, who entrusts a copy of the Gospels to the newly professed, saying: "Here is the rule you must follow for the rest of your life." These first vows, which lasted for one year, were renewed three times, after which the brother was admitted to solemn vows, that is, definitive monastic profession. We know that for these ceremonies of receiving a monastic name, being clothed with the habit, being accepted into the novitiate, as well as making temporary and definitive vows, Fr. Lebbe also composed Chinese texts.[113]

Having requested only "a lofty intention (*gaoshang zhiqi* 高尚志氣) to live the life of a Little Brother with all that is required," a certain

---

[112] Cited in Lebbe, "Nova et vetera," 7.

[113] Cf. e.g., RLB 60; 61 comments; 69 comments. The rule makes several mentions of a *Ritual* (*Lijieben* 禮節本), no longer existing, that almost certainly contained these liturgical texts.

level of education or intellectual preparation was not required for admission into community. Possessing "a specialization in some field or other special skills" (RLB 57) could be sufficient. In 1931 two Little Brothers were sent to Louvain for theological studies and to live the monastic life in the Benedictine monasteries of Saint-André (Bruges) and Mont-César (Louvain).[114] In the last months of his life Fr. Lebbe decided to move the novitiate of the Little Brothers to the monastery of Qinghe near Peking, so that the young men could benefit from the nearby intellectual center.[115]

The Spirit and the Rule

Abbot Nève, who saw the life of the community of the Little Brothers in the 1930s, testified to the spiritual quality of their fraternal life and the spirit that animated it.

> In the monastic life . . . *unum est necessarium*, one thing is necessary, indispensible for its harmonious development: the spirit, the spirit that blows in the community. . . . What is important in the monastic life and what dominates everything else is the mentality in which the soul is formed and maintained, that is, the spirit and the heart of each of the monks. . . . For a monastery to be living, it is necessary that its organism be vivified by a soul very much alive. Such a soul I have felt vibrating in Ankwo [Anguo]. . . . What characterizes their life, . . . what has enchanted me, what has captivated me is the spirit of the community.[116]

Vincent Lebbe imparted to his new monastic family the same spirit that had animated his own spiritual life for many years. Perhaps it could not be otherwise. The content of his preaching and of his extensive correspondence shows a radical and unreserved commitment to the Gospel, which can be seen explicitly in a letter Fr. Lebbe wrote in 1931, toward the end of his life, in response to a request by the vicar of the Diocese of Liège, André Boland, who asked him to offer

---

[114] Cf. Levaux, *Le père Lebbe*, 338.
[115] Cf. Claude Soetens, "Introduction," in RPF, p. xi.
[116] Nève, "L'œuvre monastique du Père Lebbe," 2–3.

a few guidelines for the spiritual formation of future priests of the Société des Auxiliaires des Missions (SAM).[117]

First there is the fundamental conviction that the spiritual life of those who follow the Lord is nothing other than an immediate and constant effort to "put the Gospel into practice . . . as the living and eminently practical law" that will perfectly direct life. This translates into a practice of the evangelical life based on three principles that the followers of Fr. Lebbe often repeated as the pillars of their discipleship: perfect detachment or total and absolute renunciation; true love (*caritas non ficta*); constant joy (*gaudete semper*). "To be a good Christian, and much more, to be a good missionary, you have to be happy, joyful." More concretely, Lebbe speaks of conformity to the life and death of Jesus "always," "in everything," and in a spirit of obedience to the church.[118]

The *Rule of the Little Brothers* that Fr. Lebbe started sketching during the 1930s and formulated in 1940 is in continuity with the program expressed in the letter of 1931. The texts of articles 4 and 5, along with Fr. Lebbe's commentary, are particularly significant for the way they treat the union between the ascetical-spiritual and apostolic-social ideals.

> *The Little Brother aspires to sanctification in asceticism, to glorify God and to save men. The objective of his work is to participate in a grandiose undertaking of the rebirth of the [Chinese] people.*
>
> . . . Sanctification (*chengsheng* 成聖) is the universal goal of the religious (*xiushi* 修士), but "holy" has two senses, one broad and the other narrow. What the Little Brother should propose to himself as his objective is the narrower sense, in other words, the desire that his heart must never abandon is to become truly and fully a saint, without the least difference as regards canonized saints. The means of sanctification are many; the one chosen by the Little Brother is asceticism (*kuxiu* 苦修). Although his work may be for the outside and he may be involved in society, basically he must be a true ascetic, like his spiritual brothers in the Cistercian Order. Nevertheless, since we are a religious

---

[117] Cf. letter of V. Lebbe to A. Boland, 26 August 1931, in Goffart and Sohier, *Lettres du père Lebbe*, pp. 276–80, no. 142.

[118] Cf. Guelluy, "La spiritualité du Père Lebbe," 466–67.

congregation with a Chinese character and our work conforms to our times, there are some differences as regards ascetical discipline. . . . To glorify God and save men, although strategies of direct evangelization should be used, the method preferred by the Little Brother will be that taught us by the Lord Jesus, who said: "May your light shine before men, so that they may see your good works and glorify your father who is in heaven" (Matt 5:16). To save men means to save the whole man, constituted inseparably of body and soul, and to accept his weaknesses, without asking him to become a Christian, so that people may not think that all our social works require something in return. As for the objective of our work, Jesus has said: "You are the light of the world. . . . A lamp is not lit to be put under a bushel basket" (Matt 5:14-15), and our Lord has also said in a parable: "The kingdom of heaven is like leaven that a woman took and mixed in three measures of flour, so as to leaven all" (Matt 13:33). The Little Brother, rooted in this holy teaching, after having first of all disposed himself to become leaven, is placed directly in society, gives his service with patience, and makes of his work the most efficacious and concrete announcement with which to introduce the Gospel. Together with all the people he aspires to the salvation of the nation, opening the way that prepares Christ's coming. . . .

The spirit required of the Little Brother is: (1) elevated, with a tenacious will to give life to great enterprises and to edify together the times; (2) radical; (3) conformed to the times. It is contained in three slogans: total sacrifice, true charity, constant joy. The motto of the congregation is: "The violent gain it" (Matt 11:12). The intention of our congregation and the objective of its works are great and arduous. If a Little Brother does not possess an eminently strong and great spirit, he will not be capable of fulfilling them. It is difficult to express in words the importance of this point. Since the Little Brother's mission is a spiritual mission, it is necessary that his spirit rise above the events of the times, otherwise it is not possible for him to persevere and to perfect himself ascetically or to have the capacity to manifest the Catholic religion before so many young non-Christian persons of impulsive spirit. In addition, since his work is carried out mostly within society, if he wants to be received by it, he will succeed only if he has lofty feelings, if he eliminates every displeasing worldly habit, if he renews his way of thinking, of speaking, and of acting in accordance with the tendencies of his times.

Fortunately, the tendencies of our times, the needs of our nation and what it legitimately seeks with ardor, are on the whole not extraneous to the spirit of the Gospel. The mission of the Little Brother, therefore, who pushes himself with all his strength to the forefront of this wave, is to carry the Catholic religion and to occupy the line of assault of this grandiose movement, so that it may receive Catholic baptism.[119]

There are, thus, three summary expressions of spirituality that Fr. Lebbe pointed to as cornerstones for his own spiritual life and that of the Little Brothers: total sacrifice (*quan xisheng* 全犧牲), true charity (*zhen airen* 真愛人), constant joy (*chang xile* 常喜樂).[120] In response to the request of one of the Little Brothers, he provided a concise explanation of what they meant.

As regards the spiritual method, we do not choose one school over another, or discuss one principle rather than another, or, much less, establish a new one in order to be different; we follow only Christ, because he is "the way, the truth, and the life." For this reason our spiritual principles and methods are Christ's Gospel and the teaching of the apostles. If we look comprehensively at the Gospels taken together, we can summarize three central ideas: (1) total sacrifice: this is what Jesus repeatedly proclaimed as the condition to be his disciples; (2) true charity: this is the central point of the entire law and of all the prophets; it is the mark that distinguishes Christians; it is our final goal; (3) constant joy: this is the fruit of following Christ and is the style that should characterize our spiritual life: "Rejoice always in the Lord!" (Phil 4:4; cf. Matt 5:12; Rom 12:12).[121]

In these catchphrases, the adjective is more important than the noun. They express the three essential features of every aspect of life

---

[119] Lebbe, *Huigui shiyi*, pp. 3–6; cf. RPF, pp. 7–9, and Lebbe, "Petits Frères," 441–43.

[120] On this theme, see Cao Lishan, *Lei Mingyuan shenfu de shenxiu gangling* [The spiritual pillars of Fr. Vincent Lebbe] (Taizhong: Tianzhujiao Yaohan xiao xiongdi hui, 1982); Zeng Lida, *Lei Mingyuan shenfu Zhongguo jiaohui bendihua de qianqu huashidai de fuchuan fangfa* [The pioneering and epoch-making method of evangelization of Fr. Vincent Lebbe in favor of the indigenization of the Chinese church] (Taizhong: Tianzhujiao Yaohan xiao xiongdi hui, 2004), 33–59.

[121] Cao Lishan, "Lei shenfu de shenxiu gangling" 雷神父的神修綱領 [The spiritual pillars of Fr. Lebbe], in *Chunfeng shinian*, 10–12, at 12.

of the Little Brother: total or absolute (*quan* 全), true (*zhen* 真), and constant (*chang* 常). These three ideograms, writ large, dominated the front of the chapel of the Monastery of the Beatitudes at Anguo.

According to the testimony of one who was very close to him and who succeeded him as head of the community, Fr. Lebbe never wrote any systematic manual of spirituality for the Little Brothers, nor did he ever use existing texts on spirituality during his classes to the novices. Significantly, he gave each novice the Chinese translation of three texts: the New Testament, in which he pointed to the Sermon on the Mount as the essential text for constant meditation; *The Story of a Soul* by St. Therese of Lisieux; and the Rule of St. Benedict.[122]

Abbot Théodore Nève wrote in 1933 that Fr. Lebbe, in his desire for an authentic monastic community, gave special attention to ancient monastic rules in drawing up the "provisional" rules of the early community of the Beatitudes. "The rule is still provisional; the community is still too young to have a definitive rule. For that the experience of years is necessary, but already now it *finds inspiration in the most authoritative monastic rules*, although it seeks to adapt itself as much as possible to Chinese life."[123]

For Lebbe, among these influential monastic rules the Rule of St. Benedict was the primary reference for his new monastic community. "The soul turns to the great patriarch of the monks. . . . We now ask St. Benedict to introduce us to the monastic life; his holy rule becomes the fundamental rule of the new institute."[124] This outlook was repeated by the brother who would succeed Lebbe as superior. "St. Benedict remains for us the ideal of the monk. For this reason we include him in the Confiteor, we celebrate his feast with solemnity, and in the beginning, before we had our own rule, we read his."[125]

Vincent Lebbe, in fact, never felt the urge to write a definitive rule for his monks, even though he often spoke of the day when he would present it to Rome for approval. A decade after the beginning of the community a definitive rule had still not been put in writing, and

---

[122] Ibid., 10.
[123] T. T. E., "Une nouvelle congrégation religieuse en Chine," 66–67 (emphasis added).
[124] Lebbe, "Nova et vetera," 5–6.
[125] Frère Alexandre, "Petits Frères de Saint Jean-Baptiste," 74.

Fr. Lebbe kept revising drafts of a provisional rule for the community. "Although the general principles and the spirit of the order were determined very early, he did not want to decide too quickly the form of life and the scope of activity. Before establishing any norms, he wanted them to be tried out for some time. He had already put in writing quite a few detailed norms for the community's way of life and activities, but they were all sporadic and fragmentary and had been corrected more than once as a result of changing times and circumstances."[126]

A manuscript copy of this type of draft of the rule is conserved in the archives of the Congregation of the Little Brothers of John the Baptist in Taizhong, Taiwan, and has been published.[127] This draft appears to have been the only reference material Fr. Lebbe consulted at the time he drew up the "definitive" rule.[128] The rule of 1940 expanded and made specific the basic contents of the primitive rule and altered the order in which they appear. While the main lines of the two rules are the same, in the rule of 1940 we find a more complex and canonically ordered structure that answers the need to systematize a reality that had become in a short time more complex.

The person who urged Fr. Lebbe to hasten the completion of a written text that would be authoritative for administering the life of the congregation was Fr. Raymond de Jaegher, an SAM priest who came to Anguo in 1931 and whom Fr. Lebbe put in charge of the two monasteries of the Beatitudes of Anguo when he left for the South

---

[126] Cao Lishan, "Qijishi de chengjiu" 奇蹟式的成就 [Miraculous accomplishments], in *Chunfeng shinian*, 418–20, at 418. See also Cao Lishan, "Huizu shouxie huigui de shenqi jingguo" 會祖手寫會規的神奇經過 [The miraculous events surrounding the manuscript of the rule (written by) the founder of the congregation], in *Huizu Lei Mingyuan shenfu shouxie Yaohan xiao xiongdi hui, Delai xiao meimei hui huigui* [Rule of the Congregation of the Little Brothers of John the Baptist and of the Congregation of the Little Sisters of Therese of the Child Jesus. Manuscript of the founder, Fr. Vincent Lebbe] (Taizhong: Taizhong zonghui Zhenfuyuan, [preface 1998]), iii–vi.

[127] Cf. Lei Mingyuan, "Jiagui chugao" [Draft of the rule of the family], *Lei Mingyuan shenfu zhuankan* 9 (1992): 44–56. An English translation is given in app. 3 (cf. *infra*, pp. 335–53).

[128] Cf. Cao Lishan, "Qijishi de chengjiu," 419: "[When he wrote up the final version of the rule, Fr. Lebbe] did not have at hand other reference works to consult, not even the Code of Canon Law. All he had with him was a fragmentary draft of the rule that he had previously written."

in 1937. Finding himself in charge of a community situated in territory that was occupied by the invader and therefore isolated and realizing that there was little possibility of communicating with the "living rule" that was Fr. Lebbe, Raymond de Jaegher felt the urgency of having a definitive written rule.

Lebbe was initially opposed to the idea, saying, "It took St. Vincent [de Paul] twenty years to write the rule for the Congregation of the Mission and the Daughters of Charity. So why are you asking me now to write the rule for the two congregations of John the Baptist and Therese of the Child Jesus?"[129] He gave in, however, to the pressures of Fr. de Jaegher and in early March 1940, in the course of one week, while he was at Yaocun in the district of Linxian (Linhsien, in the region of Henan), he compiled the rule in Chinese. Fr. de Jaegher helped him translate it into Latin.[130] He called it the *Rule of the Congregation and Commentary* (*Huigui shiyi* 會規釋義),[131] since each of the 182 articles is followed by a commentary explaining its meaning. The manuscript of the rule, consisting of ninety-nine pages, was miraculously saved when documents were burned following the arrest of Fr. Lebbe a few days after he finished writing it. It is now conserved in the archives of the Monastery of the Beatitudes of Taizhong as "the treasure of the congregation."[132] After being reproduced and translated into French in 1986,[133] the manuscript was also edited with ideograms and published.[134]

---

[129] Ibid., 419.

[130] In a letter to Bède Lebbe, dated 6 March 1940, R. de Jaegher writes: "In these days we transcribed the rules of the Little Brothers of Saint John the Baptist that I had been requesting for several months." In another letter, this one to A. Boland, dated 2 April 1940, de Jaegher says: "What I got clarified were the rules that I had clamored for and which we finished together. It was a big job and it took a lot of our time, but it will produce much fruit." Excerpts cited in Soetens, "Introduction," p. xiv, esp. n. 1.

[131] The manuscript actually has two titles. The first is *Jiagui shiyi* 家規釋義 [Rule of the family and commentary], followed by a brief introduction in three columns (this title and the introduction were not put in the printed version), followed by a second title, probably the proper one, which is *Huigui shiyi* 會規釋義 [Rule of the congregation and commentary], followed by a table of contents.

[132] *Huizu Lei Mingyuan shenfu shouxie*, i.

[133] Cf. *Recueil des archives Vincent Lebbe*, [vol. 4]: *La Règle des Petits frères de Saint-Jean-Baptiste*, ed. Claude Soetens (Louvain-la-Neuve: Faculté de théologie, 1986).

[134] Cf. *Huizu Lei Mingyuan shenfu shouxie*.

Complying with a request made by Lcbbe shortly after writing the rule, the Latin version of the rule was revised by the canonist Nicolas Wenders, an SAM priest and at the time rector of the regional seminary of Xuanhua (Suanhwa).[135] In 1942 it was translated into Chinese by the new superior of the congregation, Alexander Cao Lishan (Ts'ao Li-shan), and it was approved the following year by the bishop of Anguo. The text of the rule was revised a first time in line with the new theology of religious life based on the Second Vatican Council and a second time in order to conform to the requirements of the new Code of Canon Law of 1983. It was finally approved in its final form in 1991 by the bishop of Taizhong.[136]

A number of passages from the rule and the comments on them made by Fr. Lebbe have already been cited to indicate the main features of the spirituality contained in it. I wish to highlight briefly the specifically monastic content of the rule, which in the prologue states that "the essential nature [of the congregation] is derived from the Benedictine and Cistercian Orders."[137]

If, as already noted, Francis of Assisi is invoked especially with regard to poverty (cf. the commentary by Fr. Lebbe on arts. 28, 96, and 101) and as a model of the kind of "patience, kindness, and humility" that evangelizes (cf. art. 32 comments), Benedict, the father of Western monasticism, and his monks are evoked several times with regard to the centrality of the Divine Office, the *opus Dei*, and the social role of Benedictine monasticism (cf. art. 14 comments).[138] Benedict is also presented as an example that the Little Brothers have followed in the organization of their monasteries, in their administration, and in the allocation of tasks (cf. the comments on arts. 122 and 129). In addition, Lebbe's rule contains other

---

[135] Claude Soetens affirms that the Latin translation of the rule was only sent to Rome in 1951, in a version that had been revised only partially, and was submitted to the Congregation of Propaganda Fide for approval. Cf. Soetens, "Introduction," p. xiv, esp. n. 3.

[136] Cf. *Yaohan xiao xiongdi hui huigui* [Rule of the Congregation of the Little Brothers of John the Baptist] (Taizhong: Taizhong zonghui Zhenfuyuan, [preface 2006]). This edition is of the revised rule (with the last minimal amendments of 2006) with references to passages of the manuscript rule of 1940.

[137] The three columns of the prologue (*xu* 序) that are found in the original manuscript of 1940 (cf. the reproduction in RPF, p. 103) were omitted in the printed versions.

[138] Cf. *infra*, p. 301.

implicit, but clear, references to the Benedictine monastic model, such as that concerning the allocation of seats in choir according to the order of entry into the monastery.

The inspiration for austerity of life and the requirement of manual labor come from the Cistercians, who are explicitly mentioned in the commentary on article 4 on asceticism[139] and in the commentary on article 45 about burial without a coffin. It is interesting to note that this latter Cistercian practice is evaluated in terms of its applicability in the sociocultural context of China. "Burial without a coffin is a practice in the Cistercian Order tied to holy poverty. At the beginning we too had decided to establish this as a norm, but later we acquiesced to the general opposition of the good brothers, according to whom, on account of Chinese customs, this was to be abandoned."[140]

There are other implicit references to typical practices of Trappist monasticism. One example is the use of sign language, particularly in those times of the day when the rule of silence is absolute (cf. art. 56 comments).

The terminology of the rule also reflects a monastic influence. The most obvious example is the decision to adopt the term *kuxiu* to translate "asceticism," a term that with the arrival of the Trappists in China in 1883 had become synonymous with the Trappist form of monastic life. Another example is the choice of the term *shengong* 神工 to translate spiritual work or divine service, a clear reference to the *opus Dei* of the Rule of St. Benedict. A significant example is the decision to adopt the Buddhist term *chujia* 出家 (literally, "abandoning the family") as the Chinese expression for abandoning the world and deciding to become a monk.

The Divine Office in Chinese

It is necessary to read another article of the rule, number 14, to understand the essential elements of the spiritual life of the Little Brothers: "Among works, *opus Dei* (*shengong*, 'spiritual work') is

---

[139] Cf. *supra*, p. 293.
[140] Lebbe, *Huigui shiyi*, p. 34; cf. RPF, p. 32.

above all else. The *opus Dei* in our congregation consists of four dimensions: (1) daily meditation; (2) Divine Office; (3) the Holy Sacrifice; (4) reading of the Bible."[141]

A comment by Fr. Lebbe makes explicit the peculiarly monastic, which for Lebbe means Benedictine, origin and character of the priority given to the *opus Dei*.

> The phrase *"opus Dei* above all else" was written by St. Benedict in his rule.[142] St. Benedict did not cultivate his virtues in solitude but created a grand work, and his spiritual sons founded Christian civilization. He was a great personality of Europe, yet he gave priority to the *opus Dei*. We recognize him as the father of our congregation and, since we desire our nation to be reborn by basing itself on him who inspired a Christian epoch in Europe, we cannot but take him as our example and give the *opus Dei* an inviolable position also among us.[143]

One is certainly struck by the emphasis given to the frequent reading of and meditation on the Scriptures in speaking about the *opus Dei*. This *lectio divina* is indeed essential for a deep spiritual life.[144] Here I would like to focus on the monastic Office as liturgical prayer. In the same commentary on article 14 of the rule, Fr. Lebbe offers some precise details on the practice of the Divine Office (*Sheng rike* 聖日課) in the community of the Little Brothers, stressing in this way its centrality.

> Among the prayers that are raised [to God], particular importance will be given to the official prayer of holy church, especially to the Divine Office and the Holy Sacrifice, since they have been inspired by the Holy Spirit. . . . As regards the Divine Office, for

---

[141] Lebbe, *Huigui shiyi*, p. 15; cf. RPF, p. 15, and Lebbe, "Petits Frères," 449.

[142] Cf. RB 43.3: *Nihil operi Dei praeponatur* (Nothing is to be preferred to the work of God).

[143] Lebbe, *Huigui shiyi*, p. 15; cf. RPF, p. 15.

[144] Cf. Lebbe's comments on art. 14: "The habit that the Little Brother should foster is a continual intimacy of heart with the good Lord: for this, daily meditation is to be the first spiritual practice and it must be supported by the frequent reading of the Bible. . . . As for various other prayers that the faithful are accustomed to, the Little Brother is under no obligation to recite them; in fact, these prayers are not comparable to a more assiduous reading of the Bible and meditation on the word of God." Lebbe, *Huigui shiyi*, pp. 16–17; cf. RPF, p. 16, and Lebbe, "Petits Frères," 450.

the time being, the Little Brothers recite the little Office of the Holy Mother. When the printing of the great Office is finished, in the choir of the house only the great Office will be recited. During journeys outside and during work this can be substituted by the little Office. However, whether it is a matter of the great or the little Office, it must be recited according to ancient custom, with respect to the division of the Hours; only in the case of the night Office can the time be anticipated according to circumstances, except on Thursdays (Holy Hour).[145]

In one of his letters Lebbe further specifies the monastic nature of the communal liturgical prayer practiced in the Monastery of the Beatitudes: "Because they really were monks and their house a monastery, the idea occurred that the best common prayer for them would be the Office. Since at present we have in Chinese only the Offices of the Holy Virgin and of the Dead, we kept to the little Office [of the Holy Virgin] every day and the Office of the Dead in a few specified circumstances and three days every month. Seven times a day, hence, following David, they recite in the choir the holy hours; only Vespers is sung daily. On certain solemnities other parts of the Office are likewise sung."[146]

This praying of the Liturgy of the Hours, carried out "according to ancient custom," but also intelligible to Chinese monks who had not done any special study of Latin and the liturgy, was only possible thanks to the enormous work of Fr. Lebbe. The Chinese Office he developed using Gregorian melodies has not received much attention from scholars.[147] To appreciate what he accomplished, it is necessary to trace, at least to some degree, the itinerary of his interest in and

---

[145] Lebbe, *Huigui shiyi*, pp. 16–17; cf. RPF, p. 16.

[146] Lebbe, *En Chine, il y a du nouveau*, 174–75.

[147] The only important work specifically dedicated to this subject, but more from the musical rather than the liturgical aspect, is the extremely well-documented master's thesis of Ng Ka Chai, "The Indigenization of Gregorian Chant in Early Twentieth-Century China: The Case of Vincent Lebbe and His Congregations" (Chinese University of Hong Kong, 2007). See also the article by the same author, "Neumes and Chinese Liturgy: How Liturgical Renewal Was Brought to China by Vincent Lebbe," in *About Books, Maps, Songs and Steles: The Wording and Teaching of the Christian Faith in China*, ed. Dirk Van Overmeire and Pieter Ackerman (Leuven: Ferdinand Verbiest Institute, K. U. Leuven, 2011), 280–94.

reflection on the liturgy, an itinerary that is intertwined with his monastic journey described earlier in this chapter.

Lebbe's interest in the liturgy goes back to the days of his youth; it was closely related to his sojourns in monasteries, which in those early years of the twentieth century were the privileged place for a reform of the Catholic liturgy. His reflection on the liturgy seems to have been further stimulated by his encounter, when he arrived in China, with the centuries-old liturgical traditions of the Chinese Catholic population. Compared with the solemn atmosphere of Gregorian chant and the Latin liturgy, Chinese liturgical and devotional practices, together with the traditional Chinese music that accompanied them, must have been a huge shock to Lebbe, leading him to rethink what constitutes the very essence of the liturgy.

In letters to his Benedictine brother Dom Bède, Lebbe contributes a voice from China to the liturgical debate that was starting in Europe in those years; he was also concerned with modernist issues.[148] Recognizing a certain "petrification of the liturgy," which had become "very sad" in Europe, Lebbe proposes the vernacular in the liturgy as the only solution, not only for the West, but for China as well. To adopt the vernacular in the Catholic liturgy would be to take up a long liturgical tradition in China. For centuries Chinese Catholics recited prayers and sang hymns with great fervor several times a day, using a prayer book that was, in fact, a daily Office made up of prayers and devotions combined with materials composed in Chinese by missionaries and Chinese Christians beginning in the seventeenth century.[149] "The liturgy in China . . . it is here corrected by prayers chanted in the native language in all seasons. Our Christians have their Office, or public prayers, developed especially in those places where there is no resident priest. This keeps them in church hours and hours, without seeming to tire them, just as you do not tire of singing the Office in Latin. Gregorian chant does not say anything

---

[148] Cf. letter of V. Lebbe to B. Lebbe, written on 26 May, 10 June, and 12 June 1908, in Goffart and Sohier, *Lettres du père Lebbe*, pp. 84–88, no. 37.

[149] For the history of this prayer book, known in Chinese as *Shengjiao rike* 聖教日課, cf. Paul Brunner, *L'Euchologe de la mission de Chine. Editio princeps 1628 et développements jusqu'à nos jours* (Münster: Aschendorffsche Verlagsbuchhandlung, 1964).

to them so far. . . . Many ceremonies, directly opposed to Chinese customs, shock them and are often the cause of very painful scandals among neophytes. Liturgical formation, hence, is not yet a topic for discussion here."[150]

The fundamental problem, thus, was an ignorance of the Catholic liturgy among the common people because of a lack of liturgical education. Fr. Lebbe probably soon began to think about practical ways to bring together the liturgical and musical traditions of China and those of the West, in particular, the Western musical tradition of Gregorian chant.

Lebbe spoke publicly on this issue at the fifth Liturgical Week held at the Benedictine Abbey of Mont-César in 1913.[151] An anonymous author reports that the ideas presented by Fr. Lebbe on that occasion lead one to make a bold comparison between the devotional practices of Chinese Catholics and those of the ancient church, the *"ecclesia* of the good old days,"* and suggests that the use of the vernacular in the liturgy needs to be rethought.

In this way, Lebbe entered the liturgical debate that was emerging around the imposing figure of Dom Lambert Beauduin (1873–1960), whom he met during that liturgical week in Mont-César.[152] He entered the debate thinking about the specific situation in China. To him it was clear that the key issue was the adoption of the vernacular in the liturgy.[153]

Fifteen years later, at the end of the 1920s, Lebbe would begin to create a true Chinese liturgy, having the Chinese monks chant some texts of the Breviary, of the Benediction liturgy, and of the

[150] Goffart and Sohier, *Lettres du père Lebbe,* p. 86.

[151] A summary of Vincent Lebbe's conference is given in an article by an anonymous author, "La liturgie populaire chinoise," *Questions liturgiques* 3, no. 8 (1913): 403–6.

[152] Cf. Leclercq, *Vie du père Lebbe,* 143ff. On the question of the contribution of Lebbe to the liturgy, see also Paul Goffart, "Le Père Lebbe et la liturgie," *Église vivante* 2 (1950): 24–27. Another incident shows Fr. Lebbe's personal involvement in the area of liturgical research. In 1927 Bishop Odoricus Cheng Hede of Puqi (Hubei) named Vincent Lebbe member of a commission for the reform of prayers, which was set up during the Council of Shanghai in 1924, of which Bishop Cheng was president (cf. Leclercq, *Vie du père Lebbe,* 281).

[153] Cf. ibid., 406.

Roman Missal in a language that they could finally understand, and to chant them to Gregorian melodies. "We have here something unique in the world: the *Office chanted in Chinese* in choir—don't shout this too loudly, or good people will immediately make use of it to cause us trouble. Actually, we are perfectly in the right: since we are not obliged to have the Office, our Little Brothers may recite it in whatever language they want. But the originality (not forbidden, and everything that is not forbidden is permitted) consists in our chanting and also in our coming together in choir like authentic Benedictine monks."[154]

The singing of the Divine Office in choir is a defining characteristic of monastic orders, and from the very beginning it was Lebbe's wish that this practice should be followed by the Little Brothers of John the Baptist. For this reason the chapel was constructed to facilitate the antiphonal recitation of the Office, that is, the choir was divided into two sections that faced each other. It was also expected that in the congregation some monks would be appointed to supervise the choir (cf. RLB 128 and 153),[155] and for this reason Lebbe decided "[to set] specific standards for the choir" (RLB 50 comments).[156] We also know that the liturgical celebrations at the Monastery of the Beatitudes were recited and sung slowly to match the meditative style of Chinese religious practice.[157]

Of all the melodies chosen by Fr. Lebbe, "ninety percent consisted of Gregorian music; only a limited number used Chinese music."[158] His decision was in line with the practice most recommended by

[154] Letter of V. Lebbe to A. Cotta, 13 June 1930, in Goffart and Sohier, *Lettres du père Lebbe*, p. 272 (emphasis added). Only the priests were obliged to pray the Divine Office in Latin.

[155] *Sigelü* 司歌侶 (Lebbe, *Huigui shiyi*, pp. 87, 100; cf. RPF, pp. 77, 87).

[156] *Gelü xize guiding* 歌侶細則規定 (Lebbe, *Huigui shiyi*, p. 37; cf. RPF, p. 34).

[157] Cf. Raymond de Jaegher, "Le Père Lebbe, homme de Dieu," *Église vivante* 2 (1950): 167.

[158] Cao Lishan, "Yinyue. Neixiu de liulu" 音樂—內修的流露 [Music. Revelation of interiority], in *Chunfeng shinian*, 15–16, at 15. For this and for other details regarding the musical output of V. Lebbe, which were furnished by a member of the Congregation of the Little Brothers of John the Baptist, see also Cao Lishan, "Lei Mingyuan shenfu de yuepu" [The musical scores of Fr. Vincent Lebbe], *Lei Mingyuan shenfu zhuankan* 25 (1994): 32–42.

missionaries in those years. Moreover, the Council of Shanghai in 1924 prescribed Gregorian chant in the liturgy (cf. cc. 522–23). It allowed Chinese music, provided it was not profane and it was used in the manner and at times that were appropriate (cf. c. 525). Nevertheless, in all Chinese Catholic churches most of the music consisted of traditional melodies and vocal formulas typical of the ancient Chinese musical tradition, but these continued to be considered devotional practices and not the true liturgy of the church.

The true liturgical essence of Gregorian chant, as found in the choral singing of the monastic Divine Office, still remained unknown to the vast majority of Chinese Catholics. If Gregorian chant was to become really popular, it had to be adapted to the structure of the Chinese language. This was the liturgical task that Fr. Lebbe accomplished over the course of a decade in collaboration with his Little Brothers.[159] He was deeply convinced of what the Chinese Benedictine monk Pierre-Célestin Lu Zhengxiang[160] expressed a few years later: "In so far as among us . . . the Catholic liturgy will have been unable to adopt the Chinese literary language (which, as I like to insist, is admirably suited to the Gregorian chant), to that extent the worship which the church renders to God—the sacrifice of the Mass, the Divine Office, the liturgy of the sacraments, the admirable Catholic liturgy of the dead—will remain an absolutely closed book for the yellow race."[161]

If the singing of the Divine Office was to be at the heart of the life of the congregation, while there still was no liturgical book that could be used for singing the Office in Chinese, the practical Fr. Lebbe had to prepare one from existing materials and find ways of adapting Gregorian melodies to Chinese liturgical texts.

The Chinese texts of the Divine Office and of the Missal were for the most part taken from the elegant and erudite translations made

---

[159] On the specific musical selections to which V. Lebbe adapted the different syllabic structure of Chinese liturgical terms and the different phraseology of Chinese liturgical texts to Gregorian chant and the syllabic structure of the Latin language, see Ng Ka Chai, "The Indigenization of Gregorian Chant," 111–70.

[160] For information about Pierre-Célestin Lu Zhengxian, cf. *supra*, pp. 228–39.

[161] Lou Tseng-Tsiang, *Ways of Confucius and of Christ* (London: Burns Oates, 1948), 88.

by the Jesuit Ludovico Buglio (1606–1682) in the second half of the seventeenth century.[162] Never having been used in the liturgy, these translations were now, two and a half centuries after their composition, introduced into liturgical celebrations thanks to Fr. Lebbe.

The first compositions to be completed, probably by the end of 1929, were the Office of the Blessed Virgin Mary, whose recitation on weekdays was prescribed by Lebbe as an interim measure while waiting for the entire *Breviarium Romanum* in Chinese to be ready for singing (cf. RLB 14.3), and the Office of the Dead, which was sung at the death of a Little Brother (cf. RLB 47) and three times a month.[163] Both of these Offices were very popular among Chinese Catholics.

Lebbe then worked on musical compositions for the Office on Marian feasts and on Sundays, for the proper Offices of feasts during the liturgical year, and for the common Office of martyrs. As we have seen, in community prayer a special place was reserved for the Chinese martyrs, who were co-patrons of the congregation and who were to be commemorated with dignity and solemnity. Of the proper Offices in memory of the saints, the only ones to be prepared by Lebbe were those for the feast of the Nativity of St. John the Baptist and for the feast of his martyrdom, since the Precursor was the patron of the congregation. Lebbe himself composed the Chinese texts of these Offices, since they were not part of Buglio's translation. He also composed the music for these Offices, instead of using existing Gregorian melodies.[164]

All these compositions were then assembled to form a single large liturgical book for the choral singing of the Divine Office (*Da rike* 大日課). It had more than seven hundred pages of texts and scores,

---

[162] The translations he made use of were *Misa jingdian* 彌撒經典. *Missale Romanum auctoritate Pauli V Pont. M. Sinice redditum a P. Ludovico Buglio Soc. Iesu* (1670); *Rike gaiyao* 日課概要. *Breviarium Romanum Sinice redditum a P. Ludovico Buglio Soc. Iesu* (1674); *Shengmu xiao rike* 聖母小日課 [Little Office of the Blessed Mother, 1676]; *Yiwangzhe rike jing* 已亡者日課經 [Office of the Dead].

[163] Cf. Lebbe, *En Chine, il y a du nouveau*, 175.

[164] Cf. Cao Lishan, "Yinyue. Neixiu de liulu," 16. For a description of the constitutive parts of the sung Office prepared by Lebbe, see Ng Ka Chai, "The Indigenization of Gregorian Chant," 80–110.

was decorated with Chinese-style miniatures, and was finely bound. "[Their choir book] has been remarkably edited, printed, and bound. The characters are large and clear. The profusion of musical notation and the symbolic illuminations show that it was made as a work of love. This book contains in Chinese the little Office of the Holy Virgin, the Office of the Dead, and the Offices for the principal feasts of the year. I was surprised to learn that it was the work of the monastery print shop. Fr. Lebbe composed the musical adaptation; the Little Brothers did all the rest."[165]

Someone who closely studied this uniquely conceived and published liturgical book found it exceptional in every way: "The chant book is the most beautifully made liturgical or music book of the Chinese Catholic Church that the author has seen, whether from the point of view of the music notation, language, calligraphy, or physical appearance."[166]

On the death of Lebbe in 1940 the project of composing music and setting the entire *Breviarium Romanum* in Chinese to music came to an end. Lebbe confided to his friend Raymond de Jaegher that a true liturgy in Chinese remained his ultimate dream and something he still wanted to contribute to the Chinese church.[167] Although it is incomplete, the work of Fr. Lebbe remains a valuable contribution to the task of inculturating the Catholic liturgy in general and monastic liturgy in particular in the linguistic, ritual, and musical world of China. Its value is also highly symbolic. "[It is] a fusion of ancient Catholic liturgical practice and the Chinese language. Through the liturgies of the Christian communities enriched by Gregorian chant, the universal voice of the Catholic Church became fused with their native language."[168]

The Little Sisters of Therese of the Child Jesus

According to the same Fr. Lebbe, the characteristics of the life of the Little Brothers were adopted in full by the Congregation of the

[165] King, "Les Petits Frères," 486. The Monastery of the Beatitudes of Taizhong has two manuscript copies of this liturgical book.
[166] Ng Ka Chai, "The Indigenization of Gregorian Chant," 83.
[167] Cf. Jaegher, "Le Père Lebbe, homme de Dieu," 165.
[168] Ng Ka Chai, "The Indigenization of Gregorian Chant," 110.

Little Sisters of Therese of the Child Jesus (in Chinese *Delai xiao meimei hui* 德來小妹妹會). As the founder himself said, "They are the female counterpart of the Beatitudes,"[169] that is, of the Little Brothers of John the Baptist. In other words, "practically everything that we have said of the life, the ideal, and the spirit of the brothers also applies to the sisters, *mutatis mutandis*. There is one exception, however: some educational preparation is required of the aspirant and also a small dowry."[170] Just as the Little Brothers were a kind of "apostolic" Trappist, the Little Sisters were to be "apostolic" Carmelites.[171] "Basically, our life in the monastery and outside is similar to that of the Little Brothers. It is a life of praise and a life of prayer; only the ascetic aspect is different with regard to food and to the hour of rising. With the Office, which we chant in Chinese, the Mass, meditation, the reading of the Gospel are the principal daily spiritual exercise."[172]

In late April 1928 Bishop Sun wrote to the Carmel of Lisieux announcing the foundation and asking for prayers for this new congregation modeled on Carmelite life and the "little way" of St. Therese. Fr. Lebbe tirelessly proposed this saint as its model for spiritual growth, and she was chosen as the patroness of the congregation, together with the Chinese martyrs. "On the example of St. Therese, he wanted our love of God and of souls not to leave us any rest. . . . He used to say: 'St. Therese should be your model; you must seize every occasion to prove your attachment to Christ, bearing the cross with Jesus, not a very little cross of straw, but a *true cross* . . . not desiring anything outside of Christ.' . . . St. Therese's generosity filled him with admiration, and in his zeal he would have wanted

---

[169] Letter of V. Lebbe to A. Cotta, 13 July 1930, in Goffart and Sohier, *Lettres du père Lebbe*, p. 269.

[170] King, "Les Petits Frères," 520.

[171] Apart from the references that Vincent Lebbe makes in his correspondence, information about the Congregation of the Little Sisters of Therese of the Child Jesus were taken from: Petite sœur Louka, "Petites sœurs Thérésiennes"; Gabrielle Yang, "La congrégation des Petites Sœurs de sainte Thérèse de L'enfant-Jésus d'Anguo (Chine)," *Vies consacrées* 81, no. 1 (2009): 19–24, republished under the title "Sommaire historique de la congrégation des petites sœurs de Sainte Thérèse de L'Enfant-Jésus d'Anguo (Province de Hebei, Chine)," *Courrier Verbiest* 23 (2010): 20–22.

[172] Petite sœur Louka, "Petites sœurs Thérésiennes," 82.

all the Little Sisters to follow the 'little way' of childhood with a giant's steps."[173]

The construction of their convent, called the "Theresian monastery" (in Chinese *Delaiyuan* 德來院), and located next to that of the brothers, was funded by a patron from Liège, Paul Staes. It "is a replica of the monastery of the brothers, with the same rule, with the same radiant joy, with the same silence."[174] It was dedicated on 3 October 1929, the feast of St. Therese of Lisieux, and on that day sixteen postulants entered the novitiate. Although a sister was designated as superior, Fr. Lebbe's role as the founder and leader of the new community was crucial. "The father used to come morning and evening, to discuss with the young superior questions relative to the good order in the community. Then he would give us a course on Sacred Scripture, the life of St. Therese, or some other spiritual subject. He wanted us to know the Gospel perfectly, especially chapters 5, 6, and 7 of St. Matthew. His great desire was that each Little Sister, once she had finished her novitiate, be ready to leave on mission, ready to aid the missionaries in instructing catechumens. He also watched with particular care over each one's formation."[175]

The spirituality of the Beatitudes and the three pillars set up by Fr. Lebbe for the Little Brothers—total sacrifice, true love, and constant joy—were adopted by the Little Sisters as the basis of their spiritual life. This can be seen from the questions put to a novice at the time of her first profession.

> Are you ready to sacrifice totally your habits, your tastes, your advantages, your own will?
>
> Do you want to give yourself totally to God and for this to obey her who represents him here?
>
> Since you take God for your sole refuge, do you accept to live in poverty, chastity, obedience?
>
> Do you want to acknowledge the eight beatitudes as your only good? Do you love work, hard labor, silence, and penance? Do

[173] Ibid., 83–84.
[174] King, "Les Petits Frères," 488.
[175] Petite sœur Louka, "Petites sœurs Thérésiennes," 83.

you want to obey your superior without regard to her age, her intelligence, or her qualities?

As for your sisters, do you want to accept joyously their company, live with them in true charity?

Do you want to consider the monastery of St. Therese as your only family?[176]

A little more than a year after the construction of the monastery the number of sisters had increased to such a point that at the beginning of 1931 the founder told them they could no longer admit postulants because there was insufficient space.[177] In 1932 the community of Little Sisters was made up of twenty-two professed sisters, twenty-three novices, and twenty-four postulants.[178] In 1933 there were eighty sisters, postulants included, including a French sister from Lyons, Sr. Saint Luke. They lived in great poverty. "I do not think," wrote the founder, "that any community in the world would agree to live in the conditions in which they live, and live very happily."[179]

The Little Sisters of St. Therese responded to the needs of the missionary apostolate to such a degree that they were often overwhelmed by the many services they were called on to provide. On Sundays and public holidays they often did not even have time to eat their frugal meal.[180]

> The apostolic life of the Little Sisters consists in the direct work of evangelization in union with the clergy. In this country, where priests are so few, the Little Sister is in the midst of all a fraternal face of Christianity. . . . Generally, a Little Sister occupied a room at the house of a Christian family of the village. During the day she held classes for children and in the evening, when everyone had returned from the fields, she spoke to all about Christianity and prepared for baptism these people of the North,

[176] Ibid., 84.
[177] Cf. letter of V. Lebbe to B. Lebbe, 26 January 1931, in Goffart and Sohier, *Lettres du père Lebbe*, p. 275.
[178] Cf. King, "Les Petits Frères," 520.
[179] Letter of V. Lebbe to P. Staes, February 1928, cited in Levaux, *Le père Lebbe*, 354.
[180] Cf. King, "Les Petits Frères," 520.

so simple and so sympathetic. Occasionally, at New Year, the instructions were given outside because of the great number of hearers.[181]

Later, as they became more numerous, the Little Sisters provided staff for schools, for female catechumenates, for various dispensaries, hospitals, and orphanages, for prisons; they also dedicated themselves to sewing and embroidery.

In 1938 the Little Sisters were scattered throughout the region because of the war, offering service in four vicariates. During the war of resistance against Japan (1937–1945) five sisters worked in a hospital for the wounded. Two nuns died in 1941 during this service. Forced to leave Anguo at the end of the 1940s, some sisters took up residence in a poor neighborhood in Peking, where they ran an orphanage and a dispensary. Others provided the same services in different provinces of China. Still others, dispersed by the Communist government in 1952, had to go back to their families of origin because they lacked any means of subsistence.

A small group of three sisters who were not accepted by their families or by friends and acquaintances continued to live a community life together not far from Anguo. A Little Brother and a diocesan priest lived with them. "They lived as beggars. In spite of the persecution and the extremely difficult conditions of life, they kept up their morale. They shared their food, supporting each other in turn in the name of Jesus. Even though the sisters had been disbanded, they were very attached in spirit to their congregation."[182]

When China opened up after 1979, this "small remnant" of three elderly sisters, all older than eighty, was able to return in 1982 and live in a place close to the old convent. Two years later the elderly superior of the community of Anguo, Sr. Guiying, who had lived with a nephew during the previous years, but was able to visit her sisters occasionally, was finally able to reach the community.

When the Bureau for Religious Affairs gave them permission to recruit new candidates in 1987, some postulants from various dioceses in China began to arrive and revived the community life that

---

[181] Petite sœur Louka, "Petites sœurs Thérésiennes," 85.
[182] Yang, "La congrégation des Petites Sœurs," 22.

for several years appeared to be on the point of extinction. In 1990 the elderly Sr. Pauline, who before the Sino-Japanese War had been superior general and then had lived through the dark years with her family, was able to come back to community life. On 1 October 1996 the first group of nine sisters to enter the community after its reopening made solemn vows. That same year the government returned to the sisters a portion of the properties that had belonged to the congregation, making it possible to build a new monastery. In 2008 the congregation numbered forty-six sisters (thirty-six in solemn vows, ten in simple). Besides the work of evangelization, catechetical and pastoral, in various dioceses in China, the Little Sisters are engaged in social work, health care (management of nursing homes and clinics), dispensaries, and crafts (knitting and embroidery); they maintain themselves by working as doctors, nurses, and pharmacists. The Little Sisters continue to be "a small but bright white flower in the Chinese mission today, as the little Therese."[183]

---

[183] "Le piccole sorelle di santa Teresina dell'He Bei (De Lai), un piccolo fiore bianco ma brillante nella missione cinese di oggi," news agency Fides, 26 January 2010.

Peking, 1937.
Vincent Lebbe, founder of the
Congregation of the Little
Brothers of John the Baptist, in
the habit of the congregation.

Anguo, Monastery of the Beatitudes, 1931. The community of the Little Brothers of
John the Baptist at the end of their yearly retreat.

Anguo, Monastery of the Beatitudes, 1928 or 1929 (?). The provisional belfry with a traditional Chinese bell.

Anguo, Monastery of the Beatitudes, 1928 or 1929 (?). Praying the Divine Office in the first chapel.

1935. Vincent Lebbe with his friend Théodore Nève, abbot of the Benedictine Abbey of Saint-André (Belgium), Raymond de Jaegher (left), and Paul Gilson (right).

Manuscript of Vincent Lebbe,
in which he expounds the three
qualities he considers fundamental for the Little Brothers:
"total" (*quan* 全) sacrifice,
"true" (*zhen* 真) charity,
"constant" (*chang* 常) joy.

Anguo,
Theresian
monastery,
1930 (?).
The Little
Sisters of
Therese of the
Child Jesus
at the en-
trance of their
chapel during
a ceremony of
clothing.

Appendix 1

||||||||||||||||||||||||||||||||||||||||||||||||

Preface to the First Chinese Translation
of the Rule of St. Benedict (1894)

If we examine the five hundred years following the Incarnation, in the Far West we find a great holy monk (*yinxiu dasheng* 隱修大聖) whose name was Benedict (Bendu 本篤).[1] He dwelt in seclusion (*yinju* 隱居) for many years, during which he was silently instructed by the Lord, built a monastery (*xiuyuan* 修院),[2] framed a rule for an order (*huigui* 會規), instructed his disciples, and exerted influence on the people. His order began to flourish in Italy, France, and other countries. As happens with the bright sunshine at midday, there was nobody who was not enlightened by his light.

Those among the people of that age who wished to live in celibacy (*jieshen* 潔身)[3] and to serve the Lord cared only about gaining the most profit [from their practice] and were committed to the utmost to striving for excellence. In out-of-the-way places and deep in wild mountains they built monasteries and established hermitages where they cultivated themselves (*xiushen* 修身) and served the Lord in accordance with the rule established by the saint.[4]

---

[1] Translation of the preface contained in *Sheng Bendu huigui* 聖本篤會規 [The Rule of St. Benedict] (Beijing: Jiushitang, 1894), fols. 1a–4b. Reprinted from Matteo Nicolini-Zani, "Christian Monastic Literature in China: Preliminary Survey and Bibliography," in *Light a Candle: Encounters and Friendship with China; Festschrift in Honour of Angelo Lazzarotto P.I.M.E.*, ed. Roman Malek and Gianni Criveller (Sankt Augustin: Institut Monumenta Serica, 2010), 325–27.

[2] The Monastery of Montecassino.

[3] Lit., "to cleanse their bodies."

[4] I.e., Benedict.

317

Afterward the Holy Teaching (*Shengjiao* 聖教)[5] did not enjoy times of peace: evil groups swarmed all around, monasteries were destroyed by fire one after the other, the monks all became homeless wanderers. We have to wait until the eleventh century for a period when the situation became tranquil again and the Holy Teaching prospered once more. At that time St. Robert (Luoboerduo 羅伯爾多),[6] St. Bernard (Boernaduo 伯爾納多),[7] and other monks of the same [Benedictine] Order respectfully received from the pope the mandate to rebuild the monasteries, to reform old customs, to travel throughout all the countries of the Far West.

Among all [the monks] belonging to the order there was none who was not granted spiritual gifts, who did not succeed in saving his soul, and, excelling all other men, who did not even reach sanctity. In that generation there was no lack of men who truly can be called the "glory of God" and the "delight of the Holy Teaching."

Recently, thanks to the Lord's grace, in China the Holy Teaching enjoyed wide diffusion. In a solitary region deep in the mountains and in a land unfrequented by men, according to the admirable intention of our holy forefather (*xiansheng* 先聖),[8] a monastery was built to accommodate monks (*yinxiu zhi shi* 隱修之士). Its name is the Monastery of Our Lady of Consolation (*Shengmu shenweiyuan* 聖母神慰院). In the monastery the first duties daily are to venerate the Holy Mother and fervently to love God; the daily labors are to sing the offices (*gejing* 歌經), to devote oneself to meditation (*modao* 默禱), and to practice self-restraint (*keji* 克己) and strict abstinence (*yanzhai* 嚴齋); the final aim daily is to turn away from one's sins and to revert to good deeds, to become holy and so to ascend to Heaven. Therefore the monastery can rightly be compared to a hospital (*yaoshi* 藥室)[9] in which spiritual sickness is healed, and to a precious raft (*baofa* 寶筏)[10] that ferries people across to Heaven.

---

[5] I.e., Christianity.

[6] Robert of Molesmes (ca. 1027–1110).

[7] Bernard of Clairvaux (1090–1153).

[8] I.e., Benedict.

[9] Lit., "pharmacy."

[10] A term originally used in Buddhism to indicate the teachings of Buddha, which ferry believers across to bliss.

Unfortunately, the Rule of St. Benedict, originally written in Latin, has not yet been translated into Chinese. But if it is not translated into Chinese, how can the Chinese become acquainted with it? And if they do not understand it, they will not be able to act according to it. This makes the foundation of a monastery vain and the benefits [of the monastic life] difficult to obtain. [This situation] is like beauty losing its splendor, like willingness to put on the roof but not to build the house, and so to identify deficiency with good. How regretful!

Therefore, I considered it no small matter to obey respectfully the superior will of reverently translating into Chinese the seventy-three chapters of the rule written by St. Benedict with his own hands. The language is plain and easy to understand, and the meaning of the words is clear and simple, so that future students will easily be able to comprehend it fully and to comply with it.

This is the preface respectfully written by a brother monk (*moduo* 末鐸),[11] 1,894 years after God's incarnation, in the corresponding year Jiawu 甲午 [of the Chinese calendar], on the occasion of the feast of the Holy Mother's Assumption into Heaven.

[11] Lit., "not priest," or "not yet priest." It could more probably refer to a choir brother not yet ordained priest, rather than to a lay brother. From another source we know that the translator was Joseph Wen. Cf. Louis Brun, "La vie contemplative en Chine," in Alphonse Hubrecht, *Une trappe en Chine* (Peking: Imprimerie des Lazaristes, 1933), 104.

Title page of the first Chinese translation of the Rule of St. Benedict (1894).

Appendix 2

"The Monastery Will Be a Chinese House": Three Texts of Jehan Joliet

"A Project for a Chinese Monastery" (1922)

[A.] Guiding Ideas

The intention is to found a monastery with the Divine Office and prayer and, for work, principally intellectual work.[1]

Apart from the interest in public prayer prayed in China by Chinese, from this follow developments and fruits for the conversion and the christianization of China. Education is something laborious and long, all the more so that education which is the Christian life, and even more so when it is a matter of an entire people. Of course, God can do everything, but we see always and even at the beginning by the conversion of the Roman Empire that he works slowly, progressively, and as if submitting himself to the natural law of mankind. Christianity, substantially complete at the moment of conversion, grows strong and takes root so as to embrace the whole man and all of society. Then, by a truly divine condescension, God does not despise any man or race; he not only permits but wants the growth

---

[1] Translation of the manuscript *Projet de monastère chinois*, preserved in the archives of the Benedictine Abbey of Sint-Andries in Bruges (ASA, Chine, Joliet 4 [Personalia]). The third and final part of the manuscript ("Historique du projet") has been left out of the present translation. As stated in the first lines of the manuscript, this is a transcription of Jehan Joliet's original, dated 30 May 1922. The same text is repeated almost entirely in a letter of J. Joliet to the abbot primate, F. von Stotzingen, dated 30 May 1926, cited in Henri-Philippe Delcourt, *Dom Jehan Joliet (1870–1937). Un projet de monachisme bénédictin chinois* (Paris: Cerf, 1988), 265–67. The expressions in italics in the text are underlined in the manuscript.

of every Christian body to embrace its natural characteristics. For each person or each Christian people there is a harmonious coupling of the natural and the supernatural, and both profit from this.

Let us pass to concrete things: the conversion of *pagan Chinese* is to be made by *Christian Europeans*; the result to be obtained is the composite *Chinese Christian*. On both sides there has been a centuries-old association with interpenetration of the natural element with the religious. Because of this there is a great risk of imposing on the Chinese a European Christianity, and then the harmonious coupling will be missing. On the other hand, there is the opposite danger of pruning European Christianity too much out of excessive respect for the Chinese mentality.

The principal place where these elements can be harmoniously fused is the monastery. Because of its strong discipline and complete Christianity, and because of its solitude and retreat from the masses, Christianity can be grafted in peace and leisure on the old Chinese trunk. With Chinese and European monks living together in the fraternity of the cloister, Chinese culture will be sifted almost unnoticeably and imperceptibly from its pagan tares, while the seeds providentially deposited in it will come to bloom in Christianity. At the same time Chinese literature will be the object of a long historical and scientific scrutiny so as to bring it closer to Christianity and penetrate it with its influence. The periodical of the Kiangnan [Jiangnan] mission *L'École en Chine* noted with disappointment: Catholic Chinese literature is meager; moreover it is almost exclusively in a style very, indeed excessively, popular. This is an evil of the beginnings, which Greece and Rome have known, but the perfidious efforts of Julian and the resistance of Gregories and Basils show well how important it is that Christianity not remain at the margins of the national culture. In the monastery or under its influence writers will be formed who will not make simple translations or hasty adaptations, but will rethink in Chinese the immutable Christian truths and thus will make them penetrate more deeply among their compatriots.

This [monastery] will be a center of religious life where the best and the most highly educated local Christians will be able to come to strengthen and revive their faith. This will also be a hospitable center for all Chinese, who will find there sincere love and a knowledge of all that makes for the glory and character of their civilization. Christians in China are for the most part déclassé or very insignificant people, but God has also the right, and we have the duty to realize this right, to the worship of the great and the cultured. The monastery will show them Christianity free of all European protection, acting and expanding in a Chinese atmosphere.

With resurgence of nationalism all over the world and in China, ancient difficulties will become exacerbated. The most reverend father general of the Jesuits, in two letters of 1918 and 1919, has shown very well the special danger for China. The great number of conversions, which has doubled the Christian population in less than twenty years, makes the problem even more urgent. A Chinese monastery will contribute slowly and surely to give legitimate satisfaction to the mounting aspirations of Christians to diminish the foreign portion in their religion before it is carried out by force. It will, at the same time, increase their faith and their union with Rome.

Certain pages of the apostolic letter *Maximum Illud* of Benedict XV appear to regard China especially, and the foundation outlined here seems to respond to the aim of the Holy See.

> There are peoples already illuminated maturely by the Gospel, who have reached such a degree of civilization that in the variety of arts and sciences they vaunt eminent men, yet after several centuries of the influence of the Gospel and of the church they still do not have bishops to govern them or priests who may guide efficaciously their fellow-citizens. . . . It is not enough that they have a native clergy of whatever kind, considered to be of an inferior order. . . .
>
> It is not a case of spreading a human empire, but that of Christ, of procuring clients for the human fatherland, but citizens of the heavenly one. . . . Men, however barbarian and savage, understand well what it is that the missionary wants and demands from them, and have an extremely fine sense if he seeks something other than their spiritual good. If the missionary in some way works for terrestrial interests, if he is not exclusively an apostle, but seems to contribute also to the interests of his homeland, very soon all his zeal will give grave offense to the population and will disseminate the opinion that the Christian religion is limited to a certain foreign nation, so that in embracing it, one has the impression of passing under

the protection and dependence of a foreign country, losing thus one's own nationality. . . . One must not be content in any way with a smattering of knowledge of the language, but of knowing it so as to be able to speak it correctly and elegantly. Since the missionary is a debtor to all, to the illiterate as to the intellectuals, . . . by his perfect knowledge of the language he must preserve his own dignity, even when he is asked to deal with high functionaries and is invited to the meetings of the learned.[2]

B. The Mode for Carrying This Out

Successive indications of Providence will show the road to follow, but here I will make some basic comments on the stages that quite naturally present themselves.

1) *Recognition.* Since the enterprise is new and difficult, following authoritative and pressing advice, some preliminary steps are indispensable. Before deciding anything, two or three monks would pass six months or more in China, beginning to study the language, making contact with the people and familiarizing themselves with the tasks, examining the conditions of life, the chances of recruitment, and the like. Only after this stage, and with full agreement of the episcopal authority, will it be decided where and in what conditions this foundation will be made.

2) *The first establishment.* This will be made with money and monks from Europe. The low prices in China will mean that it will be possible at once to build a kind of monastery for twelve to twenty monks, so as to be from the beginning in an environment appro-

---

[2] Here the author cites in French, and not always literally, some passages of the apostolic letter on missionary activity in the world *Maximum Illud*, promulgated by Pope Benedict XV on 30 November 1919. Cf. the original text in *Acta Apostolicae Sedis* 11 (1919): 440–55, especially 445–49 for the passages quoted here. In the letter addressed to F. von Stotzingen of 30 May 1926 (cf. *supra*, p. 321, n. 1) immediately after mentioning *Maximum Illud*, Joliet adds: "My joy became even greater and my gratitude to God more lively at reading about the recent encyclical of His Holiness Pius XI on the missions. The precision, insistence, and vigor of the apostolic recommendations fulfill all my desires. And it is not without profound emotion that after more than thirty years of waiting I heard the moving appeal made to the superiors of monastic institutes to establish houses in China, among these populations that God has predisposed as if naturally to the contemplative life." Cited in Delcourt, *Dom Jehan Joliet*, 266.

priate to our life. The number of recruits from Europe will be what God wants, but in any case, they should be few. First of all, it is to be noted that few will want this kind of life, will want to embrace resolutely all of Chinese culture, except sin; then, it is desirable that the Chinese monks not feel they are in a milieu too full of foreigners. For recruitment, as for financial resources, after the original establishment, for which help from France and from Europe is counted upon, it will depend on China and especially on Providence.

3) *The development.* This will be as God wants. Authoritative voices, however, lead us prudently to hope for vocations among many young Chinese who have a taste for studies. Missionaries in Cheli [Zhili], in Kiangnan [Jiangnan], in Sechuen [Sichuan] consider recruitment guaranteed. Msgr. de Guébriant, with his vast experience, foretells success.[3] Chinese voices speak similarly. It is to be hoped that there will be gifts of books for the Chinese library, which will be the only luxury, but a necessary one for the monastery. Even as regards money, there are some very generous wealthy Chinese Christians. We hope that the monastery with its prominent Chinese character will especially attract their munificence. Probably there will also be some benefactors among the members of the European colony of the Far East. Thus the monastery, once founded thanks to foreigners, will be, in every aspect, a Chinese house.

"A Monastic Task" (1928)

. . . The monks who at present are attempting to plant monastic life in China do not come either to play a role or to justify a program.[4] The monastery is a place where Christians come together for prayer, retreat, and work, and to develop in peace their natural and supernatural faculties. Their external flourishing will be regulated by Providence. It happens, however, that by its very existence and

[3] Jean-Baptiste Budes de Guébriant (1860–1935) was vicar apostolic of Kientchang (Jianchang) from 1910 to 1916 and of Canton (Guangzhou) from 1916 to 1921. In 1919 he was apostolic visitor in China. In 1921 he became superior general of MEP.
[4] Partial translation of Jehan Joliet, "Un rayon d'espérance en Chine," *La vie intellectuelle* (December 1928): 5–23, republished with the title "Une tâche monastique," BM 10 (1930), supp. no. 1: *Le Courrier monastique chinois*, 15*–25*, also as a separate offprint.

in its fundamental constitution the monastery can make a real contribution to the immense effort for peace in China.

I have said that the success of every initiative of drawing closer or of union requires a precondition, treatment as equals. My thoughts are not to be misconstrued: this treatment as equals is not a tactic, a measure of prudence or of opportunity, an artifice to win goodwill. No, this is the outward manifestation of the human and Christian conviction that this equality really exists. Now, a monastery is an absurdity if it does not foster the radical equality of its members.

This is true, it will be said, of every religious house, and even of many other associations. Nevertheless, an integral element of monastic life peremptorily reinforces this equality: stability in the local context. When a monastery is fully constituted, it is autonomous, it recruits its members locally, and it chooses its own superior. A monastery in China is destined by fate to become a Chinese monastery or to disappear if the recruitment does not occur. It is not a European establishment with a limited addition of Chinese members or a play of rules that ensure the preponderance or the direction of foreign monks. Automatically, and the sooner the better, the house will become truly Chinese; even if there is a certain inequality and preference, it can be said that it will be in favor of the Chinese and not against them. . . . There is, thus, assurance of a favorable terrain, of an acceptable basis for collaboration. Neither for the monks themselves, nor for its guests, nor for the public is the monastery a fortress of foreign influence; it is autochthonous. It is not a question of creating a cyst on the Chinese body, but rather of living from the same sap and the same blood.

What is lacking for many works is time and tranquility. This double favor is assured by the monastic life. Since the monks do not exercise a regular ministry outside, but normally remain in the cloister all their life, where they have the resources of a library, they enjoy the conditions of long and profound study without having to hasten its stages. For linguistic, historical, philosophical, and religious studies, especially useful for a better understanding of the two civilizations, Western and Chinese, we can therefore hope for good results (naturally, this does not guarantee either intelligence or work). Another very necessary advantage in this kind of work is cordial and daily collaboration. It is necessary that in such delicate matters the work of one be verified and sustained by that of others, without which there is the risk that instead of differences being attenuated and harmonized, they will be made more acute and rendered irreconcilable. Such collaboration is found naturally in the cloister and will be aided also by contact with guests, whose assiduous presence is one of the traits of Benedictine monasticism. . . .

The monastery, [however], is not an academy or a meeting place of intellectuals; the vast majority of monks will have no part in this work. Only, in accordance with the tradition of the order, and, it seems, following the signs of present circumstances in China, it can be foreseen that in the future monastery fruitful intellectual activity will have a special place.

. . . The monastery appears as a place favorable to the exploration of the Chinese enigma. In fact, we will approach this mystery in its totality through fraternal life led in common. And if we should ever contribute to appreciating it, this will be much more the fruit of our simple monastic life than the result of our research and of our historical works.

. . . We Christians, who believe that Christ has received all nations as his inheritance, feel deeply that something is lacking in the fullness of the body of Jesus Christ as long as all peoples have not entered it. It is not only a question of numbers and because God wants the salvation of all people, but because each man and every people have their own beauty, which will make the beauty of others and the harmony of all shine the more. Then, when the divided West is faced by the enormous mass of Chinese, it seems impossible to those who believe in the unity of creation and the redemption of the entire human race, that such a multitude of such an ancient civilization has nothing to bring to the church except its numbers. If we are so proud of our quality as whites, are there not among the yellow race too natural virtues, which, made fertile by the blood of Christ, will bring new luster to the church of tomorrow? . . .

A young man of Canton, particularly brilliant, a zealous Catholic and convinced about Western advantages, methods, and sciences, one day said to me, in talking about missionaries: "But why do they want to westernize us? No, let the world continue to have its different kinds of beauty. It is not a question of westernizing China, no more than that of orientalizing Europe." If relations with other peoples are well conducted, they should make us more human, more Catholic, I dare to say, while preserving and even strengthening our particular racial qualities, rendered by them finer, more gracious. The European monks present in a Chinese monastery from the beginning, hence, will know that they personally have things to gain and to learn from their Chinese brothers, and they will obtain this gain by the practice of common life. Then, apart from the solely spiritual benefit of the monastic life, which comes from God, there will no longer be benefactors and those who receive benefactions, but a full and true equality and liberty, servants of the same Lord who does not know the barriers of nations. . . .

We are monks and we come to disseminate in the land of China the thousand-year-old Western monastic work. The times have changed and the peoples are different. Here there are no barbarians to civilize or nomads to settle. We come to a people of a high and ancient civilization, the most numerous and most compact that earth has known. Following our own vocation as monks we come to take root in its soil, to assimilate and incorporate ourselves into that [Chinese] race and there [in China] to lead our life, ancient and always the same, but supple, adapting ourselves to a new environment. That is the reason and the end of our monastic vocation, and not in erudite research or in lofty problems of the drawing together of civilizations. If now this dissemination and its consequences for Chinese monasticism are to be realized in some way, this would be a great honor and a serene joy for the sons of St. Benedict, of having contributed however little to bring not only to China, but to relations between China and the West a little of that *Pax* that is their motto.

"Monastic Formation in China" (1930)

Since the thirteenth century all the various religious orders and the new congregations have adopted as something natural a division [of the monks] into two categories and the institution of lay members.[5] This responds to their vocation. In fact, once there is specialization,

[5] Translation of Jehan Joliet, *Notes sur les études et la distinction des moines de chœur et convers dans le monastère chinois*, 3 September 1930, reproduced in Del-

be it preaching, education, care of the sick, or even special consecration to ritual prayer, it becomes useful and often necessary to have assistants vowed to the great and indispensable material services. In the enthusiasm of a beginning or of youth, under the personal influence and the stimulating example of the founder, there exists no doubt a heroic age, when each one gives himself to whatever work comes up, but neither the health of the members, nor good order, nor the institute's progress permit this to become the ordinary regime.

Up until the twelfth century it was different in the many monasteries of the Christian world. Primitive monastic rules make no provision for lay brothers. This is understandable: monks entered a new family, this time religious, to occupy themselves with God[6] under the direction of the abbot. Every monk can and should occupy himself with God. In the great communities, then, there inevitably arise certain specializations, the germ of a division of work. Thus, even the Rule of St. Benedict provides that the cellarer be exempted from kitchen work[7] and that the cooks for the guests remain one year at their task.[8] Ten to twenty persons can live in common as if in an enlarged family under the immediate and living direction of the father [abbot]. Make it a hundred or more, and material and moral ruin comes quickly. It is necessary to use the members' abilities, not to waste them, to favor their development. It would have truly been too bad for the church of God and for the stomach of the religious if St. Bernard or St. Thomas had taken their turn in the kitchen. Similarly, a good cellarer in a large house is a rare bird. Would you send the soloist to run after the cows in muddy fields?

Nevertheless, if there was a division of work in the monastic order, while for many centuries it remained faithful to not having a special and exclusive vocation, this was done for better or for worse to answer the needs of the day, but without instituting an organic dualism in

---

court, *Dom Jehan Joliet*, 197–201. The text was sent to Gaston Aubourg, librarian at Solesmes, with whom Joliet had been corresponding for several years.

[6] The Latin phrase, quite common in monastic literature, is *vacare Deo*, literally, "be empty for God."

[7] Cf. RB 35.5: "If the community is rather large, the cellarer should be excused from kitchen service."

[8] Cf. RB 53.17: "Each year, two brothers who can do the work competently are to be assigned to this kitchen [i.e., the kitchen for the abbot and guests]."

the community. The pressure of various converging circumstances was needed to impose everywhere the institution of lay members.

The prodigious expansion of monasticism, with its landed properties, often situated at a great distance from the monastery, was a factor in this evolution. In such places there were small groups of farmer monks dependent on the mother abbey. Not much was asked for the intellectual culture of the monks, still less of those engaged in agricultural work, isolated for many months or for their entire life from the vivifying atmosphere of the abbey.

During these same centuries in various countries the Romance languages came to be formed, with the progressive abandonment of Latin as the universal language for speaking. Doubtless, from the beginnings there were persons in the monastery who did not speak Latin and especially barbarians and country folk whose Latin was always mediocre and rudimentary. But thanks to the environment, to the daily psalmody, this could go on. Isolate a group of these illiterates in a community of farmer monks, a dead end looms, and the Latin Office becomes impossible. The disappearance of Latin rendered necessary more assiduous studies for those who wanted to speak and understand it. Thus was dug the ditch between clerks and the common folk. This language difficulty rendered the cycle of studies for the priesthood more arduous. The two categories became emphasized automatically: the Latinists more and more destined to the priesthood and the others to our modern lay members.

The final blow to the ancient equality of the monks was given by the example and the success of the new orders, which all had lay members, and rightly, as we have seen at the beginning.

This is not the place to examine in what measure this was a legitimate and desirable development or a deviation and danger for the full blossoming of monasticism without losing its family character and its repugnance at being a utilitarian organization.

At the present time, when it is a question of introducing monasticism in China, it is not superfluous to give thought to healthy conditions for its introduction.

Although China is a highly civilized country, the difference between town and country folk is much less than what it was in Greece and in the Roman Empire and also in many European lands up to our own days. Like everywhere, of course, city dwellers like to make fun of country bumpkins, but there is a great similarity or uniformity in their clothing, for example. The form and the construction of the houses is similar; schools have always sprung up spontaneously in the most remote countryside. It is also necessary to note that there are no castes, not even a hereditary nobility, much less a plutocracy among us. There is, no doubt, a refinement of language and of manners surpassing ours to mark the multiple distinctions of the social body, but all the same, there is a proximity between all that would repel us, a spirit of equality, an admirably patient tolerance, an innate politeness with a horror of brutal and violent proceedings. Finally, compared to Europe, there is infinitely less arrogance, disdainful or wounding manners, discomfiture when one is not of the same social circle. This means that those [among the Chinese] who would be lay members in Europe possess much more self-composure, social grace, and ease of manner than their Western brothers, and even than many choir religious of our country! Would not then the rigid distinction between the two categories of monks appear especially out of place here?

In China the ancient and contemporary habit is to study patiently to an age where in our country one would be ashamed to be still at a school desk. Even in the lowest class it is not rare to come across a worker, once his work is finished, without shame laboriously deciphering out loud his book. The highly cultured, like everywhere, are there in small numbers, but assuredly it is not here that one would find a monk incapable of signing his name. On the other hand, they do not feel pressured, there is nothing of that feverish haste to gain a year in one's cycle of studies. In fact, if one wants to push them in the Western manner, too often their health suffers, and above all, they don't have the time to assimilate; it is force-feeding, sometimes successful, because of an excellent memory. I have expounded elsewhere the extreme difficulty and the dangers for them of a school education hasty in the European manner.

We monks, then, who by definition do not have for our goal a special concrete work, we who by a thousand-year-old tradition are not pressured, we who are formed slowly and progressively all through our life, why would we want to impose on them [i.e., the Chinese] a method already out of harmony with our own vocation? Isn't it indicated in such a milieu [i.e., China] to return with confidence to the ancient monastic manner with its six centuries of incomparable splendor? Let us allow time and Providence to act. Let us allow specialization to come about naturally without methodically organizing it. What is wrong if one or another becomes a priest only at the age of fifty? Cases of conscience are not rare and will multiply if God, as one may think, favors religious life here [in China].

[Let us imagine that] a candidate of twenty years and more knocks at the door. In Sze-Chwan [Sichuan][9] at least it is a very rare case that he might have already done European-style secondary studies; it is unheard of, unless he comes from a seminary, that he should know Latin; for the rest, I assume he is intelligent and open. If one holds rigidly to present Western monastic customs, one has three choices in answering him: (a) "Go find your fortune elsewhere; you are beginning too late"; (b) "We will receive you as a lay brother"; (c) "Before entering the novitiate you will have to go to school for three, four, ten years." It is useless to stress how harsh and insolent these answers are. St. Benedict opened the door to him. With daily psalmody and patient studies he learned gradually the Psalter and the usual prayers. At the same time and after, according to his zeal, his capacities, and circumstances, he [the candidate] slowly began to pursue the study of Latin and other subjects. In the case of complete success, this will lead to the priesthood; others will stop along the way; finally, many will pray their whole life long the official prayer [of the church] more with the intention of their heart rather than with their understanding, like many of our religious women in the West.

For all, however, there is a marked advantage, especially for the monastery and for the church in China. We should not be reduced to [the education of] young oblates, who are so slow and so difficult to train. The foundations will never be too deep or the cadres too broad for preparing for China the recruitment of monks and, among them, of an intellectual elite rooted in prayer and doctrine.

---

[9] The central region of China, where the Xishan monastery, of which Jehan Joliet was prior, was located.

Even if the division from the beginning of the novitiate between choir novices and lay novices has only advantages and ought to be put into practice in China, there is a general law that revolutions, abrupt revolutions even, toward the good are dangerous for the equilibrium and the health of a society. It is normal and good that the Chinese church should repeat in part our experiences in Europe, that it advance from stage to stage, that it not become immobilized within limits that perhaps only imperfectly suit it, but remain supple under the direction of holy church and the Holy Spirit so as to produce in the Christian garden its native flowers and fruits in all their beauty.

MONASTÈRE·DE·SISHAN:
SHUNKING:SZECHWAN:
:CHINE::VIA·SIBÉRIE::

四川順慶西山院

Epiphanie 6 Janvier 1931

Un monastère depuis deux ans s'établit à Si Shan. Ce n'est pas un campement, ni un lieu d'étape, suivant la tradition quatorze fois séculaire des moines bénédictins, nous voulons creuser profond les bases du monachisme chinois. Penser, exprimer, vivre en Chinois l'éternelle vérité chrétienne qui s'est développée deux mille ans au sein de la prestigieuse culture gréco-occidentale : immense labeur qu'égale seule la radieuse espérance. Nous avons commencé une bibliothèque avec déjà cinq mille volumes étrangers et deux mille chinois. A tous ceux qui ont le culte de l'esprit, nous demandons de décupler ce premier effort.

fr Jehan Joliet
prieur

S'adresser au Prieur de Si Shan, ou au représentant officiel du monastère pour la bibliothèque : Monsieur Pierre Joliet, manoir de la Perrière Fixin Côte-d'Or

"A monastery was established in Si Shan [Xishan] two years ago. It is not a camp or a temporary place. Following a fourteen-centuries-old tradition of Benedictine monks, we want to dig the foundations of Chinese monasticism deeply. To think, to express, to live in Chinese the eternal Christian truth, which has developed for two thousand years within the prestigious Greek-Western culture, is an immense undertaking, which is equaled only by joyful hope. We have begun a library, which already has five thousand foreign and two thousand Chinese books. We ask all those who cultivate intellectual pursuits to render this first venture ten times greater."

Letter of 6 January 1931, written on elegant paper addressed in Chinese style and signed by Prior Jehan Joliet, in which the Xishan community asks for books for the monastery library.

Appendix 3

‖‖‖‖‖‖‖‖‖‖‖‖‖‖‖‖‖‖‖‖‖‖‖‖‖‖‖‖‖‖‖

Vincent Lebbe's
Draft of the *Rule of the Little Brothers*
of John the Baptist

(*Jiagui chugao* 家規初稿)

I. Asceticism and Its Expressions

Among the various means of sanctification, the Trappist (*Kuxiuhui* 苦修會) form has been chosen to indicate the ascetic path followed by [the members of] our congregation.[1] This means that we choose to wear rough clothing, eat plain food, live in humble dwellings, travel on foot, and do manual labor. We shall examine each of these [practices] in more detail.

a) The Habit

1. The habit of the congregation (to be worn inside and outside the monastery) is made of coarse gray material, with a leather belt tightened around the waist, white socks of coarse cotton, and shoes of coarse gray cotton.

2. Only the monastic scapular with hood is made of wool. On the scapular, below the neck, an embroidered silk cross is placed at the time of the profession. The cross will be green for the [simply] professed, red for the solemnly professed.

---

[1] Translation of the Chinese text found in Lei Mingyuan, "Jiagui chugao" [Draft of the rule of the family], *Lei Mingyuan shenfu zhuankan* 9 (1992): 44–56.

3. Apart from the hood attached to the scapular, which can be used as a headdress while working on very hot days, no other headgear may be worn.

4. Except for coats and cotton garments, there are no particular exceptions to the prohibition to wear leather clothes.

5. Except when going to bed, the complete habit must always be worn, regardless of climate, work, or place.

6. At the time of burial the brother is clothed with the complete habit; a brother who has made profession wears the scapular proper to his profession. (Interment with coffin or mat?)[2]

b) Food

1. Meals are of raw cereals (millet, maize, sorghum) with some vegetables. It is not allowed to eat meat (including eggs) or to drink alcohol or to smoke.

2. These three prohibitions (eating meat, drinking alcohol, smoking) also apply outside [the monastery].

3. In addition to the times prescribed by the church calendar of this diocese, fasting is observed on the eve of the festivals of the Holy Mother, St. John the Baptist, and the holy Chinese martyrs. Fasting is also prescribed on every Wednesday, Friday, and Saturday of Advent and Lent, and on each day of Holy Week. These fasts are chosen at our discretion[3] and thus do not require ecclesiastical approval. Therefore we will fast on the Wednesdays, Fridays, and Saturdays of Advent and Lent; on every day of Holy Week (except Saturday); on Ember Days.[4]

---

[2] This last sentence seems to refer to a question not yet resolved at the time this draft was written. In the *Rule of the Little Brothers* written in 1940, art. 45 and the related commentary of V. Lebbe have to do with burial. What is foreseen is severe poverty, manifested in the choice of less valuable wood for the coffin and the possibility (if the brother asks for it) of being buried directly in the bare earth, like the Trappist monks.

[3] That is, not imposed by the discipline of the church, but chosen by the congregation as an ascetic practice.

[4] In the Roman rite the Ember Days are four separate groups of days, originally meant to sanctify the four seasons, to invoke and thank God for the fruits of the earth and human work, in the context of the mystery of Christ as celebrated in time.

4. Both at home and away from the monastery, eating is never allowed between the three meals. Water, however, may be drunk.

5. It is not allowed to take medication on one's own initiative. At home permission from the brother nurse is needed; when away, one needs the prescription of a doctor. In any event, it should be remembered that a person who has chosen poverty should be able to put up with a little discomfort.

c) The House

1. The buildings that make up the monastery must truly be poor. It is good to be concerned about their solidity, but even the slightest decorative accessory is prohibited.

2. Solidity and durability, however, are not to be used as an excuse for violating the fundamental principle of poverty (that is, authentic, rather than hypocritical, poverty) and the spirit of poverty.

3. The furnishings must be sober, without any decorations; images and paintings on the walls should preserve the spirit of poverty.

4. The only exception is the chapel, which will be decorated as well as possible.

5. The brothers ordinarily do not live in single rooms, but occupy common rooms.

6. No heating is used in the winter. However, if lack of heating makes it impossible to work in a room, a small heater may be allowed.

7. When living outside the monastery, it is not permitted to manifest any dissatisfaction with the arrangements that are made. On the contrary, the more modest the accommodation, the better it is to be regarded. When it is possible to choose, choose what is modest, in imitation of Jesus and the saints.

Each of the four times falls on the same days of the week (Wednesday, Friday, and Saturday). The winter Ember Days occur between the third and fourth Sundays of Advent, those of spring occur between the first and second Sundays of Lent, those of summer occur between Pentecost and the feast of the Trinity, and those of fall occur between the third and fourth Sundays of September. These days are characterized by prayers of praise and thanksgiving. Before 1966, when the decree *Paenitemini* of Paul VI was promulgated, they were also days of fasting and abstinence.

d) Journeys

1. The fundamental principle for the Little Brothers is that when they go out, they walk rather than travel in sedans, on horseback, or by boat.

2. If there is a real need to save time or there is some other compelling reason, as judged by those who exercise authority, then riding a bicycle or sometimes traveling by train or ship is allowed.

3. Money for a trip is generally not to be taken, since room and board are to be requested from parishes, meeting places,[5] Catholic families, and even non-Catholics. If inconveniences along the way are anticipated, or if it is feared that asking for food and shelter might damage the reputation of the Catholic religion[6] (such circumstances are to be determined exclusively by those who exercise authority), a small amount of cash for the trip may be carried.

4. When one is traveling, the main things to avoid are breaking the three prohibitions;[7] returning home without explicit authorization; staying someplace else when there are parishes or meeting places at which to reside.

e) Work

Our beloved Jesus, King of heaven and earth, did hard manual labor for thirty years. The Holy Mother, St. Joseph, the apostles, and countless generations of monks (*xiushi* 修士) did manual labor that was hard on their bodies. During his missionary activities St. Paul supported himself by the labor of his hands [cf. 2 Thess 3:7-9]. The Little Brothers should admire these noble exemplary figures and consider the work done by their own hands to be holy.

1. During the novitiate each Little Brother will learn a craft; one who already has one should strive to perfect it.

---

[5] *Gongsuo* 公所: these are small centers where Christians gathered in the village where there was no resident priest.

[6] In the years when Lebbe was writing, the Catholic religion was commonly referred to as *Shengjiao*, literally, "Holy Teaching."

[7] That is, as mentioned above, eating the flesh of animals, drinking alcohol, smoking.

2. An effort will be made to ensure that all works in the house are gradually assumed by the brothers themselves.

3. When an activity such as teaching or mission work is done outside the monastery, if there is no time for doing manual labor, it can be replaced by the service one is engaged in. If possible, however, a craft that takes up little time should be chosen. Moreover, the proceeds or part of the proceeds of such manual work should be used to support oneself so that, like St. Paul, one can be known as someone who announces the Gospel free of charge (cf. 1 Cor 9:18).

4. It is never permitted, under any circumstances, to be served by others; one should clean one's own room, make and serve one's meals, and the like.

5. Every time during the year that a brother comes back to the family (that is, to the monastery), he should continue to work diligently and joyfully, as in the time of the novitiate.

6. Even the Little Brothers to whom intellectual work is assigned (e.g., those who have received holy orders) must learn and practice a craft, and every time they return to the family, they should do manual work for at least part of the time.

7. In their work the Little Brothers should pursue perfection and excellence. In particular, they must surpass craftsmen and possess a spirit that will edify others. Otherwise they will bring shame to the whole family, and the enemies of the Catholic religion and thieves will apply to them the words of St. Paul: "Anyone unwilling to work should not eat" (2 Thess 3:10).

II. Sanctification

The Holy Spirit says through the words of St. Paul, "For this is the will of God, your sanctification" [1 Thess 4:3]. Since there are many different kinds of holiness—in fact, no two saints are completely alike—what is the ideal spiritual goal of the Little Brothers?

a) Living the Gospel

The Little Brother reads the Gospel with reverence and in silence pours over the spirit contained in the word of God that is at work in human beings. He desires to give up everything, to renounce his very self, in order to realize the teachings of the Gospel in a way that is both radical and authentic. For this reason, the New Testament is the foundation underlying the *Rule of the Little Brothers*, the spiritual source of the Little Brothers, the holy book they love, respect, and read regularly.

b) The Virtues to Be Esteemed

Each congregation has specific virtues that it holds in the highest esteem. The Little Brothers, for their part, consider charity, work,[8] and joy as the virtues to be cultivated above all. In other words, the Little Brothers want to love sincerely (cf. Rom 12:9),[9] work hard, and always be joyful. The words given to us by our beloved Jesus are single-minded, radical, passionate. . . .

1. *To love truly.* This is what the Holy Spirit says through the words of John, the beloved disciple of Jesus. To this end the Little Brother wants to fulfill as completely as possible the commandment of our Lord: "Just as I have loved you, you also should love one another" (John 13:34). What this means concretely is that he is to do everything he can, always, everywhere, and in everything, to increase the happiness of others. To achieve this he should willingly sacrifice himself always, everywhere, and in everything.

2. *To work hard.* The Little Brother is never allowed to sit idle or have sleep in his eyes[10] but must have the working man as a model. In his special craft he should achieve a certain degree of perfection and in his work (missionary activities are also work) his objectives should be improvement and excellence. In short, he should surpass others who engage in the same activities. Two defects are absolutely to be avoided: indolence and negligence (doing the minimum, doing things carelessly, and the like).

3. *Rejoice always* (Phil 4:4), whether happy or unhappy, sick or healthy, being contradicted or agreed with. In short, regardless of the number and kind of crosses God gives him, the Little Brother should rejoice constantly and consistently show a smiling face. The Little

---

[8] *Laoku* 勞苦: literally, "hard work," implying that it is tiring.

[9] "Let love be genuine."

[10] This image seems to indicate an idle person who falls prey to sleep at work and therefore has bleary eyes, as in the case of those who sleep much.

Brother is to remember that constant joy is a great virtue that brings with it true rather than affected patience. With regard to this virtue, what is most to be avoided is putting on a sad face and saying things that express discouragement, since these defects seriously contradict charity, do harm to the spirit, and even weaken one's ability to be productive. In short, they directly threaten the sanctification that is at the very heart of the ideals of the Little Brothers. For this reason, there is no place in the Monastery of the Beatitudes for pessimism.

The Little Brother must [therefore] possess these three virtues: true charity (*zhen airen* 真愛人), total sacrifice (*quan xisheng* 全犧牲), constant joy (*chang xile* 常喜樂).

c) The Duties to Be Performed with Zeal

1. The Holy Sacrifice[11] and the Divine Office are the principal duties to be performed with zeal by the Little Brother. At Mass he prays only the prayers that correspond to what the priest recites or prays or he meditates on these prayers. The only prayers said or prayer books read are those that have a direct bearing on the Holy Sacrifice.

2. Second to the Mass in importance is the Divine Office. On weekdays the brothers recite the little Office of the Holy Mother. Three times a month the recitation of the Office of the Dead is prescribed. On major feast days the Office of the day is recited and will be prayed at the time appropriate for each Hour. Only the night Office will be prayed together before meditation.

3. Every day rising will be at an early hour and there will be a half hour of meditation.

4. Every day a rosary will be prayed.

5. Every day some verses of the New Testament will be proclaimed; [likewise] some passages from inspiring stories of the saints who imitated the Lord.

6. Every day holy books[12] are to be read or at least listened to during meals.

---

[11] That is, the Mass.

[12] *Shengshu* 聖書. This expression indicates edifying books, such as the lives of the saints or their writings.

Christian Monks on Chinese Soil

Only that which is prescribed in points 2 and 3[13] must necessarily be done before the Blessed Sacrament. If [a Little Brother is] involved in other necessities, [the above-mentioned duties] may be fulfilled during working hours. The Way of the Cross is to be made every Sunday.

7. Every year a retreat of eight days is to be made.

8. On the first Sunday of each month a general examination of conscience is to be made.

9. In the place where the Blessed Sacrament is kept, a nighttime Holy Hour is to be made.[14]

10. The zealous observance of these duties and the organization of daily work should follow a well-defined horarium. Outside of these times, the Little Brother will have to adapt himself to the circumstances of the place and the decisions of the one who has authority in the Monastery of the Beatitudes. Once these matters are established, they are to be considered God's commands and therefore to be obeyed, even if one is not in agreement with them.

11. Among the above-mentioned duties, the main ones are the Holy Sacrifice and the Divine Office. When a priest is present, neither is to be omitted. Even if no priest is present, the Divine Office is not to be omitted. When work is prolonged, there may have to be a little less sleep, but the Office should not be neglected.

Meditation follows, which, if necessary, can be done at work.

Confession is made on Friday.

d) Spiritual Direction (Opening the Heart)

Those things that our Lord wanted to convey to St. Paul he did not tell him directly, but said to him, "Get up and enter the city, and you will be told [by Ananias] what you are to do" [cf. Acts 9:6]. Furthermore, the Bible and the saints unanimously affirm that without the direction of a spiritual master it is very difficult to progress [spiritually]. For this reason, the Little Brother should recognize the

---

[13] That is, the recitation of the Divine Office and meditation.

[14] The Holy Hour, a traditional Catholic devotion, is a time of prayer in which one unites oneself to the prayer of Jesus in Gethsemani on the night before his crucifixion.

importance of the practice of opening one's heart[15] and should never neglect it.

1. The spiritual director of each Little Brother will be chosen by the bishop.

2. If a brother wishes to have a priest other than the one indicated by the bishop to whom to open his heart, he must request permission from the bishop.

3. Before profession, the brother is required to open his heart in a formal way [that is, to a spiritual director] at least six times a year; after profession, at least twice a year.

4. In addition, the Little Brother, whenever he is prey to great and persistent temptations, in particular those that contradict the vows and his vocation, he must open his heart sincerely to his spiritual master. In time of dire need, this is the most effective remedy. If it is applied with perseverance, the devil, who desires to destroy the soul of the Little Brother, cannot exercise his power. If in opening his heart the brother finds that there is no affinity [with the spiritual master], it will be necessary to look for a priest of this congregation who can accept this role.

III. Service

The scope of the service of the Little Brother is broad and unlimited, because it is completely determined by the free will and order of the bishop, who is the superior of the monastery. However, the service of a brother usually does not go beyond the following works.

a) Inside the Monastery

1. The Little Brothers must do everything possible to take upon themselves all the work pertaining to the soul, the body, the spirit, and material things. To the degree that it is possible, they should eat cereals and vegetables grown by themselves, make their own clothes and furniture, and so on.

---

[15] *Suxin* 訴心: literally, "speak [the intentions of] the heart." The term indicates a spiritual conversation.

2. It is even more necessary that there be productive activities in the monastery that can maintain the life of the whole community. Everything possible should be done to ensure that such enterprises are fully staffed by the Little Brothers. Help from outside the community should not be sought unless it is absolutely necessary.

3. In the Theresian monastery[16] all services entrusted to externs, as well as all spiritual services, such as the celebration of the Holy Sacrifice, and all the works related to the material needs, such as the porter's office and the cultivation of vegetables, should be entrusted, whenever possible, to the Little Brothers.

b) The Mission

Once the monastery is completely set up and its productive activities are sufficient to ensure its subsistence, the principal work of the Little Brother will be mission on behalf of [the people of] the Diocese of Anguo, that they may be completely converted to Christ.

1. In those places where a member of the clergy is in permanent residence, the Little Brother resides in a parish facility; otherwise he lives near the meeting place [of the local Christians] or temporarily rents a small house. He not only assumes responsibility for guiding and educating the Catholic and non-Catholic population of that village, but also should begin church services in that place, assist the faithful of the surrounding villages, and do all he can to preach the Gospel to the Gentiles. This is the sublime work entrusted to him by God. In this work the Little Brother must be solicitous, determined, and bold; he must persevere without flinching, move forward with courage, be neither negligent nor murmuring, and this until his last breath.

2. While explicit mission is fundamental, the Little Brother should consider other activities, such as education, charity, and social services, as indirect mission. Prayer, asceticism, and manual work inside and outside the monastery should also be considered tools for the mission. Moreover, although these activities are not explicitly

---

[16] The monastery of the Little Sisters of Therese of the Child Jesus was founded by Lebbe in 1929 at Anguo (cf. *supra*, pp. 308–13).

missionary, their usefulness for the glory of God and the salvation of people is not less than that of direct activities, and the intention and love of those who practice them must always be taken into consideration. With this conviction, the whole family will create a common enterprise whose unity embraces a diversity of activities. All the Little Brothers, whether at home or outside, whether in holy orders or not, will undertake intellectual or manual work, consecrating themselves to one common goal: the conversion to Christ of the Diocese of Anguo.

c) Social Service

Among the indirect [missionary] activities, the Little Brother should consider social service of prime importance.

1. At the monastery a course in practical sociology should be taught.

2. In the face of social problems, the Little Brother should create a new mentality and a vibrant spirit; he is to represent the vanguard and leadership of the working class.

3. In addition to social enterprises that the congregation may undertake in due time, if a Little Brother finds himself, in the place where he lives, confronted with social circumstances that require urgent intervention, he should consider that the task has been entrusted to him by God and that it is his personal duty to look for a remedy.

d) Education

The congregation should gradually provide the following personnel:

1. persons who are able to assume the position of teachers in schools of all levels, especially the elementary;

2. persons who are able to assume the position of professors at continuing education schools (evening classes, open schools, and others);

3. persons who are able to write and translate books, as well as contribute to various newspapers;

4. persons who know how to bind books and to print and produce materials for religious and social education.

The Little Brother, at whatever level of education he is engaged, will never sacrifice the Catholic spirit and character [of his teaching]. He will never give the impression that he accepts non-religious principles of education and will be tireless in his opposition to such principles.

e) Medical and Charitable Activities

1. The congregation must ensure that some of the Little Brothers study Chinese and Western medicine, so that they will be equipped to hold positions in Catholic clinics or work as nurses in Catholic hospitals.

2. The Little Brother should take special care about personal hygiene, paying particular attention to cleanliness, practicing Tai Chi,[17] brushing his teeth, airing out his living quarters, taking a shower, changing his clothes. There should be few things in his room. He should not spit at random.

3. Although the monastery itself is poor, one should take care of the poor as best one can, as if one were serving the Lord.

4. In case of natural disasters, every effort should be made to bring relief.

f) Rules for Carrying Out Various Ministries in Parishes

1. Whatever be [a Little Brother's] task in the parishes, the brother must agree to do whatever the bishop requests.

2. When a secular task is assumed, what is most important is that it be purified of its mundane nature and carried out with the spirit that is proper to a true and holy monk.

3. The Little Brother must not forget that in his missionary service the first thing he should offer is his example. Then he should take advantage of all favorable opportunities for missionary service, both direct and indirect, not allowing any of these [opportunities] to be lost in vain.

---

[17] *Taiji (quan)shu* 太極(拳)術. Tai Chi is a practice that consists primarily of a series of bodily movements and control of the breath for the purpose of physical well-being. Its philosophical content is rooted in the basic concepts of Taoism.

4. The humility, respect, and obedience that the Little Brother shows priests must exceed that shown by all the others and thus be an explicit example for all the faithful.

5. With regard to all the services performed in the parish, the Little Brother has no superior other than the pastor. He is not obliged to explain or report anything relating to his service in the parish to the servant[18] of the Monastery of the Beatitudes.

6. [The Little Brother] should be on his guard against talkativeness, chatter, gossip, and other such things. If, when he comes home, he starts gossiping about things that took place in the parish, in addition to being punished and given a suitable penance, he must also go to the local pastor and ask him for a penance to make reparation.

g) Other Matters

1. Among the Catholic organizations and community services to which aid is to be given, Catholic Action comes first.

2. After that, and on a provisional basis, if any situation arises in which God can be glorified and people benefited, the brother is to do so fearlessly, courageously, and without hesitation, provided that he has a mandate from those in authority. He should act with the firm conviction and sure hope that God's help will not fail.

IV. The Name

a) The Name Chosen

The name of the congregation is "Congregation of the Little Brothers of John [the Baptist]."

b) The Patrons

1. The reason John the Baptist has been chosen as the principal patron is that, just as John was the precursor[19] of Jesus, our Lord, so the Little Brothers are to be the precursors and assistants of parish

---

[18] *Gongpu*: cf. *infra*, pp. 349 and 351.
[19] *Qianfeng* 前鋒: literally, "avant-garde."

priests. Just as St. John wanted all traces of himself to disappear when Jesus was made manifest, so too the Little Brother ought to desire a position that is subordinate to that of others, to take his place behind that of the parish priests.

In the desert St. John prepared himself for his ministry with prayer, fasting, and silence. In the same way, the Little Brothers while living in the Monastery of the Beatitudes should make use of these three instruments to prepare themselves.

When he left the desert to fulfill his mission of proclamation, St. John did not change his austere and ascetic life. In the same way the Little Brother, after leaving the Monastery of the Beatitudes to fulfill his external service, should not change the austere and ascetic life he led in the monastery.

St. John, having accomplished his ministry, placed his disciples under the authority of Jesus. So too, the Little Brother must put all his accomplishments in mission, in education, and in every other service under the jurisdiction of the parish priest. The Monastery of the Beatitudes is not involved in any way in the administration of the parish. In fact, not even reports about parish [administration] are to be received.

2. The secondary patrons are the Chinese martyrs.

Because the congregation is fully Chinese and wants to fulfill the recently expressed desire of the Holy Father to promote the inculturation[20] of the Catholic Church in China, it asks for the blessing and aid of the blessed martyrs, [who are] its ancestors and fellow citizens in heaven.

3. The monastery is called "Monastery of the Beatitudes," first because its patrons are the Chinese blessed, second, because the Little Brother, from the time he is invested until his death, desires nothing more than that the eight Beatitudes be the only happiness

---

[20] The word Lebbe uses is *Zhongguohua* 中國化, literally, "to make Chinese." One of the principal means to accomplish the inculturation of the church in China is through the formation of a Chinese clergy. With regard to the policy of the Holy See vis-à-vis indigenization during the time this rule was being drafted, see the "Introduction," pp. 15–18.

in which he rejoices, and that they be the basis of his "constant joy"[21] or eternal joy.

c) The Coat of Arms

A cross is set on a yellow and white background, the colors of the flag of the pope (that is, the flag of the Catholic Church[22]). The cross is green and represents the young sprout of this small congregation that hopes to grow. On either side of the cross is engraved the motto of the congregation: "The violent take it by force." Because Jesus, our Lord said, "From the days of John the Baptist . . . the violent take it by force" (Matt 11:12), the disciples of St. John, recalling this motto, must remind each other what their goal is.

d) The Titles of the Members of the Congregation

1. The highest authority of the whole congregation is the diocesan bishop, who is called "abbot" (*yuanzhang* 院長).
2. The bishop has two representatives. The first official representative is a priest, appointed directly by the bishop, who is called "father servant" (*gongpu shenfu* 公僕神父). Since the monastery is a real family, the Little Brothers usually call him "father" (*fuqin* 父親). The second is the vice-representative, who is a brother without holy orders elected by an absolute majority in the general chapter, ratified by the abbot (bishop). His term is for three years and he is eligible for reelection. He is called "brother servant" (*gongpu xiongdi* 公僕兄弟) or, in abbreviated form, "servant" (*gongpu* 公僕).
3. The treasurer and general administrator of the material life of the monastery is called "brother in charge of poverty" (*si shenpin xiongdi* 司神貧兄弟); when the two servants are not at home, he is in charge of the entire monastery.
4. The priest in charge of the novices is called "elder brother" (*zhangxiong* 長兄), while the brother who is his deputy is called "assistant" (*gongyi* 公役).

---

[21] "Constant joy" is one of the three virtues that the Little Brother is especially to pursue, cf. *supra*, pp. 340–41.

[22] Lebbe is referring here to the flag of the Holy See.

5. All the Little Brothers, without exception, add the word "brother" (*xiongdi* 兄弟) to their monastic name and are to be called by this title. To show that after entering into the congregation, one is a new man and has broken all ties with the old man, one's family name or first name is never used.

6. Since the monastery has become the permanent residence of the Little Brother, it will be referred to as "home" (*jia* 家), while his family of origin will be referred to as his "place of birth" (*yuanji* 原籍). So, for example, one will say, "Brother so-and-so has returned to his place of birth to visit relatives and will soon come back home."

7. When one is outside the monastery and writes a letter to the servant, he writes on the envelope: "Letter of reassurance from Little Brother so-and-so." When one writes a letter to a Little Brother, however, one writes on the envelope: "To the kind attention of brother so-and-so."

8. Meeting a believer who has greeted him, [the Little Brother], according to the usage established by Catholic Action in 1930, will say, "God bless you." Meeting other Little Brothers, however, he says, "Little Brother so-and-so, be joyful in the Lord"; and the answer will be, "Ever joyful."

V. The Monastery

What Is Meant by the "Monastery of the Beatitudes"?

a) The Monastery of the Beatitudes is not a camp, much less an organization. It is the true home of the Little Brother and for that reason it is regularly to be called "home." The father servant is the elder of the house, and that is why he is called "father," while the brother servant is the older brother.

b) There is only one Monastery of the Beatitudes. The Little Brother, when he goes outside the monastery for his work, resides in a temporary dwelling, and when his work is done, he goes home. If he is involved in an ongoing ministry that cannot be completed within a year, then the Little Brother must reside at home every year for a period of one to two months or at least for an uninterrupted month. The time for retreat cannot be counted toward this month.

If in the future there are places that, in accordance with the rules, want to have a monastery, the Monastery of the Beatitudes will appoint some Little Brothers to found another monastery. Although the two monasteries should support each other amicably, they are autonomous, without any bonds of mutual dependency.

VI. Those Who Exercise (Administrative) Authority

a) [The Father Servant]

In the house there is only one person who has the absolute authority of a father. In the Monastery of the Beatitudes it is only the [father] servant who exercises absolute authority in the name of the abbot (bishop). The government of the monastery is entirely his own responsibility; all other authorities are only his assistants. For this reason, the brothers on the council,[23] since they do not have an authority that places them, according to secular custom, in a position of equals [with the father servant], cannot be regarded as on the same level [as the father servant].

b) The Brother Councilors

1. The one who first shares the labors of the father and gives him counsel is the brother servant. When the father is at home, the scope of authority of the brother servant is determined completely by the father servant. When the father servant is out, the brother servant temporarily assumes his authority. However, the father servant may also, at his discretion, restrict the scope of the authority conferred [on the brother servant]. The brother servant is also, *ex officio*, the personal secretary of the father servant.

2. The second is the brother in charge of poverty. He manages the finances of the monastery and oversees the work and material matters inside the monastery.

[23] *Weilaohui* 慰勞會: literally, "comforting committee." In the *Rule of the Little Brothers* (comment on art. 129), the following explanation is given: "The name 'council' is taken from the Benedictine Order. Its meaning is profound and inclusive: to comfort and uphold the head of the family, who wears himself out for the whole family." Lebbe, *Huigui shiyi*, p. 88; cf. RPF, p. 78.

3. Under the brother in charge of poverty there may be some brothers responsible for different areas and activities: hygiene, the chapel, the kitchen, the garden, clothing, the library, woodworking, weaving, bookbinding, and so on.

c) The Brother Servant

1. He is elected by secret ballot by the general chapter.[24]
2. As a rule, only a solemnly professed brother can be elected; however, the bishop has the right to include the simply professed.
3. The father servant is entitled to a double vote.
4. Elections shall be decided by fifty percent of the votes plus one.
5. The results of an election must be ratified by the bishop. If the bishop does not ratify the results, another vote is to be taken. However, the one who had been elected in the first round cannot be reelected.
6. The term of a brother servant shall be three years.

If two candidates obtain the same number of votes and one of the two is a solemnly professed, he is to be considered elected. Otherwise, there is to be a new election.

d) The Little Brothers Who Hold Other Offices

1. They are all appointed by the father servant, who is to consult the general chapter beforehand.
2. In addition, [the father servant] should, as far as possible, consult the Little Brothers, especially the brother in charge of poverty, to get their opinions. If there are differences of opinion and difficulties, he may, at his discretion, convoke the chapter of the professed or a general chapter.
3. All of these remain in office for one year but can be reappointed [by the father servant] at his discretion.

e) The Novitiate

1. The novice master is chosen by the abbot (bishop) from among the brother priests of the congregation; the duration of his office is unlimited.

---

[24] *Quanjia huiyi* 全家會議: "meeting of the entire family."

2. The assistant [novice master] is chosen by all the novices by secret ballot. If he has not yet expressed his willingness [to belong to the congregation],[25] he will remain in office for six months; if he has already expressed his willingness, he will remain in office until he makes vows.

3. All other positions [within the novitiate] are assigned by the novice master and last six months.

f) The Annual General Meeting

1. After the community retreat, taking advantage of the time when all the brothers [who carry out their ministry] outside the monastery come home, a meeting will be held to discuss all issues related to the reform and development [of the congregation].

2. The abbot (bishop) is to be invited to preside over [the meeting].

3. Before opening the meeting the propositions to be discussed are to be put in writing, read, and approved by the abbot (bishop).

4. The proposals will go into effect only if they have obtained the consent of more than five brothers.

5. The most important issues will be put to a secret ballot; those of secondary importance will be voted on by a show of hands. The order of the propositions is established by the father servant with the consent of the abbot (bishop).

6. The minutes recording the decisions that have been made are to be read in the chapter room during the annual retreat.

---

[25] Cf. RLB 87: "After the year of novitiate the Little Brother expresses in a liturgy his willingness (*dingzhi* 定志) [to belong to the congregation]." Fr. Lebbe comments, "Even though [such a] promise does not bind one's soul to the Lord with the same intensity as do the vows, . . . nonetheless it will greatly increase the fervent desire of the Little Brother never to be separated from our family and from the good Lord Jesus." Lebbe, *Huigui shiyi*, p. 61; cf. RPF, p. 56.

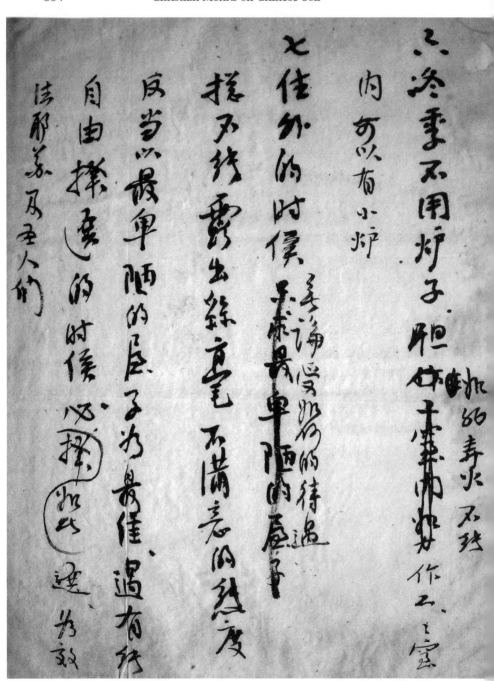

A manuscript page, written by Vincent Lebbe, of the draft of the *Rule of the Little Brothers of John the Baptist*, dated in the 1930s, known as *Jiagui chugao* 家規初稿, "Draft of the rule of the family."

Bibliography

Sources and General Works on Christianity in China

Brunner, Paul. *L'Euchologe de la mission de Chine. Editio princeps 1628 et développements jusqu'à nos jours*. Münster: Aschendorffsche Verlagsbuchhandlung, 1964.

Charbonnier, Jean-Pierre. *Christians in China. A.D. 600 to 2000*. San Francisco, CA: Ignatius, 2007.

———. "La vie de l'Église dans la province de Sichuan."*Églises d'Asie* 4 (2008): 52–65.

Chongqing shi shizhongqu zhi 重慶市市中區誌 [Chronicles of the city of Chongqing, central zone]. Chongqing: Chongqing chubanshe, 1997.

Colombel, August M. *Histoire de la mission du Kiang-nan [1840–1899]*. 3 vols. [T'ou-sè-wè]: n.p., 1900.

Crouch, Archie R., Steven Agoratus, Arthur Emerson, and Debra E. Soled. *Christianity in China: A Scholars' Guide to Resources in the Libraries and Archives of the United States*. Armonk, NY: M. E. Sharpe, 1989 (2nd ed., edited by Wu Xiaoxin, 2009).

Ducornet, Étienne. *L'Église et la Chine. Histoire et défis*. Paris: Cerf, 2003.

Handbook of Christianity in China. Vol. 1: *635–1800*. Edited by Nicolas Standaert. Leiden: Brill, 2001.

———. Vol. 2: *1800–present*. Edited by R. Gary Tiedemann. Leiden: Brill, 2009.

Hebei sheng zhi. Zongjiao zhi 河北省誌一宗教誌 [Chronicles of the province of Hebei. Chronicles about religion]. Beijing: Zhongguo shuji chubanshe, 1995.

Kunming shi zhi 昆明市誌 [Chronicles of the city of Kunming]. Beijing: Renmin chubanshe, 2003.

La Servière, Joseph de. *Histoire de la mission du Kiang-nan*. 2 vols. Zi-ka-wei: Imprimerie de l'orphelinat, [1914].

Lazaristes du Pétang. *Les missions de Chine. Seizième année (1940–1941)*. Shanghai: Procure des Lazaristes, 1942.

Lettres des nouvelles missions de la Chine. 6 vols. Paris: n.p., 1846–1868.

Myers, James T. *Enemies Without Guns: The Catholic Church in the People's Republic of China*. New York: Paragon House, 1991.

Nanchong shi zhi 南充市誌 [Chronicles of the city of Nanchong]. Chengdu: Sichuan kexue jishu chubanshe, 1994.

Tiedemann, R. Gary. *Reference Guide to Christian Missionary Societies in China: From the Sixteenth to the Twentieth Century*. Armonk, NY: M. E. Sharpe, 2009.

Xuhui qu zhi 徐匯區誌 [Chronicles of the suburb of Xuhui]. Shanghai: Shanghai shehui kexueyuan chubanshe, 1997.

Zhang Xianqing 张先清 and Zhao Ruijuan 赵蕊娟, eds. *Zhongguo difangzhi jidujiao shiliao jiyao* 中国地方志基督教史料辑要 [References to Christianity contained in local Chinese chronicles]. Shanghai: Dongfang chuban zhongxin, 2010.

Monastic Life and Mission

Auniord, Jean-Baptiste. "Dom Chautard, abbé de Sept-Fons. Vie intérieure et apostolat—Les trappistes en pays de mission." CA 6 (1935): 219–25.

Bevans, Stephen B., and Roger P. Schroeder. *Constants in Context: Theology of Mission for Today*. Maryknoll, NY: Orbis Books, 2004.

Bosch, David J. *Transforming Mission: Paradigm Shifts in Theology of Mission*. Maryknoll, NY: Orbis Books, 1991.

Bria, Ion. "Monachisme et mission." In *Dictionnaire œcuménique de missiologie. Cent mots pour la mission*, edited by Ion Bria, Philippe Chanson, Jacques Gadille, and Marc Spindler, 230–33. Paris: Cerf / Genève: Labor et Fides / Yaoundé: CLE, 2001.

Brun, Louis. "La vie contemplative en Chine." CA 3–4 (1934): 93–116. Originally published as an appendix to Hubrecht, *Une trappe en Chine*, 74–113.

Contemplation et Apostolat (offprint from the journal *Bulletin des Missions*). Lophem-lez-Bruges: Abbaye de Saint-André, 1927.

Debalus, Irene. "AIM: Fifty Years and More in Sustaining the Momentum of Monastic Life in Asia." *AIM Bulletin* 102 (2012): 30–42.

Delacroix, Jean. "Possibilités monastiques aux Indes et en Extrême-Orient." CA 12 (1947): 7–13.

"Le devoir de l'apostolat missionnaire." COCR 3 (1936): 36–37, 98–99, 168–69; 4 (1937): 31–33.

Dore, Maria Giovanna. "Il monachesimo è missionario?" *Camaldoli* 43 (1955): 135–39.

Driscoll, Jeremy. "Mission and Monasticism: Theological Reflections." In Leyser and Williams, *Mission and Monasticism*, 11–17.

Dynya, Hlib. "Annunciare il vangelo nella vita monastica." In *Le missioni della chiesa ortodossa russa. Atti del XIV Convegno ecumenico internazionale di spiritualità ortodossa, sezione russa. Bose, 18–20 settembre 2006*, edited by Adalberto Mainardi, 295–322. Magnano: Qiqajon, 2007.

L'Extrême-Orient au Sacré-Cœur. Œuvre de Messes et Croisade de Prières. Compte-rendu pour l'année 1929. N.p.: n.p., [1930].

Farrugia, Edward, and Innocenzo Gargano, eds. *Monaci e missione.* Verucchio: Pazzini, 1999.

García Paredes, José Cristo Rey. "Missione." In *Dizionario teologico della vita consacrata*, edited by Angel Aparicio Rodríguez and Joan María Canal Casas, 1038–63. Milan: Àncora, 1994.

Guébriant, Jean-Baptist de. "Le monachisme en pays de mission." *Annales des Missions Étrangères de Paris* (1929): 241–52. http://archives.mepasie.org/annales-des-missions-etrangeres/le-monachisme-en-pays-de-mission, accessed 21 August 2013.

Haverbèque, Gérard. "Pourquoi des monastères en Extrême-Orient." CA 6 (1935): 230–34.

Hendriks, Olaf. "L'activité apostolique des premiers moines syriens." *Proche-Orient Chrétien* 8 (1958): 3–25.

———. "L'activité apostolique du monachisme monophysite et nestorien." *Proche-Orient Chrétien* 10 (1960): 97–113.

Heyndrickx, Jeroom. "Les communautés religieuses contemplatives re-vivent-elles en Chine? Signes d'espérance sur un long chemin." *Vies consacrées* 81, no. 1 (2009): 8–18.

Hubrecht, Alphonse. *Une trappe en Chine.* Peking: Imprimerie des Lazaristes, 1933.

Leclercq, Jean. "Monachisme chrétien et missions." *Studia Missionalia* 28 (1979): 133–52.

———. *Nouvelle page d'histoire monastique. Histoire de l'AIM. 1960–1985.* [Vanves]: AIM, 1986.

———. "Le renouveau solesmien et le renouveau religieux du XIXe siècle." *Studia Monastica* 18, no. 1 (1976): 157–95.

Le Nouy, Guénolé. "L'Extrême-Orient au Sacré-Cœur." COCR 1 (1934): 130–37.

Le Roux (Gabriel Roux). "Centres bouddhiques et moines catholiques." BM 10 (1930), supp. no. 1: *Le Courrier Monastique Chinois*, 31*–32*.

Leyser, Conrad, and Hannah Williams, eds. *Mission and Monasticism: Acts of the International Symposium at the Pontifical Athenaeum S. Anselmo, Rome, May 7–9, 2009.* Rome: Pontificio Ateneo Sant'Anselmo / Sankt Ottilien: EOS, 2013.

M. Albert, Frère. "Notre vocation missionnaire." COCR 6 (1939): 131–39.

Mazzolini, Sandra. "Missione e monachesimo. Una prospettiva missiologica." In Leyser and Williams, *Mission and Monasticism*, 197–210.

Merton, Thomas. "The Inner Experience: Prospects and Conclusions." *Cistercian Studies* 19 (1984): 336–45.

Molette, Charles. "Mission et missions. De la Révolution française à Vatican II." In *Dictionnaire de spiritualité, ascétique et mystique, doctrine et histoire*, 10:1390–404. Paris: Beauchesne, 1980.

Il monachesimo nel terzo mondo. Rome: Edizioni Paoline, 1979.

Müller, Karl. *Kontemplation und Mission. Steyler Anbetungsschwestern 1896–1996.* Rome: apud Collegium Verbi Divini, 1996.

Neut, Édouard. "Le Christ apôtre cherche des contemplatifs." BM 9 (1928–1929): 297–311.

———. "Le Moine Apôtre." BM 6 (1920–1923): 121–26.

Nève, Théodore. "De la fondation de monastères en terre de mission." In *Autour du problème de l'adaptation. Compte rendu de la quatrième semaine de missiologie de Louvain (1926),* 36–46. Louvain: Éditions du Museum Lessianum, 1926.

Nicolini-Zani, Matteo. "La via monastica al cristianesimo cinese." *Ad Gentes* 15, no. 1 (2011): 9–22.

"Notre apostolat missionnaire monastique. Sa légitimité." COCR 6 (1939): 55–57, 128–30, 226–28.

"L'œuvre 'Contemplation et Apostolat' sous le Pontificat de SS. Pie XI." CA 11 (1939): 1*–21*.

Pantaloni, Andrea. "The Sylvestrine-Benedictine Congregation: A Monastic Pioneer in Modern Benedictine Mission." In Leyser and Williams, *Mission and Monasticism,* 133–42.

"Pour un monachisme chinois." BM 8 (1926–1927): 257.

Un religieux cistercien. *Action missionnaire d'arrière-garde. Conférences.* Godewaersvelde: Abbaye Sainte-Marie-du-Mont, 1930.

"Sa sainteté Pie XI." COCR 6 (1939): 1–5.

Schäfer, Cyrill. "Missionarietà delle congregazioni monastiche nei secoli XIX–XX." In Leyser and Williams, *Mission and Monasticism,* 99–123.

So Far yet So Near: Monasticism for a New World; Alliance for International Monasticism. Sankt Ottilien: EOS, 2013.

Sortais, Marie Gabriel. "Fonction des ordres contemplatifs en pays de missions." CA 22 (1954): 1–16.

"Les sources de l'apostolat missionnaire." COCR 4 (1937): 127–30, 210–13.

Spiller, Vsevolod. "Missionary Aims and the Russian Orthodox Church." *International Review of Mission* 52, no. 206 (1963): 195–205.

Struyven, Jean-Marie. "Œuvre de messes et croisade de prières. À propos d'un jubilé (1914–1939)." COCR 6 (1939): 254–61.

Teixeira, Manuel. "Os Franciscanos em Macau." *Archivo ibero-americano* 38 (1978): 309–75.

Vandenbroucke, François. "Monachisme missionnaire." CA 14 (1950): 12–16.

Williams, Rowan. "Monks and Mission. A Perspective from England." http://www.archbishopofcanterbury.org/articles.php/2391/monks-and-mission-a-perspective-from-england, accessed 21 August 2013.

Syro-Oriental Monasticism

Baum, Wilhelm, and Dietmar W. Winkler. *The Church of the East: A Concise History*. London: Routledge Curzon, 2003.

Berti, Vittorio. "Cristiani sulle vie dell'Asia tra VIII e IX secolo. Ideologia e politica missionaria di Timoteo I, patriarca siro-orientale (780–823)." *Quaderni di storia religiosa* 13 (2006): 117–56.

Beulay, Robert. *La lumière sans forme. Introduction à l'étude de la mystique chrétienne syro-orientale*. Chevetogne: Éditions de Chevetogne, 1987.

Borbone, Pier Giorgio. "I blocchi con croci e iscrizione siriaca da Fangshan." *Orientalia Christiana Periodica* 72, no. 1 (2006): 167–87.

———. *Storia di Mar Yahballaha e di Rabban Sauma. Un orientale in Occidente ai tempi di Marco Polo*. Turin: Zamorani, 2000.

Brock, Sebastian. "The 'Nestorian' Church: A Lamentable Misnomer." *Bulletin of the John Rylands University Library of Manchester* 78, no. 3 (1996): 23–35.

Chialà, Sabino. *Abramo di Kashkar e la sua comunità. La rinascita del monachesimo siro-orientale*. Magnano: Qiqajon, 2005.

Dauvillier, Jean. "Les Provinces Chaldéennes 'de l'extérieur' au Moyen Âge." In *Mélanges offerts au R. P. Ferdinand Cavallera*, 261–316. Toulouse: Bibliothèque de l'Institut Catholique, 1948.

Forte, Antonino. "The Edict of 638 Allowing the Diffusion of Christianity in China." In Pelliot, *L'inscription nestorienne*, 349–73.

Gillman, Ian, and Hans-Joachim Klimkeit. *Christians in Asia before 1500*. Richmond: Curzon, 1999.

Guglielminotti Trivel, Marco. "Tempio della Croce—Fangshan—Pechino. Documentazione preliminare delle fonti epigrafiche 'in situ.'" *Orientalia Christiana Periodica* 71, no. 2 (2005): 431–60.

Hage, Wolfgang. "Einheimische Volkssprachen und syrische Kirchensprache in der nestorianischen Asienmission." In *Erkenntnisse und Meinungen*, edited by Gernot Wießner, 2:131–60. Wiesbaden: Harrassowitz, 1978.

———. "Religiöse Toleranz in der nestorianischen Asienmission." In *Glaube und Toleranz. Das theologische Erbe der Aufklärung*, edited by Trutz Rendtorff, 99–112. Gütersloh: G. Mohn, 1982.

———. *Syriac Christianity in the East*. Kottayam: St. Ephrem Ecumenical Research Institute, 1988. Repr. 1996.

Jullien, Florence. *Le monachisme en Perse. La réforme d'Abraham le Grand, père des moines de l'Orient*. CSCO 622. Louvain: Peeters, 2008.

———, ed. *Le monachisme syriaque*. Paris: Geuthner, 2010.

Klimkeit, Hans-Joachim. *Die Begegnung von Christentum, Gnosis und Buddhismus an der Seidenstraße*. Opladen: Westdeutscher Verlag, 1986.

Le Coz, Raymond. *Histoire de l'église d'Orient*. Paris: Cerf, 1995.

Leyser, Conrad, and Hannah Williams, eds. *Mission and Monasticism: Acts of the International Symposium at the Pontifical Athenaeum S. Anselmo, Rome, May 7–9, 2009*. Rome: Pontificio Ateneo Sant'Anselmo / Sankt Ottilien: EOS, 2013.
Ligeti, Louis. "Les sept monastères nestoriens de mar Sargis." *Acta Orientalia Hungarica* 26, no. 2–3 (1972): 169–78.
Moffett, Samuel Hugh. *A History of Christianity in Asia*. Vol. 1: *Beginnings to 1500*. San Francisco, CA: Harper, 1992.
Moule, Arthur Christopher. *Christians in China before the Year 1550*. London / New York / Toronto: SPCK, 1930.
Nau, François. "L'expansion nestorienne en Asie." *Annales du Musée Guimet* 40 (1914): 193–383.
Nicolini-Zani, Matteo. "Eastern Outreach: The Monastic Mission to China in the Seventh to the Ninth Centuries." In Leyser and Williams, *Mission and Monasticism*, 63–70.
———. "The Tang Christian Pillar from Luoyang and Its 'Jingjiao' Inscription: A Preliminary Study." *Monumenta Serica* 57 (2009): 99–140.
———. *La via radiosa per l'oriente. I testi e la storia del primo incontro del cristianesimo con il mondo culturale e religioso cinese (secoli VII–IX)*. Magnano: Qiqajon, 2006.
Pelliot, Paul. *L'inscription nestorienne de Si-ngan-fou*. Edited with supplements by Antonino Forte. Kyoto: Scuola di Studi sull'Asia Orientale / Paris: Collège de France, Institut des Hautes Études Chinoises, 1996.
Teule, Herman. *Les Assyro-Chaldéens*. Turnhout: Brepols, 2008.
Timothy I. *Letters* = Oscar Braun, ed. *Timothei patriarchae I epistolae*. 2 vols. CSCO 74–75; Syr 30–31. Paris: Gabalda, 1914–1915. Repr. Louvain: Sécretariat du CorpusSCO, 1953.
Tisserant, Eugène. "Nestorienne (l'Église)." In *Dictionnaire de Théologie Catholique*, 11/1:157–323. Paris: Letouzey et Ané, 1931.
Thomas of Marga. *Monastic History* = E. A. Wallis Budge, ed. *The Book of Governors: The* Historia Monastica *of Thomas, Bishop of Margâ*. London: Kegan Paul / Trench / Trübner, 1893.
Vööbus, Arthur. *History of Asceticism in the Syrian Orient: A Contribution to the History of Culture in the Near East*. 3 vols. CSCO 184, 197, 500. Louvain: Sécretariat du CorpusSCO, 1958–1988.
Yin Xiaoping. "On the Christians in Jiangnan during the Yuan Dynasty according to 'The Gazetteer of Zhenjiang of the Zhishun Period.'" In *Hidden Treasures and Intercultural Encounters: Studies on East Syriac Christianity in China and Central Asia*, edited by Dietmar W. Winkler and Li Tang, 305–19. Münster: LIT, 2009.

Carmelites

A. L. "Een Missie-Karmelietessen-Klooster in China." *Kerk en Missie* 17 (1937): 18–20.

Ambrosius a S. Teresia. *Bio-bibliographia Missionaria Ordinis Carmelitarum Discalceatorum (1584–1940).* Rome: apud Curiam Generalitiam, 1940.

———. "Monasticon Carmelitanum, seu lexicon geographicum-historicum omnium fondationum universi ordinis carmelitarum ab initio eiusdem ordinis usque ad nostra tempora." *Analecta Ordinis Carmelitarum Discalceatorum* 22 (1950): 59–144, 201–96, 381–480, 569–616; 23 (1951): 145–208, 363–410.

Apis. "Il Carmelo di Yunnanfu-Yunnan." *Il Carmelo e le sue missioni all'estero* 38 (1939): 234–35.

Avertanus. "Le Carmel thérésien aux missions." CA 13 (1949): 29–31.

C. de Y. (Carmélites de Yunnanfu). "Yunnanfu (Chine). Origine de la Fondation du Carmel." *Le Carmel. Bulletin mensuel du Carmel de France et son Tiers-Ordre* 25 (1938–1939): 280–84.

Carmel de Cherbourg. *Généalogie des couvents de Carmélites de la Réforme de sainte Thérèse, 1562–1962.* N.p.: n.p., 1962.

"Le Carmel de Saint-Michel-lez-Bruges établit une fondation à Canton." CA 1 (1933): 41–44.

"La Carmélite Missionnaire." *Messager Thérésien* 21, no. 7 (1940): 158–61.

Castellan, Ilario G. "Sorge un nuovo Carmelo a Macau (Indie portoghesi)." *Il Carmelo e le sue missioni all'estero* 49 (1950): 150–52. Published also in *Analecta Ordinis Carmelitarum Discalceatorum* 22 (1950): 370–72.

The Discalced Carmelite Nuns of Chiung Lin. *It Is Good to Be Here: The Story of Our Foundation.* [Chiung Lin: Discalced Carmelite Monastery], 2004.

D'Souza, Paul. "Unforgettable Carmelite Missionaries on Asian Soil." http://www.ocd.pcn.net/mission/News17Congr4.htm, accessed 21 August 2013.

Élisabeth, Mère. *Partir. Vers la Chine, en Chine, à Dieu la Chine.* Saint-Rémy: Monastère Saint-Élie, 1998.

Fang Zhirong 房志榮. "Taiwan shengyihui yinxiuyuan sishi zhounian" 臺灣聖衣會隱修院四十周年 [The fortieth anniversary of the Carmel in Taiwan]. *Shenxue lunji* 神學論集 (*Collectanea Theologica Universitatis Fu Jen*) 102 (1994): 580.

Fortes, Antonio. *Las Misiones del Carmelo Teresiano, 1584–1799. Documentos del Archivo General de Roma.* Rome: Teresianum, 1997.

———. *Las Misiones del Carmelo Teresiano, 1800–1899. Documentos del Archivo General de Roma.* Rome: Teresianum, 2008.

Gallagher, R. "The Contemplative Life: A New 'Carmel' in Hong Kong." *The Rock* (July 1937): 305–8.

Gaucher, Guy. "La fondation des Carmels de Saïgon et d'Hanoï par le Carmel de Lisieux." *Vie Thérésienne* 39 (1999): 7–21.

"Jiaxing chuangshe shengyiyuan yi chengli" 嘉興創設聖衣院已成立 [The Carmelite monastery founded in Jiaxing is completed]. YZB 32 (1928): 12.

Li Qingmei 李慶梅. "Pan Sujing xiunü" 潘肅敬修女 [Sister Pan Sujing]. *Xinde* 信德, 1 July 2004, 3.

Molnar, Edmond. "Recherches sur l'origine du carmel de T'ou-se-we." Unpublished typewritten manuscript, Zi-ka-wei, Chang-hai, 1938.

Moussay, Gérard. "Mons. Lefebvre (1810–1865) et les Carmélites en Cochinchine." *Thérèse de Lisieux* 876 (2007): 2–3.

"Nova Missio in Sinarum imperio." *Analecta Ordinis Carmelitarum Discalceatorum* 19 (1947): 65–66.

Picard, Pierre-André. "Le climat missionnaire du diocèse de Lisieux au temps de Thérèse." *Vie Thérésienne* 187 (2007): 227–45.

"Shengyihui xiunü she xiuyuan" 聖衣會修女設修院 [Carmelite nuns establish a monastery]. YZ 12 (1948).

"Shengyiyuan xiunü di Chuan" 聖衣院修女抵川 [Carmelite nuns arrive in Sichuan]. SZ 8 (1920): 370–71.

Thérèse de Lisieux. *Lettres à mes frères prêtres*. Paris: Cerf, 1997.

———. *Yiduo xiao bai hua* 一朵小白花 [A little white flower]. Translated by Su Xuelin 蘇雪林. Hong Kong: Zhenli xuehui chubanshe, 1950.

Thomas, A. (Jean-Marie Planchet). "Projet de fondation d'un Carmel." In *Histoire de la mission de Pékin*, vol. 2: *Depuis l'arrivée des Lazaristes jusqu'à la révolte des Boxeurs*, 564–65. Paris: Vald. Rasmussen, 1933.

Tripod Staff. "Faithful Daughter of the Church." *Tripod* 110 (1999): 45–46.

Wang, Helen. "An Account of My Journey on the China Mainland in Search of Our Carmelite Sisters." Unpublished typewritten manuscript, Indianapolis Carmel, 1996.

Wu, John C. H. (Wu Jingxiong 吳經熊). *Beyond East and West*. New York: Sheed and Ward, 1951.

———. *Chinese Humanism and Christian Spirituality*. Jamaica, NY: St. John's University Press, 1965.

———. *The Science of Love: A Study of the Teachings of Thérèse of Lisieux*. Hong Kong: Catholic Truth Society, 1941. http://www.ourgardenofcarmel.org/wu.html, accessed 21 August 2013.

"Xianggang shengyihui xiunü qianju xinyuan" 香港聖衣會修女遷居新院 [The Carmelite nuns of Hong Kong take up residence in a new monastery]. *Gongjiao funü* 公教婦女 3 (1937): 246–47.

"Xianggang shengyihui yuanmen juxing fengsuo li" 香港聖衣會院門舉行封鎖禮 [Claustration ceremony celebrated at the Carmelite monastery of Hong Kong]. YZB 26 (1937): 774–75.

"Xujiahui shengyiyuan xiunü fu Chongqing" 徐家匯聖衣院修女赴重慶 [Nuns of the Xujiahui Carmel go to Chongqing]. SZ 5 (1920): 234.

"Yunnan jianzhu shengyihui xiunüyuan" 雲南建築聖衣會修女院 [A monastery of Carmelite nuns erected in Yunnan]. *Gongjiao baihua bao* 公教白話報 18 (1936): 387–88.

"Yunnan jianzhu shengyihui xiunüyuan" 雲南建築聖衣會修女院 [A monastery of Carmelite nuns erected in Yunnan]. YZB 35 (1936): 908.

"Yunnan jiaoqu chengli shengyihui yinyuan" 雲南教區成立聖衣會隱院 [A Carmelite monastery founded in the diocese of Yunnan]. *Gongjiao baihua bao* 公教白話報 20 (1936): 433.

Zhou Xiufen 周秀芬, ed. *Lishi shang de Xujiahui* 历史上的徐家汇 (*Zikawei in History*). Shanghai: Shanghai wenhua chubanshe, 2005.

Trappists

"Acte de fondation du Monastère de N.-D. de la Consolation au Tchély Septentrional." In Thomas, *Histoire de la mission de Pékin*, 2:568–70.

Arnáiz Álvarez, Eusebio. "Los monjes blancos." In *Religiosos mártires. Persecución comunista en China*, 330–464. Hong Kong: n.p., 1960. Facsimile repr. in Ren Dayi, *Yangjiaping Shengmu shenweiyuan shi*, 185–320.

Autour du problème de l'adaptation. Compte rendu de la quatrième semaine de missiologie de Louvain (1926). Louvain: Éditions du Museum Lessianum, 1926.

Baillon, Alexis. "Appel à la prière pour nos monastères de Chine." COCR 10 (1948): 57–59.

Beltrame Quattrocchi, Paolino, ed. *Monaci nella tormenta. La "passio" dei monaci trappisti di Yan-Kia-Ping e di Liesse, testimoni della fede nella Cina di Mao-Tze-Tung*. Cîteaux: n.p., 1991.

———. "The Trappist Monks in China." In Heyndrickx, *Historiography of the Chinese Catholic Church*, 315–17.

Bouton, Jean de la Croix. *Histoire de l'ordre de Cîteaux*. 3 vols. Westmalle: n.p., 1959–1968.

[Brandstetter], Ildephonse. "A Pilgrimage to the Trappist Monastery of Yang Chia Ping." BCUP 2 (1927): 23–30.

Carrasquer Pedrós, María Sira. "El Monasterio de N.tra S.ra de la Consolación (China, 1883–1983)." *Cistercium* 165 (1983): 215–49.

"Chanan kuxiu huishi shang shengcun zhe jin shisi ren" 察南苦修會士尚生存者僅十四人 [Of the Trappist monks in Southern Chahar only fourteen have survived]. YZ 25 (1948).

"Chanan kuxiuyuan jiaoshi linan ji" 察南苦修院教士罹難記 [Account of the killing of the religious of the Trappist monastery in Southern Chahar]. SB 8 (1948): 265.

"Le Cinquantenaire." In Hubrecht, *Une trappe en Chine*, 114–38.

"Le Cinquantenaire de la Fondation du Monastère de Notre-Dame de Consolation." BCP 20 (1933): 400–404.

"Les Cisterciens en Chine." BCP 29 (1942): 3–5.

Clément, Philippe. "La Trappe de Yang-kia-p'ing." BCP 3 (1916): 206–10.

Dall'Osto, Antonio. "Monaci nella tormenta." *Testimoni* 7 (1992): 21–29. Repr., with the title "La 'via crucis' dei monaci trappisti di Yangjiaping" and an introduction by Gerolamo Fazzini, in *Il libro rosso dei martiri cinesi. Testimonianze e resoconti autobiografici*, edited by Gerolamo Fazzini, 219–41. Cinisello Balsamo: San Paolo, 2006.

Danzer, Beda. "Fünfzig Jahre chinesische Trappisten." *Die Katholischen Missionen* 61 (1933): 184.

Davis, Thomas X. "Trappists," In Sunquist, *A Dictionary of Asian Christianity*, 853–54.

"La destruction de l'abbaye des trappistes de Yangkiaping par les communistes et la mort tragique de plusieurs religieux. Août–octobre 1947." *Fides documentazione* 10 (1947): 78–82.

Durand, Prosper. "Le père Alphonse, trappiste (Albert L'Heureux)." *Prêtre et Missions* 10 (1949): 132–36.

"2011 nian de Yangjiaping Shenweiyuan yizhi" 2011 年的楊家坪神慰院遺址 [The ruins of the monastery of the Consolation at Yangjiaping in 2011]. http://blog.sina.com.cn/s/blog_5eaa27e80100oi5n.html, accessed 21 August 2013.

"Une élection abbatiale à la Trappe de Yang-Kia-Ping." MC 53 (1921): 247.

Hermans, Vincent. "Dans le feu de la lutte. Le trappiste belge Jean-Marie Struyven en Chine (1934–1953)." *Courrier Verbiest* 23 (December 2010): 17–19.

Heyndrickx, Jeroom, ed. *Historiography of the Chinese Catholic Church: Nineteenth and Twentieth Centuries*. Leuven: Ferdinand Verbiest Foundation, K. U. Leuven, 1994.

"Huabei zhi xiduhui kuxiuyuan jinkuang" 華北之西都會苦修院近況 [The present situation of the Cistercian Trappist monastery in North China]. SB 6 (1947): 198.

Hubrecht, Alphonse. "De Pékin à la Trappe de Chine." MC 55 (1923): 154–56, 163–65, 176–77, 190–91, 200–201, 210–13.

———. "Le monachisme en Chine." *Les Missions des Lazaristes* 3 (1932): 73–78.

———. "Les origines de la Trappe de Chine." *Dossiers de la Commission Synodale* 6 (1933): 324–27.

———. *Une trappe en Chine*. Peking: Imprimerie des Lazaristes, 1933.

Ignace, Frère. *Au Japon. Mes premières années. Souvenirs et impressions*. Alençon: Imprimerie alençonnaise, 1907.

"Kuxiu huishi binan ji" 苦修會士避難記 [Account of a Trappist monk seeking refuge]. YZ 4 (1948): 58–59; 6 (1948): 90–91; 7 (1948): 102–5.

"Kuxiu huishi ershi ren yuhai, shijiu ren beishi di Ping" 苦修會士二十人遇害十九人被釋抵平 [Trappist monks: twenty have been killed and nineteen have been freed and have reached Peking]. YZ 6 (1948): 93.

"Kuxiushi liu ren shang zai jujin zhong" 苦修士六人尚在拘禁中 [Six Trappist monks still held prisoners]. YZ 20 (1948): 318.

"Kuxiushi zhi nongye zhuanjia" 苦修士之農業專家 [A Trappist agronomist]. SB 9 (1940): 287.

Lei, Raymond (Raymond de Jaegher). "En promenade à la trappe de Yang-Kia-P'ing." *Jeunesse chinoise. Bulletin de la Jeunesse catholique chinoise* 85 (1932): 333–37.

Lemire, J. *Une trappe en Chine*. Paris: Sécretariat de la Société d'économie sociale, 1892. Collection of articles appeared in *La Réforme sociale* 12, ser. III, tome 3 (1892), 116–27, 203–17.

Lenssen, Seraphin. *Hagiologium cisterciense*. 2 vols. Tilburg: n.p., 1948–1949.

———. *Supplementum ad hagiologium cisterciense*. Tilburg: n.p., 1951.

Leurent, Philippe. "À la Trappe de Yang kia p'ing." *Chine, Ceylan, Madagascar* 19 (1930–1931): 173–92.

Leyssen, J. "De Trappisten in China." *Kerk en Missie* 16 (1936): 144–49.

Li Dongming 李動明, "Zhili Zhuolu xian dongnan baisishi li Yangjiaping kuxiuyuan zhi" 直隸涿鹿縣東南百四十里楊家坪苦修院誌 [Chronicle of the Trappist monastery of Yangjiaping, 140 *li* southeast of Zhuolu, Zhili]. SZ 6 (1917): 252–56.

Limagne, A. *Les Trappistes en Chine*. Paris: J. de Gigord, 1911. Collection of articles appeared, with the title "La Trappe chinoise de Yang-Kia-Pinn," in MC 42 (1910): 153–56, 166–68, 173–75, 188–89, 196–97, 210–13, 224–25.

Lin Da 林达. "Xunfang Yangjiaping" 寻访杨家坪 [In search of Yangjiaping]. In *Zai bianyuan kan shijie* 在边缘看世界 [Looking at the world from the edges], 152–67. Kunming: Yunnan renmin chubanshe, 2001.

M. V. W. "La Trappe de Notre Dame de la Consolation." BCP 14 (1927): 8–13, 71–75.

Martin, Bruno-Jean. *Histoire des moines de Tamié et de quelques autres*. Saint-Étienne: Action graphique, 1991.

McCarthy, Charles J. "Trappist Tragedy: The Truth about the 'Land Reformers' in Action." *Catholic Review* (January 1948): 20–21, 34; (February 1948): 71–74. Repr. in Beltrame Quattrocchi, *Monaci nella tormenta*, 136–50, and in Heyndrickx, *Historiography of the Chinese Catholic Church*, 317–33.

Meester, Emmanuel de. "Trappistes et Missions." CA 2 (1933): 74–79.

Merton, Thomas. "Et les trappistes allèrent au martyre. . ." *Digeste Catholique* 8 (1950): 48–55.

———. *The Waters of Siloe*. New York: Harcourt Brace, 1949.

"Les Moines Cisterciens en Chine." *Revue d'Histoire des Missions* 11 (1934): 358–66.

Morelli, A. "Les Trappistes (N. D. de Liesse)." In *Notes d'histoire sur le vicariat de Tcheng-ting-fou. 1858–1933*, 169–71. Peking: Imprimerie des Lazaristes, 1934.

Ng Ka Chai (Wu Jiazhai 吳家齊). "Pax Intrantibus: The Cistercian Monks and Monastery." In *History of the Catholic Religious Orders and Missionary Congregations in Hong Kong*, vol. 2: *Research Papers*, edited by Louis Ha and Patrick Taveirne, 700–739. Hong Kong: Centre for Catholic Studies, Chinese University of Hong Kong, 2009.

The Ninth Centenary of Foundation of Cîteaux and the Seventieth Anniversary of Foundation of the Monastery of Our Lady of Joy. Hong Kong: n.p., 1999.

Pasqualini, Jean. "The Christmas Mass of Father Hsia." *Reader's Digest*, Hong Kong ed. (February 1970): 70–74. Repr. in Ren Dayi, *Yangjiaping Shengmu shenweiyuan shi*, 140–44.

———. *Prisoner of Mao.* New York: Coward, McCann and Geoghegan, 1973. French trans.: *Prisonnier de Mao. Sept ans dans un champ de travail en Chine.* Paris: Gallimard, 1975.

Peffer, [Père]. "Les Cisterciens réformés dans l'Asie Orientale." In *Autour du problème de l'adaptation*, 47–56.

Pennington, M. Basil. *The Cistercians.* Collegeville, MN: Liturgical Press, 1992.

———. "Cistercians." In Sunquist, *A Dictionary of Asian Christianity*, 180–82.

Postulatio Generalis O.C.S.O. *Dossier "China" pro capitulo generali 1980.* Montecistello: n.p., 1980.

"Une première victime sanglante de notre apostolat missionnaire en Extrême Orient." COCR 5 (1938): 40.

"Providentielle conversion d'un jeune lama." MC 43 (1911): 162–64.

Raymond, Marcel. *Trappists, the Reds, and You.* N.p.: Abbey of Gethsemani, 1949.

Ren Dayi 任達義 (Stanislaus Jen). *Shengmu shenleyuan cangsang wushi nian huashi* 聖母神樂院滄桑五十年畫史 (*Pictorial History of Our Lady of Joy [Liesse] Written for Its Golden Jubilee of Foundation, 1928–1978*). Hong Kong: Catholic Truth Society, 1978.

———. *Yangjiaping Shengmu shenweiyuan shi* 楊家坪聖母神慰院史 (*The History of Our Lady of Consolation Yang Kia Ping*). Hong Kong: n.p., 1978.

———. *Zhongguo xiduhui xundaozhe zhuanji* 中國熙篤會殉道者傳記 (*The Lives of the Martyrs of O. L. of Consolation Yang Kia Ping, 1947–1953*). Hong Kong: Dayushan Shengmu shenleyuan, 1985.

Robial, Anne-Marie. *Père Emmanuel Robial. Une vie consacrée.* Jouaville: Scripta, 2005.

Scanlan, Patrick J. *Stars in the Sky.* Hong Kong: Trappist Publications, 1984.

"A Story of Communist Terror in China." *Catholic Missions* 25 (October–November 1948): 6, 11–13, 15.

Struyven, Jean-Marie. "The Cistercian Trappist and the Rural Problem in China." *China Missionary* 1 (1949): 36–42.

———. "Martyre d'un monastère chinois. N.-D. de Consolation à Yang-Kia-Ping [codex C]." Unpublished typewritten manuscript, AGOCSO, fondo postulazione generale [archive of the general postulation], D.7, 1953. Published in abridged form in Ren Dayi, *Yangjiaping Shengmu shenweiyuan shi*, 163–203.

Sunquist, Scott W., ed. *A Dictionary of Asian Christianity*. Grand Rapids, MI / Cambridge, UK: Eerdmans, 2001.

Thomas, A. (Jean-Marie Planchet). "Enquête des autorités chinoises sur les Trappistes." In *Histoire de la mission de Pékin*, 2:570–71.

———. *Histoire de la mission de Pékin*. 2 vols. Paris: Vald. Rasmussen, 1933.

———. "Projet d'une Trappe à Pékin. Approbations reçues." In *Histoire de la mission de Pékin*, 2:565–66.

———. "La Trappe de Sept-Fonds [*sic*] accepte d'envoyer une colonie de religieux à Pékin." In *Histoire de la mission de Pékin*, 2:566–68.

"Una trappa in Cina." *Le Missioni Cattoliche* 21 (1892): 467 68.

"A Trappist Monastery in China." *Catholic Missions* 4 (1910): 105–9.

"Die Trappistenabtei U. L. Frau vom Trost in Yan-kia-pin." *Die Katholischen Missionen* 39 (1910–1911): 29–32.

"Das Trappistenkloster U. L. Frau vom Trost im Norden Chinas." *Die Katholischen Missionen* 27 (1898–1899): 193–95, 219–23.

"Das Trappistenkloster U. L. Frau vom Trost in Yan-kia-ping." *Die Katholischen Missionen* 36 (1907–1908): 58–60.

"Les Trappistes en Chine." MC 67 (1935): 148.

"Trappistes et Trappistines en Extrême-Orient." BCP 16 (1929): 269–72.

Valensin, Albert. "Monastère Cistercien en Chine du Nord. Trappe de N.-D. de la Consolation, à Yang-kia-ping." MC 70 (1938): 113–17.

———. "Une visite à Notre Dame de la Consolation, Yangkiap'ing. Chine." COCR 4 (1937): 258–61.

Vinciarelli, Raphaël. "Les trappistes de Gni-pa-to." CSA 19 (1949): 17–20.

"Wunian nei sifang Yangjiaping Shenweiyuan yougan" 五年內四访楊家坪神慰院有感 [The emotions resulting from four visits over the course of five years to the monastery of Consolation at Yangjiaping]. http://blog. sina.com.cn/s/blog_5eaa27e80100d5xu.html, accessed 21 August 2013.

Xiduhui jianshi 熙篤會簡史 [A short history of the Cistercian Order]. Taipei: Huaming shuju, 1964.

"Yangjiaping kuxiuyuan canzao dahuo" 楊傢坪苦修院慘遭大禍 [Tragic calamity at the Trappist monastery of Yangjiaping]. SB 11 (1948): 366.

"Yangjiaping kuxiuyuan daili yuanzhang Xu gong zaonan shishi" 楊傢坪苦修院代理院長徐公遭難逝世 [Dom Xu, abbot administrator of the Trappist monastery of Yangjiaping, has unfortunately died]. SB 3 (1948): 93.

"Yangjiaping kuxiuyuan dayuanzhang shishi" 楊傢坪苦修院大院長逝世 [The abbot of the Trappist monastery of Yangjiaping has died]. SB 1 (1943): 30.

"Yangjiaping kuxiuyuan jinkuang" 楊傢坪苦修院近況 [The present situation of the Trappist monastery of Yangjiaping]. SB 11 (1940): 331.

"Yangjiaping kuxiuyuan xin yuanzhang Wang siduo dangxuan" 楊傢坪苦修院新院張汪司鐸當選 [Dom Brun elected the new abbot of the Trappist monastery of Yangjiaping]. SZ 4 (1921): 182.

"Yangjiaping kuxiuyuan xin yuanzhang zhusheng jilüe" 楊傢坪苦修院新院張祝聖記略 [A brief account of the blessing of the new abbot of the Trappist monastery of Yangjiaping]. SZ 5 (1921): 228.

"Yangjiaping kuxiuyuan yi xiushi zuogu" 楊傢坪苦修院一修士作故 [A monk of the Trappist monastery of Yangjiaping has died]. SZ 3 (1920): 130.

"Yizhang zhengui de Yangjiaping Shenweihui xiushi zuihou de heying" 一張珍貴的楊家坪神慰会修士最后的合影 [A final precious photograph of the monks of Consolation at Yangjiaping]. http://blog.sina.com.cn/s/blog_5eaa27e80100l7h2.html, accessed 21 August 2013.

"Zai dao Yangjiaping" 再到楊家坪 [Again at Yangjiaping]. http://blog.sina.com.cn/s/blog_5eaa27e80100cjx3.html, accessed 21 August 2013.

"Zhengding kuxiuyuan jinwen" 正定苦修院近聞 [News of the Trappist monastery of Zhengding]. SB 3 (1945): 96.

"Zhengding kuxiuyuan xiushi quanti di Rong" 正定苦修院修士全體抵蓉 [The entire community of the Trappist monastery of Zhengding reaches Chengdu]. SB 2 (1948): 62.

Benedictines

Ackermann, Raymund. "Der Untergang der Diözese Yenki und der Abtei Heilig Kreuz in der Stadt Yenki, Mandschurei. 1945–1952." In Kaspar and Berger, *Hwan gab*, 189–93.

"L'année 1937 à Si Shan." CSA 1 (1938): 98–102.

Artus, Vincent. "Hommage au révérendissime père dom Lou Tseng-tsiang." CSA 19 (1949): 24–36.

Association Relais France-Chine, ed. *Dom Pierre Célestin Lu. Une vie toute droite*. Mesnil-Saint-Loup: Le Livre ouvert, 1993.

Ballweg, Lukas. "Abt-Bischof Theodor Breher OSB." In Kaspar and Berger, *Hwan gab*, 159–70.

"Bendu huishi yu gaihua huaren" 本篤會士欲改化華人 [Benedictine monks want to convert the Chinese]. SB 8 (1924): 248–49.

"Benduhui jiang zai Shandong Zhoucun liyuan" 本篤會將在山東周村立院 [The Benedictines will found a monastery at Zhoucun in Shandong]. SB 5 (1946): 138.

"Benduhui she Chengdu fenyuan" 本篤會設成都分院 [The Benedictines establish the dependent monastery of Chengdu]. YZ 23 (1947): 378.

"Benduhui xiunü dao Kaifeng" 本篤會修女到開封 [The Benedictine sisters arrive in Kaifeng]. *Gongjiao funü* 公教婦女 1 (1937): 75.

"I benedettini in Cina." *San Benedetto* 4 (1997): 34–38.

Benedict, Francis. "Valyermo and China." *AIM Bulletin* 70 (2000): 105–6.

La bénédiction abbatiale du reverendissime père dom Pierre-Célestin Lou Tseng-Tsiang, abbé titulaire de Saint-Pierre de Gand. Abbaye de Saint-André, le samedi 10 août 1946, fête de Saint Laurent. N.p.: n.p., [1946].

Breher, Theodor. *Erntegarben vom Acker der Yenki-Mission, Mandschurei, den Wohltätern u. Freunden gebunden.* Yenki: Bischöfliche Missionsdruckerei, 1937.

"Buildings and Grounds." BCUP 1 (1926): 11–12.

Buresh, Vitus. *The Procopian Chronicle: Saint Procopius Abbey, 1885–1985.* Lisle, IL: St. Procopius Abbey, 1985.

"Catalogo del fondo librario presso la cattedrale di Kaifeng (Henan, Repubblica popolare cinese)." Unpublished typewritten manuscript, Centro missionario PIME, Milan, 2011.

"The Catholic University of Peking." BCUP 2 (1927): 31–35.

"Cet été à Si Shan." CSA 3 (1938): 278–82.

Chang Shu-chin, Claire (Zhang Shujin 張淑勤). "Tianzhu jiaohui de zai sikao. Cong Lu Zhengxiang de jiaohui yinxiang tanqi" 天主教會的再思考—從陸徵祥的教會印象談起 [A new reflection on the Catholic Church. The repercussions (of the ideas) of Lu Zhengxiang on the church]. In *Zhong Fan waijiao guanxi shi guoji xueshu yantaohui lunwenji* 中梵外交關係史國際學術研討會論文集 [Proceedings of the international scholarly meeting on the history of the diplomatic relations between China and the Vatican], 267–80. Taipei: Furen daxue lishi xuexi, 2002.

———. "When Confucius Meets Benedictus: The Destiny of a Chinese Politician, Lou Tseng-tsiang (1871–1949)." Master's thesis in history, Katholieke Universiteit Leuven, 1994.

Chen Fang-chung. "Lou Tseng-Tsiang, A Lover of His Church and of His Country." *Tripod* 153 (2009): 45–66.

Chen Shujie, John. *The Rise and Fall of the Fu Ren University, Beijing: Catholic Higher Education in China.* New York: Routledge, 2004.

"Chengtu. Inauguration et Bénédiction de l'Oratoire du Monastère bénédictin de Sischan." *Bulletin M.E.P.* (1930): 161–63.

Chin, Lucas. "Benedictines in Taiwan." *AIM Bulletin* 98 (2010): 11–13. German trans.: "Benedektinerinnen in Taiwan." *Erbe und Auftrag* 1 (2011): 108–9.

"Chronicle of Events Connected with the Origin of the Catholic University of Peking." BCUP 1 (1926): 63–70.

Clougherty, Francis. "The Publications of the Catholic University of Peking." BCUP 6 (1929): 67–91.

Coomans, Thomas. "La création d'un style architectural sino-chrétien. L'œuvre d'Adalbert Gresnigt, moine-artiste bénédictin en Chine (1927–1932)." *Revue Bénédictine* 123, no. 1 (2013): 128–70.

"Courrier de Chine." CSA 7 (1940): 72–81.

De Crombrugghe, Albéric. "La mort en Chine." CSA 18 (1948): 133–39.

De Grunne, François. "En Chine par l'Amérique." *CSA* 20 (1949): 74–85.

Delacroix, Jean. "Passage au Szechoan." *CSA* 16 (1948): 17–25.

Delcourt, Henri-Philippe. "Dom Jehan Joliet (1870–1937). Un projet de monachisme bénédictin chinois." *Mélanges de science religieuse* 43, no. 1 (1986): 3–19.

———. *Dom Jehan Joliet (1870–1937). Un projet de monachisme bénédictin chinois.* Paris: Cerf, 1988.

———. "The Grain Dies in China," *AIM Bulletin* 40 (1986): 45–55.

"Diyiwei guoji benduhui xiunü" 第一位國籍本篤會修女 [The first Chinese Benedictine sister]. *Gongjiao funü* 公教婦女 2 (1937): 148–49.

"Dom Jehan Joliet." *Bulletin M.E.P.* (1938): 245–47.

Doppelfeld, Basilius. *Mönchtum und kirchlicher Heilsdienst, Entstehung und Entwicklung des nordamerikanischen Benedektinertums im 19. Jahrhundert.* Münsterschwarzach: Vier-Türme-Verlag, 1974.

Duhamelet, Geneviève. *Dom Lou. Homme d'État, homme de Dieu.* Brussells: Foyer Notre-Dame, [1954].

Dysinger, Luke. "Abbot Peter Celestine Lou Tseng-tsiang, O.S.B.: Chinese Diplomat and Benedictine Monk." *Valyermo Benedictine* 1, no. 4 (1990): 4–12.

———. "The Benedictine Foundations in Xishan and Chengdu, 1929–1952." *The Valyermo Chronicle* 235 (2012): 8–10; 236 (2012): 9–11; 237 (2012): 5–7. Repr. in Leyser and Williams, *Mission and Monasticism*, 184–95.

Endres, David J. "The Legacy of Thaddeus Yang." *International Bulletin of Missionary Research* 34, no. 1 (2010): 23–27.

Fang Hao 方豪. "Lu Zhengxiang" 陸徵祥. In *Zhongguo tianzhujiao shi renwu zhuan* 中國天主教史人物傳 [Biographies of important figures in the history of Chinese Christianity], 3:326–29. Taizhong: Guangqi chubanshe, 1973.

Flint, James. "A Benedictine Missionary's Journey Out of Wartime China." *American Benedictine Review* 46, no. 4 (1995): 367–87.

"A General Prospectus of the Institution." *BCUP* 1 (1926): 13–16.

Germann, M. Consolatrix. "Die Mission der Schwesternkongregation Heiligkreuz Cham in der Mandschurei." *Katholisches Missionsjahrbuch der Schweiz* 2 (1935): 82–84.

———. "Die Missionstätigkeit der Schwestern von Heiligkreuz, Cham, in Mandschukuo." *Katholisches Missionsjahrbuch der Schweiz* 4 (1937): 132–34.

———. "Die Schwestern von Heiligkreuz Cham in Mandschukuo." *Katholisches Missionsjahrbuch der Schweiz* 3 (1936): 94–95.

Handl, Matilda, and Cyrill Schäfer, eds. *Der Gründer. Briefe von P. Andreas Amrhein OSB (1844–1927).* 2 vols. St. Ottilien: EOS, 2010.

Healy, Sylvester. "The Plans of the New University Building." *BCUP* 6 (1929): 3–12.

Heilig Kreuz Schwestern. *Aus Cham in Manchukuo.* Yenki: Bischöfliche Missionsdruckerei, n.d.

Heyndrickx, Jeroom, ed. *Historiography of the Chinese Catholic Church: Nineteenth and Twentieth Centuries.* Leuven: Ferdinand Verbiest Foundation, K. U. Leuven, 1994.

Huyghebaert, Nicolas. "Le 'Cahier' du Szechoan." CSA 11 (1946): 271–76; 18 (1948): 159–64; 23 (1950): 14–20.

———. "Nouvelles de Chine." CSA 8 (1945): 118–23.

———. "Voix de Chine." CSA 9 (1946): 172–77.

"In Memoriam Dom Gabriel Roux." BM 15 (1936), supp. no. 1: *Le Courrier de l'Apostolat Monastique,* 1*–5*.

Joliet, Jehan. "L'avenir du haut enseignement catholique en Chine." BM 9 (1928–1929): 32–38.

———. "La civilisation chinoise et l'apostolat du missionnaire." *Bulletin Joseph Lotte* 72 (November 1936): 81–86 (also repr. as offprint).

———. "Un rayon d'espérance en Chine." *La vie intellectuelle* (December 1928): 5–23. Repr., with the title "Une tâche monastique," in BM 10 (1930), supp. no. 1: *Le Courrier Monastique Chinois,* 15*–25* (also repr. as offprint).

"Kaifeng xinjian benduhui xiunüyuan" 開封新建本篤會修女院 [A monastery for Benedictine women recently built in Kaifeng]. SB 4 (1941): 131.

Kaspar, Adelhard. "Die Veröffentlichungen der Benediktiner-Missionare in Tokwon und Yenki." *Zeitschrift für Missionswissenschaft und Religionswissenschaft* 42 (1958): 108–25.

———, and Placidus Berger, eds. *Hwan gab. 60 Jahre Benediktinermission in Korea und in der Mandschurei.* Münsterschwarzach: Vier-Türme-Verlag, 1973.

Koss, Nicholas. "The Benedictine Commission for China," *AIM Bulletin* 70 (2000): 101–4.

Lenz, Philipp. "Benediktiner-Mission Yenki—Mandschurei." In Kaspar and Berger, *Hwan gab,* 171–93.

Leyser, Conrad, and Hannah Williams, eds. *Mission and Monasticism: Acts of the International Symposium at the Pontifical Athenaeum S. Anselmo, Rome, May 7–9, 2009.* Rome: Pontificio Ateneo Sant'Anselmo / Sankt Ottilien: EOS, 2013.

Loriers, Gaëtan. "Les émotions d'une étape." CSA 20 (1949): 85–89.

Lou Tseng-Tsiang and His Contribution to China = *Tripod* 152 (2009).

Lu Zhengxiang 陸徵祥 (Pierre-Célestin Lou Tseng-Tsiang). *Benduhui shilüe* 本篤會史略 [Brief history of the Benedictine Order]. Shanghai: Shengjiao zazhi she, 1935.

———. *Benduhui xiushi Lu Zhengxiang zuijin yanlunji* 本篤會修士陸徵祥最近言論集 [Collection of the most recent conferences of the Benedictine monk Lu Zhengxiang]. Shanghai: Guangqi xuehui, 1936.

————. *La rencontre entre humanités et la découverte de l'évangile.* [Bruges]: DDB, 1949.

————. *La vie et les œuvres du grand chrétien chinois Paul Siu Koang-k'i.* Lophem-lez-Bruges: Abbaye de Saint-André, [1934].

————. *Ways of Confucius and of Christ.* London: Burns Oates, 1948.

Luo Guang 羅光. *Lu Zhengxiang zhuan* 陸徵祥傳 [A biography of Lu Zhengxiang]. Hong Kong: Zhenli xuehui, 1949.

Ma Wan Sang (Hildebrand Marga). "Le Monastère de Si shan en Chine." BM 13 (1934), supp. no. 1: *Le Courrier de l'Apostolat Monastique*, 4*–14*.

"The MacManus Academy of Chinese Study." BCUP 1 (1926): 39–49.

Mahr, Johannes. *Aufgehobene Häuser. Missionsbenediktiner in Ostasien.* 3 vols. Sankt Ottilien: EOS, 2009.

Marga, Hildebrand. "Inauguration du monastère chinois." BM 10 (1930), supp. no. 1: *Le Courrier Monastique Chinois*, 26*–30*.

Martin, Vincent. "La Chine, empire du milieu." *La revue nouvelle*, 15 April 1948, 3–16 (also repr. as offprint).

McDonald, M. Grace. *With Lamps Burning.* St. Joseph, MN: Saint Benedict's Convent, 1957.

Un moine de Saint-André. "Dom Jehan Joliet." CSA 1 (1938): 30–52 (also repr. as offprint).

"Le monastère de Si Shan dans le conflit sino-japonais." CSA 4 (1939): 65–70.

Monestier, Alphonse. "The Monk Lu Cheng-Hsiang: An Ex–Prime Minister of China Enters the Benedictine Order." BCUP 5 (1928): 11–21.

Muehlenbein, M. Wibora. *Benedictine Mission to China.* St. Joseph, MN: Saint Benedict's Convent, 1980.

————. "China Memoirs: The Sisters of St. Benedict's Mission to China, 1930–1950." Unpublished typewritten manuscript, n.p., preface 1962.

Neut, Édouard. *Jean-Jacques Lou, Dom Lou. Quelques ébauches d'un portrait, quelques aspects d'un monde.* Brussells: Synthèses, 1962.

Nève, Théodore. "À travers le Szechwan." BM 14 (1935), supp. no. 1: *Le Courrier de l'Apostolat Monastique*, 1*–9*.

————. "En remontant le 'Yangtzekiang.'" BM 15 (1936): 31–46.

————. "Le Monastère des SS. Pierre et André de Si Chan." BM 9 (1928–1929): 289–96.

————. "Le monastère des SS. Pierre et André de Si-Shan." BM 15 (1936), supp. no. 1: *Le Courrier de l'Apostolat Monastique*, 6*–11*.

————. "Le Prieuré des SS. Pierre et André de Si Chan." BM 10 (1930), supp. no. 1: *Le Courrier Monastique Chinois*, 1*–14*.

————. "Vicariats européens et vicariats chinois au Szechwan." BM 16 (1937): 1–16.

"Notice sur la fondation du prieuré des SS. Pierre et André de Sischan, Shunking." *Bulletin M.E.P.* (1929): 484–88.

"Nouvelles de Si Shan." CSA 2 (1938): 186–87.

O'Donnell, W. "Progress at the Catholic University of Peking." BCUP 7 (1930): 115–19.

Oetgen, Jerome. *An American Abbot: Boniface Wimmer O.S.B., 1809–1887.* 2nd ed. Washington, DC: The Catholic University of America Press, 1997.

———. *Beijing Furen daxue chuangban shi. Meiguo benduhui zai Zhongguo* 北京輔仁大學創辦史—美國本篤會在中國 (1923–1933) (*History of the Foundation of the Peking Furen University. The American Benedictines in China, 1923–1933*). Translated by Zhang Yan 張琰. Taipei: Furen daxue chubanshe, 2001 (trans. of the English original: *Mission to America*, chaps. 6–7).

———. *Mission to America: A History of Saint Vincent Archabbey, The First Benedictine Monastery in the United States.* Washington, DC: The Catholic University of America Press, 2000.

O'Toole, George Barry. "The Spiritual Lineage of the Catholic University of Peking." BCUP 1 (1926): 17–22.

Papeians de Morchoven, Christian. *L'abbaye de Saint-André Zevenkerken.* 2 vols. Tielt: Lannoo, 1998–2002.

———. "The China Mission of the Benedictine Abbey of Sint-Andries (Bruges)." In Heyndrickx, *Historiography of the Chinese Catholic Church,* 305–10.

Papeians de Morchoven, Werner. "Inondation à Chengtu." CSA 15 (1947): 226–29.

———. "Omeï, montagne sacrée." CSA 14 (1947): 144–50.

Paragon, Donald. "Ying Lien-chih (1866–1926) and the Rise of Fu Jen, The Catholic University of Peking." *Monumenta Serica* 20 (1961): 165–225.

"'Pei-ching Kung Chiao Ta Hsüeh'. The Chinese Name of the Catholic University of Peking." BCUP 1 (1926): 7–9.

Perez, Bernardo. "Benedictines." In Sunquist, *A Dictionary of Asian Christianity,* 70–73.

Pfiffner, M. Januaria. "Überblick über die Schwesterntätigkeit in der Yenki-Mission von 1931–1945." In Kaspar and Berger, *Hwan gab,* 194–97.

"Le premier bénédictin chinois." BM 9 (1928–1929): 238–40.

"Le R. P. Dom Jehan Joliet (1870–1937)." *La Vie diocésaine,* 2 April 1938 (also repr. as offprint).

"Rinascita di un vecchio monastero." *Asia News* 8 (1999): 31.

Schäfer, Cyrill, ed. *Der Gründer. Schriften von P. Andreas Amrhein OSB (1844–1927).* St. Ottilien: EOS, 2006.

Schramm, Gregory. "The Laying of the Corner Stone." BCUP 7 (1930): 19–30.

Schröder, Jeremias. "The Benedictines in China," *AIM Bulletin* 98 (2010): 15–28. Repr. in *Courrier Verbiest* 28 (December 2010): 15–17.

"Sheng benduhui shicha woguo Xishan fenyuan" 聖本篤會視察我國西山分院 [The Order of St. Benedict inspects the dependent monastery of Xishan in our country]. SB 9 (1947): 299.

Shi Jianguo 石建國. *Lu Zhengxiang zhuan* 陸徵祥傳 [A biography of Lu Zhengxiang]. Shijiazhuang: Hebei renmin chubanshe, 1999.

"Shunqing Xishan benduhui chuangbanzhe ji diyi ren yuanzhang Yu siduo shishi" 順慶西山本篤會創辦者及第一任院長余司鐸逝世 [The founder and first prior of the Benedictine monastery of Xishan, Shunqing, has died]. SZ 3 (1938): 166.

"Sichuan jiang jian benduhui xiuyuan zhi didian" 四川將建本篤會修院之地點 [The place where a Benedictine monastery will be constructed in Sichuan]. YZB 32 (1928): 8.

"Sichuan Shunqing Xishan benduhui xiudaoyuan yuanzhang shishi" 四川順慶西山本篤會修道院院長逝世 [The prior of the Benedictine monastery of Xishan, Shunqing, Sichuan has died]. SZ 7 (1936): 441.

"Sichuan Xishan sheng benduhui xiuyuan chuangli ji" 四川西山聖本篤會修院創立記 [Information on the foundation of the Benedictine monastery in Xishan, Sichuan]. YZB 6 (1935): 9–11; 7 (1935): 6–8.

Sieber, Godfrey. *The Benedictine Congregation of St. Ottilien*. St. Ottilien: EOS, 1992.

Sisters of St. Benedict. *Beyond the Horizon*. N.p.: n.p., 1980.

Les solennités de l'ordination sacerdotale du r. p. dom Pierre-Célestin Lou Tseng-Tsiang O.S.B. Abbaye de Saint-André, le 29 juin 1935. N.p.: n.p., [1935].

Standaert, Benoît. "P. Dominique Van Rolleghem (1904–1995). Un des pionniers sur la voie de la rencontre avec l'hindouisme?" *Dilatato Corde* 1 (2011): 117–31.

"Statuta scholae puellarum, dictae 'P'ei-Kenn', in municipio Peiping privatim erectae." *Collectanea Commissionis Synodalis* 5 (1932): 224–31.

Stehle, Callistus. "The Catholic University of Peking." *The Call of the Mission*, 20 October 1929, 1–2.

Sunquist, Scott W., ed. *A Dictionary of Asian Christianity*. Grand Rapids, MI / Cambridge, UK: Eerdmans, 2001.

Tatsachenbericht aus dem Missionsgebiet Yenki (Mandschurei). St. Ottilien: EOS, 1954.

Vanderhoven, Hubert. "L'Université Catholique Chinoise de Péking." BM 8 (1926–1927): 174–79.

———. "L'Université Catholique de Péking." BM 8 (1926–1927): 207–12.

Vansteelandt, Anne. "Lou Tseng-tsiang: zijn contactenen en zijn invloed als monnik in de Sint-Andriesabdij (1927–1949)." *Zevenkerken* 176 (1991): 5–23.

————. "Lu Zhengxiang (Lou Tseng Tsiang), a Benedictine Monk of the Abbey of Sint-Andries." In Heyndrickx, *Historiography of the Chinese Catholic Church,* 223–30.

Vetter, Francetta. "Oral History Tape Interview, Tokyo, Japan, ca. 1955–1958." Unpublished typewritten manuscript.

Vinciarelli, Raphaël. "Au monastère de Si Shan." CSA 5 (1939): 155–60; 6 (1939): 227–30.

————. "Dom Jehan Joliet et son œuvre monastique en Chine." CA 10 (1938): 6*–11*.

————. "Jubilé du prieuré Saint-Benoît de Chengtu." CSA 31 (1952): 119–34.

————. "Lettre du Szechwan." CSA 12 (1947): 49–54.

————. "Profession de foi d'un jeune moine bénédictin chinois." CSA 31 (1952): 135–39.

————. "Une réalisation." CSA 21 (1949): 131–37.

————. "Témoin du Christ en Chine communiste. Le Prieuré de Saint-Benoît de Chengtu." BM 26 (1952): 191–219.

Walter, Bernita. *Sustained by God's Faithfulness: The Missionary Benedictine Sisters of Tutzing.* Vol. 1: *Founding and Early Development of the Congregation.* St. Ottilien: EOS, 1987.

Wang Huaimao 王怀茂 and Yang Jun 杨君. "Xinian qingcong jin cheng qiaomu. Tianzhujiao Nanchong Xishan benduyuan" 昔年青葱今成乔木一天主教南充西山本笃院 [The shrubs of the past have now become trees. The Catholic Benedictine monastery of Xishan, Nanchong]. *Zhongguo zongjiao* 中国宗教 (*China Religion*) 7 (2007): 51–53.

Winance, Eleuthère. *The Communist Persuasion: A Personal Experience of Brainwashing.* New York: P. J. Kenedy and Sons, 1959.

————. "L'enseignement catholique au Szechuan." BM 21 (1947): 100–108.

————. "Une séance de police." CSA 35 (1953): 82–89.

Wolf, Notker. "An Experience of Cooperation with Chinese Church Institutions." In *Papers and Materials of the European Catholic China Meeting "Prospects of Catholic Cooperation with China in the Present International Context" (Verona, December 12–14, 1992),* edited by China-Zentrum, 84–87. Sankt Augustin: China-Zentrum, 1994.

————. "In Geduld Ängste abbauen—Das Engagement der Benedektiner in heutigen China." *Forum Weltkirche* 1 (2003): 20–23.

————. "Mission als Partnerschaft. Die Mitwirkung der Benedektinerkongregation von St. Ottilien in der Diözese Jilin." In *"Fallbeispiel" China. Ökumenische Beiträge zu Religion, Theologie und Kirche im chinesischen Kontext,* edited by Roman Malek, 665–76. Sankt Augustin: China-Zentrum / Nettetal: Steyler, 1996.

Wong, Joseph. "Teaching in China," *AIM Bulletin* 70 (2000): 107–9.

Wu Ching-hioung, Jean (Wu Jingxiong 吳經熊). *Dom Lou. Sa vie spirituelle.* N.p.: DDB, 1949.

Wu Xiaoxin. "A Case Study of the Catholic University of Peking during the Benedictine Period (1927–1933)." PhD diss., University of San Francisco, 1993.

Xishan sheng bendu xiuyuan chuangli ji 西山聖本篤修院創立記 [Information on the foundation of a Benedictine monastery in Xishan]. Shanghai: Tushanwan yinshuguan, n.d.

Yang, Thaddée (Yang Anran 楊安然). "The Chinese Adventure of an Indonesian Monk." http://www.valyermo.com/monks/yang2.html, accessed 21 August 2013.

———. "From Buddha to Benedict." http://www.valyermo.com/monks/yang1.html, accessed 21 August 2013.

———. "L'inauguration du Prieuré de Saint-Benoît à Chengtu." CSA 21 (1949): 127–30.

———. "Le paradis de l'abbé T'ai-K'ung." CSA 22 (1950): 191–95.

———. "Le Szetchoan grenier du Ciel." CSA 15 (1947): 221–25.

———. "T'ai-K'oung Fa-Che. L'opinion d'un abbé bouddhiste." CSA 10 (1946): 213–16.

———. "Le thé chez les taoïstes." CSA 20 (1949): 67–73.

Zhang Weibing 張維屏. "Ji Zhonghua diyizuo sheng benduhui xiuyuan zhi yuanqi ji chengli" 記中華第一座聖本篤會修院之緣起及成立 [Information on the origin of the foundation of the first Benedictine monastery in China]. SZ 10 (1929): 419–24.

"Zhongguo diyiwei benduhui yinxiushi Yang Anran siduo xiaozhuan" 中國第一位本篤會隱修士楊安然司鐸小傳 [A brief biography of Dom Yang Anran, first Chinese Benedictine monk]. SZ 2 (1933): 117–18.

Zhou Bangjiu, Pierre. "Chine: une lettre émouvante." CSA 43–44 (1955): 165.

———. *Dawn Breaks in the East: One Spiritual Warrior's Thirty-Three Year Struggle in Defense of the Church.* Upland, CA: Serenity, 1992. French trans., with additions: *L'aube se lève à l'Est. Récit d'un moine bénédictin chinois emprisonné pendant 26 ans dans les camps de la Chine communiste au nom de la foi.* Paris: Pierre Téqui, 2000.

———. "A Skiff Cuts through the Waves. A Discourse on October 15, 2000." http://www.valyermo.com/monks/peter.html, accessed 21 August 2013.

Vincent Lebbe, the Little Brothers of John the Baptist, and the Little Sisters of Therese of the Child Jesus

Barra, Giovanni. *Padre Lebbe. L'apostolo della Cina.* Brescia: Acqua Viva, 1955.

Un Bénédictin. "Huit jours au monastère des petits frères de St-Jean-Baptiste." *Société des Auxiliaires des Missions* 23 (1937): 11.

Cao Lishan 曹立珊 (Alexander Ts'ao). *Chunfeng shinian* 春風十年 [Ten years of spring breeze]. Taizhong: Tianzhujiao Yaohan xiao xiongdi hui, 1977.

———. "Father Lebbe's Principles Live On." *Worldmission* 13, no. 3 (1962): 109–14.

———. *Lei Mingyuan shenfu de shenxiu gangling* 雷鳴遠神父的神修綱領 [The spiritual pillars of Fr. Vincent Lebbe]. Taizhong: Tianzhujiao Yaohan xiao xiongdi hui, 1982.

———. "Lei Mingyuan shenfu de yuepu" 雷鳴遠神父的樂譜 [The musical scores of Fr. Vincent Lebbe]. *Lei Mingyuan shenfu zhuankan* 雷鳴遠神父專刊 25 (1994): 32–42.

———. "Petits Frères de Saint Jean-Baptiste." *Perspectives de catholicité* 15, no. 3 (1956): 73–79.

Chen Ganfu 陳幹夫. "Dao Zhenfuyuan hou" 到真福院後 [After having been at the Monastery of the Beatitudes]. YZB 36 (1936): 946–48.

Chen Hui 晨暉. "Qinghe Zhenfuyuan sumao" 清河真福院素描 [Sketch of the Monastery of the Beatitudes at Qinghe]. YZ 11 (1948): 172.

Duoma xiongdi 多馬兄弟 (T. Song Zhiqing 宋稚青). "Yaohan xiao xiongdi hui de chuangli ji chuqi de huodong" 耀漢小兄弟會的創立及初期的活動 [The foundation and the first activities of the Congregation of the Little Brothers of John the Baptist]. *Lei Mingyuan shenfu zhuankan* 雷鳴遠神父專刊 17 (1993): 21–26.

Fang Hao 方豪. "Lei Mingyuan" 雷鳴遠. In *Zhongguo tianzhujiao shi renwu zhuan* 中國天主教史人物傳 [Biographies of important figures in the history of Chinese Christianity], 3:314–21. Taizhong: Guangqi chubanshe, 1973.

Goffart, Paul. "Manuscrit définitif de la Vie du P. Lebbe." Unpublished typewritten manuscript, Vincent Lebbe Archives, Université catholique de Louvain, Fonds I, sect. II, 2 A 2.

———. "Le Père Lebbe et la liturgie." *Église vivante* 2 (1950): 24–27.

———, and Albert Sohier, eds. *Lettres du père Lebbe*. Tournai / Paris: Casterman, 1980.

Guelluy, Robert. "La spiritualité du Père Lebbe." *Revue théologique de Louvain* 21, no. 4 (1990): 455–71.

Heyndrickx, Jeroom, ed. *Historiography of the Chinese Catholic Church. Nineteenth and Twentieth Centuries*. Leuven: Ferdinand Verbiest Foundation, K. U. Leuven, 1994.

Hu Yu 胡愈. "Anguo Zhenfuyuan canguan hou zhi jianwen ji" 安國真福院參觀後之見聞記 [An account of what was seen and heard during a visit to the Monastery of the Beatitudes in Anguo]. YZB 21 (1934): 8–10.

Jaegher, Raymond de. "De vrais Moines et de vrais Chinois. Les petits Frères de Saint Jean Baptiste." *Église vivante* 1 (1949): 196–99.

———. *Father Lebbe: A Modern Apostle*. Louvain / New York: SAM, 1950. Repr. London: Catholic Truth Society, 1954.

———. "Le Père Lebbe, homme de Dieu." *Église vivante* 2 (1950): 155–74.

King, Clifford. "Little Brothers and Sisters." *Fu Jen Magazine* 3 (1932): 18–25. French trans.: "Les Petits Frères de St Jean-Baptiste et les Petites Sœurs de Ste Thérèse." *Jeunesse chinoise. Bulletin de la Jeunesse catholique chinoise* 91–92 (1932): 482–92; 93–94 (1932): 514–20; 95–96 (1932): 550–56.

Kuijlaars, Frans. "Ein Bahnbrecher der einheimischen Kirche Chinas: Vincent Lebbe—Lei Mingyuan (1877–1940)." *China heute* 51 (1990): 129–41.

"Laodong shengchan de Zhenfuyuan" 勞動生產的真福院 [The Monastery of the Beatitudes that produces by working]. *Shiguang zazhi* 世光雜志 3–4 (1943).

Lebbe, Vincent (Lei Mingyuan 雷鳴遠). "Bushi. Wo lixiang zhong de Zhenfuyuan" 布施—我理想中的真福院 [Bushi. My ideal Monastery of the Beatitudes]. YZB 37 (1936): 963–65; 39 (1936): 1028–30.

———. *En Chine, il y a du nouveau. Le Père Lebbe nous écrit...* Liège: La Pensée Catholique, 1930.

———. *Huigui shiyi* 會規釋義 [Rule of the congregation and commentary] = *Huizu Lei Mingyuan shenfu shouxie Yaohan xiao xiongdi hui, Delai xiao meimei hui huigui* 會祖雷鳴遠神父手寫耀漢小兄弟會、德來小妹妹會會規 [Rule of the Congregation of the Little Brothers of John the Baptist and of the Congregation of the Little Sisters of Therese of the Child Jesus. Manuscript of the founder, Fr. Vincent Lebbe]. Taizhong: Taizhong zonghui Zhenfuyuan, [preface 1998].

———. "Jiagui chugao" 家規初稿 [Draft of the rule of the family]. *Lei Mingyuan shenfu zhuankan* 雷鳴遠神父專刊 9 (1992): 44–56.

———. "Nova et vetera. Du vieux neuf." CA 9 (1937): 5–12.

———. "Petits Frères." *Église vivante* 17 (1965): 439–50.

Leclercq, Jean. *Vie du père Lebbe. Le tonnerre qui chante au loin.* Tournai / Paris: Casterman, 1955. English trans.: *Thunder in the Distance: The Life of Père Lebbe.* N.p.: Congregation of St. John the Baptist, 1958.

Levaux, Léopold. *Le père Lebbe, apôtre de la Chine moderne (1877–1940).* Brussells / Paris: Éditions universitaires, 1948.

"La liturgie populaire chinoise." *Questions liturgiques* 3, no. 8 (1913): 403–6.

Liu Lingyun 劉陵雲. "Zhenfuyuan de kuxiu shenghuo" 真福院的苦修生活 [The ascetic life at the Monastery of the Beatitudes]. *Gongjiao yuekan* 公教月刊 14 (1934): 18–19; 15 (1934): 25–26; 16 (1934): 21–22.

Lou Tseng-Tsiang, Pierre-Célestin (Lu Zhengxiang). "Hommage au Père Vincent Lebbe." BM 19 (1940–1945): 89–98.

Louka, Petite sœur. "Petites sœurs Thérésiennes." *Perspectives de catholicité* 15, no. 3 (1956): 81–87.

Martin, Vincent. "Mes souvenirs sur le Père Lebbe." CSA 14 (1947): 151–60.

Merten, Peter, and Hugh O'Donnel, "Lebbe, Frederic Vincent." In Sunquist, *A Dictionary of Asian Christianity*, 475–76.

"Nan yuanzhang zai Anguo Zhenfuyuan sanri zhong zhi jiayan shanbiao" 南院長在安國真福院三日中之嘉言善表 [Words of praise from Abbot Nève during his three days at the Monastery of the Beatitudes in Anguo]. YZB 17 (1935): 1–3.

Nève, Théodore. "Moine et Abbé." In *Le Père Lebbe, missionnaire de Chine. Témoignages à l'occasion de sa mort*, 13–19. Louvain: SAM, [1941].

———. "L'œuvre monastique du Père Lebbe." CA 9 (1937): 1–4.

———. "S. Benoît et l'Action Catholique Chinoise." BM 9 (1928–1929): 419–20.

Ng Ka Chai (Wu Jiazhai 吳家齊). "The Indigenization of Gregorian Chant in Early Twentieth-Century China. The Case of Vincent Lebbe and His Congregations." Master's thesis, Chinese University of Hong Kong, 2007.

———. "Neumes and Chinese Liturgy. How Liturgical Renewal Was Brought to China by Vincent Lebbe." In *About Books, Maps, Songs and Steles: The Wording and Teaching of the Christian Faith in China*, edited by Dirk Van Overmeire and Pieter Ackerman, 280–94. Leuven: Ferdinand Verbiest Institute, K. U. Leuven, 2011.

"Les Petits Frères de Saint Jean-Baptiste." CA 13 (1949): 32–34.

Renirkens, C., ed. *Les Monastères du Père Lebbe. Deux lettres du P. Lebbe*. Louvain: SAM, n.d.

Rivinius, Karl Josef. "Lebbe, Frédéric Vincent." In *Biographisch-Bibliographisches Kirchenlexikon*, 4:291–96. Nordhausen: Traugott Bautz, 1992.

Soetens, Claude. "Apôtre et chinois: Vincent Lebbe (Lei Mingyuan)." In Heyndrickx, *Historiography of the Chinese Catholic Church*, 206–21.

———. "Chinois et chrétiens chinois dans l'optique du Père Lebbe, jeune missionnaire (1901–1914)." *Neue Zeitschrift für Missionswissenschaft* 40 (1984): 161–73.

———, ed. *Recueil des archives Vincent Lebbe*. [Vol. 4]: *La Règle des Petits frères de Saint-Jean-Baptiste*. Louvain-la-Neuve: Faculté de théologie, 1986.

Sohier, Albert. "Profetismo e missioni: la figura di padre Lebbe." *Concilium* 4, no. 7 (1968): 131–49.

Sunquist, Scott W., ed. *A Dictionary of Asian Christianity*. Grand Rapids, MI / Cambridge, UK: Eerdmans, 2001.

T. T. E. "Une nouvelle congrégation religieuse en Chine." CA 2 (1933): 63–73.

Thoreau, Vincent. *Le tonnerre qui chante au loin. Vie et mort du père Lebbe, apôtre des chinois (1877–1940)*. Brussells: D. Hatier, 1990.

Wei Tsing-sing, Louis. "Le Père Lebbe et l'Abbaye de Saint-André-lez-Bruges (1877–1949)." *Rythmes du monde* 34 (1960): 218–24.

Wiest, Jean-Paul. "The Legacy of Vincent Lebbe." *International Bulletin of Missionary Research* 23, no. 1 (1999): 33–37.

Yang, Gabrielle. "De congregatie van de Kleine Zusters van de Heilige Theresia van het Kind Jezus in Anguo. Een historisch overzicht." *Verbiest Koerier* 23 (September 2010): 10–12.

———. "La congrégation des Petites Sœurs de sainte Thérèse de L'enfant-Jésus d'Anguo (Chine)." *Vies consacrées* 81, no. 1 (2009): 19–24.

Yang Di 楊堤. "Zhenfuyuan canguan ji" 真福院參觀記 [Notes after a visit to the Monastery of the Beatitudes]. *Gongjiao baihua bao* 公教白話報 11–12 (1944): 152.

Yaohan xiao xiongdi hui huigui 耀漢小兄弟會會規 [Rule of the Congregation of the Little Brothers of John the Baptist]. Taizhong: Taizhong zonghui Zhenfuyuan, [preface 2006].

Yaohan xiao xiongdi xiushi 耀漢小兄弟修士 [A Little Brother of John the Baptist]. "Yaohan xiao xiongdi hui jianshi" 耀漢小兄弟會簡史 [A brief history of the Congregation of the Little Brothers of John the Baptist]. *Shensi* 神思 (*Spirit*) 98 (2013): 81–99.

Yilu xiongdi 義祿兄弟. "Wo suo renshi de Zhenfuyuan" 我所認識的真福院 [The Monastery of the Beatitudes that I know]. YZB 5 (1937): 123–25.

Zeng Lida 曾麗達. *Lei Mingyuan shenfu Zhongguo jiaohui bendihua de qianqu huashidai de fuchuan fangfa* 雷鳴遠神父中國教會本地化的前驅劃時代的福傳方法 [The pioneering and epoch-making method of evangelization of Fr. Vincent Lebbe in favor of the indigenization of the Chinese Church]. Taizhong: Tianzhujiao Yaohan xiao xiongdi hui, 2004.

Zhao Yabo 趙雅博 (Albert Chao). *Lei Mingyuan shenfu zhuan* 雷鳴遠神父傳 [A biography of Fr. Vincent Lebbe]. Taizhong: Tianzhujiao Yaohan xiao xiongdi hui, 1963 (2nd ed., 1977; 3rd ed., 1990).

Index of Names

The index contains names of persons and of places mentioned in the text. In case of Chinese names, the terms are transliterated according to the Hanyu Pinyin romanization system, which now has become the most common, and are accompanied by the corresponding Chinese characters in traditional writing, sometimes also, in parentheses, by one or more transliterations according to alternative systems, such as Wade-Giles, EFEO, and others, depending on how they are found in the sources quoted in this book.

Guangxi 廣西 (Koangson), 100, 131n48

Guangyuan 廣元, 102n147

Guangzhou 廣州. *See* Canton

Guébriant, Jean-Baptiste Budes de, 11n37, 23, 33, 130, 325, 325n3

Guelluy, Robert, 266n19

Guénat, Jérôme, 118–19

Guéranger, Prosper, 194

Guillot, Joséphine. *See* Anne de Jésus, nun

Guiying, nun, 312

Guizhou 貴州 (Kweitchow), 131n48

Guizzo, Virginio. *See* Gioacchino di Maria Bambina, monk

Hakodate, 124

Hangzhou 杭州 (Hangchow), 89

Hanoi, 60, 96

Hanyang 漢陽, 157n115

Hao Huaxian 郝華賢, 102

Haverbèque, Gérard, 30

Healy, Sylvester, 183, 185, 188–89

Hebachang 河壩場 (Hopachang, Hopatch'ang), 210–11, 255, 257

Hebei 河北 (Hopeh, Hopei), 131n48, 148, 149n98, 157, 194, 197, 268

Helmstetter, Ernest, 172, 173n7

Henan 河南 (Honan), 131n48, 147, 183, 185–86, 189, 189n59, 278, 298

Henry, Yves, 90n105

Herat, 48

Hetan 河灘, 148

Hohenburg, 243

Hokkaido, 124

Hong Kong, xi, 62n11, 75, 86, 88n99, 92–93, 93nn114–15, 94, 94n120, 95, 95n122, 104n152, 114, 131n48, 132, 145, 153, 156, 158, 158n119, 159,

159nn120–21, 160, 160nn122–24, 161–62, 185n45, 223, 241, 282

Hossart, Jeanne. *See* Marie-Anne de Saint Paul, nun

Hou, Benedict Labre 侯世恩 (Hou Shi'en), 144

Hu Ruoshan, Joseph 胡若山, 197

Huangzhou 黃州 (Hwangchow), 105

Hubei 湖北 (Hupeh), 105, 157n115, 304n152

Hubrecht, Alphonse, ix, xi, 131

Hülegü, 54

Ilario del Sacro Cuore e di Maria (Guglielmo Castellan), monk, 105, 105n153

Indianapolis, IN, 106

Inner Mongolia, 145, 278, 278n73

Irénée, monk, 124

Isabelle de Jésus (Poncelet), nun, 62n11, 81–82, 88, 88nn96–97

Jaegher, Raymond de, 297–98, 298n130, 308, 315

Jalpaigury, 84n84

Janssen, Arnold, 32n104

Janssens, Léon, 124

Jantzen, Louis-Gabriel-Xavier, 80, 82–83, 200, 216

Jarlin, Stanislas, 127, 132, 133n56

Java, 223

Jeanne de Jésus-Maria, nun, 82, 82n80, 83n81, 84n84

Jerusalem, 56

Jianchang 建昌 (Kientchang), 325n3

Jiang Jieshi 蔣介石. *See* Chiang Kai-shek

Jiangnan 江南 (Kiangnan, Kiang-nan), 64–65, 67, 68n34, 69, 322, 325